THE CAMBRIDGE COMPANION TO
LEVINAS

Each volume in this series of companions to major philosophers contains specially commissioned essays by an international team of scholars, together with a substantial bibliography, and will serve as a reference work for students and non-specialists. One aim of the series is to dispel the intimidation such readers often feel when faced with the work of a difficult and challenging thinker.

Emmanuel Levinas is now widely recognized alongside Heidegger, Merleau-Ponty and Sartre as one of the most important Continental philosophers of the twentieth century. His abiding concern was the primacy of the ethical relation to the other person and his central thesis was that ethics is first philosophy. His work has also had a profound impact on a number of fields outside philosophy such as theology, Jewish studies, literature and cultural theory, psychotherapy, sociology, political theory, international relations theory and critical legal theory. This volume contains overviews of Levinas's contribution in a number of fields, and includes detailed discussions of his early and late work, his relation to Judaism and Talmudic commentary, and his contributions to aesthetics and the philosophy of religion.

New readers will find this the most convenient, accessible guide to Levinas currently available. Advanced students and specialists will find a detailed conspectus of recent developments in the interpretation of Levinas.

OTHER VOLUMES IN THE SERIES OF CAMBRIDGE COMPANIONS:

AQUINAS   *Edited by* NORMAN KRETZMANN *and*
ELEONORE STUMP
HANNAH ARENDT   *Edited by* DANA VILLA
ARISTOTLE   *Edited by* JONATHAN BARNES
AUGUSTINE   *Edited by* ELEONORE STUMP *and*
NORMAN KRETZMANN
BACON   *Edited by* MARKKU PELTONEN
DESCARTES   *Edited by* JOHN COTTINGHAM
EARLY GREEK PHILOSOPHY   *Edited by* A. A. LONG
FEMINISM IN PHILOSOPHY   *Edited by* MIRANDA
FRICKER *and* JENNIFER HORNSBY
FOUCAULT   *Edited by* GARY GUTTING
FREUD   *Edited by* JEROME NEU
GALILEO   *Edited by* PETER MACHAMER
GERMAN IDEALISM   *Edited by* KARL AMERIKS
HABERMAS   *Edited by* STEPHEN K. WHITE
HEGEL   *Edited by* FREDERICK BEISER
HEIDEGGER   *Edited by* CHARLES GUIGNON
HOBBES   *Edited by* TOM SORELL
HUME   *Edited by* DAVID FATE NORTON
HUSSERL   *Edited by* BARRY SMITH *and*
DAVID WOODRUFF SMITH
WILLIAM JAMES   *Edited by* RUTH ANNA PUTNAM
KANT   *Edited by* PAUL GUYER
KIERKEGAARD   *Edited by* ALASTAIR HANNAY *and*
GORDON MARINO
LEIBNIZ   *Edited by* NICHOLAS JOLLEY
LEVINAS   *Edited by* SIMON CRITCHLEY *and*
ROBERT BERNASCONI
LOCKE   *Edited by* VERE CHAPPELL
MALEBRANCHE   *Edited by* STEPHEN NADLER
MARX   *Edited by* TERRELL CARVER
MILL   *Edited by* JOHN SKORUPSKI
NEWTON   *Edited by* I. BERNARD COHEN *and*
GEORGE E. SMITH
NIETZSCHE   *Edited by* BERND MAGNUS *and*
KATHLEEN HIGGINS
OCKHAM   *Edited by* PAUL VINCENT SPADE
PLATO   *Edited by* RICHARD KRAUT
PLOTINUS   *Edited by* LLOYD P. GERSON
ROUSSEAU   *Edited by* PATRICK RILEY
SARTRE   *Edited by* CHRISTINA HOWELLS
SCHOPENHAUER   *Edited by* CHRISTOPHER
JANAWAY
SPINOZA   *Edited by* DON GARRETT
WITTGENSTEIN   *Edited by* HANS SLUGA *and*
DAVID STERN

The Cambridge Companion to
LEVINAS

Edited by Simon Critchley
University of Essex

and Robert Bernasconi
University of Memphis

CAMBRIDGE
UNIVERSITY PRESS

PUBLISHED BY THE PRESS SYNDICATE OF THE UNIVERSITY OF CAMBRIDGE
The Pitt Building, Trumpington Street, Cambridge, United Kingdom

CAMBRIDGE UNIVERSITY PRESS
The Edinburgh Building, Cambridge CB2 2RU, UK
40 West 20th Street, New York, NY 10011-4211, USA
477 Williamstown Road, Port Melbourne, VIC 3207, Australia
Ruiz de Alarcón 13, 28014 Madrid, Spain
Dock House, The Waterfront, Cape Town 8001, South Africa

http://www.cambridge.org

First published 2002

Printed in the United Kingdom at the University Press, Cambridge

Typeface Trump Medieval 10/13 pt   *System* LATEX 2ε [TB]

A catalogue record for this book is available from the British Library

ISBN 0 521 66206 0 hardback
ISBN 0 521 66565 5 paperback

CONTENTS

vii

CONTRIBUTORS

ROBERT BERNASCONI is Moss Professor of Philosophy at the University of Memphis. He is co-editor with Simon Critchley of *Re-Reading Levinas* and with Adriaan Perperzak and Simon Critchley of *Emmanuel Levinas: Basic Philosophical Writings*. He is the author of two books on Heidegger and of numerous articles on twentieth-century Continental philosophy and race theory.

RUDOLF BERNET is Professor of Philosophy at the University of Leuven (Belgium) and Director of the Husserl archives. He is the editor of E. Husserl's collected works (*Husserliana*) and of the series Phaenomenologica (Kluwer). He has published Husserl's posthumous writings on time and numerous articles in the fields of phenomenology, psychoanalysis and contemporary philosophy. His books include *An Introduction to Husserlian Phenomenology* (1993) and *La vie du sujet* (1994).

RICHARD J. BERNSTEIN is Vera List Professor of Philosophy and Chair at the Graduate Faculty, New School University. His recent books include *Freud and the Legacy of Moses*, *Hannah Arendt and the Jewish Question*, and *The New Constellation: the Ethical Political Horizon of Modernity/Postmodernity*. He is currently writing a book on radical evil.

GERALD L. BRUNS is the William P. and Hazel B. White Professor of English at the University of Notre Dame. His most recent books include *Maurice Blanchot: the Refusal of Philosophy* (1997) and *Tragic Thoughts at the End of Philosophy: Language, Literature, and Ethical Theory* (1999).

ix

CATHERINE CHALIER teaches philosophy at Paris X-Nanterre. Her main fields are moral philosophy and Jewish thought. She has published thirteen books on these subjects and a few translations from Hebrew. The most recent books she has published are *Pour une morale au-delà du savoir. Kant et Levinas* (Albin Michel, 1998) (a translation into English is about to be published by Cornell University Press); *De l'intranquillité de l'âme* (Payot, 1999); *L'écoute en partage. Judaïsme et Christianisme* (with M. Faessler, Le Cerf, 2001).

SIMON CRITCHLEY is Professor of Philosophy and Head of Department at the University of Essex, and Directeur de Programme at the Collège International de Philosophie, Paris. He is author of *The Ethics of Deconstruction* (1992), *Very Little . . . Almost Nothing* (1997), *Ethics–Politics–Subjectivity* (1999), *Continental Philosophy: a Very Short Introduction* (2001) and *On Humour* (2002).

PAUL DAVIES teaches philosophy at the University of Sussex. Over the past ten years, he has written many articles on issues in the work of Levinas, Heidegger, Blanchot and Kant. He is currently researching for a book on Kant and philosophical continuity, and completing a monograph on aesthetics.

JOHN LLEWELYN has been Reader in Philosophy at the University of Edinburgh and Visiting Professor at the University of Memphis and Loyola University of Chicago. Among his publications are *Beyond Metaphysics?*, *Derrida on the Threshold of Sense*, *The Middle Voice of Ecological Conscience*, *Emmanuel Levinas: the Genealogy of Ethics*, *The HypoCritical Imagination* and *Appositions of Jacques Derrida and Emmanuel Levinas*. He is currently preparing a book to be entitled *Seeing Through God*.

HILARY PUTNAM is Cogan University Professor Emeritus at Harvard University. His books include *Reason, Truth and History*, *Realism with a Human Face*, *Renewing Philosophy*, *Words and Life*, *Pragmatism* and *The Threefold Cord: Mind, Body and World*.

STELLA SANDFORD is Lecturer in Modern European Philosophy at Middlesex University, London. She is the author of *The Metaphysics of Love: Gender and Transcendence in Levinas* (Continuum, 2000), and a forthcoming study of Plato and feminist philosophy. She is a member of the *Radical Philosophy* editorial collective and the *Women's Philosophy Review.*

BERNHARD WALDENFELS is Emeritus Professor of Philosophy at Ruhr University of Bochum. Some of his writings include *Phänomenologie in Frankreich* (1983, 1998); *Ordnung in Zwielicht* (1987, in English *Order in Twilight*, 1996); *Antwortregister* (1994); *Deutsch-Französische Gedankengänge* (1995); *Studien zur Phänomenologie des Fremden*, 4 vols. (1997–1999); *Das leibliche Selbst* (2000); *Verfremdung der Moderne* (2001). His research interests in phenomenology include topics such as life-world, corporeality, otherness, strangeness and responsivity.

EDITH WYSCHOGROD is J. Newton Rayzor Professor of Philosophy and Religious Thought at Rice University. Her works include *An Ethics of Remembering: History, Heterology and the Nameless Others* (1998), *Saints and Postmodernism* (1990) and *Emmanuel Levinas: the Problem of Ethical Metaphysics* (second edn 2000). Her current research interest is biological and phenomenological theories of altruism.

ACKNOWLEDGEMENTS

The editors would like to thank Hilary Gaskin for her editorial guidance and support, Noreen Harburt for all her secretarial help on the project and especially Stacy Keltner for preparing the bibliography and getting the manuscript into a state that could be delivered to the publishers.

ABBREVIATIONS

AT	*Alterity and Transcendence*
BPW	*Emmanuel Levinas: Basic Philosophical Writings*
BV	*Beyond the Verse: Talmudic Readings and Lectures*
CP	*Collected Philosophical Papers*
DEH	*Discovering Existence with Husserl*
DF	*Difficult Freedom: Essays on Judaism*
EE	*Existence and Existents*
EN	*Entre Nous: On Thinking-of-the-Other*
EI	*Ethics and Infinity: Conversations with Philippe Nemo*
GCM	*Of God Who Comes to Mind*
GDT	*God, Death, and Time*
LR	*The Levinas Reader*
NTR	*Nine Talmudic Readings*
OB	*Otherwise than Being or Beyond Essence*
OS	*Outside the Subject*
PM	'The Paradox of Morality' in *The Provocation of Levinas*
PN	*Proper Names*
TE	'Transcendence and Evil' in *Collected Philosophical Papers*
TI	*Totality and Infinity*
TIHP	*The Theory of Intuition in Husserl's Phenomenology*
TO	*Time and the Other*
TN	*In the Time of Nations*
TRO	'The Trace of the Other' in *Deconstruction in Context*
US	'Useless Suffering' in *The Provocation of Levinas*
WES	'What Would Eurydice Say? / Que dirait Euridice?'
WO	'Wholly Otherwise' in *Re-Reading Levinas*

EMMANUEL LEVINAS:
A DISPARATE INVENTORY

SIMON CRITCHLEY*

'Cet inventaire disparate est une biographie.'

Levinas, 'Signature' in DF

1906   On 12 January, born in Kovno (Kaunas), Lithuania (or, according to the Julian calendar used in the Russian empire at the time, on 30 December 1905). Eldest of three brothers: Boris (born in 1909) and Aminadab (born in 1913, whose name – probably coincidentally – was later the title of a novel by Maurice Blanchot); both were murdered by the Nazis. The Levinas family belonged to Kovno's large and important Jewish community, where, as Levinas later recalled, 'to be Jewish was as natural as having eyes and ears'. The first language Levinas learned to read was Hebrew, at home with a teacher, although Russian was his mother tongue, the language of his formal education and remained the language spoken at home throughout his life. Levinas's parents spoke Yiddish. As a youth, Levinas read the great Russian writers, Lermontov, Gogol, Turgenev, Tolstoy, Dostoevsky and Pushkin. The last was the most important influence, and it is these writers whom Levinas credits with the awakening of his philosophical interests. Shakespeare was also and would remain an influence on his thinking.

1915–16 During World War I, after the Germans occupied Kovno in September 1915, the Levinas family became refugees and moved to Kharkov in Ukraine, after being refused entry to Kiev. Levinas was one of very few Jews admitted to the Russian *Gymnasium*. The Levinas family experienced the upheavals of the revolutions of February and October 1917.

1920   The Levinas family returned to Lithuania, where Levinas attended a Hebrew *Gymnasium* in Kovno.

1923   After initially considering studying in Germany, Levinas went to the University of Strasbourg in France. When asked why he chose France, Levinas replied 'Parce que c'est l'Europe!' Bizarrely enough, Strasbourg was apparently chosen because it was the French city closest to Lithuania. His subjects included classics, psychology and a good deal of sociology, though he soon came to concentrate on philosophy, studying Bergson and Husserl in particular. In autobiographical reflections, he mentioned Charles Blondel, Henri Carteron, Maurice Halbwachs and Maurice Pradines as the four professors who most influenced his thinking. What made a very strong impression on the young Levinas was the way in which Pradines, who would later be his thesis supervisor, used the example of the Dreyfus affair to illuminate the primacy of ethics over politics.

1926   Beginning of his lifelong friendship with Maurice Blanchot who arrived in Strasbourg as a student in 1926.

1927   Obtained his *Licence* in philosophy and thanks to Gabrielle Pfeiffer began a close study of Husserl's *Logical Investigations* and eventually chose Husserl's theory of intuition as his dissertation topic.

1928–9 Spent the academic year in Freiburg, Germany, where he gave a presentation in Husserl's last seminar and attended Heidegger's first seminar as Husserl's successor. Levinas attended Heidegger's lecture course that has been published as *Einleitung in die Philosophie* [Introduction to Philosophy] (Klostermann, 1996). His time in Freiburg was marked by an intense reading of Heidegger's *Being and Time* (1927) to which he was introduced by Jean Héring, Professor of Protestant Theology at Strasbourg and former student of Husserl. As Levinas puts it in an interview,

'I went to Freiburg because of Husserl, but discovered Heidegger'.

1929   First publication, a review article on Husserl's *Ideas I* in *Revue Philosophique de la France et de l'Etranger.*

Attended the famous encounter between Heidegger and Cassirer at Davos that took place between 18 and 30 March, which was actually part of a wider Franco-German philosophical meeting attended by younger philosophers such as Jean Cavaillès, Maurice de Gandillac, Eugen Fink and Rudolf Carnap. At the end of two weeks of discussion, the Freiburg students organized a satirical *soirée* where they re-created the debate. Levinas assumed the role of Cassirer, allegedly with flour in his abundant black locks and repeating the words 'Humboldt Kultur, Humboldt Kultur'. Cassirer's wife was apparently offended, and Levinas later very much regretted this act of mockery. However, in another version of events, given in a late interview from 1992, Levinas says that he repeated the words 'I am a pacifist. I am a pacifist', and that this could be interpreted as some sort of response to Heidegger, who was present at the *soirée.*

Returned to Strasbourg, completed and defended his doctorate, *The Theory of Intuition in Husserl's Phenomenology.* On 4 April 1930 it received a prize from the Institute of Philosophy and was published by Vrin in Paris later in 1930. It is this work which introduced Jean-Paul Sartre to phenomenology. As Levinas put it, with some wry humour, 'It was Sartre who guaranteed my place in eternity by stating in his famous obituary essay on Merleau-Ponty that he, Sartre "was introduced to phenomenology by Levinas".'

1930   Became a French citizen, and performed his military service in Paris. Married Raïssa Levi, whom he had known from schooldays in Kovno. Obtained a teaching position at the Alliance Israélite Universelle in Paris. Because Levinas did not have the *Agrégation* in philosophy he could not apply for a university position or indeed a teaching position in a *lycée.* In private conversation, Levinas admitted that his ignorance of Greek prevented him from sitting the *Agrégation*. The Alliance was established in France in 1860 by a group of Jews prominent in French life. They wished to promote the integration of Jews everywhere as full citizens within their states, with equal rights and freedom from persecution. The Alliance saw itself as having a civilizing mission through the education of Jews from the Mediterranean basin (Morocco, Tunisia, Algeria, Turkey, Syria) who were not educated in the Western tradition.

1931   He co-translated Husserl's *Cartesian Meditations* with a fellow Strasbourg student Gabrielle Pfeiffer. Levinas was responsible for the Fourth and Fifth Meditations, which contain Husserl's famous discussion of intersubjectivity.

1932   Began work on a book on Heidegger but abandoned it when Heidegger became committed to National Socialism. A fragment of the projected book was published as 'Martin Heidegger and Ontology' in 1932, the first article on Heidegger in French. Levinas wrote in a Talmudic reading from 1963, 'One can forgive many Germans, but there are some Germans it is difficult to forgive. It is difficult to forgive Heidegger.'

1931–2 Participated in the monthly philosophical Saturday evening *soirées* of Gabriel Marcel where he met Sartre and other members of the intellectual avant-garde.

1933   Intermittently attended Kojeve's famous lectures on Hegel at the Ecole des Hautes Etudes (1933–7), and met Jean Hippolyte and others.
           Published his only extant original article in Lithuanian, an intriguing essay called 'The Notion of Spirituality in French and German Culture'.

1934   Levinas publishes a fascinating philosophical meditation on National Socialism, called 'Some Reflections on the Philosophy of Hitlerism', in a special issue of *Esprit*, a newly founded French left Catholic journal. It was republished in 1997 with a study by Miguel Abensour (Paris: Payot-Rivages).

1935   Birth of daughter, Simone, who later trained to become a doctor.

   Publication of Levinas's first original, thematic essay, 'De l'évasion', in *Recherches Philosophiques*, which represents his first understated attempt to break free from Heideggerian ontology. Reissued with an extensive commentary by Jacques Rolland with Fata Morgana publishers in 1982.

1939   Drafted into the French army, and served as an interpreter of Russian and German.

1940–5   Taken prisoner of war in Rennes with the Tenth French Army in June 1940 and held captive there in a *Frontstalag* for several months. Levinas was then transferred to a camp in Fallinpostel, close to Magdeburg in Northern Germany. Because Levinas was an officer in the French army, he was not sent to a concentration camp but to a military prisoners' camp, where he did forced labour in the forest. His camp had the number 1492, the date of the expulsion of the Jews from Spain! The Jewish prisoners were kept separately from the non-Jews and wore uniforms marked with the word 'JUD'. Most members of his family were murdered by the Nazis during the bloody pogroms that began in June 1940 with the active and enthusiastic collaboration of Lithuanian nationalists. Although it is not certain, it would appear that his brothers, mother and father were shot by Nazis close to Kovno. The names of close and more distant murdered family members are recalled in the Hebrew dedication to his second major philosophical work, *Otherwise than Being or Beyond Essence*. Raïssa and Simone Levinas were initially protected by a number of brave French friends, notably Suzanne Poirier, M. and Mme Verduron and Blanchot. It would appear that Levinas somehow got a message through to Blanchot from the prison camp in Rennes. Blanchot lent his apartment to Raïssa and Simone for some time before Simone received an extremely courageous offer of refuge from the sisters of a Vincentian convent outside Orléans. Raïssa Levinas was supported financially throughout the war by the Alliance

Israélite Universelle. She stayed in hiding in Paris until 1943 when she joined her daughter, adopting the name 'Marguerite Bevos'. Raïssa's mother, Amélia Frieda Levi, who had been living with the Levinas family before the war, was deported from Paris and murdered. There exist *carnets de guerre* from this period, as yet unpublished. Levinas vowed never to set foot on German soil again.

1945 Levinas returned to Paris and rejoined his family. Thanks to the intervention of René Cassin, Levinas became Director of the Ècole Normale Israélite Orientale (ENIO), the school established by the Alliance in Paris in 1867 to train teachers for its schools in the Mediterranean basin. As a former student of the ENIO points out in a memoir of Levinas as a teacher, the school was neither normal, nor truly Israeli nor completely oriental. The ENIO was located at 59 rue d'Auteuil and later on the rue Michel-Ange in the 16th *arrondissement*. The family lived above the school on the seventh floor, in an apartment in which they remained until 1980, when they moved to another apartment on the same street. It should be recalled that Levinas did not have a university position until 1964 when he was in his late fifties. Because of his professional position and his pedagogical commitments, he dedicated a number of essays to the problems facing Jewish education and the need for a renaissance of Jewish spirituality after the catastrophe of the *Shoah*. This also explains why in this period Levinas's growing importance in discussions of Jewish affairs was not matched by an equal prominence in philosophical circles. These interests are well reflected in his 1963 collection, *Difficult Freedom*. The ENIO corresponded to and fostered the vision of Judaism that Levinas would defend with increasing vigour in the post-war years: rigorously intellectual, rooted in textual study, rationalistic, anti-mystical, humanist and universalist. However, it should be recalled that most of Levinas's professional life was spent as a school administrator with extensive and rather routine responsibilities for the day-to-day welfare of ENIO students. Levinas took responsibility for Talmudic

study in the ENIO and gave the famous public 'cours de
Rachi' on Saturdays which were followed by smaller study
groups where Levinas would as readily discuss Dostoevsky
or an article in *Le Monde* as a Judaic theme.

1945–80   Although they met before the war in 1937, after the war
Levinas developed a very close friendship with Henri
Nerson, a doctor who lived near the Levinas family and
with whom he had daily contact. It was Nerson who introduced Levinas to the enigmatic Monsieur Chouchani,
his eventual teacher and *maître*, with whom he studied
Talmud and who renewed his interest in Judaism. Nerson
died in Israel in 1980 and in an interview from 1987,
Levinas said 'I miss him every day'.

1946–7   Levinas was invited by his good friend and supporter
Jean Wahl, Professor of Philosophy at the Sorbonne (the
1961 book *Totality and Infinity* was dedicated to Jean
and Marcelle Wahl) to give four lectures at the Collège
Philosophique. *Time and the Other* was published in 1948
in a collective volume and reappeared in 1979 as a separate
volume with a revealing new preface. The initial publication was famously criticized by Simone de Beauvoir in the
preface to *The Second Sex* for its understanding of the feminine as the other to the masculine. These lectures express
many of the core ideas of Levinas's later work, the central-
ity of the other, and the claim that time determines the
relation between the other and oneself.

1947–9   Studied Talmud, in its original languages, Hebrew and
Aramaic, with Monsieur Chouchani, who is the 'master'
whom Levinas frequently mentions in his Talmudic commentaries. Chouchani actually lived with the Levinas
family in their apartment during this period and
Emmanuel effectively stopped writing philosophy in order
to concentrate on Talmudic study. One should not under-
estimate the great influence that Chouchani exerted over
Levinas and the great affection that he inspired among his
students, another of whom was Elie Wiesel. Chouchani
died in South America in 1968 at the moment of the

publication of *Quatres Lectures Talmudiques*, Levinas's first collection of Talmudic essays. The reader of Levinas's commentaries will realize that he does his own translations of the passages chosen for discussion.

1947   Publication of his first original book, *De l'existence à l'existant [Existence and Existents]* which had been written in captivity during the war. The book was published by Georges Blin in Editions de la Revue Fontaine after being refused by Gallimard. In contradistinction to the intellectual context of the *libération* dominated by the existentialism of Sartre and Camus, the book was published with a red banner around it with the words 'où il ne s'agit pas d'angoisse' ('where it is not a question of anxiety'). In 1946, Levinas had published a fragment of this book under the title 'Il y a', in the first issue of a new journal called *Deucalion* founded by Jean Wahl. The *il y a* is Levinas's name for the nocturnal horror of existence prior to the emergence of consciousness. Levinas later called the *il y a*, the 'morceau de résistance' in this book. The original publication appeared with the dedication P. A. E., which means 'Pour Andrée Eliane', the daughter born to the Levinases after the war who lived for just a few months.

1948   'Reality and its Shadow', Levinas's controversial critique of art, published in *Les Temps Modernes*, with a critical prefatory note, possibly written by Merleau-Ponty or Sartre.

   Publication of *Discovering Existence with Husserl and Heidegger*, a collection of pre-war and unpublished pieces on phenomenology. It was reissued in a second edition in 1967 with a number of important new essays added, such as 'Language and Proximity'.

1949   Birth of son, Michaël, now a recognized composer, concert pianist and Professor of Musical Analysis at the Paris Conservatory.

1951   'Is Ontology Fundamental?' is published in *Revue de Métaphysique et de Morale*. It is here, finally, that Levinas makes explicit his critique of Heidegger in ethical terms.

1952   First visit to Israel, where he later returned to give papers
        in the late 1970s and early 1980s, but where he was not
        really recognized as an original thinker.

1956   Elected *Chevalier de la Légion d'honneur.*

1957   'Philosophy and the Idea of Infinity' published in *Revue
        de Métaphysique et de Morale*. This essay is the best
        overview of Levinas's work in the 1950s, anticipating
        many of the theses of *Totality and Infinity*, and develop-
        ing Levinas's appropriation of the concept of infinity from
        Descartes.
            Co-founder of the *Colloque des intellectuels juifs de
        langue française*, which met annually and with which
        Levinas was closely involved until the early 1990s. The
        idea of this meeting was to reconstitute the French intel-
        lectual Jewish community after the war by identifying the
        links between contemporary social, political and philo-
        sophical issues and the Jewish tradition.

1960   Begins giving Talmudic commentaries as the concluding
        address of the yearly meetings of the *Colloque des intellec-
        tuels juifs de langue française*, a habit he continued until
        1991. Far from being devotional exercises, these commen-
        taries often see Levinas using the Talmud to discuss the
        intellectual and political events of the time. As well as ex-
        emplifying a highly rationalistic hermeneutic approach,
        inspired by Chouchani, the commentaries are also note-
        worthy for their informality and for their often wry hu-
        mour. For example, his 1972 commentary, 'Et Dieu créa
        la femme', alludes to Roger Vadim's 1957 film, starring
        Brigitte Bardot.

1961   *Totality and Infinity* published in Holland by Martinus
        Nijhoff publishers as part of their famous Phaenomenolo-
        gica series, under the patronage of the Husserl archives in
        Leuven and with the crucial support of Father Herman Leo
        Van Breda. Its principal thesis is described below in the in-
        troduction. With the encouragement and crucial support
        of Jean Wahl, Levinas presented this book as the main
        thesis for his *doctorat d'état*, while a collection of his

previously published philosophical works was accepted as a complementary thesis. In addition to Wahl, Vladimir Jankélévitch, Gabriel Marcel, Paul Ricœur and Georges Blin were members of the jury, which was also due to include Merleau-Ponty, who died one month prior to the *soutenance*. Although this is not widely known, *Totality and Infinity* was not originally intended as a thesis, but as an independent book. Levinas had given up the idea of submitting a thesis and only renewed the idea at the prompting of Jean Wahl after the manuscript had been refused for publication by Brice Parain at Gallimard in 1960. An English translation of *Totality and Infinity* by Alphonso Lingis appeared in 1969.

1961–2   Publication of three texts by Blanchot in *La Nouvelle Revue Française* more or less directly inspired by *Totality and Infinity*: 'Connaissance de l'inconnu', 'Tenir parole' and 'Être juif'.

1962   Shortly after the publication of *Totality and Infinity*, Levinas was invited by Jean Wahl to speak to the Société Française de Philosophie, where he presented 'Transcendence and Height', a very useful summary of the early arguments of the book from an epistemological perspective.

1963   Publication of *Difficult Freedom*, a very important collection of Levinas's writings on Jewish topics, dedicated to Henri Nerson. Besides the essays on Jewish education, the volume contains a wide assortment of observations and polemics on contemporary issues and figures, and includes Levinas's first Talmudic commentaries, which deal with messianic themes. It also contains 'Signature', Levinas's elliptical but revealing autobiographical reflections.

1964   Appointed Professor of Philosophy at the University of Poitiers. His colleagues included Mikel Dufrenne, Roger Garaudy, Jacques D'Hondt and Jeanne Delhomme. Levinas remained Director of the ENIO until 1980 but delegated more and more of the administrative tasks. It is widely thought that Levinas was appointed to Poitiers in 1961, which is not true. He was also unsuccessful in a candidature for a professorship at the University of Lille because of the opposition of Eric Weil, who appointed Henri Birault instead of Levinas.

'Meaning and Sense' published in *Revue de Métaphysique et de Morale*, which, via an interesting debate with Merleau-Ponty and the question of decolonization, shows the beginnings of the philosophical transition from *Totality and Infinity* to *Otherwise than Being*. It is here that the notion of the trace and the critique of the idea of presence, so important for Jacques Derrida's work, makes its appearance in Levinas.

Publication of Derrida's 'Violence and Metaphysics' in two parts in *Revue de Métaphysique et de Morale*. It was republished in a slightly revised form in the 1967 volume, *Writing and Difference*. It is worth pointing out that this essay – effectively a monograph – was one of Derrida's first essays, and would for a long time be the most extensive discussion of Levinas's work.

1965   Member of the committee of direction for 'l'Amitié Judéo-Chrétienne de France'. The topic of Jewish–Christian friendship would preoccupy Levinas in his later writings.

1967   Appointed Professor of Philosophy at the newly established University of Paris-Nanterre, where his colleagues included Dufrenne, Paul Ricœur and Jean-François Lyotard in philosophy and Alain Touraine, Henri Lefebvre and the young Jean Baudrillard in sociology.

'Substitution' given as one of two lectures in Brussels in November and published in the *Revue Philosophique de Louvain* in 1968. The text expresses the core idea of *Otherwise than Being or Beyond Essence*, namely the idea of the subject as hostage, where responsibility to the other is seen as something interior to the self. The original version, contained in *Basic Philosophical Writings*, is easier to follow than the more developed version published in the 1974 book.

1968   *Quatre lectures talmudiques* (contained in *Nine Talmudic Readings* in English) published by Jérôme Lindon in

Editions de Minuit, as were all of Levinas's subsequent 'confessional' writings.

Although Levinas distanced himself from the events of 1968, where his friend Ricœur, at that point Dean of Faculty at Nanterre, was obliged to bring in the police to protect the campus in 1969, Levinas responded philosophically to the events of 1968 and to the anti-humanism of structuralist and post-structuralist thought in 'Humanism and Anarchy' (1968) and 'No Identity' (1970), both contained in *Collected Philosophical Papers*. A fascinating Talmudic response to Marxism and student radicalism can be found in 'Judaism and revolution' (1969), contained in *Nine Talmudic Readings*.

1970   Awarded an honorary doctorate at Loyola University of Chicago, on the same day as Hannah Arendt, which was the only time they met, and where Levinas was somewhat perplexed by the enthusiasm with which Arendt joined in the singing of the American national anthem. Honorary doctorates followed from the universities of Leiden, Holland (1975), Leuven, Belgium (1976), Fribourg, Switzerland (1980) and Bar-Ilan, Israel (1981).

Appointed to a visiting professorship at the University of Fribourg, where he taught for short periods for many years.

1971   Awarded the Albert Schweitzer philosophy prize.

1972   *Humanisme de l'autre homme.*

1973   Appointed Professor of Philosophy at the Sorbonne (Paris IV) and became honorary professor after his retirement in 1976. He continued his seminar at the Sorbonne until 1980. His colleagues included Ferdinand Alquié, Henri Birault, Pierre Aubenque and Jacques Rivelaygue.

1974   *Otherwise than Being or Beyond Essence* published by Nijhoff. English translation by Alphonso Lingis in 1981. Its principal innovations are discussed below in the introduction. Many commentators claim that this is Levinas's most important philosophical work; it is certainly his most difficult.

Publication of first book-length study of Levinas in English, by Edith Wyschogrod: *Emmanuel Levinas: the Problem of Ethical Metaphysics* (The Hague: Nijhoff).

Elected *Officier de l'ordre national du Mérite* in November.

1975   *Sur Maurice Blanchot*, a collection of three articles and a conversation about his great friend.

1976   *Proper Names*, a very interesting and accessible collection of short articles on Agnon, Buber, Celan, Delhomme, Derrida, Jabès, Lacroix, Laporte, Picard, Proust, van Breda and Wahl.

1977   *Du sacré au saint. Cinq nouvelles lectures talmudiques* (contained in *Nine Talmudic Readings* in English).

1980   *Textes pour Emmanuel Levinas* published (Paris: Jean-Michel Place), with important contributions by Blanchot, Derrida, Edmond Jabès, Jean-François Lyotard, Paul Ricœur and others.

Levinas met Jean-Paul II, during the Pope's visit to Paris in May. The Pope (Karol Wojtyla) wrote a thesis on the phenomenologist Max Scheler in 1959 and had strong interests in the relation of phenomenological ethics to Christian metaphysics. In 1980, Levinas wrote an article on 'The Philosophical Thought of Cardinal Wojtyla'. Along with other philosophers, Levinas took part in conferences at Castel Gandolfo, the Papal summer residence, at which the Pope presided, in 1983 and 1985, giving the paper 'Transcendence and Intelligibility' on the occasion of the second conference.

1982   *Beyond the Verse*, a collection of five Talmudic commentaries and a very interesting series of texts on Judaism, Zionism and politics.

Of God Who Comes to Mind published by Vrin, an important collection of essays, which makes explicit the more theological orientation of Levinas's later work. This can best be seen in 'God and Philosophy', from 1975, which is a wide-ranging essay that better than any other provides a powerful summary of Levinas's mature thought. The book was awarded the Charles-Lévêque prize.

Ethics and Infinity, a series of conversations with Philippe Nemo, originally broadcast on French radio. Highly illuminating, they provide an excellent review and entry point to Levinas's work.

1983   Awarded the Karl Jaspers prize in Heidelberg which Michaël Levinas accepted on his father's behalf because of Levinas's vow never to enter Germany after the war.

1984   'Transcendence and Intelligibility' published, providing a concise and useful summary of Levinas's later thinking. It can profitably be read alongside his other attempts to provide an overview and a point of entry to his thinking.

1985   Elected *Commandeur des Arts et Lettres* in April.

1986   A ten-day conference or 'decade' at Cerisy-la-Salle, organized by Jean Greisch and Jacques Rolland, published by Editions du Cerf in 1993.

Face to Face with Levinas, edited by Richard A. Cohen, an important collection of articles on Levinas, with many useful translations.

1987   *Collected Philosophical Papers* published in English, translated and introduced by Alphonso Lingis.

At the invitation of Miguel Abensour, President of the Collège International de Philosophie, Levinas presents 'Dying For'. This is a wonderfully measured paper on Heidegger given at the hysterical height of the Heidegger affair in Paris, when many intellectuals were caught up in the scandal over Heidegger's political commitment to National Socialism. Derrida presented an early version of his *Of Spirit* at the same meeting. This was only the second time that Levinas had given a public lecture on Heidegger, the first being at Jean Wahl's seminar at the Sorbonne early in 1940.

Outside the Subject, a late collection of philosophical papers, with interesting pieces on Husserl.

1988   *The Hour of Nations* published, in a similar format to *Beyond the Verse*, with five Talmudic readings, and a series of theological writings touching in particular on the relation of Judaism to Christianity and essays on Moses Mendelssohn and Franz Rosenzweig.

1991   *Entre Nous: On Thinking-of-the-Other* published, a collection of Levinas's papers and interviews with some very important early pieces such as 'Is Ontology Fundamental?' and 'Ego and Totality'.

Publication of the *Cahier de l'Herne*, on Levinas, edited by Catherine Chalier and Miguel Abensour. In addition to important studies of Levinas's work, it contains unpublished original texts by Levinas, and the transcription by Jacques Rolland of his final lecture course at the Sorbonne, 'Dieu, la mort et le temps'.

Elected *Officier de la Légion d'honneur*.

1994   *Les imprévus de l'histoire* published, a collection of previously published journal articles, including important pieces such as Levinas's first publications on Husserl, and his critique of art, 'Reality and its Shadow'.

1995   *Alterity and Transcendence* published, a collection of occasional texts, encyclopaedia entries and interviews.

Night of 24–5 December, death in Paris after a long struggle with illness. The funeral oration, 'Adieu', was given by Jacques Derrida at the interment on 28 December.

1996   *New Talmudic Readings* published just a few weeks after Levinas's death, containing three Talmudic readings, from 1974, 1988 and 1989.

Basic Philosophical Writings published.

December, *Hommage* to Levinas, organized by Danielle Cohen-Levinas and the Collège International de Philosophie in the Amphithéâtre Richelieu at the Sorbonne.

NOTE

* I would like to thank Michaël Levinas, Catherine Chalier, Miguel Abensour and Robert Bernasconi for their help in confirming and adding facts to this chronological table. Certain facts have been taken from a number of sources: Adriaan Peperzak's preface to *Emmanuel Levinas: Basic Philosophical Writings*, Anette Aronowicz's introduction to

Nine Talmudic Readings, Marie-Anne Lescourret's *Emmanuel Levinas* (Paris: Flammarion 1994), François Poirié's *Emmanuel Levinas* (Arles: Actes Sud, 1996 [1987]), *L'arche. Le mensuel du judaïsme français*, 459 (February 1996), *Emmanuel Levinas. Philosophe et pédagogue* (Paris: Alliance Israélite Universelle, 1998) and Roger Burggraeve's *Emmanuel Levinas. Une bibliographie primaire et secondaire (1929–1985)* (Leuven: Peeters, 1986).

1   Introduction

One might speculate about the possibility of writing a history of French philosophy in the twentieth century as a philosophical biography of Emmanuel Levinas. He was born in 1906 in Lithuania and died in Paris in 1995. Levinas's life-span therefore traverses and connects many of the intellectual movements of the twentieth century and intersects with some of its major historical events, its moments of light as well as its point of absolute darkness – Levinas said that his life had been dominated by the memory of the Nazi horror (*DF* 291).[1]

The history of French philosophy in the twentieth century can be described as a succession of trends and movements, from the neo-Kantianism that was hegemonic in the early decades of the twentieth century, through to the Bergsonism that was very influential until the 1930s, Kojève's Hegelianism in the 1930s, phenomenology in the 1930s and 1940s, existentialism in the post-war period, structuralism in the 1950s and 1960s, post-structuralism in the 1960s and 1970s, and the return to ethics and political philosophy in the 1980s. Levinas was present throughout all these developments, and was either influenced by them or influenced their reception in France.

Yet Levinas's presence in many of these movements is rather fleeting, indeed at times shadowy. It is widely agreed that Levinas was largely responsible for the introduction of Husserl and Heidegger in France, philosophers who were absolutely decisive for following generations of philosophers, if only in the opposition they provoked. Levinas even jokingly suggested that his place in philosophical immortality was assured by the fact that his doctoral thesis on Husserl had introduced the young Jean-Paul Sartre to phenomenology.[2] However, for a variety of reasons – a certain reticence, even diffidence, on Levinas's part, his professional position outside the French university system until 1964, and his captivity in the *Stalag* between 1940 and 1945 – Levinas's work made little impression prior to the publication of *Totality and Infinity* in 1961, and not much immediately after it. In the exuberance of the *libération*, and the successive dominance of existentialism, phenomenology, Marxism, psychoanalysis and structuralism on the French scene, Levinas's work played in a minor key, where he was known – if at all – as a specialist and scholar of Husserl and Heidegger. As can be seen from his 1963 collection, *Difficult Freedom*, in the 1950s and after Levinas was much more influential in Jewish affairs in France than in philosophy.

Indeed, even after the appearance of *Totality and Infinity*, apart from some rich, if oblique, texts by Levinas's lifelong friend Maurice Blanchot, the first serious and extensive philosophical study of Levinas's work was by a then 34-year-old philosopher, relatively unknown outside scholarly circles, called Jacques Derrida.[3] First published in 1964, nothing remotely comparable to Derrida's brilliant essay, 'Violence and Metaphysics', was published on Levinas during the next decade. A measure of the obscurity enjoyed by Levinas's work can be seen from the fact that in Vincent Descombes's otherwise excellent presentation of the history of philosophy in France during the period 1933–77, published in 1979, Levinas is barely even mentioned.[4] How is it, then, that Jean-Luc Marion, Professor of Philosophy at the Sorbonne (Paris *IV*), was able to write in an obsequy from February 1996, 'If one defines a great philosopher as someone without whom philosophy would not have been what it is, then in France there are two great philosophers of the twentieth century: Bergson and Levinas'?[5]

The situation began to change, and change rapidly, from the early to the mid-1980s. The reasons for this are various. First and foremost, the word 'ethics', which had either been absent from intellectual discussion, or present simply as a term of abuse reserved for the bourgeoisie in the radical anti-humanism of the 1970s, once again became acceptable. The collapse of revolutionary Marxism, from its short-lived structuralist hegemony in Althusser, to the Maoist delusions of the *Tel Quel* group, occasioned the rise of the so-called *nouveaux philosophes*, André Glucksmann, Alain Finkielkraut and Bernard Henri-Lévy, who were critical of the enthusiastic political myopia of the 1968 generation. Although the debt that philosophical posterity will have to the latter thinkers is rather uncertain, by the early 1980s questions of ethics, politics, law and democracy were back on the philosophical and cultural agenda and the scene was set for a reappraisal of Levinas's work. A convenient landmark is provided by the radio interviews with Philippe Nemo that were broadcast on France Culture and published in 1982 as *Ethics and Infinity*. Another crucial event in the reception of Levinas was the Heidegger affair of the winter of 1986–7, which was occasioned by the publication of Victor Farias's *Heidegger and Nazism* and new revelations about the extent of Heidegger's involvement with National Socialism. This affair is significant because much of the criticism of Heidegger was also, indirectly, a criticism of the alleged moral and political impoverishment of the thinking he inspired, in particular that of Derrida. The alleged ethical turn of Derrida's thinking might be viewed simply as a return to Levinas, one of the major influences on the development of his thinking, as is amply evidenced by the 1964 essay.

The renewed interest in Levinas can also be linked to two other factors on the French scene: a return to phenomenology that begins in the 1980s and which gains pace in the 1990s, and a renewal of interest in religious themes. These two factors might be said to come together in what Dominique Janicaud has diagnosed as a theological turn in French phenomenology, evidenced in different ways in the work of Michel Henry, Jean-Luc Marion and Jean-Louis Chrétien.[6] By the mid to late 1980s, Levinas's major philosophical works, which hitherto had only been available in the handsome, yet expensive, volumes published by Martinus Nijhoff in Holland and Fata Morgana in Montpellier, were beginning to be reissued in cheap *livre de poche* editions. *En bref*, Levinas begins to be widely read in France for the first time.

Another highly significant factor in the contemporary fascination for Levinas's work is its reception outside France. A glance at Roger Burggraeve's helpful bibliography of Levinas confirms the fact that the first serious reception of Levinas's work in academic circles took place in Belgium and Holland, with the work of philosophers like Alphonse de Waelhens, H. J. Adriaanse, Theodore de Boer, Adriaan Peperzak, Stephen Strasser, Jan De Greef, Sam IJselling and Jacques Taminiaux.[7] It is perhaps ironic that Levinas is first taken up by Christian philosophers, whether Protestants like De Boer, or Catholics like Peperzak.[8] The first honorary doctorates presented to

Levinas were from the Jesuit faculty of Loyola University Chicago in 1970, the Protestant theologians of the university of Leiden in 1975 and the Catholic University of Leuven in 1976. In Italy, from 1969 onwards, Levinas was a regular participant in meetings in Rome organized by Enrico Castelli, which often dealt with religious themes. Also, in 1983 and 1985, after meeting with the Pope briefly on the occasion of his visit to Paris in May 1980, Levinas, along with other philosophers, attended the conferences held at the Castel Gandolfo at which the Pope presided. The positive German reception of Levinas, with the notable exception of phenomenologists like Bernhard Waldenfels and critical theorists like Axel Honneth, was largely thanks to Freiburg Catholic theologians such as Ludwig Wenzler and Bernhard Caspar, and has obviously been dominated by the question of German guilt for the *Shoah*.

The vicissitudes of the Anglo-American reception of Levinas might also be mentioned in this connection. The reception begins in the Catholic universities in the USA, many of which enjoyed strong connections with the Dutch and Belgium Catholic academic milieux such as Duquesne University and Loyola University Chicago. But Levinas was also being read from the early 1970s onwards in Continental philosophy circles in non-Catholic universities such as Northwestern, Pennsylvania State and the State University of New York (Stonybrook), which produced Levinas scholars such as Richard A. Cohen. The first book-length study of Levinas in English was by Edith Wyschogrod from 1974, although it was published by Nijhoff in Holland.[9] As an undergraduate at the University of Essex in the 1980s, I was introduced to Levinas's work by my present co-editor, as were many others, such as Tina Chanter. At that time, one had the impression that an interest in Levinas was a passion shared by a handful of initiates and rare senior figures such as John Llewelyn, Alan Montefiore or David Wood. It is fair to say that in the English-speaking world many people came to Levinas through the astonishing popularity of the work of Derrida. The turn to Levinas was motivated by the question of whether deconstruction, in its Derridian or De Manian versions, had any ethical status, which in its turn was linked to a widespread renewal of interest in the place of ethics in literary studies.[10]

Although Levinas could hardly be so described, another influential strand of the Anglo-American reception of his work has been feminist, in the work of scholars such as Noreen O'Connor, Tina Chanter, Jill Robbins and younger philosophers such as Stella Sandford.[11] They were in turn inspired by the early work of Catherine Chalier on figures of femininity in Levinas and Judaism, and also by Luce Irigaray's commentaries on Levinas in the context of discussions of the ethics of sexual difference.[12] Levinas was introduced to sociology through the pathbreaking work of Zygmunt Bauman and his influence is felt in the work of Homi Bhabha and Paul Gilroy.[13] For good or ill, Levinas has become an obligatory reference point in theoretical discussions across a whole range of disciplines: philosophy, theology, Jewish studies, aesthetics and art theory, social and political theory, international relations theory, pedagogy, psychotherapy and counselling, and nursing and medical practice.

As the theme of ethics has occupied an increasingly central place in the humanities and the social sciences, so Levinas's work has assumed an imposing profile. For example, Gary Gutting's excellent new history of French philosophy in the twentieth century, which supplants Descombes's on the Cambridge University Press list, concludes with a discussion of Levinas.[14] There is now a veritable flood of work on Levinas in a huge range of languages, and his work has been well translated into English. The more recent translations of Levinas build on the work of Alphonso Lingis, Levinas's first and best-known English translator. Indeed, in many ways it now looks as if Levinas were the hidden king of twentieth-century French philosophy. Such are the pleasing ironies of history.

It is a reflection of Levinas's growing importance that philosophers with a background in analytic philosophy and American pragmatism such as Hilary W. Putnam, Richard J. Bernstein or Stanley Cavell, should be taking up Levinas.[15] Even someone like Richard Rorty, although deeply hostile to the rigours of infinite responsibility, which he calls a 'nuisance', now feels obliged to refute him.[16] It is our hope that this Cambridge Companion will consolidate, deepen and accelerate the reception of Levinas in the English-speaking world and along its edges. In the selection of essays, we have sought a balance between the more usual phenomenological or Continental approaches to Levinas's work and more analytic approaches, the ambition being to shun that particular professional division of labour. Attention has also been paid to the significant consequences of Levinas's work for aesthetics, art and literature, and to representing the specifically Judaic character of Levinas's work, both his concern for religious issues and his practice of Talmudic commentary.

LEVINAS'S BIG IDEA

Levinas's work, like that of any original thinker, is possessed of a great richness. It was influenced by many sources – non-philosophical and philosophical, as much by Levinas's Talmudic master Monsieur Chouchani as by Heidegger – and it deals with a wide and complex range of matters. Levinas's work provides powerful descriptions of a whole range of phenomena, both everyday banalities and those that one could describe with Bataille as 'limit-experiences': insomnia, fatigue, effort, sensuous enjoyment, erotic life, birth and the relation to death. Such phenomena are described with particularly memorable power by Levinas in the work published after the war: *Existence and Existents* and *Time and the Other*.

However, despite its richness, once more like that of any great thinker, Levinas's work is dominated by one thought, and it seeks to think one thing under an often bewildering variety of aspects. Derrida, in an image that Richard Bernstein takes up later in this book, compares the movement of Levinas's thinking to that of a wave on a beach, always the same wave returning and repeating its movement with deeper insistence. Hilary Putnam, picking up on a more prosaic image from Isaiah Berlin, *via* Archilochus, compares Levinas to a hedgehog, who knows 'one big thing', rather than a fox, who knows 'many small things'. Levinas's one big thing is expressed in his thesis that ethics is first philosophy, where ethics is understood as a relation of infinite responsibility to the other person. My task in this introduction is to explain Levinas's big idea. Let me begin, however, with a remark on philosophical method.

In a discussion from 1975, Levinas said, 'I neither believe that there is transparency possible in method, nor that philosophy is possible as transparency' (GCM 143). Now, while the opacity of Levinas's prose troubles many of his readers, it cannot be said that his work is without method. Levinas always described himself as a phenomenologist and as being faithful to the spirit of Husserl (OB 183). What Levinas means by phenomenology is the Husserlian method of intentional analysis. Although there are various formulations of the meaning of the latter in Levinas's work, the best definition remains that given in the preface to *Totality and Infinity*. He writes,

Intentional analysis is the search for the concrete. Notions held under the direct analysis of the thought that defines them are nevertheless, unbeknown to this naïve thought, revealed to be implanted in horizons unsuspected by this thought; these horizons endow them with meaning – such is the essential teaching of Husserl. [*TI* 28]

Thus, intentional analysis begins from the unreflective naïvety of what Husserl calls the natural attitude. Through the operation of the phenomenological reduction, it seeks to describe the deep structures of intentional life, structures which give meaning to that life, but which are forgotten in that naïvety. This is what phenomenology calls the concrete: not the empirical givens of sense data, but the *a priori* structures that give meaning to those seeming givens. As Levinas puts it, 'What counts is the idea of the overflowing of objectifying thought by a forgotten experience from which it lives' (*TI* 28). This is what Levinas meant when he used to say, as he apparently often did at the beginning of his lecture courses at the Sorbonne in the 1970s, that philosophy, 'c'est la science des naïvetés' ('it's the science of naïveties'). Philosophy is the work of reflection that is brought to bear on unreflective, everyday life. This is why Levinas insists that phenomenology constitutes a deduction, from the naïve to the scientific, from the empirical to the *a priori* and so forth. A phenomenologist seeks to pick out and analyse the common, shared features that underlie our everyday experience, to make explicit what is implicit in our ordinary social know-how. On this model, in my view, the philosopher, unlike the natural scientist, does not claim to be providing us with new knowledge or fresh discoveries, but rather with what Wittgenstein calls *reminders* of what we already know but continually pass over in our day-to-day life. Philosophy reminds us of what is passed over in the naïvety of what passes for common sense.

Mention of the spirit of Husserlian phenomenology is important since, from the time of his 1930 doctoral thesis onwards, Levinas could hardly be described as faithful to the letter of Husserl's texts. He variously criticized his former teacher for theoreticism, intellectualism and overlooking the existential density and historical embeddedness of lived experience. Levinas's critically appropriative relation to Husserl is discussed at length below by Rudolf Bernet, with special reference to time-consciousness. If the fundamental axiom of phenomenology is the intentionality thesis, namely that all thought is fundamentally characterized by being directed towards its various matters, then Levinas's big idea about the ethical relation to the other person is not phenomenological, because the other is not given as a matter for thought or reflection. As Levinas makes clear in an essay from 1965, the other is not a phenomenon but an enigma, something ultimately refractory to intentionality and opaque to the understanding.[17] Therefore, Levinas maintains a methodological but not a substantive commitment to Husserlian phenomenology.

LEAVING THE CLIMATE OF HEIDEGGER'S THINKING

Levinas is usually associated with one thesis, namely the idea that *ethics is first philosophy*. But what exactly does he mean by that? The central task of Levinas's work, in his words, is the attempt to describe a relation with the other person that cannot be reduced to comprehension. He finds this in what he famously calls the 'face-to-face' relation. But let me try and unpack these slightly mysterious claims by considering his somewhat oedipal conflict with Heidegger, which is discussed by a number of contributors below, such as Gerald Bruns.

As is well known, Heidegger became politically committed to National Socialism, accepting the position of Rector of Freiburg University in the fateful year 1933. If one is to begin to grasp how traumatic Heidegger's commitment to National Socialism was to the young Levinas and how determinative it was for his future work, then one has to understand the extent to which Levinas was philosophically convinced by Heidegger. Between 1930 and 1932 Levinas planned to write a book on Heidegger, a project he abandoned in disbelief at Heidegger's actions in 1933. A fragment of the book was published in 1932 as 'Martin Heidegger and Ontology'.[18] By 1934, at the request of the recently founded French left Catholic journal *Esprit*, Levinas had written a memorable meditation on the philosophy of what the editor, Emmanuel Mounier, called 'Hitlerism'.[19] So if Levinas's life was dominated by the memory of the Nazi horror, then his philosophical life was animated by the question of how a philosopher as undeniably brilliant as Heidegger could have become a Nazi, for however short a time.

The philosophical kernel of Levinas's critique of Heidegger is most clearly stated in the important 1951 paper, 'Is Ontology Fundamental?'[20] Levinas here engages in a critical questioning of Heidegger's project of fundamental ontology, that is, his attempt to raise anew the question of the meaning of Being through an analysis of that being for whom Being is an issue: *Dasein* or the human being. In Heidegger's early work, ontology – which is what Aristotle called the science of Being as such or metaphysics – is fundamental, and *Dasein* is the fundament or condition of possibility for any ontology. What Heidegger seeks to do in *Being and Time*, once again in the spirit rather than the letter of Husserlian intentional analysis, is to identify the basic or *a priori* structures of *Dasein*. These structures are what Heidegger calls 'existentials', such as understanding, state-of-mind, discourse and falling. For Levinas, the basic advance and advantage of Heideggerian ontology over Husserlian phenomenology is that it begins from an analysis of the factual situation of the human being in everyday life, what Heidegger after Wilhelm Dilthey calls 'facticity'. The understanding or comprehension of Being (*Seinsverständnis*), which must be presupposed in order for Heidegger's investigation into the meaning of Being to be intelligible, does not presuppose a merely intellectual attitude, but rather the rich variety of intentional life – emotional and practical as well as theoretical – through which we relate to things, persons and the world.

There is here a fundamental agreement of Levinas with Heidegger which can already be found in his critique of Husserl in the conclusion to his 1930 doctoral thesis, *The Theory of Intuition in Husserl's Phenomenology* and which is presupposed in all of Levinas's subsequent work. The essential contribution of Heideggerian ontology is its critique of intellectualism. Ontology is not, as it was for Aristotle, a contemplative theoretical endeavour, but is, according to Heidegger, grounded in a fundamental ontology of the existential engagement of human beings in the world, which forms the anthropological preparation for the question of Being. Levinas writes with reference to the phenomenological reduction, 'This is an act in which we consider life in all its concreteness but no longer live it' (*TIHP* 155). Levinas's version of phenomenology seeks to consider life as it is lived. The overall orientation of Levinas's early work might be summarized in another sentence from the opening pages of the same book, 'Knowledge of Heidegger's starting point may allow us to understand better Husserl's end point' (*TIHP* xxxiv).

However, as some of the writings prior to the 1951 essay make clear (for example, the introduction to the 1947 book *Existence and Existents*), although Levinas's work is to a large extent inspired by Heidegger and by the conviction that we cannot put aside *Being and Time* for a philosophy that would be pre-Heideggerian, it is also governed by what Levinas calls, 'the profound need to leave the climate of that philosophy' (*EE* 19). In a letter appended to the 1962 paper, 'Transcendence and Height', with an oblique but characteristic reference to Heidegger's political myopia, Levinas writes,

The poetry of the peaceful path that runs through fields does not reflect the splendour of Being beyond beings. The splendour brings with it more sombre and pitiless images. The declaration of the end of metaphysics is premature. The end is not at all certain. Besides, metaphysics – the relation with the being (*étant*) which is accomplished as ethics – precedes the understanding of Being and survives ontology. [*BPW* 31]

Levinas claims that *Dasein*'s understanding of Being presupposes an ethical relation with the other human being, that being to whom I speak and to whom I am obliged before being comprehended. Fundamental ontology is fundamentally ethical. It is this ethical relation that Levinas, principally in *Totality and Infinity*, describes as metaphysical and which survives any declaration of the end of metaphysics.

Levinas's Heidegger is essentially the author of *Being and Time*, 'Heidegger's first and principal work', a work which, for Levinas, is the peer of the greatest books in the history of philosophy, regardless of Heidegger's politics (*CP* 52). Although Levinas clearly knew Heidegger's later work, much more than he liked to admit, he expresses little sympathy for it. In the important 1957 essay, 'Philosophy and the Idea of Infinity', the critique of Heidegger becomes yet more direct and polemical: 'In Heidegger, atheism is a paganism, the pre-Socratic texts are anti-Scriptures. Heidegger shows in what intoxication the lucid sobriety of philosophers is steeped' (*CP* 53).

'Is Ontology Fundamental?' demonstrates for the first time in Levinas's work the *ethical* significance of his critique of Heidegger. It is in this paper that the word 'ethics' first enters Levinas's philosophical vocabulary. The importance of this essay for Levinas's subsequent work can be seen in the way in which its argumentation is alluded to and effectively repeated in crucial pages of *Totality and Infinity*.[21] The central task of the essay is to describe a relation irreducible to comprehension, that is, irreducible to what Levinas sees as the *ontological* relation to others. Ontology is Levinas's general term for any relation to otherness that is reducible to comprehension or understanding. On this account, Husserl's phenomenology is therefore ontological because the intentionality thesis assumes a correlation between an intentional act and the object of that intention, or *noema* and *noesis* in the later work. Even the Heideggerian ontology that exceeds intellectualism is unable to describe this non-comprehensive relation because particular beings are always already understood upon the horizon of Being, even if this is, as Heidegger says at the beginning of *Being and Time*, a vague and average understanding. Levinas writes that *Being and Time* essentially advanced one thesis: 'Being is inseparable from the comprehension of Being' (*CP* 52). Thus, despite the novelty of his work, Heidegger rejoins and sums up the great Platonic tradition of Western philosophy, where the relation to particular beings is always understood by way of mediation with a third term, whether universal form or *eidos* in Plato, Spirit in Hegel or Being in Heidegger.

Yet how can a relation with a being be other than comprehension? Levinas's response is that it cannot, 'unless it is the other (*autrui*)' (*BPW* 6). *Autrui* is arguably the key term in all of Levinas's work and, in line with common French usage, it is Levinas's word for the human other, the other person. The claim here is that the relation with the other goes beyond comprehension, and that it does not affect us in terms of a theme (recall that Heidegger describes Being as 'thematic' in the early pages of *Being and Time*) or a concept. If the other person were reducible to the concept I have of him or her, then that would make the relation to the other a relation of knowledge or an epistemological feature. As the two allusions to Kant in 'Is Ontology Fundamental?' reveal – and this is something taken up by Paul Davies in his contribution to this volume – ethics is not reducible to epistemology, practical reason is not reducible to pure reason. As Levinas puts it in a discussion from the mid-1980s, ethics is otherwise than knowledge.[22] Levinas revealingly writes, 'that which we catch sight of seems suggested by the practical philosophy of Kant, to which we feel particularly close'.[23] To my mind, this suggests two possible points of agreement between Levinas and Kant, despite other obvious areas of disagreement such as the primacy of autonomy for Kant and Levinas's assertion of heteronomy as the basis for ethical experience. First, we might see Levinas's account of the ethical relation to the other person as an echo of Kant's second formulation of the categorical imperative, namely respect for persons, where I should act in such a way as never to treat the other person as a means to an end, but rather as an end in him or herself.[24] Second, we should keep in mind that Kant concludes the *Groundwork of the Metaphysic of Morals* by claiming the incomprehensibility of the moral law: 'And thus, while we do not comprehend the practical unconditioned necessity of the moral imperative, we do comprehend its *incomprehensibility*. This is all that can fairly be asked of a philosophy which presses forward in its principles to the very limit of human reason.'[25]

For Levinas, this relation to the other irreducible to comprehension, what he calls the 'original relation' (BPW 6), takes place in the concrete situation of speech. Although Levinas's choice of terminology suggests otherwise, the face-to-face relation with the other is not a relation of perception or vision, but is always linguistic. The face is not something I see, but something I speak to. Furthermore, in speaking or calling or listening to the other, I am not reflecting upon the other, but I am actively and existentially engaged in a non-subsumptive relation, where I focus on the particular individual in front of me. I am not contemplating, I am conversing. It is this event of being in relation with the other as an act or a practice – which is variously and revealingly named in 'Is Ontology Fundamental?' as 'expression', 'invocation' and 'prayer' – that Levinas describes as 'ethical'. This leads to a significant insight: that Levinas does not posit, *a priori*, a conception of ethics that then instantiates itself (or does not) in certain concrete experiences. Rather, the ethical is an adjective that describes, *a posteriori* as it were, a certain event of being in a relation to the other irreducible to comprehension. It is the relation which is ethical, not an ethics that is instantiated in relations.

Some philosophers might be said to have a problem with other people. For a philosopher like Heidegger, the other person is just one of many: 'the they', the crowd, the mass, the herd. I know all about the other because the other is part of the mass that surrounds and suffocates me. On this picture, there is never anything absolutely challenging, remarkable or even, in a word Levinas uses in his late work, traumatizing about the other person. The other might at best become my colleague, comrade or co-worker, but not the source of my compassion or the object of my admiration, fear or desire. Levinas's point is that unless our social interactions are underpinned by ethical relations to other persons, then the worst might happen, that is, the failure to acknowledge the humanity of the other. Such, for Levinas, is what took place in the *Shoah* and in the countless other disasters of this century, where the other person becomes a faceless face in the crowd, someone whom the passer-by simply passes by, someone whose life or death is for me a matter of indifference. As Levinas succinctly puts it in one of his last published interviews from *Le Monde* in 1992, 'The absence of concern for the other in Heidegger and his personal political adventure are linked'.[26]

So, where Levinas puts ethics first, Heidegger puts them second. That is, the relation to the other person is only a moment in a philosophical investigation of which the ambition is the exploration of the basic question of philosophy, the question of Being. Of course, the danger in all this is that the philosopher risks losing sight of the other person in his or her quest for ontological truth. It is perhaps no accident that the history of Greek philosophy begins with Thales, who falls into a ditch because he would rather gaze at the starry heavens that at what is under his nose.

WHY TOTALITY? WHY INFINITY?

Levinas's first full-length systematic philosophical book, what Derrida calls 'the great work', is *Totality and Infinity*, which is discussed below by a number of contributors, especially Bernhard Waldenfels. Why does it have this title? For Levinas, all ontological relations to that which is other are relations of comprehension and form totalities. The claim is that if I conceive of the relation to the other in terms of understanding, correlation, symmetry, reciprocity, equality and even, as has once again become fashionable, recognition, then that relation is totalized. When I totalize, I conceive of the relation to the other from some imagined point that would be outside of it and I turn myself into a theoretical spectator on the social world of which I am really part, and in which I am an agent. Viewed from outside, intersubjectivity might appear to be a relation between equals, but from inside that relation, as it takes place at this very moment, you place an obligation on me that makes you higher than me, more than my equal. It might be argued that much philosophy and social theory persistently totalizes relations with others. But for Levinas, there is no view from nowhere. Every view is from somewhere and the ethical relation is a description from the point of view of an agent in the social world and not a spectator upon it.

In the work of the later 1950s onwards, the ethical relation to the other is described by Levinas in terms of infinity. What does that mean? Levinas's claim is very simple, but even quite sophisticated readers still get it muddled. The idea is that the ethical relation to the other has a *formal* resemblance to the relation, in Descartes's Third Meditation, between the *res cogitans* and the infinity of God.[27] What interests Levinas in this moment of Descartes's argument is that the human subject has an idea of infinity, and that this idea, by definition, is a thought that contains more than can be thought. As Levinas puts it, in what is almost a mantra in his published work, 'In thinking infinity the I from the first *thinks more than it thinks*' (CP 54).

It is this formal structure of a thought that thinks more than it can think, that has a surplus within itself, that intrigues Levinas because it sketches the contours of a relation to something that is always in excess of whatever idea I may have of it, that always escapes me. The Cartesian picture of the relation of the *res cogitans* to God through the idea of the infinite provides Levinas with a picture or formal model of a relation between two terms that is based on height, inequality, non-reciprocity and asymmetry. However, Levinas is making no substantive claim at this point, he is not saying that I actually do possess the idea of the infinite in the way Descartes describes, nor is he claiming that the other is God, as some readers mistakenly continue to believe. As Putnam rightly points out below, 'It isn't that Levinas accepts Descartes's argument, so interpreted. The significance is rather that Levinas transforms the argument by substituting the other for God.'

As Levinas is a phenomenologist, it then becomes a question for him of trying to locate some concrete content for this formal structure. Levinas's major substantive claim, which resounds in different ways throughout his mature work, is that the ethical relation of the self to the other corresponds to this picture, concretely fulfilling this model. One might say that the ethical relation to the face of the other person is the *social* expression of this formal structure. Levinas writes, 'the idea of infinity is the social relationship', and again, 'The way in which the other presents himself, exceeding *the idea of the other in me*, we here name face' (CP 54; TI 50). Thus, the ethical relation to the other produces what Levinas calls, in a favourite formulation, rightly picked up by Blanchot, 'a curvature of intersubjective space', that can only be totalized by falsely imagining oneself occupying some God-like position outside of that relation (TI 291).

WHAT IS THE SAME? WHAT IS THE OTHER?

Ethics, for Levinas, takes place as the putting into question of the ego, the self, consciousness or what he calls, in the term that he borrows from Plato, the same (*le Même, to auton*). What is the same? It is important to note that the same refers not only to subjective thoughts, but also to the objects of those thoughts. In Husserlian terms, the domain of the same includes not only the intentional acts of consciousness, or *noeses*, but also the intentional objects which give meaning to those acts, or *noemata*. Again, in Heideggerian terms, the same refers not only to *Dasein*, but also to the world which is constitutive of the Being of *Dasein*, where the latter is defined as Being-in-the-world. So, the domain of the same maintains a relation with otherness, but it is a relation in which the ego or consciousness reduces the distance between the same and the other, in which, as Levinas puts it, their opposition fades (TI 126).

The same is therefore called into question by an other that cannot be reduced to the same, by something that escapes the cognitive power of the subject. The first time that Levinas employs the word 'ethics' in the text proper – excluding the preface – of *Totality and Infinity*, he defines it as 'the putting into question of my spontaneity by the presence of the Other (*Autrui*)' (TI 43). Ethics, for Levinas, is critique. It is the critical putting into question of the liberty, spontaneity and cognitive emprise of the ego that seeks to reduce all otherness to itself. Ethics is the location of a point of otherness, or what Levinas calls 'exteriority', that cannot be reduced to the same. *Totality and Infinity* is subtitled 'An essay on exteriority'. In his brief autobiographical reflections, Levinas remarks 'Moral consciousness is not an experience of values, but an access to exterior being' (DF 293).

This exterior being is named 'face' by Levinas and is defined, bringing to mind what was said above about the notion of infinity, as 'the way in which the other presents himself, exceeding *the idea of the other in me*' (*TI* 50). In the language of transcendental philosophy, the face is the condition of possibility for ethics. Levinas makes a distinction between two forms of otherness, distinguished by *autre* and *autrui* in French, which are sometimes capitalized and sometimes not in Levinas's rather unsystematic prose style. *Autre* refers to anything which is other, this computer at which I am typing, the window panes and the buildings I can see across the street. *Autrui* is reserved for the other human being with whom I have an ethical relation, although it remains a moot point to what extent, if any, Levinasian ethics is capable of being extended to non-human beings, such as animals.[28]

As well as being critique, Levinasian ethics bears a critical relation to the philosophical tradition. For Levinas, Western philosophy has most often been ontology, of which Heidegger's work is only the most recent example, and by which Levinas means any attempt to comprehend the Being of that which is. On this account, epistemology, in either its realist or idealist versions, is an ontology in so far as the object of cognition is an object *for* consciousness, an intuition that can be placed under a concept, whether that intuition is the empirical given of a sense-datum or is transcendentally constituted by the categories of the understanding. For Levinas, the ontological event that defines and dominates the philosophical tradition from Parmenides to Heidegger consists in suppressing or reducing all forms of otherness by transmuting them into the same. In ontology, the other is assimilated to the same like so much food and drink – 'O digestive philosophy!', as Sartre exclaimed against French neo-Kantianism.[29] Taking up the analysis of separated existence in part II of *Totality and Infinity*, ontology is the movement of comprehension, which takes possession of things through the activity of labour, where conceptual labour resembles manual labour. Ontology is like the movement of the hand, the organ for grasping and seizing, which takes hold of (*prend*) and comprehends (*comprend*) things in a manipulation of otherness. In 'Transcendence and Height', Levinas outlines and criticizes this digestive philosophy, where the knowing ego is what he calls 'the melting pot' of Being, transmuting all otherness into itself. Philosophy is defined by Levinas as that alchemy whereby otherness is transmuted into sameness by means of the philosopher's stone of the knowing ego.[30]

WHAT IS THE SAYING? WHAT IS THE SAID?

For want of a better term, 'non-ontological philosophy' would consist in the resistance of the other to the same, a resistance that Levinas describes as ethical. It is this resistance, this point of exteriority to the appropriative movement of philosophical conceptuality, that Levinas seeks to describe in his work. In *Totality and Infinity*, such a point of exteriority is located in the face of the other, but this exteriority is still expressed in the language of ontology, as when Levinas writes that 'Being is exteriority' (*TI* 290). Thus, in Heideggerian terms, the meaning of the Being of beings, the basic question of metaphysics, is determined as exteriority. The contradiction, where that which is meant to escape ontology is still expressed in ontological language, was powerfully pointed out by Derrida in 'Violence and Metaphysics'. He argued that the attempt to leave the climate of Heidegger's thinking was doomed from the start because Levinas still employs Heideggerian categories in the attempt to exceed those categories. Derrida extended the same argument to Levinas's critique of Hegel and Husserl. Levinas confessed that he had been 'tormented' by Derrida's questions in 'Violence and Metaphysics'.[31] Accepting Derrida's point, Levinas writes in 'Signature' that 'The ontological language which is still used in *Totality and Infinity* in order to exclude a purely psychological signification of the proposed analyses is henceforth avoided' (*DF* 295). Again, in an interview with some English graduate students, published in 1988, Levinas reiterates the point, '*Totality and Infinity* was my first book. I find it very difficult to tell you, in a few words, in what way it is different from what I've said afterwards. There is the ontological terminology. I have since tried to get away from that language' (*PM* 171).

In his second major philosophical book, from 1974, *Otherwise than Being or Beyond Essence*, Levinas tries to avoid this problem of ontological language, in a sinuous self-critique, by coining the distinction between the saying and the said (*le dire et le dit*). The conception of language at work in this book and elsewhere is discussed below by John Llewelyn and Edith Wyschogrod. Crudely stated, the saying is ethical and the said is ontological. Although Levinas can hardly be said to offer dictionary definitions of these terms, we might say that the saying is my exposure – both corporeal and sensible – to the other person, my inability to resist the other's approach. It is the performative stating, proposing or expressive position of myself facing the other. It is a verbal and possibly also non-verbal ethical performance, of which the essence cannot be captured in constative propositions. It is, if you will, a performative *doing* that cannot be reduced to a propositional description. By contrast, the said is a statement, assertion or proposition of which the truth or falsity can be ascertained. To put it another way, one might say that the content of my words, their identifiable meaning, is the said, while the saying consists in the fact that these words are being addressed to an interlocutor, at this moment each of you. The saying is a non-thematizable ethical residue of language that escapes comprehension, interrupts ontology and is the very enactment of the movement from the same to the other.

Given that philosophy as ontology speaks the language of the said – it is propositional, it fills papers, chapters and books such as this one – the methodological problem facing the later Levinas, and which haunts every page of the rather baroque prose of *Otherwise than Being*, is the following: how is the saying to be said? That is, how is my ethical exposure to the other to be given a philosophical exposition that does not utterly betray this saying? In *Otherwise than Being*, Levinas's thinking and, more especially his style of writing, become increasingly sensitive to the problem of how the ethical saying is to be conceptualized – and necessarily betrayed – within the ontological said. One might call this Levinas's deconstructive turn.

The solution to this methodological problem is found, I would suggest, in a notion of *reduction*. In brief, it is a question of exploring the ways in which the said can be unsaid, or reduced, thereby letting the saying circulate as a residue or interruption within the said. The philosopher's effort, Levinas claims, consists in the reduction of the said to the saying and the continual disruption of the limit that separates the ethical from the ontological (*OB* 43–5). Ethics is not, as it perhaps seemed in *Totality and Infinity*, the overcoming or simple abandonment of ontology through the immediacy of ethical experience. It is rather the persistent deconstruction of the limits of ontology and its claim to conceptual mastery, while also recognizing the unavoidability of the Said. *Traduire, c'est trahir* (to translate is to betray) as Levinas was fond of pointing out, but the translation of the saying into the said is a necessary betrayal. So, whereas *Totality and Infinity* powerfully articulates the non-ontological experience of the face of the other in the language of ontology, *Otherwise than Being* is a performative disruption of the language of ontology, which attempts to maintain the interruption of the ethical saying within the ontological said. Whereas *Totality and Infinity* writes about ethics, *Otherwise than Being* is the performative enactment of an ethical writing which endlessly runs up against the limits of language. This puts me in mind of the following remark from Wittgenstein's 1929 'Lecture on Ethics': 'I can only describe my feeling by the metaphor, that, if a man could write a book on Ethics which really was a book on Ethics, this book would, with an explosion, destroy all the other books in the world.'[32] Reading the tortuously beautiful, rhapsodic incantations of *Otherwise than Being*, one sometimes wonders whether it is Levinas's attempt to write such a book. For Wittgenstein, human beings feel the urge to run up against the limits of language, and such an urge has an ethical point. It reveals that the ethical saying is nothing that can be said propositionally and that ethics cannot be put into words. Strictly speaking, ethical discourse is nonsense, but it is serious nonsense.

So, with what his great friend Blanchot sees as a continual refinement of reflection on the possibilities of philosophical language, Levinas gives expression to the primacy of ethics, that is, the primacy of the interhuman relationship, 'an irreducible structure upon which all other structures rest' (*TI* 79).[33] For Levinas, excepting what he calls certain *instants merveilleux* in the history of philosophy, notably the Good beyond Being in Plato and the idea of infinity in Descartes, it is ethics that has been dissimulated within the philosophical tradition. Philosophy is not, as Heidegger maintained, a forgetfulness of Being, as much as a forgetfulness of the other. Hence, the fundamental question for philosophy is not Hamlet's 'To be or not to be', or Heidegger's 'Why are there beings at all and why not rather nothing?', but rather 'How does Being justify itself?' (*LR* 86).[34]

WHO IS THE SUBJECT?

Against Heidegger, but also against structuralists like Levi-Strauss and anti-humanists like Foucault and Deleuze, Levinas presents his work as a defence of subjectivity (*TI* 26). What is this Levinasian conception of subjectivity? As Robert Bernasconi shows in his contribution below, subjectivity is a central and constant theme in Levinas's work. In his first post-war writings, *Existence and Existents* and *Time and the Other*, Levinas describes the advent of the subject out of the impersonal neutrality of what he calls the *il y a*, the anonymous rumbling of existence, the sheer 'there is' of the night of insomnia. However, staying with *Otherwise than Being*, another innovation of the latter work is that whereas *Totality and Infinity* describes ethics as a relation to the other, *Otherwise than Being* describes the structure of ethical subjectivity that is disposed towards the other, what Levinas calls 'the other within the same'.

In *Otherwise than Being*, Levinas begins his exposition by describing the movement from Husserlian intentional consciousness to a level of preconscious sensing or sentience, a movement enacted in the title of the second chapter: 'From Intentionality to Sensing'. As we saw above, from the time of his doctoral thesis on Husserl, Levinas had been critical of the primacy of intentional consciousness, claiming that the latter was theoreticist, where the subject maintains an objectifying relation to the world mediated through representation. The worldly object is the *noema* of a *noesis*. Such is Husserl's intellectualism. Now, in a gesture that remains faithful to Heidegger's ontological undermining of the theoretical comportment toward the world, what he calls the present-at-hand (*Vorhandenheit*), the movement from intentionality or sensing, or, in the terms of *Totality and Infinity*, from representation to enjoyment, shows how intentional consciousness is, to put it simply, conditioned by *life*. Life is sentience, enjoyment and nourishment. It is *jouissance* and *joie de vivre*. It is a life that lives from (*vivre de*) the elements: 'we live from good soup, air, light, spectacles, work, sleep, etc. These are not objects of representations' (*TI* 110). Life, for Levinas, is love of life and love of what life lives from: the sensible, material world. I would argue that Levinas's work offers a material phenomenology of subjective life, where the conscious ego of representation is reduced to the sentient self of enjoyment. The self-conscious subject of intentionality is reduced to a living subject that is subject to the conditions of its existence. Now, for Levinas, it is precisely this self of enjoyment that is capable of being claimed or called into question ethically by the other person. As we have seen, Levinasian ethics is simply this calling into question of myself – of my spontaneity, of my *jouissance*, of my freedom – by the other. The ethical relation takes place at the level of sensibility, not at the level of consciousness. The Levinasian ethical subject is a sensible subject, not a conscious subject.

For Levinas, the subject is subject, as it were, and the form that this subjection assumes is that of sensibility or sentience. Sensibility is what Levinas calls 'the way' of my subjection. This is a sentient vulnerability or passivity towards the other that takes place 'on the surface of the skin, at the edge of the nerves' (OB 15). The entire phenomenological thrust of *Otherwise than Being* is to found intentionality in sensibility (ch. 2) and to describe sensibility as a proximity to the other (ch. 3), a proximity whose basis is found in what Levinas calls substitution (ch. 4, what Levinas describes as 'the centrepiece' of the book). The ethical subject is an embodied being of flesh and blood, a being that is capable of hunger, who eats and enjoys eating. As Levinas writes, 'only a being that eats can be for the other' (OB 74). That is, only such a being can know what it means to give its bread to the other from out of its own mouth. In what must be the world's shortest refutation of Heidegger, Levinas complains that *Dasein* is never hungry, and the same might be said of all the various heirs to the *res cogitans*. As Levinas wittily puts it, 'The need for food does not have existence as its goal, but food' (TI 134).

Levinasian ethics is not therefore an obligation toward the other mediated through the formal and procedural universalization of maxims or some appeal to good conscience. Rather, and this is what is truly provocative about Levinas, ethics is *lived* in the sensibility of an embodied exposure to the other. It is because the self is sensible, that is to say, vulnerable, passive, open to the pangs of both hunger and eros, that it is worthy of ethics. Levinas's phenomenological claim, in the sense of intentional analysis clarified above, is that the deep structure of subjective experience, what Levinas calls the 'psychism', is structured in a relation of responsibility or, better, responsivity to the other. This deep structure, what Levinas calls the 'psychism' and what other traditions might call the 'soul', is the other within the same, in spite of me, calling me to respond.

Who, then, is the subject? It is *me* and nobody else. As Dostoevsky's underground man complains, I am not an instance of some general concept or genus of the human being: an ego, self-consciousness or thinking thing. Levinas phenomenologically reduces the abstract ego to me, to myself as the one who undergoes the demand or call of the other. As Levinas puts it, 'La subjectivité n'est pas le Moi, mais moi' ('Subjectivity is not the Ego, but me') (*CP* 150). That is, my first word is not Descartes's 'ego cogito' ('I am, I think'), it is rather 'me voici!' ('here I am!' or 'see me here!'), the word with which the prophet testifies to the presence of God. For Levinas, the subject arises in the response to the other's call. To put it another way, ethics is entirely my affair, not the affair of some hypothetical, impersonal or universal I running through a sequence of possible imperatives. Ethics is not a spectator sport. Rather, it is my experience of a demand that I both cannot fully meet and cannot avoid.

IS LEVINAS A JEWISH PHILOSOPHER?

One of the prevailing and potentially misleading assumptions about Levinas's work is that he is a Jewish philosopher. Often the people most eager to categorize him as a Jewish philosopher have little understanding of Judaism, and even less of Levinas's particular version of it, which owes a good deal to his Lithuanian heritage and to a highly specialized technique of Talmudic interpretation that owes more than a little to that heritage. Although Levinas's thinking is quite inconceivable without its Judaic inspiration, one should be careful not to categorize him simply as a Jewish philosopher. He once said, 'I am not a Jewish thinker. I am just a thinker.'[35] Levinas was a philosopher *and* a Jew, a point underlined by the fact that his philosophical work and his Talmudic readings even appear with different French publishers. Because Levinas was a practising Jew, and wrote extensive Talmudic interpretations, as well as being a skilled commentator on Jewish affairs in France and Israel, he exercises careful discretion about his Judaism when speaking as a philosopher. It is a discretion that is only surpassed by the economy of his remarks about the *Shoah*.

However, that said, Levinas's declared philosophical ambition was no less than the translation of the Bible into Greek. What he meant by this was the rendering of the ethical message of Judaism into the language of philosophy. But what is essential here is the act of translation: philosophy speaks Greek in the sense in which the great discovery of Greek philosophy is the primacy of reason, universality, evidence and argument. The philosopher cannot rely upon the experience of faith or the mystery of revelation. Levinas's Judaism was extremely hostile to mysticism, whether what he saw as the pagan mysticism of the sacred in the later Heidegger, or the Jewish mysticism of the Kabbala and the Hassidic tradition, which was one of the sources of his disagreement with Martin Buber. I think this basic belief in reason explains why the most cited texts in Levinas's *magnum opus, Totality and Infinity*, are not the Jewish scriptures, but the dialogues of Plato. I know of only three direct references to Talmudic or Biblical sources in *Totality and Infinity* (*TI* 201, 267, 277).[36]

As Putnam points out below, there is a deeply paradoxical claim implicit in Levinas's writing, namely that all human beings are Jews. Thus, rather than reducing philosophical universality to the particularism of a specific religious tradition, Levinas universalizes that particularism, which is another way of expressing the idea of translating the Bible into Greek. When it comes to the delicate topic of Levinas and Judaism, Catherine Chalier is surely right in her essay when she claims that the peculiarity of Levinas's thinking is its double fidelity, both to a Hebrew source and to a Greek source, both to Talmudic hermeneutics and philosophical rationality. The more time that one spends reading Levinas, and the more that one becomes familiar with his biography and the background of his work, the less sense it makes to argue for a hierarchy of his philosophical over his confessional work, or to argue that the latter provides the key to understanding the former or vice versa. Neither claim is true: Levinas was a philosopher and a Jew.

WHAT IS THE RELATION BETWEEN ETHICS AND POLITICS?

A question that is often rightly raised – and more often than not intended as a criticism – with regard to Levinas's conception of ethics is the following. What is the relation between the exceptional experience of the face-to-face relation and the more mundane and prosaic spheres of rationality, law and justice – spheres which, at least in the Western liberal tradition, are at the basis of the political organization of society, ensuring the legitimacy of institutions and underwriting the rights and duties of citizens? In other words, the ethical relation seems very nice, but isn't it a little abstract? What, then, is the relation between ethics and politics?

Far from this being a blind spot in his work, one finds – and with an increasing insistence – an attempt to traverse the passage from ethics to politics. In each of his two major philosophical works, *Totality and Infinity* and *Otherwise than Being*, Levinas tries to build a bridge from ethics, conceived as the non-totalizable relation to the other human being, to politics, understood as the relation to what Levinas calls the third party (*le tiers*), that is, to all the others that make up society.[37] Although the account of justice, law and politics is more developed in *Otherwise than Being* than in *Totality and Infinity*, both books begin with the statement that the domination of totalizing politics is linked to the fact of war, both the fact of the Second World War, and equally the Hobbesian claim that the peaceful order of society, the commonwealth, is constituted in opposition to the threat of the war-of-all-against-all in the state of nature. For Levinas, the domination of the category of totality in Western philosophy, from the ancient Greeks to Heidegger, is linked to the domination of totalizing forms of politics, whether Plato's adventure with the tyrant Dionysus in Syracuse, or in Heidegger's commitment to National Socialism which, in his 1933 rectoral address, was steeped in the language of Plato's *Republic*. For Levinas, totality reduces the ethical to the political. As Levinas writes in *Totality and Infinity*, 'Politics left to itself bears a tyranny within itself' (*TI* 300).

One might conclude, then, that Levinas's ethical thinking is a critique of politics. If this were so, then the above critical question would be justified. However, as becomes clear in *Otherwise than Being* or a revealing late text like 'Peace and Proximity' from 1984, Levinas does not at all want to reject the order of political rationality, and its consequent claims to legitimacy and justice.[38] Rather, Levinas wants to criticize the belief that *only* political rationality can answer political problems. He wants to indicate how the order of the state rests upon the irreducible ethical responsibility of the face-to-face relation. Levinas's critique of totalizing politics leads to the deduction of an ethical structure that is irreducible to totality: the face-to-face, infinite responsibility, proximity, the other within the same, peace. Thus, Levinas's thinking does not result in an apoliticism or ethical quietism, which, incidentally, is the core of his critique of Martin Buber's I–Thou relation. Rather, ethics leads back to politics, to the demand for a just polity. Indeed, I would go further and claim that ethics is ethical for the sake of politics, that is, for the sake of a more just society.

In 'Peace and Proximity', the question of the passage from ethics to politics is discussed in relation to the theme of Europe, and more specifically what Levinas refers to as 'the ethical moment in the crisis of Europe'. This crisis is the result of an ambiguity at the heart of the European liberal tradition, where the attempt to found a political order of peace on the 'Greek wisdom' of autonomy, equality, reciprocity and solidarity has become a guilty conscience that recognizes how this political order often legitimized the violence of imperialism, colonialism and genocide. With the rise of anti-ethnocentric discourse, say in cultural anthropology, we see Europe turned against itself and forced to recognize a deficiency in its ethical resources. Responding to this crisis, Levinas wonders whether one might not ask if the ambiguous Hellenic peace of the European political order presupposes another order of peace, located not in the totality of the state or nation, but rather in the relation to the other human being, an order of sociality and love. So, if the ethical crisis of Europe is based in its unique attachment to a Greek heritage, then Levinas is suggesting that this heritage needs to be supplemented by a Biblical tradition, which would be rooted in the acknowledgement of peace as the responsibility to the other. It is never a question, for Levinas, of shifting from the paradigm of Athens to that of Jerusalem, but rather of recognizing that both are simultaneously necessary for the constitution of a just polity. As Levinas states in the discussion that follows 'Transcendence and Height', 'Both the hierarchy taught by Athens and the *abstract* and slightly *anarchical* ethical individualism taught by Jerusalem are simultaneously necessary in order to suppress violence' (BPW 24).

CONCLUSION

Levinas's big idea is that the relation to the other cannot be reduced to comprehension and that this relation is ethical, structuring the experience of what we think of as a self or subject. But is he right? In concluding, let me shift emphasis here and try and explain Levinas's point with reference to the old epistemological chestnut of the problem of other minds. How can I know that another person is truly in pain? In Stanley Cavell's memorable restatement of the problem, let's imagine that I am a dentist drilling a patient's tooth and the patient suddenly screams out as a response to what seems like the pain caused by my clumsy drilling. And yet, in response to my embarrassed show of remorse, the patient says, 'It wasn't hurting, I was just calling my hamsters.'[39] Now, how can I know that the other person is being sincere, short of his hamsters scuttling obediently into my dental surgery? The point is that ultimately *I cannot*. I can never *know* whether another person is in pain or simply calling his hamsters.

That is to say, there is something about the other person, a dimension of separateness, interiority, secrecy or what Levinas calls 'alterity' that escapes my comprehension. That which exceeds the bounds of my knowledge demands *acknowledgement*. Taking this a little further, one might say that it is the failure to acknowledge the other's separateness from me that can be the source of tragedy. Let me take the Cavellian example of Shakespeare's *Othello*. Most people would say that Othello murdered Desdemona because he believed that he *knew* that she had been unfaithful. Prompted by his own green-eyed monster and by the sly intrigues of Iago, Othello murders Desdemona. So, if the consequence of Othello's alleged knowledge is tragic, then in what does the moral of this tragedy consist? One might say that it simply consists in the fact that we cannot ultimately know everything about the other person, even and perhaps especially when it comes to the people we love. I think this means that in our relation to other persons we have to learn to acknowledge what we cannot know and that the failure to do this was Othello's tragic flaw. The end of certainty can be the beginning of trust.

In this sense, the lesson of Shakespearean tragedy and the vast human tragedies of this century, is to learn to acknowledge what one cannot know and to respect the separateness or what Levinas calls the *transcendence* of the other person, a transcendence that is very much of this world and not part of some other-worldly mysticism. If the other gets lost in the crowd, then their transcendence vanishes. For Levinas, an *ethical* relation is one where I *face* the other person. It is this ethical relation to the other person that was lost in both the fact of National Socialist anti-semitism and in its philosophical apologias. And this is why Levinas wants to leave the climate of both Heidegger's philosophy and an entire Greek tradition, in order to return to another source for thinking, namely the more Biblical wisdom of unconditional respect for the other human being.

As Levinas was fond of putting it, the entirety of his philosophy can be summarized in the simple words, 'Après vous, Monsieur'. That is, by everyday and quite banal acts of civility, hospitality, kindness and politeness that have perhaps received too little attention from philosophers. It is such acts that Levinas qualifies with the adjective 'ethical'. Now, it is to be hoped that it goes without saying that the achievement of such an ethical relation with the other person is not *just* a task for philosophy, but it *is* a philosophical task, namely to understand what we might call the moral grammar of everyday life and to try and teach that grammar. The other person is not simply a step on the philosopher's ladder to metaphysical truth. And perhaps the true source of wonder with which, as Aristotle claimed, philosophy begins, is not to be found by staring into the starry heavens, but by looking into another's eyes, for here is a more palpable infinity that can never exhaust one's curiosity...

... And yet, despite the power of Levinas's basic intuition, is ethics the right word to describe the experience that he is trying to express? In his funeral oration for Levinas, Derrida recalls a conversation with Levinas at his apartment in Paris. Levinas said, 'You know, they often speak of ethics to describe what I do, but what interests me when all is said and done is not ethics, not only ethics, it's the holy, the holiness of the holy (*le saint, la sainteté du saint*)'.[40]

Is holiness or saintliness a better word for what Levinas is after? Maybe. Maybe not. But if such a substitution is at least conceivable, and we might be able to conceive of yet other substitutes – peace, love or whatever – then does this not suggest a possible weakness with Levinas's account of ethics? Levinas's work cannot be said to provide us with what we normally think of as an ethics, namely a theory of justice or an account of general rules, principles and procedures that would allow us to assess the acceptability of specific maxims or judgements relating to social action, civic duty or whatever. Levinas tells us that his ethics must lead to some theory of justice without telling us in any detail what this theory might be. The best we get is several pages of interesting adumbrations, the gist of which was described above.

So, is Levinas really doing ethics at all? Following Cavell once again, we might respond that there are two species of moral philosophers: legislators and moral perfectionists.[41] The former, like John

Rawls and Jürgen Habermas, provide detailed precepts, rules and principles that add up to a theory of justice. The latter, like Levinas and Cavell, believe that ethics has to be based on some form of basic existential commitment or demand that goes beyond the theoretical strictures of any account of justice or any socially instituted ethical code. The moral perfectionist belief is that an ethical theory that does not give expression to this basic demand will simply spin in a void and, moreover, have no compelling way of explaining the source of one's motivation to act on the basis of that theory.

Although Levinas might not have approved of this terminology, I think that he is seeking to give an account of a basic existential demand, a lived fundamental obligation that should be at the basis of all moral theory and moral action.[42] In my view, it is a powerful and compelling account. Levinas describes this demand, like other moral perfectionists, in exorbitant terms: infinite responsibility, trauma, persecution, hostage, obsession. The ethical demand is impossibly demanding. It has to be. If it were not so demanding then it would let us off the moral hook, as it were, and ethics would be reduced to a procedural programming where we justified moral norms by either universalizing them, assessing them in the light of their consequences, or referring them to some already given notion of custom, convention or contract. Surely the entire difficulty of moral theory and moral life consists in the fact that we require *both* legislators *and* moral perfectionists, both a compelling description of the ethical demand and a plausible theory of justification for moral norms. We need both Levinasians and Habermasians, both Cavellians and Rawlsians.

Levinas's big idea does not suffice for the solution of all our pressing and often conflicting ethical problems, and surely it would be nothing short of miraculous if it did. We can be good Levinasians and still be genuinely uncertain about which course of action to follow in a specific situation. But the strength of Levinas's position lies, I would claim, in reminding us of the nature of the ethical demand, a demand that must be presupposed at the basis of all moral theories if those theories are not to lose all connection with both the passions and the apathy of everyday life. Levinasian ethics might not be a sufficient condition for a complete ethical theory, but it is, in my view, a necessary condition for any such theory.

NOTES

1 See Levinas's telegraphically brief autobiographical reflections in 'Signature', in DF.

2 The story about Sartre reading Levinas on Husserl can be found in Simone de Beauvoir, *The Prime of Life*, trans. P. Green (Cleveland and New York: The World Publishing Company, 1962), p. 112.

3 Blanchot's essays on *Totality and Infinity*, originally published in *La Nouvelle Revue Française* in 1961–2, were reprinted in slightly modified form in the 1969 collection, *The Infinite Conversation*, trans. S. Hanson (Minneapolis: University of Minnesota Press, 1993), pp. 49–71. Derrida's 'Violence and Metaphysics' was published in two parts in *Revue de Métaphysique et de Morale* in 1964 and then reprinted with slight but significant modifications in the 1967 collection *Writing and Difference*, trans. Alan Bass (London and New York: Routledge, 1978), pp. 79–153. Derrida's second essay on Levinas, 'At this very Moment in this Work Here I Am', was originally published in *Textes pour Emmanuel Levinas* (Paris: Editions Jean-Michel Place, 1980) and an English translation is included in Robert Bernasconi and Simon Critchley (eds.) *Re-Reading Levinas* (Bloomington: Indiana University Press, 1991), pp. 11–48. Although there are many references to Levinas in Derrida's published work, particularly from the late 1980s onwards, Derrida's most extensive subsequent engagement with Levinas is *Adieu to Emmanuel Levinas*, trans. P.-A. Brault and M. Naas (Stanford: Stanford University Press, 1997), which includes both Derrida's funeral oration for Levinas and the full text of a paper given on the occasion of a commemorative conference on Levinas held at the Sorbonne in 1996.

4 Vincent Descombes, *Modern French Philosophy* (Cambridge: Cambridge University Press, 1981).

5 See *L'arche. Le mensuel du judaïsme français*, 459 (February 1996), p. 65.

6 Dominique Janicaud, *Le Tournant théologique de la phénoménologie française* (Paris: Editions de l'éclat, 1991). For a collection of articles which represent this phenomenological approach to Levinas, see Emmanuel Levinas, *Positivité et transcendance suivi de Levinas et la phénoménologie* (Paris: Presses Universitaires de France, 2000).

7 Roger Burggraeve, *Emmanuel Levinas. Une bibliographie primaire et secondaire (1929–1985) avec complément 1985–1989* (Leuven: Peeters, 1986).

8 See Theodore de Boer's 'An Ethical Transcendental Philosophy', in Richard A. Cohen (ed.), *Face to Face with Levinas* (Albany: State University of

New York Press, 1986), pp. 83–115; and Adriaan Peperzak, *To the Other: an Introduction to the Philosophy of Emmanuel Levinas* (West Lafayette: Purdue University Press, 1993).

9 Edith Wyschogrod, *Emmanuel Levinas: the Problem of Ethical Metaphysics* (The Hague: Martinus Nijhoff, 1974).

10 The key text here is J. Hillis Miller's *The Ethics of Reading* from 1987, which sought to argue for the ethical significance of De Manian deconstruction or rhetorical reading (New York: Columbia University Press, 1987). A representative overview of this ethical turn in literary studies can be seen in collections such as D. Rainsford and T. Woods (eds.), *Critical Ethics* (Basingstoke: Macmillan, 1999) and Robert Eaglestone, *Ethical Criticism: Reading after Levinas* (Edinburgh: Edinburgh University Press, 1997). My own contribution to this debate was *The Ethics of Deconstruction: Derrida and Levinas* in 1992 (Oxford: Blackwell; 2nd edn, Edinburgh: Edinburgh University Press, 1999).

11 See Noreen O'Connor, 'Being and the Good: Heidegger and Levinas', *Philosophical Studies*, 27 (1980), pp. 212–20, and 'Intentionality, Analysis and the Problem of Self and Other', *Journal of the British Society for Phenomenology*, 13 (1982), pp. 186–92; Tina Chanter, *The Ethics of Eros: Irigaray's Re-reading of the Philosophers* (London and New York: Routledge, 1995); Jill Robbins, *Prodigal Son/Elder Brother: Interpretation and Alterity in Augustine, Petrarch, Kafka, Levinas* (Chicago: University of Chicago Press, 1991) and *Altered Reading: Levinas and Literature* (Chicago: University of Chicago Press, 1999); Stella Sandford, *The Metaphysics of Love: Gender and Transcendence in Levinas* (London: Athlone, 2000).

12 See Catherine Chalier, *Figures du féminin. Lecture d'Emmanuel Levinas* (Paris: La Nuit Surveillée, 1982), 'Ethics and the Feminine', in Critchley and Bernasconi, *Re-Reading Levinas*, pp. 119–28; Luce Irigaray, 'The Fecundity of the Caress', trans. C. Burke, in Cohen, *Face to Face with Levinas*, pp. 231–56, and 'Questions to Emmanuel Levinas: on the divinity of love', trans. M. Whitford, in *Re-Reading Levinas*, pp. 109–18.

13 See Zygmunt Bauman, *Modernity and the Holocaust* (Cambridge: Polity, 1989) and *Postmodern Ethics* (Oxford: Blackwell, 1993); see the preface to Homi K. Bhabha, *The Location of Culture* (London and New York: Routledge, 1994), pp. 15–17; and Paul Gilroy, *Between Camps: Nations, Cultures and the Allure of Race* (London: Penguin, 2000).

14 Gary Gutting, *French Philosophy in the Twentieth Century* (Cambridge: Cambridge University Press, 2001).

15 Papers by Putnam and Bernstein are included below. Cavell gave a paper on Levinas in Amsterdam in June 2000, with the title 'What is the Scandal of Scepticism?'

16 Richard Rorty, *Achieving our Country* (Cambridge: Harvard University Press, 1998), pp. 96–7.

17 See 'Enigma and Phenomenon', in BPW 65–77.

18 Published in *En découvrant l'existence avec Husserl et Heidegger*, 3rd edn (Paris: Vrin, 1974). An English translation appeared as 'Martin Heidegger and Ontology', trans. Committee of Public Safety, *Diacritics*, 26, 1 (1996), pp. 11–32.

19 Levinas's 1934 essay has been very usefully and extensively discussed by Miguel Abensour in his new edition of this essay: *Quelques refléxions sur la philosophie de l'hitlérisme* (Paris: Payot-Rivages, 1997). An English translation appeared with a revealing prefatory note by Levinas in *Critical Inquiry*, 17 (1990), pp. 62–71.

20 Included in BPW, 1–10.

21 See 'Metaphysics Precedes Ontology' and 'Ethics and the Face', TI 42–8, 172–5.

22 See *Autrement que savoir* (Paris: Editions Osiris, 1987).

23 *Ibid.*, p. 10, but see also p. 8.

24 Kant, *The Moral Law*, ed. H. J. Paton (London: Hutchinson, 1948), p. 91.

25 *Ibid.*, p. 123.

26 Reprinted in *Les imprévus de l'histoire* (Montpellier: Fata Morgana, 1994), p. 209.

27 On this point, see TI, 53, and 'Philosophy and the idea of infinity', in CP 79–80.

28 Derrida has criticized Levinas on this point in ' "Eating Well", or the Calculation of the Subject: An Interview with Jacques Derrida', in E. Cadava, P. Connor and J.-L. Nancy (eds.), *Who Comes After the Subject?* (London and New York: Routledge, 1991), pp. 105–8. But the most detailed and nuanced account of Levinas and the problem of ethical obligations towards animals is in the work of John Llewelyn. See his 'Am I Obsessed By Bobby? Humanism of the Other Animal', in Critchley and Bernasconi, *Re-Reading Levinas*, pp. 234–45; and *The Middle Voice of Ecological Conscience* (London and Basingstoke: Macmillan, 1991).

29 See Jean-Paul Sartre, 'Intentionality: A Fundamental Idea of Husserl's Phenomenology', *Journal of the British Society for Phenomenology*, 1 (1970), p. 4.

30 For Levinas's critique of epistemology, see his important 1962 lecture, 'Transcendence and Height', in BPW 11–31.

31 *Autrement que savoir*, p. 68.

32 L. Wittgenstein, 'Lecture on Ethics', *The Philosophical Review*, 74 (1965), p. 7.

33 Also see M. Blanchot, 'Our Clandestine Companion', in Cohen, *Face to Face with Levinas*, p. 45.

34 See Levinas's 'Ethics as first philosophy' in LR.

35 *Autrement que savoir*, p. 83.
36 For a balanced and informed account of the relation between Levinas and Jewish philosophy, see Tamra Wright, *The Twilight of Jewish Philosophy* (Amsterdam: Harwood, 1999).
37 See *TI*, 212–14, and *OB*, 156–62.
38 See *BPW*, 161–9.
39 *The Claim of Reason* (New York and Oxford: Oxford University Press, 1979), p. 89.
40 Derrida, *Adieu to Emmanuel Levinas*, p. 4.
41 See *Conditions Handsome and Unhandsome: the Constitution of Emersonian Perfectionism* (Chicago: University of Chicago Press, 1990) for this distinction, which is employed below with respect to Levinas by Putnam.
42 In this regard, see Knud Ejler Løgstrup's remarkable book, *The Ethical Demand* (Notre Dame: University of Notre Dame Press, 1997), which contains a helpful introduction by Hans Fink and Alastair MacIntyre. The link between Løgstrup and Levinas was first established by Bauman in *Postmodern Ethics* (Oxford: Blackwell, 1993).

HILARY PUTNAM*

2 Levinas and Judaism

Levinas survived the Second World War under difficult and humiliating circumstances,[1] while his family, with the exception of his wife and daughter, perished. These experiences may well have shaped his sense that what is demanded of us is an 'infinite' willingness to be available to and for the other's suffering. 'The Other's hunger – be it of the flesh, or of bread – is sacred; only the hunger of the third party limits its rights', Levinas writes in the preface to *Difficult Freedom*. To understand fully what Levinas means here would be to understand his whole philosophy. I want to make a beginning at such an understanding.

LEVINAS'S MISSION TO THE GENTILES

Levinas's audience is typically a gentile audience. He celebrates Jewish particularity in essays addressed to Christians and to modern people generally. He is fully aware of this. Thus he writes 'Lest the union between men of goodwill which I desire to see be brought about only in a vague and abstract mode, I wish to insist here on the particular routes open to Jewish monotheism' (*DF* 21–2) – and again,

A truth is universal when it applies to every reasonable being. A religion is universal when it is open to all. In this sense the Judaism that links the Divine to the moral has always aspired to be universal. But the revelation of morality, which discovers a human society, also discovers the place of election, which in this universal society, returns to the person who receives this revelation. This election is made up not of privileges but of responsibilities. It is a nobility based not on an author's rights [*droit d'auteur*] or on a birthright [*droit d'aînesse*] conferred by a divine caprice, but on the position of each human I [*moi*]...The basic intuition of moral growing-up perhaps

33

consists in perceiving that I am not *the equal* of the Other. This applies in
a very stict sense: I see myself *obligated* with respect to the Other; consequently I am infinitely more demanding of myself than of others... This
'position outside nations' of which the Pentateuch speaks is realized in the
concept of Israel and its particularism. It is a particularism that conditions
universality, *and it is a moral category rather than a historical fact to do
with Israel* [my emphasis]. [DF 21–2]

In this passage we see Levinas reinterpreting the doctrine of the
election of Israel in terms of Levinasian ethics/phenomenology, so
that it becomes a 'particularism that conditions universality' – becomes, that is, the asymmetry that Levinas everywhere insists on
between what I require of myself and what I am entitled to require
of anyone else; and he tells us that so reinterpreted, election 'is a universal moral category rather than a historical fact to do with Israel'.
Here and elsewhere, Levinas is universalizing Judaism. To understand him, one has to understand the paradoxical claim implicit in
his writing that, in essence, all human beings are Jews.

In one place, we see this universalization of the category of 'Jew'
connected with Levinas's own losses in the Holocaust. The dedication page to *Otherwise than Being or Beyond Essence* bears two
dedications. The upper dedication is in French and reads (in translation), '*To the memory of those who were closest among the six
million assassinated by the National Socialists, and of the millions
and millions of all confessions and all nations, victims of the same
hatred of the other man, the same anti-semitism.*'

The other dedication is in Hebrew, and using traditional phraseol-
ogy dedicates the volume to the memories of his father, his mother,
his brother, his father-in-law and his mother-in-law. What is most
striking about this page is the way in which Levinas dedicates the
book to the memory of 'those closest' (to himself) among the six
million Jews assassinated by the Nazis, those whom he lists in the
Hebrew dedication, and the way in which he simultaneously identifies all victims of the same 'hatred of the other man', regardless of
their nation and religious affiliation, as victims of anti-semitism.

ETHICS AS FIRST PHILOSOPHY

Levinas is famous for the claim that ethics is first philosophy[2] –
by which he means not only that ethics must not be derived

from any metaphysics, not even an 'ontic' metaphysics (i.e. an 'anti-ontological' anti-metaphysics) like Heidegger's, but also that all thinking about what it is to be a human being must *begin* with such an 'ungrounded' ethics. This doesn't mean that Levinas wishes to deny the validity of, let us say, the 'categorical imperative'. What he rejects is any formula of the form 'Behave in such and such a way *because*.' In many different ways, he tell us that it is a disaster to say 'treat the other as an end and not as a means *because*'.[3]

Yet to most people there seems to be an obvious 'because'. If you ask someone 'Why *should we* act so that we could will the maxims of our actions as universal laws?' or 'Why should we treat the humanity in others always as an end and never as a mere means?' or 'Why *should we* attempt to relieve the suffering of others?', ninety-nine times out of a hundred the answer you will be given is 'Because the other is fundamentally the same as you'. The thought – or rather the cliché – is that if I realized how much the other was like me I would automatically feel a desire to help. But the limitations of such a 'grounding' of ethics only have to be mentioned to become obvious.

The danger in grounding ethics in the idea that we are all 'fundamentally the same' is that a door is opened for a Holocaust. One only has to believe that some people are not 'really' the same to destroy all the force of such a grounding. Nor is there only the danger of a denial of our common humanity (the Nazis claimed that Jews were vermin in superficially human form). Every good novelist rubs our noses in the extent of human dissimilarity, and many novels pose the question 'If you really knew what some other people were like, could you feel sympathy with them at all?'

But Kantians will point out that Kant saw this too. That is why Kant grounds ethics not in 'sympathy' but in our common rationality. But then what becomes of our obligations to those whose rationality we can more or less plausibly deny?

These are ethical reasons for refusing to base ethics on either a metaphysical or a psychological 'because'. Levinas sees metaphysics as an attempt to view the world as a totality, from 'outside', as it were.[4] And like Rosenzweig, whom he cites, Levinas believes that the significance that life has for the human subject is lost in such a perspective.[5] Thus he tells Philippe Nemo,

There have been few protestations in the history of philosophy against this totalization. For me, it is in Franz Rosenzweig's philosophy, which is essentially a discussion of Hegel, that for the first time I encountered a critique of totality…In Rosenzweig there is thus an explosion of the totality and the opening of quite a different route in the search for what is reasonable. [*EI* 75–6]

Levinas's daring move is to insist that the impossibility of a metaphysical grounding for ethics shows that there is something wrong with metaphysics, and not with ethics. But I will defer further discussion of Levinas's attitudes to philosophy for the moment.

LEVINAS AS A 'MORAL PERFECTIONIST'

It is possible to distinguish two species of moral philosophers. One species, the legislators, provide detailed moral and political rules. If one is a philosopher of this sort, then one is likely to think that the whole problem of political philosophy (for example) would be solved by devising a constitution for the Ideal State.

But, as Stanley Cavell has emphasized, there are philosophers of another kind, the philosophers whom he calls 'moral perfectionists'. It is not, he hastens to tell us, that the perfectionists deny the value of what the legislative philosophers are attempting to do; it is that they believe there is a need for something *prior* to principles or a constitution, without which the best principles and the best constitution would be worthless.[6] Emmanuel Levinas is a 'moral perfectionist'.

Moral perfectionists believe that the ancient questions – 'Am I living as I am supposed to live?' 'Is my life something more than vanity, or worse, mere conformity?' 'Am I making the best effort I can to reach (in Cavellian language) my unattained but attainable self?' – make all the difference in the world. Emerson, Nietzsche and Mill are three of Cavell's principal examples. (Cavell also detects perfectionist strains in Rousseau and in Kant.)

When Emerson and Mill attack 'conformity', what they object to isn't the principles to which the conformist pays lipservice. What they tell us is that if conformity is all one's allegiance comes to, then even the best principles are useless. Such a philosopher is a 'perfectionist' because s/he always describes the commitment we ought to have in ways that seem impossibly demanding; but such a philosopher is also a realist, because s/he realizes that it is only by keeping an 'impossible' demand in view that one can strive for one's 'unattained but attainable self'.

When I teach Jewish philosophy, I stress that the great Jewish philosophers, including the great twentieth-century Jewish thinkers (particularly Buber, Cohen, Levinas and Rosenzweig) are moral perfectionists. The famous 'I–Thou' in Buber is a relation that Buber believes is *demanded* of us, and without which no system of moral rules and no institution can have any real value. For Levinas there is a different 'I–Thou' relation, one that is more important than Buber's I–Thou, and for Rosenzweig, in contrast to both, there is a complex system of such relations.[7] But one cannot understand any of these systems without understanding this 'perfectionist' dimension.

For Levinas, the distinction between these two moments in ethics[8] is also a distinction of tasks. He sees *his* task as describing the fundamental obligation to the other. The further task of proposing moral/political rules belongs to a later stage, the stage of 'justice', and while Levinas tells us how and why there are two stages, it is not his task to write a textbook of ethics like Rawls's *A Theory of Justice*. Almost always in Levinas's writing the term 'ethics' refers to what I called the moral perfectionist moment, the moment when he describes what I just called 'the fundamental obligation'.

The fundamental obligation

Consider the question, 'Imagine you were in a situation in which your obligations to others did not conflict with focusing entirely on one other human being. What sort of attitude, what sort of relation, should you strive for towards that other?' Like Buber, Levinas believes this is the fundamental question that must be addressed, that must be answered before discussing the complications that arise when one has to consider the conflicting demands of a number of others (when what Levinas calls 'the hunger of the third party' limits the demands of the other), or even the complications that arise when you consider that you yourself are an 'other' to others. To describe Levinas's answer in full would require a description of his entire philosophy. (In particular, one would have to describe the puzzling notion of 'infinite responsibility'.) For now I shall focus on two elements.

The first element is best explained by a Hebrew word: *hineni*. The word is a combination of two elements: *hine* (pronounced *hiné*) and *ni*, a contraction of the pronoun *ani*, I. *Hine* is often translated 'behold', but there is no reference to seeing in the root meaning. It might be translated as 'here', but unlike the Hebrew synonyms for 'here', *kan* and *po*, it cannot occur in a mere descriptive proposition. *Hine* is used only presentationally; that is, I can say *hine hameil*, here is the coat, when I point to the coat (hence the translation: 'Behold the coat!'), but I cannot say, *Etmol hameil haya hine* ('yesterday the coat was *hine*') to mean 'Yesterday the coat was here'; I have to say *Etmol hameil haya po* or *Etmol ha meil haya kan*. Thus *hine* performs the speech-act of calling attention to, or *presenting*, not describing. *Hine hameil!* performs the speech-act of presenting the coat (*meil*) and thus *hineni!* performs the speech-act of presenting myself, the speech-act of making myself available to another.

The places in which *hineni* is used in this way in the Jewish Bible are highly significant. The most tremendous of these occurs at the beginning of Genesis 22 which tells the story of the binding of Isaac. 'And it came to pass after these things that God did test Abraham, and said to him Abraham: and he said *hineni*' (22:1). Note that here Abraham is offering himself to God *unreservedly*. (That Abraham also says *hineni* to Isaac in 22:7 is an essential part of the paradox of this text.)

When Levinas speaks of saying *me voici*[9] what he means is virtually unintelligible if one is not aware of the Biblical resonance. The fundamental obligation we have, Levinas is telling us, is the obligation to make ourselves available to the neediness (and especially the suffering) of the other person. I am commanded to say *hineni* to the other (and to do so without reservation, just as Abraham's *hineni* to God was without reservation). This does *not* presuppose that I sympathize with the other, and certainly does not presuppose (what Levinas regards as the self-aggrandizing gesture) a claim to 'understand' the other. Levinas insists that the closer I come to another by all ordinary standards of closeness (especially, for example, in a love relationship),[10] the more I am required to be aware of my distance from grasping the other's essential reality, and the more I am required to respect that distance. As I have already said, this fundamental obligation is a 'perfectionist' obligation, not a code of behaviour or a theory of justice. But, Levinas believes that if the taking on of this fundamental obligation is not present, then the best code of behaviour or the best theory of justice will not help.

In contrast, according to Buber what I should seek is a relation which is reciprocal. But Levinas stresses the asymmetry of the fundamental moral relation. 'I see myself *obligated* with respect to the other; consequently I am infinitely more demanding of myself than of others.' Before reciprocity must come ethics; to seek to base ethics on reciprocity is once again to seek to base it on the illusory 'sameness' of the other person.

Turning to the second element, I have spoken of a fundamental obligation in connection with Levinas (and a fundamental relation in connection with Buber). The choice of the word 'obligation' was deliberate: for Levinas; to be a human being in the normative sense (to be what Jews call a *mensch*) involves recognizing that I am commanded to say *hineni*. In Levinas's phenomenology, this means that I am commanded without experiencing a commander (my only experience of the commander is the experience of being commanded), and without either a metaphysical explanation of the nature of the command or a metaphysical justification for the command. If you have to ask, '*Why* should I put myself out for him/her?' you are not yet human. This is why Levinas must contradict Heidegger: Heidegger thinks that fully appreciating my own death ('being-toward-death') makes me a true human being as opposed to a mere member of the 'they'; Levinas believes that what is essential is the relation to the other (*TO*).[11] Again, there is a universalization of a Jewish theme here: just as the traditional Jew finds his dignity in obeying the divine command, so Levinas thinks that every human being should find his or her dignity in the obeying of the fundamental ethical command (which will turn out to be 'divine' in the only sense Levinas can allow), the command to say *hineni* to the other, to say *hineni* with what Levinas calls 'infinite' responsibility.

Saying precedes the said

The foregoing explains Levinas's puzzling statement that 'the saying has to be reached in its existence antecedent to the said' (*OB* 46). For, if by a 'said' we mean the content of a proposition, then when I say *hineni* there is no 'said'. What I do is make myself available to the other person; I do this by uttering a verbal formula, but the content of the verbal formula is immaterial, provided it succeeds in presenting me as one who is available.[12]

LEVINAS'S PHILOSOPHICAL EDUCATION

One reason that analytic philosophers find Levinas hard to read is that he takes it for granted that reading Husserl and Heidegger is part of the education any properly trained philosopher must have, just as analytic philosophers take an education which includes reading Russell, Frege, Carnap and Quine to be what any properly trained philosopher must have. Certainly there are passages in Levinas's writing which can only be understood against the background of their explicit or implicit references to the writings of these two philosophers. Yet his thought is strikingly independent. For in the respects that are essential from Levinas's point of view, he finds Husserl and Heidegger inadequate. In this essay, I shall try to explain what Levinas is doing with a minimum of reliance on any prior knowledge of the two great 'H's.

Husserl and Levinas

'A minimum' does not mean zero, however. But what I shall say about Husserl to illustrate the way in which Levinas breaks with him will refer only to the aspect of Husserl's thought that ought to be familiar to analytic philosophers (even if it isn't) because it had great influence on one of the founding fathers of their movement, Rudolf Carnap. (Carnap's *Der Raum* is clearly a Husserlian work, and even the *Aufbau* contains acknowledgements of Husserl's influence – e.g. the striking claim,[13] 'This is *epoché* in Husserl's sense'.)

Especially in *Ideen*, Husserl portrays the world as being in some sense a construction.[14] The notion of construction isn't Carnap's, but there is no doubt that Carnap saw the *Aufbau* as a way of rectifying Husserl's project with the aid of mathematical logic, just as *Der Raum* was Carnap's way of constructing a 'Husserlian' philosophy of space with the aid of mathematical logic.

A problem that arises in both of these philosophies is that even if the construction succeeded in its own terms – even if, *per impossibile*, one were to succeed in (re)constructing 'the world' in terms of the philosopher's ontology – the primitive elements of that ontology would be *one's own* experiences. And there is something morally disturbing about this.

To put the point in terms of Carnap's rather than Husserl's notion of construction, suppose that my friend is a phenomenalist and believes that all I am is a logical construction out of *his* sense-data. Should I feel reassured if he tells me that the relevant sentences about his sense-data (the ones that 'translate' all of his beliefs about me into the system of the *Aufbau*) have the same 'verification conditions' as the beliefs they translate? Am I making a mistake if I find that that just isn't good enough?[15]

If his avowals of friendship and concern are avowals of an attitude to his own sense-data, then my friend is narcissistic. A genuine ethical relation to another presupposes that you realize that the other person is an independent reality and not in any way your construction. Here is one of Levinas's many critical descriptions of Western metaphysics cum epistemology:

Whatever the abyss that separates the psyche of the ancients from the consciousness of the moderns . . . the necessity of going back to the beginning, or to consciousness, appears as the proper task of philosophy: return to its island to be shut up there in the simultaneity of the eternal instant, approaching the *mens instanea* of God. [*OB* 78]

The note of scorn is unmistakable. In contrast, according to Levinas,

'Subjectivity of flesh and blood in matter is not . . . a 'mode of self-certainty'. The proximity of beings of flesh and blood is not their presence in 'flesh and bone', is not the fact that they take form for a look, present an exterior, quiddities, forms, give images, which the eye absorbs (and whose alterity the hand that touches or holds suspends easily or lightly, annulling it by the simple grasp, as though no one contested this appropriation). Nor are material beings reducible to the resistance they oppose to the effort they solicit. [Think of a Carnapian 'analysis' of the sentence 'a man is in front of me'.] Subjectivity of flesh and blood in matter . . . the-one-for-the-other itself – is the preoriginal signifyingness that gives sense, because it gives. [*OB* 78][16]

Descartes's proof of God's existence

The significance that the independence of the other (*l'autrui*) has for Levinas is perhaps best brought out by looking at Levinas's interpretation[17] of Descartes's proof of the existence of God in the

Third Meditation. There Descartes argued that the 'infinity' involved in the idea of God could not have been so much as *conceived* of by his mind by means of its own unaided powers, but could only have been put into his mind by God Himself.[18]

If this looks like an outrageous fallacy to a philosopher, one reason is likely to be that the philosopher thinks of 'infinite' as having the meaning it has in such statements as 'there are infinitely many prime numbers'. But this is not what Descartes means. Rather, as Kant also saw, to speak of God as 'infinitely wise' or 'infinitely great' is not to speak mathematically at all.[19]

What then is it to do? Descartes is conventionally thought to have invoked the existence of God because his argument 'ran into trouble'. But Levinas believes that what Descartes is reporting is not a step in a deductive reasoning, but a profound religious experience, an experience which might be described as an experience of a *fissure*, of a confrontation with something that disrupted all his categories. On this reading, Descartes is not so much proving something as *acknowledging* something, acknowledging a Reality that he could not have constructed, a Reality which proves its own existence by the very fact that its presence in my mind turn out to be a phenomenological impossibility.

It isn't that Levinas accepts Descartes's argument, so interpreted. The significance is rather that Levinas transforms the argument by substituting the other for God. So transformed, the 'proof' becomes: I know the other (*l'autrui*) isn't part of my 'construction of the world' because my encounter with the other is an encounter with a *fissure*, with a being who breaks my categories.

The analogy between Levinas's account of what he calls 'a direct relation with the Other' (*EI* 57) and Descartes's account of his relation to God extends still farther, however. Just as, for Descartes, the experience of God as, in effect, a violator of his mind, as one who 'breaks' his *cogito*, goes with a profound sense of obligation, and with an experience of glory, so, for Levinas, the experience of the other as, in effect, a violator of his mind, as one who breaks his phenomenology, goes with what I called the 'fundamental obligation' to make oneself available to the other, and with the experience of what Levinas calls 'the Glory of the Infinite'.[20] Indeed, it is a part of Levinas's strategy to regularly transfer predicates to the other that traditional theology ascribes to God (hence Levinas's talk of my 'infinite responsibility' to the other, of the impossibility of really seeing the face of the other, of the 'height' of the other, etc.).

WHAT TO MAKE OF THIS

WHAT TO MAKE OF THIS

It is important to keep in mind that Levinas does not intend to replace traditional metaphysics and epistemology with a different, non-traditional, metaphysics and epistemology. Merely replacing the phenomenalism of Carnap or the phenomenology of Husserl with the kind of realism currently favoured by many analytic philosophers would not satisfy Levinas at all. Such a metaphysics does just as much violence to the agent point of view as does the phenomenalism of Carnap or the transcendental phenomenology of Husserl. In the metaphysical realist picture, as Thomas Nagel has stressed (but without abandoning that picture himself), the agent point of view disappears in favour of 'the view from nowhere'.

What Levinas wants to remind us of is precisely the underivability of what I called the fundamental obligation from any metaphysical or epistemological picture. Each of Levinas's principal tropes – 'infinite responsibility', 'face versus trace', 'height' – connects with the two fundamental ideas that ethics is based on obligation to the other, not on any empirical or metaphysical 'sameness' between myself and the other and that this fundamental obligation is asymmetrical.

Infinite responsibility

I have already explained what I think Levinas means by talk of 'infinity' in this connection. But what of 'responsibility'?

An ancient Jewish principle holds that *kol Israel 'arevim zeh lazeh* – every Israelite is responsible for every other. The corresponding Levinasian claim is that every human being is responsible for every other. Levinas puts it in just these terms. In a discussion of a passage in the Talmud (Sotah 37), which talks about the various occasions upon which Israel covenanted with God, Levinas writes:

A moment ago, we saw a part played [in a remark by Rabbi Mesharsheya] by something resembling the recognition of the Other, the love of the Other. To such an extent that I offer myself as a guarantee of the other, of his adherence and fidelity to the Law. His concern is my concern. But is not my concern also his? Isn't he responsible for me? And if he is, can I answer for his responsibility for me? *Kol Ysrael 'arevim zeh lazeh*, 'All Israel is responsible one for the other', which means, all those who cleave to the divine law, all men worthy of the name, are responsible for each other. [*LR* 225–6]

'[A]ll men worthy of the name, are responsible for each other.' But Levinas in the next sentences immediately stresses the theme of asymmetry:

I always have, myself, one responsibility more than anyone else, since I am responsible, in addition, for his responsibility. And if he is responsible for my responsibility, I remain responsible for the responsibility he has for my responsibility. *Ein ladavar sof*, 'it will never end'. In the society of the Torah, this process is repeated to infinity; beyond any responsibility attributed to everyone and for everyone, there is always the additional fact that I am responsible for that responsibility. It is an ideal, but one which is inseparable for the humanity of human beings . . .

Face versus trace

Levinas speaks of the 'non-phenomenality of the face' (*OB* 89), and he goes on to say:

In the obsession with this nudity and this poverty, this withdrawal or this dying, where synthesis and contemporaneousness are refused, proximity, as though it were an abyss, interrupts being's unrendable essence.[21] A face approached, a contact with a skin – a face weighed down with a skin, and a skin in which, even in obscenity, the altered face breathes – are already absent from themselves . . .

And on the very next page,

Phenomenology defects into a face, even if, in the course of this ever am-biguous defecting of appearing, the obsession itself shows itself in the said.[22] The appearing is broken by the young epiphany, the still essential beauty of a face. But this use is already past in this youth; the skin is with wrinkles, a trace of itself, the ambiguous form of a supreme presence attending to its appearing, breaking through its plastic form with youth, but already a fail-ing of all presence, less than a phenomenon, already a poverty that hides its wretchedness and orders me. [*OB* 90]

Here part of the idea is that even when I stare at your physical face, at your skin itself, I do not 'see you face to face' in the Biblical sense, do not and cannot encounter the you that 'hides its wretchedness and orders me'. I see in this the Levinasian trope of transferring attributes of God[23] to the other. Just as we never see God, but at best traces of God's presence in the world, so we never see the 'face' of the other, but only its 'trace'. But the emphasis on 'wretchedness and suffering' isn't connected *only* with awareness that the other is mortal, although it is textually connected with that.[24] It is also connected with Levinas's emphasis on the neediness of others and the corresponding obligation on the 'me' who always has 'one responsibility more than anyone else' to sacrifice for others, to the point of substituting for them, to the point of martyrdom – a demand I shall comment on at the end of this essay. In Levinas's image of man, the *vulnerability* of the other is what is stressed, in contrast to what Levinas sees as the Enlightenment's radiant image of the human essence.

Height

Here is Levinas's own explanation of this trope, in one of the conversations with Philippe Nemo:

Ph. N.: In the face of the Other you say there is an 'elevation', a 'height'. The Other is higher than I am. What do you mean by that?

E. L.: The first word of the face is the 'Thou shalt not Kill.' It is an order. [Again the other is given a God-like attribute.] There is a commandment in the appearance of the face, as if a master spoke to me. However, at the same time, the face of the Other is destitute; it is the poor for whom I can do all and to whom I owe all. And me, whoever I may be, but as a 'first person', I am he who finds the resources to respond to the call.

Ph. N.: One is tempted to say to you: yes, in certain cases. But in other cases, to the contrary, the encounter with the Other occurs in the mode of violence, hate and disdain.

E. L.: To be sure. But I think that whatever the motivation which explains this inversion, the analysis of the face such as I have just made, with the mastery of the Other and his poverty, with my submission and my wealth, is primary. It is the presupposed in all human relationships. If it were not that, we would not even say, before an open door, 'after you, sir!' It is an original 'After you, sir!' that I have tried to describe. [*EI* 88–9]

THE VALUE OF JUDAISM (FOR GENTILES)

The thesis I am defending is that in understanding the thought of this profoundly original thinker it is essential to understand two facts:

that Levinas is drawing on Jewish sources and themes, and (paradoxically, since he is an Orthodox Jew), that Levinas is universalizing Judaism.

It is necessary, however, to keep in mind that Levinas's Judaism exhibits a 'Lithuanian' distrust of the charismatic.[25] If Christianity valorizes the moment when an individual feels the charismatic presence of the Saviour entering into his/her life, Judaism, as Levinas presents it, distrusts the charismatic. Thus he writes in 'A Religion for Adults'

But all [Judaism's] efforts – from the Bible to the closure of the Talmud in the sixth century and throughout most of its commentators from the great era of rabbinical science – consists in its understanding the saintliness of God in a sense that stands in sharp contrast to the numinous meaning of this term . . . Judaism remains foreign to any offensive return of these forms of human elevation. It denounces them as the essence of idolatry.

The numinous or the Sacred envelops and transports man beyond his powers and wishes, but a true liberty takes offense at this uncontrollable surplus . . . This somehow sacramental power of the Divine seems to Judaism to offend human freedom and to be contrary to the education of man, which remains *action on a free being*. Not that liberty is an end in itself, but it does remain the condition for any value man may attain. The Sacred that envelops and transports me is a form of violence. [*DF* 11–23]

And in 'For a Jewish Humanism', Levinas writes, 'The *no* with which the Jews, so dangerously over the centuries, replied to the calls of the Church does not express an absurd stubbornness, but the conviction that important human truths in the Old Testament were being lost in the theology of the New' (*DF* 275).

What are these 'important human truths' that Levinas is universalizing? Obviously, Levinas's notion of 'Judaism' is both selective[26] and idiosyncratic. But it is not without a basis. Rabbinic Judaism was utterly transformed after the fall of the Temple. The transformation involved subjecting all religious texts, including the Jewish Bible itself, to a literally unending process of interpretation (David Hartman has recently described the Jewish people as a 'community of interpretation').[27] The founding generation of rabbinic Judaism, the generation that saw the destruction of Jerusalem and that began the construction of a new, non-Temple-based mode of worship at Jabne, included such figures as Rabbi Johanan ben Zakkai, Rabbi Gamaliel,

Rabbi Joshua ben Hananiah and the immensely learned Rabbi Eliezer ben Hyrcanus. A story in the Talmud (Baba Metzia 59a–b) relates that in a dispute with some of the other members of the group at Jabne, Eliezer ben Hyrcanus called for a series of miracles (which then occurred) including a 'heavenly voice' (*bat kol*) to prove that he was right and that he lost the debate in spite of the heavenly voice and the miracles. 'We pay no heed to a heavenly voice', the rabbis told God – 'for you have already written in the Torah at Mount Sinai, "to incline after a multitude".'[28] The Talmud goes on to give us God's reaction. Rabbi Nathan, it relates, 'happening upon' the prophet Elijah, asked what God had done at that hour. 'He smiled', Elijah said, 'and said: My children have vanquished me, my children have vanquished me!'

While some of the commentators in the Talmud itself assert that the miracles were only dreamt and did not actually occur, there is no question that at this crucial meeting at Jabne Judaism took a turn away from what Levinas calls the 'numinous'. Human autonomy was henceforth to have a voice in determining what the Divine Commandment meant.[29] It is true that in the Pentateuch Moses is described as having a numinous experience at Sinai, but that experience is not taken as a model for the religious experience of the traditional Jew. Rather, the position of the traditional Jew is one of feeling a profound experience of being commanded by a God (s)he has *not* had a numinous experience of. The 'trace' of God's presence is the tradition which testifies to the commandment and the interpretive community which continues to work out what it means.

Levinas modifies this picture, for at least two reasons. First of all, his intended audience, as I have stressed, is not just Jews but humanity as a whole. And, secondly, even if he universalizes certain Jewish themes, he doesn't attempt to convert the gentiles to Judaism. He isn't trying to emulate St Paul. The detailed *mitzvot* ('commandments') are not what he wants his 'universal' audience to learn about or obey (which is what they would have to do, among other things, to convert to Judaism), but rather the fundamental commandment which Rabbi Hillel the Elder gave in two famous forms: 'Love mankind'[30] and 'What is hateful to you do not do to your fellow man; this is the whole Torah, the rest is mere commentary.'[31]

Thus the 'important human truths in the Old Testament', as interpreted by Levinas, include the following: (1) that every human being should experience him/herself as *commanded* to be available to the neediness, the suffering, the vulnerability of the other person. This is to be as binding upon one's very soul as the commandments to love God and to love your neighbour as yourself are in the eyes of someone who lives up to the normative Jewish ideal of piety; indeed, like Hillel, Levinas thinks 'the rest is mere commentary'. (2) One can – indeed, one must – *know* that this is commanded of one without a philosophical account of how this is possible. What makes this strain in Levinas's thought 'Jewish' is the remarkable fact that the Talmud, although produced in a Hellenistic environment in which scholars claim that every educated person was somewhat acquainted with Platonic and post-Platonic philosophy, fails to refer to that philosophy in any way. Only a handful of Jewish figures – Philo of Alexandria, for example – attempted to synthesize Greek philosophy and Jewish religion, and not until the tenth, eleventh and twelfth centuries (with such figures as Saadia Gaaon, Bahya ibn Paquda and Abraham Ibn Ezra, as well as, of course, Maimonides) did the attempt have any significant influence (and even then, Maimonides' codification of Jewish law was more influential than his philosophy). (3) My knowledge that 'I myself' have received a divine command not only lacks a metaphysical basis; it is also not based on anything like a personal epiphany. I have only a 'trace' of the Commander, never an epiphany.

THE VALUE OF JUDAISM (FOR JEWS)

If Levinas is trying to universalize fundamental Jewish values when he speaks to the gentile world, it is also true that, to a certain extent, he resists universalism when speaking to the Jewish world – especially to Jews who participate in modern culture and who, like himself, value many of the achievements of that culture. Thus in a moving essay titled 'Judaism and the Present', Levinas writes,

In the wake of the Liberation, Jews[32] are grappling with the Angel of Reason who often solicited them and who for two centuries now has refused to let go. Despite the experience of Hitler and the failure of assimilation, *the great vocation in life resounds like the call of a universal and homogenous society.* [LR 255]

Levinas goes on to urge resistance to this call of the Angel of Reason. However, Levinas's notion of resisting 'a universal and homogeneous society' does not require combating liberalizing movements within Judaism such as Reform Judaism. In the next sentences, in fact, Levinas writes,

We do not have to decide here if the nature of modern life is compatible with respect for the Sabbath and rituals concerning food or if we should lighten the yoke of the Law. These important questions are put to men who have already chosen Judaism. They chose between orthodoxy and reform depending on their ideas of rigor, courage and duty. Some are not necessarily hypocrites, others do not always take the easy way out. *But it is really a domestic quarrel* [emphasis added].

Nor does resistance to the Angel of Reason require that one believe in the literal truth of the doctrine that the Pentateuch – and, in the traditional Jewish account, the 'oral Torah', the Talmud, as well – were given to Moses by God on Mount Sinai. On the next page and its sequel Levinas writes:

Judaism had been threatened before. Cosmology and scientific history in their time had compromised the Bible's wisdom, while philology had questioned the special character of the Bible itself, dissolved in a sea of texts, pitching and rolling through its infinite undulations. Apologetics chose to reply to these attacks by discussing the arguments put forward. But believers have all resisted them by interiorizing certain religious truths. Why worry about science's refutations of Biblical cosmology, when the Bible contains not cosmology but images necessary to an unshakable inner certainty, figures that speak to the religious soul that dwells in the absolute? Why worry about philology and history challenging the supposed date and origin of the sacred texts, if these texts are intrinsically rich in value? The sacred sparks of individual revelations have produced the light needed, even if they were thrown up at different points in history. The miracle of their convergence is no less marvelous than the miracle of a unique source. [*LR* 255–6]

At this point, Levinas enters into an intricate dialectic. 'The eternity of Israel is not the privilege of a nation that is proud or carried away by illusions', he tells us, 'it has a function in the economy of being. It is indispensable to the work of reason itself.' Justice, he argues, 'needs a stable base', and this stable base cannot be a mere abstraction, not even abstract reason, but can only be 'an interiority, a person'. 'A person is indispensable to justice prior to being indispensable to himself.' He briefly digresses to criticize Sartre, pointing out that those who stress commitment in Sartre's work forget that Sartre's main concern was to guarantee disengagement (*degagément*) in the midst of engagement. But 'dumping ballast in the face of the problems posed by existence, in order to gain even greater height over reality, leads ultimately to the impossibility of sacrifice, that is to say the annihilation of self', Levinas argues (*LR* 256).

What is Judaism's alternative to this *degagément*, to the attempt to stand above reality or to bring justice down to reality from some abstract level? Judaism affirms 'the fidelity to a law, a moral standard'. But 'This is not the return to the status of a thing, for such fidelity breaks the facile enchantment of cause and effect and allows it to be judged' (*LR* 256). And in a passage strikingly reminiscent of Rosenzweig's claim in *The Star of Redemption* that Judaism stands completely outside the Hegelian dialectic of 'world historic' religions and civilizations, Levinas writes,

Judaism is a non-coincidence with its time, within coincidence: in the radical sense of the term, it is an *anachronism*, the simultaneous presence of a youth that is attentive to reality and impatient to change it, and an old age that has seen it all and is returning to the origin of things. The desire to conform to one's time is not the supreme imperative for a human, but is already a characteristic expression of modernism itself; it involves renouncing interiority and truth, resigning oneself to death, and, in base souls, being satisfied with *jouissance*. Monotheism and its moral revelation constitute the concrete fulfillment, beyond all mythology, of the primordial anachronism of the human. [*LR* 256–7][33]

It is noteworthy that this defence of Jewish particularism is itself couched in universalist language. That ethics cannot be founded on reason but must be founded on the aspiration to be 'face to face with the other' (even if all we actually see is the 'trace' of one another's faces), on the willingness to sacrifice for the other, to substitute ourselves for the other's suffering, and that this one commandment is analogous to a fissure in being, and that the aspiration of Western thought to include everything in its 'view from nowhere' (to revert to Nagel's phrase) must be resisted on *moral* grounds, are things that, if true, are true for everyone. Yet the essay from which I have been quoting is an appeal to young Jews not to 'turn their backs on Judaism because, like a waking dream, it does not offer them sufficient enlightenment concerning contemporary problems'. They forget, Levinas tells them,

that revelation offers clarification but not a formula; they forget that commitment alone – commitment at any price, headlong commitment that burns its bridges behind it... is no less inhuman than the disengagement dictated by the desire to be comfortable which ossifies a society that has transformed the difficult task of Judaism into a mere confession, an accessory of bourgeois comfort.[34]

Is Levinas simply reducing what he calls 'Judaism' to his own unique brand of ethical monotheism?

If asked what *really* characterizes Orthodox Judaism (and Levinas was an Orthodox Jew, even if a rather heterodox one), I suppose most Jews would reply 'study and *mitzvot*'. Where do these enter, if they do, into what Levinas is here calling 'Judaism'? But I need to explain 'study and *mitzvot*'.

Mitzvah (plural *mitzvot*) is translated 'commandment' but the translation is doubly misleading (although literally correct). It is misleading, first, because 'commandment' cannot help evoking 'the Ten Commandments', and the Ten Commandments are referred to in the Jewish Bible as the ten *d'varim*, the ten sayings, not the ten *mitzvot*. It is misleading, secondly, because while every religion has 'commandments', not every religion has *mitzvot*. What is characteristic of *mitzvot* is that they form a system, a system whose function is to sanctify every possible portion of life, including the parts described as 'profane'. 'Keeping *mitzvot*' is an entire way of life, a way which is supposed to glorify God and exemplify justice.

The image of the fundamental obligation as analogous to a commandment from God (a commandment from the Infinite) is central to Levinas's whole way of thinking. But Levinas certainly does not say that everyone should keep *mitzvot*, e.g. by keeping the Jewish Sabbath or observing the Jewish dietary laws. Indeed, he is surprisingly tolerant of Jews who think that 'modern life' requires that 'we should lighten the yoke of the Law' (the determination of just what *mitzvot* an observant Jew is required to keep), perhaps because he sees them as Jews who left traditional devotional life in order to respond to calls for justice.

Study is one of the *mitzvot*, but it is also described as 'equal to all' the *mitzvot* and good deeds put together, because it leads to them.[35]

What is most distinctive about traditional Jewish religiosity is the emphasis placed on study, and especially study of the Talmud (after the Bible itself, the founding text, or rather texts, of Judaism), and upon interpretation of the Jewish law.

Whereas I have not been able to find in Levinas any sustained discussion of *mitzvot*, in his emphasis on study of the Jewish texts he is at one with the tradition. Levinas (although not, by scholarly standards, a distinguished Talmudist) never tired of lecturing on and interpreting passages in the Talmud, often reading his own philosophy into these passages, but none the less communicating the joy of Talmud study. In 'Judaism and the Present', after stressing the 'anachronistic' character of Judaism, and explaining how this differs from 'this false eternity' (the eternity of 'dead civilizations such as Greece or Rome' (LR 257)), Levinas goes on to say,

But this essential content, which history cannot touch, cannot be learned like a catechism or resumed like a credo. Nor is it restricted to the negative and formal statement of the categorical imperative. It cannot be replaced by Kantianism, nor, to an even lesser degree, can it be obtained from some particular privilege or racial miracle. It is acquired through a way of living that is a ritual and a heart-felt generosity, wherein a human fraternity and an attention to the present are reconciled with an eternal distance in relation to the contemporary world. It is an asceticism, like the training of a fighter. It is acquired and held, finally, in the particular type of intellectual life known as study of the Torah, that permanent revision and updating of the content of Revelation, where every situation within the human adventure can be judged. And it is here precisely that the Revelation is to be found: the die is not cast, the prophets or wise men of the Talmud knew nothing about antibiotics or nuclear energy; but the categories needed to understand these novelties are already available to monotheism. It is the eternal anteriority of wisdom with respect to science and history. Without it, success would equal reason and reason would just be the necessity of living in one's own time. [LR 257]

Here, then, is where the universalization of Judaism stops, and the resistance to universalism begins. True, when Levinas is addressing gentiles (or the so-called 'general public'), he also opposes the universalization of abstract reason, he also teaches that 'interiority, a person' are where we should look to find a stable foundation for justice and ethics. But he never attempts to tell gentiles what *their* equivalent to the 'ritual and the heart-felt generosity' of traditional

Judaism, their equivalent to 'the particular type of intellectual life known as study of the Torah', might be.

GOD IS WITHOUT CONTENT APART FROM THE RELATION TO THE OTHER

For Levinas, God, or 'the Infinite', is unthematizable.[36] That does not mean the notion is contentless; for there is the possibility (which Buber is accused of overlooking) that 'transcendence without any dogmatic content can receive a content from the dimension of height' (LR 70), i.e. from my experiencing 'the glory of the Infinite' through the 'height of the other'.

Here is a description of this possibility:

The ego stripped by the trauma of persecution of its scornful and imperialist subjectivity, is reduced to the 'here I am' [hineni] as a witness of the Infinite, but a witness that does not thematize what it bears witness of, and whose truth is not the truth of representation, is not evidence.[37] There is witness, a unique structure, an exception to the rule of being,[38] irreducible to representation, only of the Infinite. The infinite does not appear to him that bears witness to it. It is by the voice of the witness that the glory of the Infinite is glorified. [OB 146]

Yet, in spite of the religious feeling we sense here, the Infinite has no content beyond its ethical content. Levinas is emphatic about this. For example, in one of his discussions with Philippe Nemo, Levinas himself raises the question of the content of the word 'God' in his writing, and answers:

You are thinking: what becomes of the Infinity that the title Totality and Infinity announced? To my mind the Infinite comes in the signifyingness of the face. The face signifies the Infinite. It never appears a theme, but in this ethical signifyingness itself; that is the fact that the more I am just the more I am responsible; one is never quits with regard to the Other. [EI 105]

The question a religious person will want to ask is: how is this not atheism? Certainly, I find in Levinas's writings on religion not an intolerance for other religions but an intolerance for other religious *sensibilities* than his own that reminds me of the atheist's intolerance.

APPRECIATION AND SOME OBJECTIONS

How is one to identify Levinas's unique contribution to twentieth-century thought? To say, as the dustjacket of *The Levinas Reader* does, that he provided 'inspiration for Derrida, Lyotard, Blanchot and Irigaray' is not, for all of us, an unmixed compliment!

I shall begin with a remark by Harry Frankfurt (in conversation) to the effect that there is a certain similarity between Levinas's thought and the thought of the ethical intuitionists. What I want to do is identify both the element of truth in the comparison and the limits of any such comparison.

Like the intuitionists, Levinas does not appeal to abstract arguments to ground ethics. What I called 'the fundamental obligation to say *hineni* to the other' is something one is expected to feel, not arrive at by abstract reason. But there is an important difference, especially from Moore: perception of my obligation to the other in all its dimensions is grounded in my relation to the other as a *person*. For Moore, the ethical intuition is almost Platonic: I perceive a 'nonnatural quality'. For other intuitionists it is not Moorean 'goodness' that I am supposed to intuit but *obligation as such*. But for Levinas if there is anything I 'intuit' it is the presence of the other person.

In this respect it might appear that Levinas is closer to Hume than to the intuitionists. For Hume too, after all, ethics is grounded on our reactions to people, not to Platonic universals or other 'nonnatural' entities. But, as we have already seen, there is an important difference: for Hume, it is the perception of the sameness of the other person, my sympathy for the other person, that is the *sine qua non*. But, Levinas tells us, that isn't good enough. If you only feel obliged to those with whom you sympathize, or if you only sympathize with those who you can see as 'like me', then you aren't ethical at all (a point already made by Kant). Indeed, Levinas would say, you are still trapped within your own ego – that is, your 'ethics' is, at bottom, narcissism.

At the same time, Levinas is very far from Kant. For Kant ethics is fundamentally a matter of principles and of reason; the experience of the 'dignity' of accepting a principle and acting on a principle from reason alone is the ethical experience *par excellence*. For Levinas – and I agree with him here – the indispensable experience is the experience of responding to another person, where neither the other person nor my response are seen at that crucial moment as instances of universals. The other is not an instance of any abstraction, not even 'humanity'; she is who she is. And my response is not an instance of any abstract rule, not even the categorical imperative. It is simply a matter of doing what I am 'called on' to do, then and there.

What is original (and I think important and powerful) here is the idea that ethics can – and must – be based on a relation to people, but a relation which is totally free of narcissism, and the further emphasis that to be free of narcissism one must respect the 'alterity' of the other, the other's manifold difference. My awareness of my ethical obligation must not depend on any 'gesture' of claiming (literally or figuratively) to 'comprehend' the other. I do not know any other ethical philosopher who has so powerfully combined the idea that ethics is based on the perception of persons, not of abstractions, with the idea that the ethical perception must fully respect alterity.

The third central Levinasian idea – so central that it is hard to find any place where Levinas responds to an interlocutor without mentioning it – is the asymmetry of the ethical relation. The primordial attitude (I shall call it an 'attitude' even if Levinas wouldn't) that is the Levinasian *sine qua non* for entering the ethical life – which is to say, entering *human* life, in any sense that is 'worthy of the name' – involves recognizing that one is obliged to make oneself available to the neediness of the other *without* simultaneously regarding the other as so obliged. Levinas is the very opposite of a 'contractarian' in this respect.

When I say that, for Levinas, the ethical life is the only life that can, in a normative sense, be called 'human', I do not merely mean to be 'paying a compliment' to the ethical life (as Richard Rorty might put it). In Levinas's phenomenology, not to have entered the ethical life, not to have been 'obsessed' by 'the height of the other', is to be trapped within one's own ego. Without ethics one cannot even enter into the world, in this picture.

All of this I find powerful and compelling. But I shall conclude with some criticisms of certain aspects of Levinas's philosophy that I find problematic.

In another of the discussions with Philippe Nemo, Levinas says:

I have previously said elsewhere – I do not like mentioning it for it should be completed by other considerations – that I am responsible for the persecutions that I undergo. But only me! My 'close relations' or 'my people' are already the others and, for them, I demand justice.

[Philipe Nemo] You go that far!

[Levinas] Since I am responsible even for the Other's responsibility. These are extreme formulas which must not be detached from their context. In the concrete, many other considerations intervene and require justice even for me. Practically, the laws set certain consequences out of the way. But justice only has meaning if it retains the spirit of disinterestedness which animates the idea of responsibility for the other man. In principle the I does not pull itself out if its 'first person'; it supports the world. Constituting itself in the very movement wherein being responsible for the other devolves upon it, subjectivity goes to the point of substitution for the Other. It assumes the condition – or the uncondition – of hostage. Subjectivity as such is inherently hostage; it answers to the point of expiation for others.

One can appear scandalized by this utopian and, for an I, inhuman conception. But the humanity of the human – the true life – is absent. [*EI* 99–100][39]

I must admit to being one of those who are 'scandalized by this Utopian...inhuman conception'. That is not what I want to focus on in this quotation, but let me say that I can accept all of the Levinasian insights that I find compelling without agreeing that, in the absence of the conditions which 'intervene in the concrete', I am responsible to the point of responsibility for my own persecution (in other contexts: to the point of offering myself as a substitute for the other – think of a concentration camp – to the point of martyrdom). It is true that someone who would not give his life for anyone else, for his family or his friends or even his whole people, has not reached the level of 'the human – the true life'. This is something it does not take Levinas to say; the Utilitarians know this full well. It is also true that someone who would give his life for an ideology or an abstraction but not for another person has, in a different way, missed 'the human – the true life'. But, the 'asymmetry' of the ethical relation need not be carried as far as Levinas carries it. And – incorrigible Aristotelian that I am – I would not carry it that far. It is, I think, because Levinas thinks of ethics as the *whole* of 'the true life' that he does so. But to be *only* ethical, even if one be ethical to the point of martyrdom, is to live a one-sided life.

But I said that that was not what I wanted to focus on in this quotation. What I want to focus on is a few words that may seem almost incidental: 'In the concrete, many other considerations intervene and require justice even for me.'

My quarrel is not with the idea that justice is required by the need to reconcile conflicting ethical demands. (The idea that one can explain the need for justice in purely naturalistic terms seems to me mistaken.) What troubles me is the fact that this dialectic of an extreme statement followed by a vague statement to the effect that 'in the concrete, many other considerations intervene and require justice even for me' occurs more than once in Levinas's writing. For example, in *Otherwise than Being*, 'This condition or unconditionality of being a hostage will then at least be an essential modality of freedom, the first, and not an empirical accident of the freedom, proud in itself, of the ego.' This is immediately followed by:

To be sure – but this is another theme – my responsibility for all can and has to manifest itself also in limiting itself. The ego can, in the name of this unlimited responsibility, be called on to concern itself also with itself. The fact that the other, my neighbor, is also a third party with respect to another, who is also a neighbor, is the birth of thought, consciousness, justice and philosophy. [*OB* 128]

Here Levinas seems to simultaneously restate his 'utopian', his 'unlimited' vision of human responsibility and reassure us that in practice it isn't so utopian after all. I agree that one shouldn't demand unlimited responsibility in practice; but not only because I am a neighbour of my neighbour.

I mentioned Aristotle. It is Aristotle who taught us that to love others one must be able to love oneself. The thought seems utterly alien to Levinas, for whom, it seems, I can at best see myself as one loved by those whom I love.[40] But I think Aristotle was right. I also described Levinas's ethics cum phenomenology as 'one-sided'. It is because it is one-sided that, I think, Levinas's relation to Buber is fundamentally a competitive one. Rather than seeing Buber as someone who identified a different 'I–Thou' relation from Levinas's, someone who identified a different *sine qua non* of the 'true life', Levinas must see Buber as someone who (had insights to be sure, but) got it wrong. But the ethical life has more than one *sine qua non*.

Isaiah Berlin famously divided thinkers into 'hedgehogs' (who know 'one big thing') and foxes (who know 'many small things'). But, *pace* Berlin, it isn't just a choice between hedgehogs and foxes. Where the ethical life is concerned, there are quite a few 'big things' to be known. We need many hedgehogs. But certainly one of the 'hedgehogs' we need to listen to is Emmanuel Levinas.

NOTES

* My special thanks to Ephraim Meir and Abe Stone for taking the time to read successive drafts with great care, and for extremely valuable suggestions.

1 In 'A Religion for Adults', Levinas speaks of 'my feelings in a Stalag in Germany when, over the grave of a Jewish comrade *whom the Nazis had wanted to bury like a dog*, a Catholic priest, Father Chesnet, recited prayers which were, in the absolute sense of the term Semitic' (*DF* 12). (I have added emphasis to call attention to the sort of captors Levinas had (not 'German soldiers' but 'Nazis') and to the attitude of these captors to their Jewish prisoners of war.)

2 Cf. 'Ethics as First Philosophy' in *LR* 75–87.

3 This is the gravamen of Levinas's most famous work, *Totality and Infinity*.

4 This is a major theme in *Totality and Infinity*.

5 This is a theme that has also been sounded in Anglo-American philosophy, e.g. by pragmatists and also by Thomas Nagel in *The View from Nowhere* (Oxford: Oxford University Press, 1986).

6 Cf. Stanley Cavell, *Conditions Handsome and Unhandsome* (Chicago: University of Chicago Press, 1990). 'Perfectionism, as I think of it, is not a competing theory of the moral life, but something like a dimension or tradition of the moral life that spans the course of Western thought, and concerns what used to be called the state of one's soul, a dimension that places tremendous burdens on personal relationships and of the transforming of oneself and of one's society' (p. 2).

7 Cf. my foreword to Franz Rosenzweig, *Understanding the Sick and the Healthy* (Cambridge: Harvard University Press, 1999).

8 As the examples of Kant and Mill illustrate, the fact that a philosopher is a Cavellian 'perfectionist' need not preclude his also making a 'legislative' contribution.

9 'The ego ... is reduced to the "here I am" [*me voici*], in a transparency without opaqueness, without heavy zones propitious for evasion. "Here I am" as a witness of the Infinite, but a witness that does not thematize what it bears witness of, and whose truth is not the truth of representation,

is not evidence' (*OB* 146). In a note to this paragraph (n. 11), Levinas cites Isaiah, writing, ' "Here I am! send me." (Isaiah, 6:8). "Here I am!" means "send me".' Note that 'send me' is not a proposition.

10 Cf. 'Love and Filiation', in *EL* 63–72.

11 Of course, fully appreciating the relation with the other requires fully appreciating the *mortality* of the other; the contrast with Heidegger could not be more complete.

12 Ephraim Meir has remarked (private communication) that this also presents me as one who hears the basic commandment 'Thou shalt not kill', and that in Levinas's philosophy this basic commandment is also saying. Levinas deconstructs the commandment as a 'Said' in order to point to the saying.

13 *Der Logische Aufbau der Welt*, (4th edn) (Hamburg: Felix Meiner, 1974), section 64, p. 86.

14 I am indebted to Abe Stone for convincing me of the extent of Husserl's influence on Carnap, up to and including the period of the *Aufbau*. Stone observed that even the expression '*Aufbau der Welt*' occurs in Husserl (vol. VII of the *Husserliana* volumes, pp. 175, ll. 33–4).

15 Abe Stone reminds me that Carnap didn't want to simply use mathematical logic to reproduce Husserl's system constitution, but to get it out of exactly this problem. 'In particular, he wants to replace alleged metaphysical truths, including those that have to do with metaphysical *priority*, with (conventional) truths about language. (Hence he approvingly quotes Nietzsche as saying that the "ego" is an artefact of our language, resulting from the fact that every sentence must have a subject' (personal communication from Stone).) Stone is right, but the fact remands that the 'primitive experiences' (*Urerlebnisse*) of Carnap's system are what we in ordinary language call *my* experiences, and not the experiences of human beings in general. (For a discussion of Carnap's failure successfully to avoid solipsism, see my 'Logical Positivism and Intentionality', collected in my *Words and Life* (Cambridge: Harvard University Press, 1994), pp. 85–98). This is one of the reasons that Levinas would not have been satisfied with Carnap's attempt any more than he was satisfied with Husserl's.

16 Explanations in square brackets are mine.

17 I am indebted once again to Abe Stone for pointing out the significance of Levinas's discussions of Descartes's proof (e.g. *EI* 91–2, *OB* 146, *LR* 112, 173–5). Stone writes (personal communication), 'What needs noticing, I think (as much for the proper understanding of Descartes as for the proper understanding of Levinas) is the moment at the end of the First Meditation where Descartes speaks of being like a prisoner who awakens

in a dark prison. Levinas notes that this represents a stage *before* the cogito argument.'

18 In a different reference to this argument from the one given in the previous note, Levinas writes: '[knowledge] is by essence a relation with what one equals and includes, with that whose alterity one suspends, with what becomes immanent, because it is to my measure and to my scale. I think of Descartes, who said that the *cogito* can give itself the sun and the sky; the only thing it cannot give itself is the idea of the Infinite' (*EI* 60). Here Levinas is in the midst of answering a series of questions about his own discussion not of God but of the relation to other people in the lectures published as *Time and the Other*.

19 'The concept of the infinite', Kant says, 'is taken from mathematics and belongs only to it.' And although 'I might call the divine understanding "infinite" ... this does not help me in the least to be able to say determinately how great the divine understanding is. Thus we see that I cannot come a single step further in my cognition of God by applying the concept of mathematical infinity to Him.' The quotation is from pp. 361–2 of the '*Lectures on the Philosophical Doctrine of Religion*' collected in *The Cambridge Edition of the Works of Immanuel Kant: Religion and Rational Theology*, translated and edited by Allen Wood and George Di Giovanni (eds.) (Cambridge: Cambridge University Press, 1996), pp. 345–451, delivered in the 1870s after the First Critique was published. I am grateful to Carl Posy for helping me track down this passage.

20 See ch. V, section 2, 'The Glory of the Infinite' (*OB* 140–62).

21 I see the idea of 'interrupting' being's 'unrendable essence' as reflecting the idea we encountered in Levinas's reading of Descartes's proof, the idea that the other breaks all my categories, like a 'fissure of being'.

22 In Levinas's footnote at this point the notion of 'obsession' – a Levinasian term for the recognition of the other as obliging me, the ethical relation *par excellence* – is connected with 'infinity' and also with going beyond 'intentionality', i.e. once again with going beyond the metaphysical categories.

23 In this case the attribute that 'Thou shalt not see my face; for no man can see me and live' (Exodus 33: 20).

24 Two sentences later, Levinas writes that 'life is still not arrested in the absolute immobility of a death mask. The ending up of finitude is not an appearance, which Hegel was able to designate as "a being which *immediately* is its own nothingness".'

25 Places in Lithuania – Vilna and Kovno in particular – were the great centres of Ashkenazi Jewish learning. The Lithuanian Jews were famous for their insistence on rigorous argument, and their contempt for the

enthusiastic and charismatic religiosity associated with Hassidism. Levinas himself was born in Kovno.

26 E.g., it isn't true that there are no 'charismatic' streams in Judaism. (Think of Hassidism, of various strains of Messianism.) However, it must be admitted that when Judaism is referred to, most often it is the austere variety that is meant; Hassidism is regularly marginalized, with Buber and Herschel being the great exceptions to this rule.

27 *A Heart of Many Rooms: Celebrating the Many Voices Within Judaism* (Woodstock: Jewish Lights Publishing, 1999).

28 Exodus 23:2, which the rabbis took out of context to justify the principle that the Jewish law is decided by majority vote of the great scholars.

29 On this, see *Judaism a Living Covenant* (Woodstock: Jewish Lights Publishing, 1997) by Hartman, and *Rational Rabbis* (Bloomington: Indiana University Press, 1997) by Menahem Fisch.

30 Babylonian Talmud (BT), Pirqei Avot, I:12.

31 BT, Shabbat 31a.

32 The reference to the Liberation shows that it is French Jews who are here addressed, but what Levinas goes on to say clearly concerns all Jews who live in modern times.

33 As Ephraim Meir pointed out to me, it is because Levinas makes Judaism's function an *ethical* one that it must stand outside the dialectic; there needs to be a standpoint from which historical 'development' can itself be criticized, and that standpoint is the ethical standpoint. But Levinas is not naïve; the ethical standpoint is not a set of timeless principles and codes, but something more basic than all principles and codes. Concerning the relation between ethics and politics, see 'Paix et proximité' in *Emmanuel Levinas*, Les Cahiers de la nuit surveillée 23 (Lagrasse: Verdier, 1984), pp. 339–46, and 'Liberté et commandement' (1953), reprinted in E. Levinas, *Liberté et commandement* (Paris: 1994), pp. 27–53. On this subject see also Ephraim Meir, 'milhama v'shalom behagut shel levinas', *Iyyun*, 48 (1997), pp. 471–9.

34 *LR* 258.

35 BT, Kiddushin 40b.

36 'No theme, no present, has a capacity for the Infinite' (*OB* 146).

37 Here Levinas uses the word 'evidence' in the sense of a presence or a disclosure, not in the sense of 'evidence for a hypothesis'.

38 In the next paragraph Levinas connects this idea of an 'exception to the rule of being' with Descartes's proof that we discussed above: 'The idea of the Infinite, which in Descartes is lodged in a thought that cannot contain it, expresses the disproportion between glory and the present' (*OB* 146).

39 Levinas means that the true life (human life in the normative sense of human) is absent if one rests with being 'scandalized'. The passage continues: 'The humanity in historical and objective being, the very breakthrough of the subjective, of the human psychism in its original vigilance or sobering up, is being which undoes its condition of being: *disinterestedness*.'

40 A criticism of Levinasian ethics that I heard voiced by Millie Heyd in conversation.

3   Levinas and the face of the other

The human face we encounter first of all as the other's face strikes us as a highly ambiguous phenomenon. It arises here and now without finding its place within the world. Being neither something real inside, nor something ideal outside the world, the face announces the corporeal absence (*leibhaftige Abwesenheit*) of the other. In Merleau-Ponty's terms we may call it the corporeal emblem of the other's otherness.[1] But we do not thereby resolve the enigma of the other's face. This enigma may be approached in different ways. In contrast to the later Merleau-Ponty, who tries to deepen our experience more and more, looking for the invisible within the visible, the untouchable within the touchable, Levinas prefers a kind of thinking and writing which may be called eruptive. Many sentences, especially in his last writings, look like blocks of lava spat out by a hidden vulcan. Words like 'evasion', 'rupture', 'interruption' or 'invasion' indicate a thinking which is obsessed by the provocative otherness of the other. They suggest a special sort of immediacy. In contrast to Hegel's immediacy, which is only the beginning of a long process of mediation, Levinas's immediacy breaks through all kinds of mediations, be it laws, rules, codes, rituals, social roles or any other kind of order. The otherness or strangeness of the other manifests itself as the extraordinary par excellence: not as something given or intended, but as a certain disquietude, as a *dérangement* which puts us out of our common tracks. The human face is just the foyer of such bewilderments, lurking at the borderlines which separate the normal from the anomalous. The bewildering effects lose their stimulating force if the face is taken either as something too real or as something too sublime. Although Levinas explicitly repudiates both possibilities, we will see that he has more problems avoiding the latter. He pays

63

much more attention to the breaking of orders than to the orders themselves. But phenomenologically orientated ethics, approaching the demand of the other, turns into moralism when starting immediately from the other, instead of trying to show that it has always already done so. Similar to Merleau-Ponty's claim that ontology can approach Being only in terms of an indirect ontology, we may assume that ethics can approach the other only in terms of an indirect ethics. What deviates from certain orders and exceeds them will turn to nothing unless supported by something which it exceeds and deviates from. Otherwise the extra-ordinary will turn into another order, and we are still there where we began. So we must be careful not to get into such traps, and Levinas would be the last to deny that.

THE COMMON FACE

Close to certain theological traditions, Levinas initially approaches the face of the other by the double way of *via negationis* and of *via eminentiae*. In his view the human face is *not* simply what it seems to be, and it is much *more* than that. So it may be useful to give a first idea of that manifold pre-understanding which gets transformed by Levinas's philosophy of the other.

What is called 'face' in English is less common than it seems to be. There is no basic face in the sense of Danto's basic actions. Even on the linguistic level the connotations differ from one language to the other. Let us take the languages Levinas spoke. The French word *visage*, like the German *Gesicht*, refers to seeing and being seen. The Hebrew expression *panim*, not unlike the German *Angesicht* or *Antlitz*, emphasizes the face facing us or our mutual facing.[2] The Russian term *lico* means face, cheek, but also person, similar to the Greek *prosôpon* which literally refers to the act of 'looking at' and which stands not only for the face, but also for masks and roles, rendered in Latin by *persona*.

In general, we may distinguish a narrow, rather common meaning, from a wider, more emphatic, meaning.[3] To the ordinary meaning belongs the frontal view, the face-to-face or even the façade of a building. The face itself constitutes the central zone of the body where our eyes and our mouth are located and the play of features takes place. We cannot close our face as we close our eyes, we can only protect it by visible or invisible masks. The emphatic sense of the word comes forth when the face is understood not simply as something present, but as the other's corporeal self-presence, performed by the gaze or appeal we are exposed to. What we call 'face' is culturally over-determined, marked by certain aesthetic, moral and sacred features. We are living in the face of the other, seeking or fleeing it, running the risk of losing our own face. In connection with our whole body the face is subjected to all kinds of face preserving, face restoring and face making, including modern techniques of image care. At the same time the face plays its part in acts of facing another, performed on the stage of life.

Although Levinas is looking for 'another scene', as Freud would put it, he does not simply skip the everyday scenes and their cultural equipment. The 'face' is no mere metaphor transporting a figurative sense into a higher sphere, delivering it from its corporeal chains. Levinas's ethics are rooted in a phenomenology of the body, close to that of Husserl, Sartre and Merleau-Ponty, even when he goes his own way. It is the hungering, thirsting, enjoying, suffering, working, loving, murdering human being in all its corporeality (*Leibhaftigkeit*) whose otherness is at stake. The otherness does not lie behind the surface of somebody we see, hear, touch and violate. It is just his or her otherness. It is the other as such and not some aspect of him or her that is condensed in the face. So the whole body expresses, our hands and shoulders do it as well as our face taken in its narrow sense.

But this leads us to the crucial question of how it may happen that the other appears to us without being reduced to somebody or something in the world. At this point where our world, crowded as it is with persons and things, explodes, the common face turns into the uncommon, into the unfamiliar, even into the uncanny (*Unheimliche*). Husserl's *Fremderfahrung*, the experience of what is strange, shifts into the estrangement of experience itself. The positing of the other gets undermined by the deposition of myself. The face we are confronted with can be understood as the turning point between the own and the alien where a certain dispossession takes place.[4] But the adventure of the other which starts here runs through a long and complicated story. I shall restrict myself to showing in which way the face of the other is figured out in Levinas's two major works, *Totality and Infinity* and *Otherwise than Being or Beyond Essence*. As we shall see, there is a clear change of tonality in the passage from the earlier to the later work, notwithstanding a certain continuity which is maintained from the early sketch in *Time and the Other* up to the last essays. So the topic of the other's face may be seen as a thread running through Levinas's whole work.

The ground-plan of Levinas's first major work is marked by a contrast, clearly announced by the title of the book. *Totality* has to be understood as the reign of the same[5] wherein everything and everybody exists as part of a whole or as case under a law. For Levinas it makes no great difference whether the totality is represented by the archaic form of religious or mythical participation or by the modern forms of rational mediation, achieved by economics, politics and culture. Even under these modern forms nobody becomes him- or herself because everyone is reduced to what he or she achieves in an anonymous way: life and work are nothing more than masks (*TI* 178). The totality, which forces everybody into certain roles, is based on violence, on a general war which does not end when the individual's striving for self-preservation makes use of rational means. This totality contrasts with the *infinity* of the other whose otherness exceeds the limits of any order whatsoever. Such a sharp contrast would harden into a manichaeist duality if it were not moved by an ongoing process of totalization which is itself balanced by a counter-process of excedence. Levinas presents this double process in terms of a drama, composed of two acts (see chs. II and III). In the first act the self gets separated from the totality by retiring to the *interiority* of an *oíkos*, to an enlarged self-sphere where everyone is at home, *chez soi*. Being at home, I am capable of receiving the other whose interpellation originates from outside, from an exteriority which in the end leaves every order behind. As soon as we enter the second act where the totality breaks in pieces, the face of the other plays a central role. 'The glean of exteriority or of transcendence' happens 'in the face of the Other' (*TI* 24), requiring a new 'thinking *in the face* of the Other' (*TI* 40).

But what does 'face' mean, and what sort of being should we attribute to the face? First of all, Levinas demonstrates that this traditional way of questioning goes wrong because it just misses the point. If the other's face transcends the ontological reign of more or less defined entities we are able only to say *what it is not*, or more precisely: we can only show *that it is not something at all*. The list of negations is long and sometimes tiresome. We are told that the face is not something we can see and touch, while moving within open horizons, passing through changing perspectives, transforming it into a content we embrace and manipulate (*TI* 190, 194). It has no 'plastic' form to be transformed in images; it has no *eidos*, no 'adequate idea' by which we could represent and grasp it. The face does not fall into the outer world, open the way to an inner world (*TI* 212), or take hold in a third world of ideas. But what else could we say about that strange phenomenon?

Only that before we speak about the face, 'the face speaks' (*TI* 66). This simple truth changes the whole situation. Platonists may evoke the conversion (*periagôgê*) of the soul's eyes, mentioned in Plato's *Republic*, and Heideggerians may be tempted to speak of a turning (*Kehre*). But what is decisive for Levinas is neither a change of our own attitude, nor a shift in the history of Being, but my being interpellated by the other. We start far off, subdued by the forces of gravity fields whose centre lies outside us (*TI* 183). Levinas continues to take the face as phenomenon, but not without redefining it: 'The phenomenon is the being that appears, but remains absent' (*TI* 181). It originates from a sort of epiphany, as Levinas likes to say, using a religious term.

The new concept of face raises a host of problems. Levinas seems to recast the old definition of the human being. Modifying the old formula we could state: 'The human being is a being which has a face.' Even if we leave more sophisticated questions aside (What do 'being' and 'having' mean?), we are confronted with the problem of how to distinguish between God's face and that of the human other. 'The dimension of the divine opens forth from the human face', Levinas writes (*TI* 78). It is obvious what Levinas has in mind: the way to God passes through the face of the other. But this is no answer to the question of how to distinguish the invisibility of God (see *TI* 78) from the invisibility of the human face.[6] Further, there are many faceless beings: there are things (*TI* 139–40), elements and mythical gods, the last evoking Being without beings, the horror of the *il y a* (*TI* 142), and there are finally our own works. Whatever sinks down into the anonymous, the impersonal, the neutral, is faceless. What is challenged by this philosophy of the face is the false spell of a 'philosophy of the neuter' (*TI* 298). However, apart from the general problem that 'faceless', like *alogon* or 'irrational', gives only a negative qualification, not specifying what it qualifies, we wonder why animals and plants should be omitted. The Cartesian dualism seems to throw its shadow on this philosophy of the face. We recall that Martin Buber's dialogical philosophy, whose shortcomings are not to be discussed here, concedes the role of Thou to all creatures.[7]

But let us ask what the face's speaking really means. The primacy of the face does not depend on the fact that somebody else addresses me, speaking *about* something or *about* somebody. In this case the other would communicate with me on equal terms. A simple philosophy of dialogue or of communication remains faceless because everybody would be reduced to what he or she said and did. Our intercourse would be restricted to the circulation of words, gestures and things. Giving which exceeds such a pure exchange presupposes more: the face 'expresses itself' (*TI* 51). The face is not the site from which a sender delivers certain messages by means of linguistic tools. Whenever the face speaks to us, 'the first content of expression is this expression itself' (*TI* 51). At this point we assist the birth of the other out of the Word and the birth of the Word out of the other. The Logos does not just become flesh, it becomes face.[8] Merleau-Ponty would say that we move on the level of the speaking language (*parole parlant*), not on the level of the spoken language (*parole parlée*), and Levinas would continue: we are concerned with saying, not with the said. Yet Levinas goes a step further. He personalizes the speaking language in terms which sound rather unusual in the ears of Saussurian linguistics.[9] Sign systems consist of signs, splitting into signifier and signified, and communicative systems consist of processes in which signs are used in order to exchange messages. What Levinas has in mind is nothing like that. He avoids any established linguistic system until reaching the point where the speaking face functions as the primordial signifier. 'The face, expression simpliciter, forms the first word, the face is the signifier which appears on the top of his sign, like eyes looking at you' (*TI* 153). So the other is the giver of a sense which precedes my own *Sinngebung*. Consequently we learn from the other what we cannot learn by ourselves. Levinas calls it teaching (*enseignement*), in contrast to Socratic *maieutics* (*TI* 51).

Now, speaking which speaks *to me* before and beyond speaking *about something* takes the features of appeal, call, interpellation, and it privileges grammatical forms like the imperative, the vocative and personal pronouns. Obviously, Levinas picks up motifs which have been developed long ago by the German philosophers of dialogue and their predecessors.[10] But in opposition to any kind of intimacy and reciprocity between I and Thou, Levinas maintains the distance of the other's face. 'The immediate is the interpellation and, if we may speak thus, the imperative of language. The idea of contact does not represent the primordial mode of the immediate' (TI 52).

If we reflect on the fact that the speech of the other's face privileges the imperative, we understand that the face is not something seen, observed, registered, deciphered or understood, but rather somebody responded to. I can only and only I can respond to the injunction of a face (see TI 305); disregarding it would be a response as well. When Levinas obstinately affirms that the relation between the other and myself is marked by an irrevocable asymmetry, he refers to the primary situation of the call which opens a dimension of height (TI 35, 86). The other's voice comes from above, like God's voice at the Sinai. But in opposition to any hierarchization of human relations we must admit that the interhuman asymmetry is a double-sided one. Levinas explicitly states that the other's command commands me to command (TI 213). The obedience he has in mind is a mutual one. We are all 'masters'. This is an unusual idea. We are accustomed to suppose that every order is endorsed by some authority whose legitimacy can and has to be checked. So in the end every order goes back to a law I have given by myself. Since Kant we call this autonomy. But, according to Levinas, things are less simple.

To begin with, the grammatical form of the imperative can be used in different ways. 'Come!' may express an invitation, a request, a demand or a strict command. When Levinas refers to the 'look that supplicates and demands' (TI 75), we must add the look which commands. But in Levinas's eyes these are mere variants which make no great difference. With regard to the genuine speech of the face, the question of legitimation does not yet arise. This question only arises in so far as in the face of the other expressing itself the third party intervenes and as far as through the other's face it is 'the whole of humanity which looks at us' (see TI 213, 305). The face of the other who commands justice for others, dwells itself on this side of right and wrong, of good and evil. The other's face is not a case of justice, but its very source. Justice, too, has its blind spot which will never be filled by sufficient reasons.[11]

However, that is not because one demand is not like another. The other's demand culminates in a negative command, facing the extreme possibility of murder and averting it by force of a resistance whose quality is not physical, but ethical. The other resists violence not as somebody belonging to the totality of beings, but as an infinite which is beyond all we can do to the other. The otherness of the other manifests the impossibility of our own possibilities.[12] What Levinas calls the face is just the expression of this lived impossibility. So he writes: 'This infinite, stronger than the murder, resists to us already in the face, it is its face, it is the original expression, the first word: "Thou shalt not commit murder" [*tu ne commettras pas de meurtre*]' (*TI* 199), or more simply: 'Thou shalt not kill [*tu ne tueras pas*]' (*CP* 55).

These formulas are full of strange implications which cannot be dealt with by theologization, referring to the seventh command of the decalogue, nor by anthropologization, comparing it to Hobbes's *homo homini lupus*. The speaking face would all too quickly disappear behind traditional *Ideenkleidern*. Leaving many aspects aside, I only want to lead the reader's attention to some central issues concerning the power of the face. First, the quoted command sentences are formulated in the future tense. One may take this future as an especially strong sort of imperative or as a concession to the Hebrew, whose grammar does not allow for a negative imperative such as 'Do not ...!' But it seems to me that there is even more at stake here. The quoted sentences are not normal imperatives, uttered by and addressed to somebody, as if the face were the partner of a dialogue or the opponent in a dispute. The resistance which 'gleams in the face of the other' (*TI* 199) is not directed to our seeing, knowing or doing, it does not affect our *vouloir dire* or *savoir faire*, but our *vouloir tuer* (*TI* 199). It changes our power (*pouvoir*) to kill into a sort of powerlessness (*impuissance*). 'The expression the face introduces into the world does not defy the feebleness of my powers, but my ability for power [*mon pouvoir de pouvoir*]' (*TI* 198). This peculiar resistance is not based on what the other says and on the reasons the other gives, it coincides with the very fact that the other addresses me (what the later Levinas attributes to saying in contrast to the said).

We can certainly contradict what the other says because the other is not a dogmatic authority, but we cannot contradict the call and demand of the other's face which precedes any initiative we may take.

Corresponding to that, the nakedness of the face, which is extended to the nakedness of the whole body (TI 74), does not mean that there is *something behind* the masks and clothes the other wears, it rather means that the other's otherness eludes every qualification we may apply. Compared to cultural, symbolic and social roles which mask the face, the face has something of a *visage brut*. Its nakedness is not factual, so that it could be eliminated, but is due to an 'essential poverty' which makes the poor and the stranger equal to us (TI 213).[13]

The drama which takes place between myself and the other does not stop here. The ascension to the other's face has a postface entitled 'Beyond the Face' (see ch. IV). We descend into the limbus of erotics and sexuality, of fertility and generativity. This descent resembles the philosopher's return into the cave described in *Republic* VII. What distinguishes the 'night of the erotic', from the 'night of insomnia', belonging to the faceless *il y a* (TI 258), is the fact that the human lover presupposes the face of the other even if he tries to 'enjoy the Other' as if she (not he!) were a mere element (TI 255). But this up and down, this above and beyond, does not exclude certain ambiguities, inherent to love as such, attaining even the face and leading to a special *fémininité* of the loved face. 'The feminine presents a face that goes beyond the face' by sinking into the 'equivocation of the voluptuous' (TI 260). This is not the place to discuss this odd attempt to gender the face. In any case, the oscillation between the different genders conforms to a general ambiguity ascribed to the face as staying 'at the limit of holiness and caricature' (TI 198), i.e. between the in-formal and the de-formed.

Looking back towards this first presentation of the other's otherness we may ask if the ambiguity of the face is always a good one.[14] Although Levinas emphasizes the transcendence of the face, he also declares that this transcendence does not take place outside the world and outside the economy which regulates our living in the world (see TI 172). But if so, we would better refrain from affirmations like this: 'The true essence of man is presented in his [her?] face, in which he is infinitely other than a violence like unto mine' (TI 290–1). Is it possible to transform the infinite process of othering into a true essence? Has the plurality of beings not to be completed by the pluralization of the face, following different ways to transcend the order in question? Is it really possible to put the metaphysics of the same and the other on this side, the psychology or psychoanalysis and the sociology (and we add: the cultural anthropology) of the *œuvres* on the other side (*TI* 228)?

We should contextualize the otherness or – as I would say – the *Fremdheit* as well as the selfhood, not by integrating them into certain contexts, but by relating them to those contexts which are burst apart by the extra-ordinary demand of the other. This pluralization of the face would also undermine the dubious duality of what is faceful and what faceless. With regard to the speech of the face I could further ask if we do not need a broader concept of appeal, of *Anspruch* which includes the gaze, the *Anblick*, referring to a kind of seeing which transcends what is seen. Levinas's allusion to the 'whole body' as constituting the face should be taken seriously in order to develop a sort of responsiveness which penetrates all our senses and our bodily behavior *in toto*.

Finally, what does Levinas have in mind when he proclaims the command: 'Thou shalt not murder' as the 'first word'? Reckoning with the worst when speaking of human affairs is one thing, relying on it is something other. Even the worst may differ from one culture, epoch or age to the other. Besides, why should somebody listen to the voice of the other when the prohibition would be the 'first word'? What about Virgil's *risu cognoscere matrem*?[15] Does this mean anything more than the expression of a primary narcissism, love loving itself? I recommend reading *Totality and Infinity* in a less linear way so that the postface, entitled 'Beyond the Face', would partly pass into a 'pre-face', partly into an 'inter-face', contaminating the pretended purity of the face from the beginning.[16]

THE FUGITIVE FACE: THE TRACE OF THE OTHER

Passing to the second major book *Otherwise than Being or Beyond Essence*, published seventeen years later, we feel that the tone has changed. Let us begin with the dedication which presents the book as written in the face of certain others or seeking their faces. The first book had been dedicated to Jean Wahl and his wife. Jean Wahl was a French Jewish philosopher to whom Levinas was indebted for his early support.[17] The second book is not dedicated to friends who are still alive, but to the 'closest' among so many people killed by the Nazis; the dedication is extended to the millions of victims from all confessions and nations, 'victims of the same hatred of the other man, the same anti-semitism',[18] and it is completed by an address to the 'closest', name by name, written (and for most of the readers hidden) in Hebrew. The polar air of violent death penetrates this book. The faces that the author addresses are already effaced. The 'proximity' evoked by the dedication is a delicate one. Furthermore, 'proximity', one of the key-words of the book, belongs to the occasional or indexical expressions which have to be instantiated from case to case, including recent genocides like those in Bosnia or Rwanda which each has its own singularity. In the dedication, mourning and premonition are interlaced. Finally, the fact that our speaking of the other is preceded by our being exposed to the other's call diminishes the risk of instrumentalizing morals. This risk belongs to a special amorality inherent to morals, depicted by Nietzsche's sharp pen better than by anybody else.

Now, the change of tone reflects Levinas's recasting of his own thinking, following the publication of *Totality and Infinity*. Not unlike the first great book, the second one emerges from detailed studies which are composed only afterwards. Levinas is like a wanderer who sketches his map not in advance but while marching ahead. The recasting of earlier ideas may be characterized in different ways. For me it is especially striking that dualisms like existence (Being) against existent (being) or totality against infinity are replaced with an internal intrigue, transforming opposition into entanglement.[19] Oppositions turn into internal splittings like that of speech into the saying (*dire*) and the said (*dit*). Finally, all of this is accompanied by processes of retardation and dislocation which reinforce our (dis)embodiment. In sum, the later philosophy of the other is much less Cartesian than the earlier one. This has the effect that the exteriority of the other penetrates the interiority of the self, generating certain whirls which are verbally reflected in an endless series of self-referential, paradoxical and hyperbolic expressions – as if everything has been infected by a virus of otherness. In what follows, I shall illustrate this change, still following the motif of the face.

As we have seen, in *Totality and Infinity* the other is immediately present and self-present. Otherness keeps the character of a phenomenon, or more precisely, the other, being separated from the totality of beings, is the phenomenon *par excellence* whose epiphany includes absence. The 'absence of the Other is just his or her presence as of another', so Levinas puts it in his early writings (*TO* 93–4). But in *Otherwise than Being* he clearly maintains the not-presence of the other and the non-phenomenality of the face. Does he change only the terms? We will see that much more is at stake here.

First, it has to be noticed that, compared with the earlier work, the motif of the face loses its dominant place and gets much more entangled in different topics, mostly in the central topic of proximity (see *OB* 89–90). Proximity, as understood by Levinas, does not have a socio-ontological meaning. It does not refer to beings within space, approximating each other when the distance between them diminishes, and touching upon each other when the distance reaches zero. This kind of nearness and remoteness is always relative. Even persons are more or less close to each other, corresponding to their bodily position, to their affinities and to the functions or interests they share. This kind of nearness and remoteness can be observed, compared and even measured by a third party. It belongs to what Husserl calls a *Nah-* and *Fernwelt*, both being sections of the one world, and it belongs to the social world, which in Alfred Schutz's view is divided into *Mitwelt, Umwelt, Vorwelt* and *Nachwelt*. It is interesting to see that the face-to-face relationship which guarantees the highest degree of individuality and intimacy is defined by Schutz as spatial and temporal co-presence, mediated by the mutual understanding of the other's expression.[20] Mundane and social orders leave place only for relative forms of otherness or strangeness. The face-to-face is embedded into the horizons of a common world. Everybody understands everything in his or her own way, but the exchange of positions leads to a reciprocity of perspectives. The social world is ruled by the law of symmetry. Obviously all of that is far away from what Levinas is looking for. The proximity that he has in mind originates from the otherness as such in terms of a *Fernnähe*, a proximity which not only includes distance, but even increases it. Levinas develops this idea along classical topics like time, space, body and senses. In doing so, he leaves, as he often does, many things behind which could be helpful in order to place such eruptive findings in a more satisfying way. To make only one point, when Husserl, Heidegger, Karl Bühler and other phenomenologists distinguish between 'here' and 'there' they certainly do not distinguish between positions within a given space.

The 'there' has no distance to the 'here'. For me, as the speaker, being 'there' means being elsewhere, being there where I am not, and the other is just there where I cannot be. Merleau-Ponty radicalizes this insight by referring to an 'original of the elsewhere'.[21] This assumption could be corroborated by Paul Celan's appellative poetry to which Levinas explicitly refers, or by Paul Valéry's and Jacques Lacan's reflections on the mutual look which implies that nobody is there where the other sees him or her.

But let us turn to the question of how Levinas introduces the other's face, being 'otherwise than Being'. He prefers again an unusual way, and he is forced to do so. 'Otherwise than Being' does not mean 'something other than Being' by which the reign of Being would only be doubled or multiplied. That is why Levinas's speaking of the other while rising from the other, often sounds so tautological. In order to prevent saying, which is more and other than the said, from turning into pure saying, saying nothing, certain differences are needed. Levinas tends to obtain such differences by a sort of hyperbolic paradoxical speaking which submits the related phenomena (or hyper-phenomena) to an internal iteration and gradation. Frequent formulations like 'trace, past, shadow of itself' or 'more passive than any passivity' or 'immediacy which is more immediate' might spread like a fever of thinking; they should be taken as hints, not as results. Indeed, Levinas himself does not stop there. The royal road towards the withdrawal of such phenomena gets opened by the power of time, more precisely, by a special time of the other which will never be recuperated. 'In proximity is heard a command come as though from an immemorial past, which was never present, began in no freedom. This *way* of the neighbor is face' (*OB* 88). A hard text which should not be changed into a soft reading. The term 'proximity' reminds us of the Biblical neighbour who has more to do with the stranger's than with the friend's face. Proximity does not coincide with affinity. Further, 'one hears a command' or it 'is heard (*s'entend*)'. The author uses a sort of medium beyond active and passive. Hearing the command is presented as an event which arrives, not as an act which is performed by individual subjects, the one speaking, the other listening – as if someone who receives the command were already somebody before responding to the command. The event of command is neither a neutral fact nor a responsible act. Instead, it is pregnant with responsiveness and responsibility, provoking our 'response of

responsibility' (OB 142). *Comme d'un passé immémorial*: the immemorial past echoes Schelling's *Unvordenklichkeit* and Merleau-
Ponty's reference to the pre-beginning of one's birth.[22]

'As though': this strange past is present. It is present, but it is so
in the paradoxical way of being more present than ourselves who are
always in delay. We are not only too late to begin by ourselves and
to fulfil what Kant calls freedom of spontaneity. We are also too late
to remember the command in the way we remember what has been
possible for us. What Levinas suggests is a redefinition of freedom in
terms of beginning oneself, but beginning elsewhere. Without this
redefinition things would only be reversed in such a way that my
initiative would be exchanged for that of the other whose otherness
would finally be abolished itself in want of a counterpart.[23] The passage concludes with a kind of résumé, presenting the face not as
something or somebody we can grasp, but as a mere way or mode,
i.e. as the other's proximity. In order to characterize this irrevocable
proximity which surprises, befalls, occupies us, Levinas often uses
terms like traumatism, obsession or even madness. This application of terms, taken over from pathology, remains problematic. We
should take this idiom as a hyperbolic *façon de parler*, required by
the extra-ordinary character of this 'intrigue'. But we neglect suffering, the pathos of special pathologies, if we simply blur the difference
between the normal and the pathological, notwithstanding the fact
that both are never separated by clear-cut borderlines.[24]

The temporal delay which separates the other's demand from our
own response explains why Levinas now denies phenomenality to
the face. The face is 'the very collapse of phenomenality', not because
of some strength or brutality, but because of its 'feebleness', because
of its being 'less' than a phenomenon (OB 88). The 'feebleness' of the
ethical resistance shrinks into a sort of fading, a withdrawal.[25]

The absence of the other is evoked by a kaleidoscope of quasi-
descriptions. What we find is again the nakedness of the face, its
non-form, but now its absence is much more dynamized in terms
of self-*abondement*, self-retirement, emptiness, hollowness, abyss,
ex-cession. It finds its non-place (*non-lieu*) in its homelessness, its
strangeness. Levinas himself becomes aware of certain affinities to
the negative theology which he, however, explicitly repudiates (see
OB 12). He steers in the opposite direction, considering a 'concrete
abstraction' (OB 91). Torn away from the horizons, contexts and

conditions of the world, the face keeps some threads and fringes of the webs and textures from which it is absolved. The face is not at all reduced to an abstract content, ab-straction is rather an ongoing process.

This endless process of ab-solution culminates in approximating the face which speaks to the skin we touch and caress. The sense of touching is traditionally defined as *Nahsinn*, as if by touching we could contact reality in a direct manner.[26] Once more Levinas takes the opposite direction. 'Because the contact with skin is still a proximity of the face' (OB 90), and because it creates a 'quasi transparent divergency between the visible and the invisible' (OB 89), this skin-close contact intensifies the *Fernnähe*. The closer to the other, the more distant we are. The never completely, yet nearly reached, co-incidence between touching and touched produces, so to speak, an electrifying effect.[27] In this context Levinas resumes the results of his earlier phenomenology of Eros, but gives it a new switch. Eros beyond the face is transformed into an Eros moving towards the face. 'In the approach of a face the flesh becomes word, the caress a saying' (OB 94). This approximation is not reserved for the touch: 'In every vision contact is announced: sight and hearing caress the visible and the audible' (OB 80). We are invited to treat our whole *sensorium* as a *responsorium*.[28] But if this is true we should even more ask if Levinas is right to restrict the 'face' to the human face, neglecting the appeal of things, the call of other living beings.

In the end, Levinas's reflections on the proximity and remoteness of the other's face are focused on the crucial motif of trace. The trace 'shines (*luit*) as face of the other' (OB 12). Being present only as remnant of somebody who has passed, thus referring to an immemorial past, the trace of the other marks and even constitutes the other's face. The high presence of the face-to-face yields to the *ritardando* of a mere after-face. The other enters through a back-door. Levinas emphasizes again the corporeality of the trace. The face is growing old, even while being young; as a wrinkled face, it is a 'trace of itself' (OB 88). It says adieu, à-dieu – or simply farewell. In Levinas's view the mark of interrogation which points to the enigmatic character of the trace cannot be eliminated by changing the other's demand into something we know. 'A face is not a presence announcing a "non-said," which will be said from behind it' (OB 154). But even if the mark of interrogation cannot be eliminated it must be questioned.[29]

As the trace of the other, the face keeps the ambiguous character of an enigma. This has nothing do with riddles we have not yet solved. The enigma, as understood by Levinas, is a borderline phenomenon, located between the visible and the invisible, the said and the saying. In his article 'Enigma and Phenomenon' Levinas writes: 'The enigma extends as far as the phenomenon that bears the trace of the *saying* which has already withdrawn from the already *said*' (BPW 73). We thematize what is absent, but doing so we inevitably betray what is only present as being absent. So we betray the other's face too. The enigma of the face persists. It functions as a bridge to the third party, to the claim of justice. But this bridge has become more of an expedience than it was in *Totality and Infinity*, where the third and finally the whole of humanity look at us through the other's eyes. The compatibility between the other's demand and the claim of justice has become much more fragile; in a certain sense both are incompatible, being irreducible to each other. The trace of the infinite which 'shines' as the face of the other shows the ambiguous feature of somebody before whom (or to whom) and for whom I am responsible. The enigma of the other's face, its ex-ception, consists in the incompatible fact that the other is judge and accused at once (OB 12). Any previous division of roles would spill and even poison the source of justice. The justice which is required by all others of the other takes the paradoxical form of a 'comparison of the incomparables'. 'The neighbour that obsesses me is already a face, both comparable and incomparable, a unique face and in relationship with faces, which are visible in the concern for justice' (OB 158). Whereas the proximity to the other's face is the source of justice, 'the relationship with the third party is an incessant correction of the asymmetry of proximity in which the face is ef-faced [se dé-visage]' (OB 158).[30] However, we must admit that political, juridical, linguistic or cultural orders are neither created by the other's demand nor by its correction. They require a sort of creative response to the other. Because Levinas simply presupposes such orders without questioning their origin a hole seems to open in Levinas's ethics of the other which should not be papered over. On the other side, the tension between *visage* and *dé-visagement*, between the respect of the other's otherness and the requirements of equality, marks the point where ethics and politics are insolubly entangled without covering each other.[31]

NOTES

1 Cf. M. Merleau-Ponty, *The Visible and the Invisible*, trans. A. Lingis (Evanston: Northwestern University Press, 1968), p. 147: the flesh has to be thought as 'the concrete emblem of a general mode of being'.

2 On the Biblical background, which is only implicitly present in Levinas's philosophical writings, see M. C. Srajek, *In the Margins of Deconstruction: Jewish Conceptions of Ethics in Emmanuel Levinas and Jacques Derrida* (Dordrecht/Boston/London: Kluwer, 1998); see ch. 4 which deals partly with the 'Phenomenology of Face'.

3 The visual understanding of the common face is well presented in Georg Simmel's 'Soziologie der Sinne' (1907), in *Aufsätze und Abhandlungen 1901–1908*, Ges. Ausgabe, 8 (Frankfurt am Main: Suhrkamp, 1993), pp. 276–92.

4 Husserl describes the body as 'the point of conversion' (*Umschlagstelle*) from spiritual to natural causality. See *Ideas Pertaining to a Pure Phenomenology and to a Phenomenological Philosophy*, trans. R. Rojcewicz and A. Schuwer (Dordrecht: Kluwer, 1989), p. 299.

5 More exactly we should speak of 'the Self and the Other *as the Same*'. Levinas tends to blur the difference between same (*même*) and self (*soi*); similarly other (*autre*) can also be understood in a double way.

6 Concerning the traditional Jewish and Christian background cf. Edith Wyschogrod, 'Corporeality and the Glory of the Infinite in the Philosophy of Emmanuel Levinas', in Marco O. Olivetti (ed.), *Incarnation* (Padua: Cedam, 1999).

7 This problem has been repeatedly discussed by John Llewelyn. See, for example, 'Am I Obsessed by Bobby? Humanism of the Other Animal', in Robert Bernasconi and Simon Critchley (eds.), *Re-Reading Levinas* (Bloomington: Indiana University Press, 1991).

8 On the theological and philosophical background of this distinction, see Olivetti, *Incarnation*.

9 For a comparison between Levinas's philosophy and modern linguistics and linguistic philosophies, see Thomas Wiemer, *Die Passion des Sagens* (Freiburg/Munich: Alber, 1988).

10 See Michael Theunissen, *The Other*, trans. Christopher MacCann (Cambridge: MIT Press, 1984).

11 Cf. my discussion of this problem from a Nietzschean and Levinasian point of view: 'Der blinde Fleck der Moral', in *Deutsch-Französische Gedankengänge* (Frankfurt am Main: Suhrkamp, 1995).

12 See Levinas's debate with Heidegger in *TO* 70.

13 Sartre uses the same terms *pauvreté essentielle* to characterize the image of representation in contrast with perception. See *The Psychology of the*

Imagination, trans. B. Frechtman (New York: Washington Square, 1966), p. 19. This is not the only example for Levinas's use of Sartrean terms, based on a certain Cartesian legacy that they both share.

14 I refer to Merleau-Ponty's self-criticism in 1952 in 'An unpublished text', trans. A. Dallery, in James M. Edie (ed.), *The Primacy of Perception and Other Essays* (Evanston: Northwestern University Press, 1964), pp. 3–11.

15 René Spitz uses this famous verse as *leitmotiv* for his research on the baby's discovering of the other and on the illness of hospitalism which arises when the primary relation is disturbed. See *The First Year of Life: a Psychoanalytic Study of Normal and Deviant Development of Objective Relations* (New York: International Universities Press, 1965).

16 In this context I refer to Monique Schneider's attempt to counterbalance Levinas's ethical approach by a psychoanalytic procedure; see 'En déça du visage', in J. Greisch and J. Rolland (eds.), *L'éthique comme philosophie première* (Paris: Cerf, 1993), pp. 133–53.

17 *The Time and the Other* are not the only lectures he gave at the Collège Philosophique at the invitation of Jean Wahl. In 1961 he gave another lecture at the same place on 'Le visage humain', followed by a debate in which Merleau-Ponty took part.

18 On these dedications cf. Robert Bernasconi's penetrating comment, turning around the ambiguous face-to-face of persecution; see 'Only the Persecuted . . . : Language of the Oppressor, Language of the oppressed', in A. T. Peperzak (ed.), *Ethics as First Philosophy* (New York/London: Routledge, 1995), pp. 82–3.

19 At this point Levinas comes very close to Husserl's *Ineinander* and Merleau-Ponty's *entrelacs* or *chiasme*. See my essay on 'Verflechtung und Trennung. Wege zwischen Merleau-Ponty und Levinas', in *Deutsch-Französische Gedankengänge*.

20 See A. Schutz, *The Phenomenology of the Social World*, trans. G. Walsh and F. Lehnert (Evanston: Northwestern University Press, 1967).

21 Merleau-Ponty, *The Visible and the Invisible*, p. 254.

22 ' . . . an original past, a past which has never been present': *Phenomenology of Perception*, trans. Colin Smith (London: Routledge, 1962), p. 242.

23 See my arguments in 'Response and Responsibility in Levinas', *L'ethique comme philosophie première, op. cit.*, pp. 39–52.

24 See further Elisabeth Weber, *Verfolgung und Trauma* (Vienna: Passagen, 1990).

25 Cf. Socrates' ironical response to the question of how he should be buried: 'As you like, he said, if you will really catch me and if I do not slip away from you' (*Phaedo*, 115 c).

26 This everyday materialism has been long since undermined by authors like David Katz and Erwin Straus, from whom Merleau-Ponty learned much.

27 Merleau-Ponty's reflections in *The Visible and the Invisible* are less far from that than Levinas suggests. Cf. Antje Kapust's excellent exposition and continuation of this debate in *Berührung ohne Berührung. Ethik und Ontologie bei Merleau-Ponty und Levinas* (Munich: W. Fink, 1999). On the initial role of the touch cf. also Edith Wyschogrod, 'Doing before Hearing: On the Primacy of Touch', in F. Laruelle (ed.), *Textes pour Emmanuel Levinas* (Paris: Editions Jean-Michel Place, 1980), pp. 179–203.

28 See my chapter 'Leibliches Responsorium' in *Antwortregister* (Frankfurt am Main: Suhrkamp, 1994).

29 With regard to the (a-)theological background of Levinas's ethics cf. Hent de Vries, *Theologie im Pianissimo Zwischen Rationalität und Dekonstruktion* (Kampen: KoK, 1989) and John Llewelyn, *Emmanuel Levinas: the Genealogy of Ethics* (London/New York: Routledge, 1995), ch. 12.

30 Translation modified. Concerning the relation between ethics and politics I refer to the related studies by Robert Bernasconi, Fabio Ciaramelli, Simon Critchley and others.

31 Even the role of aesthetics should be reconsidered, including the difference between the sacred and the holy, and the relation between face and mask.

4   Levinas's critique of Husserl

It seems to be generally accepted that the analysis of 'internal time-consciousness' is not only the foundation on which the entire edifice of Husserl's transcendental phenomenology rests, but that it also remains an obligatory reference point for any phenomenologist concerned with the question of time. This is certainly true of Merleau-Ponty and Ricœur, but it is also true of Heidegger, Levinas and Derrida, who are nevertheless reluctant to subscribe entirely to the Husserlian analysis of temporality and temporalization.[1] It is almost as if the Husserlian descriptions of the experience of time contained within themselves the seeds of a surpassing of the philosophical framework in which Husserl had inserted them. We are then confronted with the paradox whereby an analysis of time that was to have provided a foundation for a phenomenology of an egological transcendental consciousness constitutive of objects by justifying their *epistemological* validity also retains a large part of its value in an *ontological* phenomenology of *Dasein* or in an *ethical* phenomenology of the other person who appears in the form of the 'face' or the 'appeal'.

I

One could be forgiven, then, for thinking that Husserl's analysis of internal time-consciousness, far from conclusively justifying the idea of an egological, intentional transcendental consciousness, on the contrary pushes it towards its outermost limit. None the less, we should bear in mind that what is being pushed to its limit here

Translated by Dale Kidd

should not be confused with consciousness as understood by late nineteenth-century psychology (however much it inspired Husserl), nor with the transcendental in the neo-Kantian sense. The characterization of Husserlian phenomenology as a 'transcendental empiricism' is a perfect acknowledgement of this double difference.

By essentially distinguishing transcendental consciousness from any empirical consciousness, Husserl's phenomenology overcomes the aporias of psychologism, and this for two principal reasons: (1) the objects of consciousness are intentional objects which, instead of belonging to consciousness as its constitutive moments, are on the contrary recognized in their transcendence and ideality; (2) the intentional consciousness which is directed to these objects is a consciousness purified of all empirical apperception. By purifying consciousness of its apperception as a psychophysical fact, the phenomenological reduction at the same time safeguards the transcendence of the intentional object. As a consequence, transcendental phenomenology is devoted to a study of the correlation between the acts of a pure consciousness and noematic objects, i.e. objects just in so far as they are aimed at by such acts. By investigating objects as correlates of the acts of a pure consciousness, transcendental phenomenology deprives them of their autonomy, of their independence with respect to consciousness, but it does not deprive them of their transcendence. Their transcendence is preserved not only because the object of a punctual intentional act is not itself a constitutive part of that act, but also because various acts succeeding one another in time can still relate to the unity of one and the same object.

While Husserl's transcendental phenomenology is distinguished from the empirical psychology of its day both by its safeguarding the transcendence of the intentional object as well as by the transcendental purity of the consciousness that it studies, this does not mean that it should be confused with the transcendental philosophy of the Marburg school (the form of neo-Kantianism to which it is closest). The famous correspondence between Husserl and Natorp is a particularly telling testimony to this difference. Transcendental phenomenology does not rest on the unquestioned validity of scientific objects and works its way back, in the form of a 'reconstruction', to subjective spirit as their formal condition of possibility. On the contrary, it is immediately and exclusively interested in the transcendental subject's *effective life*, and in the way in which (scientific and natural) objects are 'given' or are presented as 'phenomena' to the transcendental subject. In this way, the transcendental acquires an 'empirical' value, in the sense that phenomenology studies the particular content of an experience, primarily its sensible content. For transcendental phenomenology, the experience that is constitutive of intentional objects is perceptual or pre-predicative before it is an experience of thought or judgement. Yet the fact that this experience or consciousness is the object of a transcendental science in no way implies that it is considered as simply the formal or logical possibility condition for the validity of objects of experience. The source of validity for these objects is not provided by the 'principles' (*Grundsätze*) of the understanding, but by the effective life of a pure intentional consciousness within which objects are given and constituted as transcendent unities. In this way, transcendental phenomenology brings to appearance an effective transcendental life, which underlies empirical life as its hidden foundation. Contrary to neo-Kantianism, the transcendental for Husserl is a specific mode of life with its own mode of appearing, in which sensibility plays a privileged role.

We must now ask what place a transcendental phenomenology of constituting consciousness will reserve for the phenomenon of temporality, and in what forms this phenomenon will be given. It cannot but occupy a central place, since transcendental consciousness is a life that is constantly evolving, and its realizations are temporal events. It is not for no reason that Husserl speaks of the 'flux' (*Fluss*) of consciousness. The rhythm of this flux is articulated by the emergence of a new intentional act succeeding the previous one, which is thus pushed into the past. In most cases, this new act is not without links to the previous act; it was already present in the form of an anticipated future before being effectively realized in the present. And what is true of the act in its temporal duration is equally true of each instant within this duration: consciousness of the present is always intertwined with consciousness of the past and of the future, and this is the very reason why consciousness is a flux and not a succession of separate punctual instants. We should therefore bear in mind that, for Husserl, even before time is related to objects, it already characterizes transcendental consciousness itself in its effective accomplishment. The being of transcendental life is the incessant movement of its own self-temporalization. We should also bear in mind that this process of self-temporalization is articulated by the indefinitely renewed emergence of a new presence or a new present.

Having thus established the fundamentally temporal character of the life of intentional constituting consciousness, Husserl's investigations then proceed in two opposing directions. The first is an interrogation of the way in which the temporality of intentional consciousness constitutes the temporal determinations of objects and, more generally, the objective time of the world as the horizon in which empirical objects manifest themselves. It is a question of understanding how, in the incessant movement of intentional life, the immutable identity of a temporal order is constructed in which each object or event is assigned its own place, once and for all, with respect to all other contemporary, prior or posterior objects or events. In particular, Husserl shows that rememorative re-presentation (*wiedererinnernde Vergegenwärtigung*) plays a crucial role in this process. The second direction, by contrast, leads towards an investigation of that ultimate or 'absolute' consciousness in which, or for which, the flowing temporality of intentional acts appears. This ultimate consciousness turns out to be the 'inner' consciousness that accompanies the temporal accomplishment of intentional acts as its shadow or, more precisely, as its own specific mode of manifestation. The flowing temporality of the intentional acts of constituting consciousness appears in a way that is fundamentally different from the way in which the fixed temporal features of constituted objects appear. The appearance of the flowing temporality of intentional acts is no longer a matter of rememoration and a synthesis of recognition, it is a matter of sensibility, of the intimacy of an immediate 'feeling' (*Empfindnis*) that is an auto-affection of consciousness by itself. It should also be mentioned that the flux of absolute consciousness within which the flowing temporality of intentional acts appears, at the same time appears to itself in the form of a 'retentional' auto-affection. This 'longitudinal intentionality' of retention explains what one could call the 'ageing' of the present: it is a reserve whose 'freshness' grows dim and then 'dies', and whose possible 'resurrection' hinges on the advent of an 'awakening' which takes place by virtue of an associative link with a novelty that resembles it.

This edifice formed by the Husserlian analysis of time-consciousness, whose outlines we have just described, has been the object of various sorts of criticism. Those formulated by Heidegger are undoubtedly the best known, and they have found the greatest echo among the thinkers of the phenomenological movement. For example, Heidegger accuses Husserl of limiting himself to a phenomenological clarification of the consciousness of time, and of overlooking time as an originary accomplishment of transcendence. Heidegger also believes that this consciousness of time always has the form of an intentional consciousness, and he concludes from this that Husserl's analysis of temporality is only concerned with time as an object of theoretical knowledge. This purely theoretical approach to time is also held responsible for the exorbitant privilege granted to the present time and to the presence of beings in the mode of *Vorhandenheit*. This double reproach that Heidegger directs at Husserl contains, in an embryonic form, the entire project of *Sein und Zeit*. Was it not the intention of 'fundamental ontology' to arrive at a new understanding of the temporal meaning of being by examining the way in which *Dasein*, in the effective accomplishment of a life governed by care, understands the temporal meaning of its own existence? By moving from Husserl to Heidegger, then, the phenomenological analysis of temporality undergoes a shift towards *ontological* preoccupations concerned in the first place with human existence and, more specifically, with its most significant moments, such as death.[2]

The criticisms that Levinas addresses to Husserl's comprehension of temporality are more difficult to delimit, for although they are sometimes inspired by Heidegger, they often turn against Heidegger and end up by at least partially rehabilitating Husserl. This deceptive appearance of an oscillation between Husserl and Heidegger can be explained primarily by the fact that Levinas essentially shares neither the epistemological preoccupations of Husserl nor the ontological preoccupations of Heidegger. Even before he raised ethics to the rank of first philosophy, Levinas had already exhibited in his first writings on time a particular attention to the question of alterity. In his debate with Husserl and Heidegger about the question of the other (*aliud*) at the heart of the sameness of my experience of time, it is already always the other person (*alter*) that Levinas is aiming at.

Before proceeding to examine his analysis of the other person's appearance at the heart of this temporalization which is the fundamental mode in which my existence is accomplished, let us pause and look more closely at the objections Levinas formulates against the Husserlian analysis of temporality. It will quickly become clear that all of these accusations are directed to the analysis of temporality within the framework of intentional consciousness, and that everything Husserl says about temporality as a mode in which sensibility is accomplished will be spared.

The first objection has to do with the exclusively theoretical character of the Husserlian analysis of temporality, and here Levinas reiterates Heidegger's criticisms, without, however, subscribing to the Heideggerian conception of practical care. According to Levinas, the transcendence of care is not any less egocentric than the intentionality of representational consciousness. An intentional consciousness that opposes itself to an object the better to dominate and appropriate it, and a *Dasein* that is preoccupied with things by utilizing them for its own designs are both, for Levinas, afflicted with the same inability to do justice to the alterity of what they are related to. They are both inscribed within the same logic of power, assimilation and enjoyment which ends up by stripping things of their autonomy and hence their reality. The temporal sense of Husserl's intentional consciousness and Heidegger's care would then consist of unfolding around oneself a horizon of possibilities of one's own life, to which things are required to conform if they want to enjoy the right to appear and to acquire a meaning. What is true of things is also true of other persons when one deals with them in the mode of intentional consciousness or care: they become either an other constituted by me or an other whom I make into my partner in view of a common task.

The second objection Levinas formulates to the Husserlian analysis of temporality tends in the same direction and is once again addressed to Heidegger as well. Levinas accuses both of them of developing an understanding of temporality that does not take sufficient account of novelty, unpredictability and impossibility. For Husserl, the event in which a new present suddenly emerges is understood as the fulfilment of a preceding anticipatory intention, which means that the new is never truly new. At first sight, the same objection could not be made to Heidegger, who carefully distinguishes *Vorlaufen* from anticipation and who specifies that the death to which this *Vorlaufen* is related belongs to the order of the impossible. To which Levinas replies that, for Heidegger, death is still the *possibility* of an impossibility, not the *impossibility* of every possibility. It is clear that, for Levinas, what is at issue in the novelty of the present and, in a death that takes away our power of possibilization, is the alterity of an event that unexpectedly strikes us and that places us in a position of impotent passivity. The temporality of the new, i.e. that which interrupts and tears apart the continuity of my life, is a temporalization that comes to me from the outside. The same can be said of the event of death, which determines the temporality of my life in a way that is just as constraining, without my being either author or actor.

The third objection that Levinas levels against the Husserlian conception of time has to do with yet another way of mistaking the role of alterity in the self-temporalization of intentional consciousness. Contrary to what has been said about the dominating, egoistic power of intentional consciousness and care in their interaction with things and with persons, and contrary to what has just been said about the failure to acknowledge the novelty of the present and the impossibility of the future, this third objection – which is still of a Heideggerian inspiration – can no longer be turned against Heidegger. What is now being questioned in Husserl is the 're-presentation' (*Vergegenwärtigung*) of the *past* in 'rememoration' (*Wiedererinnerung*). The Husserlian analysis of memory is primarily concerned with assuring continuity between the present and the past: the originary meaning of the past is determined by my elapsed intentional lived experiences, and because all of these experiences are 'retained' by my present consciousness in their original fluidity, they can for that reason be made present again at any moment in the form of a memory. For Husserl, then, the past is a displaced present, pushed back from the centre of present consciousness towards its periphery by the emergence of a new lived experience. For Levinas, this conception of the past is unable to do justice to its alterity, which has to do with temporal distance, interruption and loss. While it does not really deny the difference between the present and the past, Husserl's conception of retention and rememorative representation is nevertheless an effort to 'recuperate' the past, by re-establishing or safeguarding the continuity of the flux of intentional consciousness. Does this mean that Levinas would restrict himself to reappropriating the Heideggerian conception of a forgetting which is more original than all remembering and which memory deepens rather than eradicates? Not at all: the irreducible and irrecoverable alterity of my past should pave the way for a recognition of the other as the one who necessarily co-determines the meaning of my past. And as one might have expected, Levinas does not stop at simply acknowledging this presence of the other in my past, he also attempts to establish that the past itself, in its most originary sense, is not my past but the other's past. The famous analyses of the 'trace' and the 'immemorial' do nothing else than establish the idea of a past which, to use another famous formulation, 'has never been present'. The past, in this way, testifies to the other's precedence over self-presence.

III

We can try to summarize the three objections expressed by Levinas – the appropriation of the presence of things and persons, the subjective possibilization of the present and the future, and the recuperation of the past – by citing the following sentence from *Otherwise than Being*: 'A subject would then be a power for re-presentation in the quasi-active sense of the word: it would draw up the temporal disparity into a present, into a simultaneousness' (*OB* 133).[3] Yet, for Levinas, this critique of what Derrida has called Husserl's 'metaphysics of presence' is not a critique of the present for the sake of the future (as it is for Heidegger) or of the past (as the idea of the trace might suggest). The present maintains all of its privileges in Levinas, as the event of an unpredictable novelty, and as the gift of an infinite renewal of my life. We know that this new understanding of the present was already sketched out by Husserl himself in his analysis of the 'originary impression' (*Urimpression*), and Levinas deals with Husserl in the same way that he dealt with Heidegger: he turns Husserl against himself, that is, he turns the originary impression against intentional representation.

By contrast, however, Levinas's new conception of the alterity of the future and of the past no longer owes anything to Husserl or to Heidegger, but is rather reminiscent of certain pages in Hannah Arendt. We shall see that the possibility of a future which remains my own while also being indebted to the other will be illustrated by a phenomenological analysis of hope and promise, but also eroticism and fecundity. Regarding the possibility that the sense of my own past might be determined by the other, Levinas most often appeals to the example of forgiveness (*pardon*). The ethical content of these examples is apparent, and this is clearly not by accident. In substituting the time of hetero-affection for the time of auto-affection, and in substituting the time of passivity for the time of intentional representation, what Levinas is aiming for is a transformation of the egological transcendental subject into an ethical subject, one which is characterized not by its spontaneous, free power, but by a responsibility *for* the other which comes *from* the other. This responsibility accrues to a subject that is marked, at the deepest level of its experience, by its sensibility, which brings it into the other's proximity, or by its vulnerability with respect to the other. This vulnerable sensibility is thus an affectivity that is always already inhabited by the other, and delivered up to the other. As a consequence, ethical sensibility is an affectivity that comes to me entirely from the other; it is the result of being affected by the other's imperative, traumatizing demand. Instead of being open to the other in the mode of intentionality or ecstatic transcendence, I am, in the very intimacy of my affectivity, always already the other's 'hostage'.

In the Husserlian analysis of temporality and temporalization, what is it that prepares the ground for understanding such a 'heterological' or 'an-archic' sensibility? Paradoxically, it is precisely what Husserl has said about the originary impression of the present as 'originary source point' (*Urquellpunkt*) – and hence as *archè* – of the temporalization of the time of intentional consciousness.[4] We should recall that the temporality of intentional acts is constituted by an even more fundamental consciousness, 'absolute consciousness', i.e. a kind of inner sense that temporalizes itself by living through intentional lived experiences. Even though it may be sensible and pre-objectifying, how does this self-temporalization of absolute consciousness lend itself to a reading in terms of an an-archic heteroaffection? For Levinas, it is precisely because it rests entirely on consciousness being affected by a present that imposes itself from the outside and in an unpredictable manner, by exhibiting its discontinuity with what precedes it or comes after it. On this view, then, everything turns on a heterological interpretation of the *impressional* character of the originary impression, which is supposed to account for alterity as novelty, distance and rupture, difference and deferral, or – to say it with the terms that Levinas most readily uses – 'interval' and 'lapse'. One hardly need point out, however, that this form of alterity which is constitutive of the originary impression is not yet the alterity of another man or woman for whom I might feel responsible. There is nothing in Husserl that would permit us to conclude that it is another subject that affects me in this originary impression. Even if we were to extrapolate from the letter of Husserl's texts and admit that originary impression is indeed the experience of a hetero-affection, and not an auto-affection, it would still need to be established that this initial form of temporal hetero-affection maintained an essential link with the traumatic hetero-affection by the suffering of the other person.

Levinas's most precise (and most favourable) interpretation of Husserl's originary impression, as well as of the 'retention' and 'protention' that surround it, can undoubtedly be found in a brief text entitled 'Intentionality and Sensation' that was written between *Totality and Infinity* and *Otherwise than Being*.[5] According to this text, the originary impression is the 'needlepoint', the 'acute punctuality' of the 'event' of the present (*DEH* 142) in its 'unforeseeable novelty' (*DEH* 144), in which the 'passivity' of being gratified 'beyond all conjecture, all expectation' coincides with the 'absolute activity' of the beginning's spontaneous genesis (*DEH* 144). As one would expect of him, Levinas places both this activity and this passivity on the side of alterity: the passivity of the originary impression signifies that novelty comes to consciousness from elsewhere, or from a beyond; while the activity of the originary impression's spontaneous genesis signifies that, in coming to consciousness, it poses and imposes itself as different and 'separated' from any other present, as breaking with what has preceded it and with what will come after it. In so far as it is a sensible impression or a 'sensation' of the present, the originary impression also precedes the intentional apperception of an object. It receives the present without imposing on it the categories of a subjective understanding. Sensibility, discontinuity and passivity – these are the characteristics that make the originary impression a paradigmatic example of self-alterity.

Associated with retention and protention, the alterity of this originary impression either deepens or disappears, depending on whether we follow the text of 'Intentionality and Sensation' or that of *Otherwise than Being*. According to the Husserlian conception of absolute consciousness, retention and protention are inseparable from the originary impression. It is because of them that absolute consciousness, even in the 'most radical punctuality' of the present, is conscious of a present that is prolonged or 'extended' towards the past and the future. For 'Intentionality and Sensation', the indissoluble association between the originary impression and retention, the unity of the present and the past in the same instant, means that even at the very 'needlepoint' of the present of absolute consciousness, this consciousness diverges from itself and breaks with its immediate attachment to itself. It is, and it is already no longer; it is, by virtue of being no longer. In this connection, Levinas speaks of being 'dephasing', of being 'after-the-fact' (*DEH* 143) and of a 'consciousness [being] delayed in relation to itself' (*DEH* 144), and he attempts to show that, with this, we have reached not only the originary moment of the movement of temporalization, but also the root of all alterity and all difference. The inseparable unity of a new originary impression with the elapsed originary impressions at the heart of one and the same present is understood by Levinas as the originary experience of 'passage' and 'transition' (*DEH* 142), which he sees, however, as the experience of a transgression rather than the affirmation of a continuity. This allows him to announce that it is not immanence but rather *transcendence* that constitutes the essence of temporality: 'Should we not understand transcendence... as a passing over, an overstepping, a gait, rather than as a representation...?' (*DEH* 148). Clearly, this transcendence is the transcendence of infinity, of consciousness as a 'fundamental iteration' (*DEH* 143), of a 'diachrony stronger than structural synchronism' (*DEH* 148), rather than Heidegger's ecstatic transcendence.

It would be possible to show how much these extremely dense pages from 'Intentionality and Sensation', devoted to the originary impression and retention, already expose the temporal foundation of Levinas's conception of the trace of the infinite. It is all the more interesting to note, then, that when this conception really comes into its own – in *Otherwise than Being* – Levinas appears to be much more reserved about the resources provided by the Husserlian analysis of the originary impression and retention:

There is consciousness insofar as the sensible impression differs from itself without differing; it differs without differing, is other within identity...Differing within identity, modifying itself without changing, consciousness glows in an impression inasmuch as it diverges from itself, to *still* be expecting itself, or *already* recuperating itself. Still, already – are time; time in which nothing is lost...To speak of consciousness is to speak of time. It is in any case, to speak of a time that is recuperated. [*ob* 32]

One cannot say more clearly what the Husserlian conception of temporality can and cannot contribute to an ethical conception of the alterity of the other. Its limits have to do essentially with the fact that it envisages temporal alterity within the framework of a phenomenology of consciousness. Though this consciousness is sensible and non-objectifying, originally divided and thus separated from itself, it will always seek to re-unite with itself in order to preserve its identity. It can be other *for itself*, but it cannot be entirely and infinitely *for the other*, as Levinas demands of the ethical subject.

IV

If consciousness does not allow us to conceive of a temporality that would do sufficient justice to the alterity of the other, it is tempting to turn towards a phenomenological analysis of existence. This is exactly what Levinas does in two early texts, significantly entitled *Time and the Other* and *Existence and Existents*. As far as our subject is concerned, these texts are particularly illuminating because they largely anticipate the analyses of *Totality and Infinity*, while dealing with the temporality of the alterity of the other within a perspective that still subordinates ethics to ontology. The descriptions of the temporal modality of hope and forgiveness, but also of death, eroticism and fecundity, already occupy an important place in these early texts. What Levinas wants, above all, to show is how the subject, considered in its existence, can permit us to think what will always remain unthinkable in a philosophy of consciousness, namely the way in which the other liberates the subject from its captivity within the immanence of its own self-belonging.

Levinas concedes, however, that it is through a movement of appropriating existence that the life of the subject begins. Birth is the event of a 'hypostasis' which carries out the passage 'from existence to the existent'; it is the avenue of the subject as interruption of the 'Heraclitean flux' of being, of the anonymous buzzing of the *il y a*. The subject is a (self-)beginning. Its consciousness has its origin in a divergence from being, and because being is understood as continual vigilance, Levinas paradoxically concludes that the act of falling asleep is the originary act of consciousness. Yet the subject does not merely sleep; in order to survive, the subject must feed itself and work, which makes it dependent on the things of the world. In the enjoyment obtained by satisfying its needs, and in the exertion of labour, a division of the subject takes place that Husserl had already analysed in intentional consciousness. However, whether enjoying its existence or suffering under its weight, the subject still remains self-enclosed, Levinas says. It cannot do otherwise than to relate everything other to itself. So the accomplishment of ontological difference in the form of a separation from being, and the division of self implied by its relation to the world, do nothing to end the suffocating and solitary egoism of the subject. Only the appearance of another man or woman can change anything about this existence coiled up within itself. This sudden appearance of the other produces, for the first time, what neither Husserl nor Heidegger succeeded in thinking fully, namely a subject totally liberated from itself and from its imprisonment in the present time of its own beginning. The other who enters my life not only delivers me from the weight of my own solitude, but also opens within my life the dimension of a present, a future and a past whose meaning is no longer established in me, and which for this very reason I cannot appropriate. The alterity of this present, this past and this future is thus affirmed by my utter passivity with respect to this other time that comes to me from the other person.

It is hardly surprising, then, that Levinas, already in his earliest texts, invokes *re*-commencement, forgiveness and hope in order to illustrate how the present, past and future of my life come to me from the other. Only the 'instant' linked to the unexpected upsurge of the other can change my life to the point of forcing or allowing me to re-commence from the beginning. Such a fragmentation of my existence into a multiplicity of discontinuous instants is testimony to my essential dependence on the other. (It goes without saying that, by reasoning in this way, Levinas is following the path of Descartes and Jean Wahl more than that of Kierkegaard and Heidegger.)[6] However, the other who interrupts the continuity of my present life also radically transforms the meaning of my *past and future* existence. For instance, the forgiveness that is granted me by the other (and which only the other can grant) modifies my past to the point of transforming it into a past that has never been present as such for me. The same is true of hope which, even when it is still related to my life, can only come to me from the other and not from my anticipation of my future life on the basis of my previous life. Riveted to myself, I am neither permitted to re-commence, nor to feel forgiven, nor to hope; nor, for that matter, am I permitted to make a promise or to engender a new life. This is not the place to examine more extensively these analyses, to which Levinas devotes some of his most beautiful pages. But I would like to consider for a moment what Levinas says about the temporality of death, since it is less easy to understand how it, too, depends fundamentally on the other.

It is true that death does not come to me from myself. And it is no less true that I am incapable of representing my own death or even predicting it. The advent of death is indeed the event of a traumatic hetero-affection, which I undergo in the most extreme passivity and powerlessness. Levinas is also right to emphasize that simply the thought of my death shatters the framework of a life turned in upon itself and upon the continuous flux of its own living present. And one cannot dispute his remark which stresses that the temporality of death is that of a deferred threat: death 'pushes on, and it leaves time' (*TI* 235). However near my death may be, it is beyond my power to cross the temporal distance separating me from it. The time of my own life, then, is indeed a temporality 'in suspense', engendered by death's deferral. But by saying that the temporality of my life is engendered by the threat of my death, does it follow that it comes to me from the other, or simply that it escapes my own power and that I undergo it in the most complete destitution? By saying that death, even before its advent, interrupts the life of enjoyment and exertion lived by a subject imprisoned in its own self-presence, does it follow that death comes from the other? On this point, Levinas seems not to have had the slightest doubt, either in *Time and the Other* or in *Totality and Infinity*: because death cannot come from myself, it must come from the other. He accepts as proof of this the fact that I undergo death not only as a threat, but also as an adversity: as he says in *Totality and Infinity*, with death I am 'faced with what is *against me'*, with 'a foreign will' (*TI* 234). Which is to say that in being a hostage to death, I am already, as he will say in *Otherwise than Being*, a 'hostage to the other'. With the threat of my own death, it is already the other who threatens me, which ultimately comes down to linking the temporal meaning of my mortality with the threat of murder. In the implacable logic that characterizes his writings, Levinas does not shrink from this consequence: 'The Other, inseparable from the very event of transcendence, is situated in the region from which death, possibly murder, comes' (*TI* 233).

V

The question that we used as a clue in our reading of Levinas concerned the way in which the other intervenes in the temporality of my life and, more specifically, the relation between alterity to oneself and the alterity of the other within this temporalization. What did we discover? Mainly two things: an analysis of the experience of time as diachrony, and an analysis of the experience of the alterity of the other in terms of an-archic passivity and traumatic heteroaffection. The link between these two things appears less clearly: is it an analogy or a deduction?[7] In other words, is the diachrony of my life a consequence of the other's intervention or is the way in which I experience the diachrony of my life only *similar* to the way in which I am subjected to the command of an other who appeals to my ethical responsibility? The discussion between Levinas and Husserl exhibits a similar ambiguity: on the one hand, the self-alterity of the originary impression seems to open on to a recognition of the alterity of the other, while on the other hand the originary impression associated with retention is accused of being a way of recuperating difference, and thus an obstacle to recognizing the alterity of the other.

If we are now able to accept, thanks to Levinas's analyses, that temporality of whatever sort always implies a spacing, a discontinuity, a difference, something unpredictable or after the fact – all various forms of alterity – the nature of this alterity nevertheless remains ambiguous. We have not always succeeded in clearly separating what, in temporalization, can be attributed to *self-alterity* from what depends directly on the *alterity of the other*. In any case, it has not seemed possible to purely and simply reduce the experience of temporal self-alterity to the encounter with the alterity of the other. If the temporalization of my life by forgiveness or hope is unthinkable without a gift coming from the other, the same certainly cannot be said of the transition from one present to another present, or of a present memory of my past life. Nor have we been able to settle the question of the nature of the link which makes the experience of temporality and the experience of alterity depend on each other: is *time* the initial horizon that presides over any appearance of alterity, or on the contrary is it the advent of an *alterity* or an alteration that allows time to appear? It is clear that Levinas rejects the relevance of this question: for him it is far too phenomenological and ontological, hence ill adapted or even unfaithful to his project of an ethics as first philosophy. But did we not just discover in his own texts some signs of hesitation between an ontological approach and an ethical approach to the appearing of the other and the appearing of time? And have we not just seen how the self-alterity put forward in a phenomenological and ontological meditation on the difference between the same and the other which constitutes the movement of temporalization is suddenly transformed into the other's alterity when these same analyses are re-examined from an ethical perspective? By imposing from the outset the alterity of the other as the origin of any alterity whatsoever, ethics as first philosophy seems to foreclose the possibility of any ontological and phenomenological investigation of self-alterity's openness on to the alterity of the other. By the same stroke, any attempt to make a considered judgement, within the experience of time, between what derives from the transcendence of the other, what is due to the division or the constitutive transcendence of the subject, and what might belong to the essence of time itself as a transcendence that cannot be assigned to any conceivable subject, is stripped of all relevance.

It would be easy to show, however, that this phenomenological and ontological questioning of the temporal meaning of transcendence and of the difference between self-alterity and the alterity of the other is, despite everything, still pursued in *Totality and Infinity*, a work whose ethical content can hardly be challenged. It is significant that this questioning reaches its climax in the section entitled 'Beyond the Face', devoted to eroticism and fecundity. Is not paternity presented in the form of a 'trans-substantiation' of the self into an other, and in the form of a resurrection from death? The 'son' that I engender is, one could say, an intermediary between my self-alterity (constitutive of the meaning of my death) and the alterity of an other who remains a stranger to me. This son releases me from my imprisonment in the finitude of my life without subjugating me to the commandment of an other. By virtue of fecundity, then, my life is inscribed in the perspective of the infinite, without undergoing the trauma of a hetero-affection by the completely other. The transition from my time to the time of the other then becomes a gift, an enrichment, rather than a threat. Is this to say that the characterization of ethics as first philosophy, solemnly proclaimed in *Otherwise than Being*, is responsible for the disappearance of the distinction between self-alterity and the alterity of the other? That would be true only if one ignored the pages that this book devotes to an analysis of justice as a new form of mediation between the other and myself. Such justice is inconceivable without the intervention of a third term that makes an other person the other's other. This does not shelter me from having to bear an infinite responsibility for the other, but now I *share* this responsibility with others. These others are, like myself, responsible for the other. While this new form of responsibility always comes to me from the other, it does not refer me *directly* to the other. The alterity of the other as stranger, then, is reconcilable with the self-alterity of a community of the just. But what, then, would be the time of this justice which was no longer my own time nor simply the time of the other? What 'time' and what 'things' did Anaximander have in mind when he said 'they give justice and retribution to each other for their injustice according to the order of time'?

NOTES

1 See R. Bernet, 'Einleitung', in E. Husserl, *Texte zur Phänomenologie des inneren Zeitbewusstseins (1893–1917)* (Hamburg: Meiner ('Philosophische Bibliothek'), 1985), pp. LVIII–LXVII; R. Bernet, *La vie du sujet. Recherches sur l'interprétation de Husserl dans la phénoménologie* (Paris: Presses Universitaires de France ('Epiméthée'), 1994), pp. 187–251, 281–92 and 323–5.

2 See Bernet, *La vie du sujet*, pp. 189–214.

3 Cf. also pp. 28 ff., 32, 140.

4 See *OB* 33: 'Rather, objectifying consciousness, the hegemony of representation, is paradoxically surmounted in the consciousness of the present.'

5 See especially pp. 140 ff. Cf. also *OB*, 32 ff.

6 See Jean Wahl's additional thesis, *Du rôle de l'idée de l'instant dans la philosophie de Descartes* (1920), a text which Levinas must have known about. For instance, one can read the following remark adorning a quote by Descartes: 'Les instants sont indépendants les uns des autres, et pour que je subsiste, il faut que je sois conservé, il faut qu'en ce moment quelque chose me produise et me crée pour ainsi dire derechef c'est-à-dire me conserve.' (*Du rôle de l'idée de l'instant* (Paris: Descartes & Cie, 1994), p. 62). Or the following sentence: 'Il semble que l'œuvre [de Descartes] ait consisté ici à unir profondément à l'idée de la création continuée, telle qu'elle se présentait dans la scolastique, l'idée de temps discontinu, telle qu'elle se formait dans la mécanique et dans la physique de la Renaissance' (p. 70). Levinas was fond of saying how close he felt to the 'unusual work' of his friend Jean Wahl 'in which the saying accommodates an unsaying' where the 'tension' between finitude and the infinite was sustained until the very end, and where the movement went 'from the traumatism of experience to categories, from some categories to other categories, and from categories to a new ecstasy' ('Jean Wahl: Neither Having nor Being', *OS* 79, 72, 78, respectively). And the homage paid to Jean Wahl in the form of the (rhetorical) question, 'A point of light – is it a *being* that shines or possesses itself with an absolute having, or is it the impact of a breakthrough, the beyond of being with neither having nor being?' (*OS* 80), might also be read as a commentary on the Levinasian notion of the instant. On the other hand, we know that Levinas attached little importance to 'tension on oneself' and to 'the egotism of salvation' which characterize the Kierkegaardian conception of the instant of decision ('Existence and Ethics', *PN* 71 and 73, respectively).

7 The 1979 'preface' to *Time and the Other* speaks of 'the analogy between the transcendence that signifies dia-chrony and the distance of the Other's alterity' (*TO* 33). By contrast, the same text's edition of 1948 reads: 'Relationship with the future, the presence of the future in the present, seems all the same accomplished in the face-to-face with the Other. The situation of the face-to-face would be the very accomplishment of time' (*TO* 79). And also: 'I do not define the other by the future, but the future by the other' (*TO* 82).

5   Levinas and the Talmud

Quite a few readers of Levinas's work either do not know his Talmudic readings[1] or relegate them to a secondary position. They consider that despite the possible interest the exegetical effort exhibited in them might evoke, these readings remain of no major value for a philosopher. There would be, on the one hand, the *philosophical* work – the only work worthy of attention – and, on the other, the books consecrated to Judaism. The firmness of this line of demarcation seems none the less highly open to question, if one remembers that Levinas defines Europe by a double loyalty, a loyalty made up of tensions and conflicts between the Bible and the Greeks; the prophets and the philosophers; the good and the true (*TI* 24). But if borders are also created to be crossed, the one which separates philosophy from the Talmud can be crossed either legally or clandestinely, as in every crossing of a border. But in the present case, who has the authority to decide which is which? Given the question marks attending what is 'proper' to the philosopher and what is 'proper' to the Talmudic scholar, it would seem that this authority does not exist, despite the often violent stands taken by one or the other side to chase the stranger off its territory. The fact that Levinas himself wanted to publish his philosophical writings and his Jewish writings with different publishers should not lead us to think that Jewish sources were foreign to his philosophy or that his questioning of the Hebrew word remained free of all contamination by Greek influences. If, in his philosophical works, Levinas crosses the border at crucial moments, without necessarily warning his readers through explicit references, it goes without saying that he also does this, in

Translated by Annette Aronowicz

the opposite direction, in his Jewish writings. Within this perspective, a reflection on Levinas and the Talmud should ask itself how and why the philosopher finds, precisely in the Talmudic tractates, 'the extraordinary trace that Revelation leaves in a thought that, beyond the vision of being, hears the word of God' (TN 51). But it must also ask about how this trace decisively orients Levinas's thought without allowing him – and thus not allowing the reader either – to stand watch constantly over the intangible nature of borders. If it is true, as Leo Strauss asserts, that the conflict between the Bible and philosophy 'is the secret of the vitality of the West',[2] it does not appear as though this thesis concerns the opposition between the Talmud and philosophy for, because of the lack of knowledge that still predominates, rare are those who are able to study the philosophical texts and the Talmudic texts with equal competence. By disregarding the anathema of those who fear the consequences of breaching the frontier between the Talmud and philosophy, Levinas inscribes his thought in the wake of that vitality; he gives it a new breath of life. None the less, since he makes uneasy those whom a clear division between the disciplines reassures, those who make a clear distinction between what comes from the Greeks and what can be said only in Hebrew, Levinas requires also that we think out the framework justifying this opening of the borders.

THE INCESSANT RENEWAL OF THE LETTER BY THE INTELLECT

If a Jewish reading of the Bible is inseparable from the oral law,[3] the discussions of the sages *hahakhanim* in the tractates of the Talmud none the less do not have as their object a continuation of the Bible; they do not propose a coherent commentary of it or a fulfilment of its meaning, in the sense in which Christians understand commentary regarding the New Testament. Levinas presents them as going back to the meanings of Scripture 'in a rational spirit', resolutely watchful and open to the potential of the renewal (*hidoush*) of the meaning that the Hebrew letter offers. 'The life of a Talmudist', he says, 'is nothing but the permanent renewal of the letter through the intelligence' (NTR 79). But it is an uneasy life for, if the letter bears meaning, this meaning never imposes itself as evident. It must be sought for, even ferreted out, without giving in to the desire to possess definitive truths which, always, ratify the defeat of the intellect. 'The Oral Torah speaks "in spirit and in truth", even when it seems to pulverize the verses and letters of the Written Torah', says Levinas. Thus, in his Talmudic readings, the philosopher sets himself the very task of showing this spirit and this truth at work, within the perspective of what he calls 'ethical meaning as the ultimate intelligibility of the human and even of the cosmic' (NTR 93).

This framework is not self-evident to the person who, wishing to understand the diverse opinions of the sages on a given topic – a topic which very often seems limited in scope – and wishing to clarify the question the sages are trying to address by means of verses cited in order to shed light upon it – does not perceive the global coherence of the discussion. But this, according to Levinas, is the essential task: to seek that in their 'sovereign freedom' (NTR 55) the sages are borne by a unique concern to convey the sense of the human as illuminated by Revelation. But this thought, in contrast to philosophical categories which are universalist from the start, builds itself patiently on the basis of the concrete and particular attitudes of those who confront the question of the legitimacy of this or that attitude, from the point of view of the Torah. Casuistry thus constitutes an essential dimension of these debates. Levinas maintains, however, that this is not an objection to the cogency of a reading concerned with rationality, for he says: 'It is doubtful that a philosophical thought has ever come into the world independent of all attitudes or that there ever was a category in the world which came before an attitude' (NTR 15). Besides, the style of the Talmudic tractates – often sharp and passionate discussions, opinions always expressed in the name of their authors – incites us to claim that 'real thought is not', as Plato would have it, 'the silent dialogue of the soul with itself' but rather 'a discussion between thinkers'. Thinkers who keep their own names for 'the totality of the true is made up of multiple persons: the uniqueness of each way of hearing bearing the secret of the text; the voice of Revelation, precisely insofar as it is inflected by the ear of each person, would be necessary to the All of truth' (BV 49 and 133–4). These discussions, finally, are inseparable from a reflection on the spiritual relation that binds the master and his disciple, a relation so deep that Levinas describes it as 'as strong as the conjugal relation' (BV 43). But, unless it wants to destroy itself as such, this relation is forever irreducible to a fusion or a communion because its

meaning – almost always full of pathos – doesn't consist in neutral-
izing the alterity of the other but in joining oneself to it, against
the background of an unbreachable duality. As a result, thanks
to the fruitfulness of this relation, the perspective of a future opens
for the human being as well. He becomes capable of transcending the
irremediable finitude of his time (see *TO* 85–94). Understood within
this perspective, the relation master–disciple can thus not be fulfilled
without standing guard over the irreducible plurality of the persons
gathered to study under the leadership of a master. Fertile study –
a study that doesn't sterilize through the dogmatism or intolerance
of a master – depends on an incessant questioning, filled with the
queries of all, of both the master and the disciples. 'When I give answers instead of deepening the questions, I take away from my text'
(*NTR* 62), Levinas says. This points out how much the quest for truth
and the concern for universality, in the context of the Talmud, remain inseparable from the light shed upon it by each person. This
light conditions the fertility of study, that is to say, its passage into
the time of future generations. One must watch over this light for,
in contrast to the Platonic idea in which particular opinions must
be given up in order to accede to the truth – a truth whose brilliance
attracts the philosopher but at the expense of its separation from the
multiplicity of opinions, always denounced as blind to the truth –
Talmudic thought settles itself at the heart of this multiplicity, not
to delight in relativism but because the Word it asks questions of
has an infinite density, a density which requires the multiplicity of
persons in order to express itself and unfold in the course of time.

Talmudic discussions make sense, in fact, only in relation to a
prior text – the Torah – of which they ask particular questions, often
very practical and concrete ones, with which human beings are faced.
For a Jew, this density of the Bible letter – 'the folded wings of the
spirit' – unfolds only as a result of the power and insistence of human questions. The Bible breathes thanks to the oral tradition, and
the Talmud, through its discussions, is thus essential to the task
of giving breath. Moreover, in several instances, it teaches that 'the
Bible speaks the language of human beings' which means, according to Levinas, that the Word of God has contracted itself within
Scripture, thus giving it that infinite density, lying in wait for the
questions of human beings who, by enquiring of it, will make it
meaningful for today's lives. No erudition, no critical or historical

knowledge can substitute for the unceasing work of asking questions of the letter, unless it wishes to dry up the living source from which this letter proceeds. Or, more precisely, this is the feeling the human being will have, the feeling of a dead letter. He will then close a book whose letter has rigidified into a knowledge and will see in the Talmud only obscurities without interest. On the other hand, he who is convinced of the 'prophetic dignity of language, always capable of meaning more than it says, of the marvel of an inspiration in which the human being listens, surprised by what it says, in which, already, he *reads* what is said and interprets it, in which human speech is already writing' (BV x–xi), will turn to the Talmud as the site in which this dignity continues to challenge human beings.

In order to stay alive, the link of the modern interpreter with the harmonics of Talmudic discussions implies the effort of constantly demythologizing Scripture and the concern of the whole (BV 136). This is crucial to Levinas's Talmudic readings. The temptation to approach the texts as if they were mythological would be, according to the philosopher, that of modernity. Since modernity cannot speak directly with the masters of the Talmud – which is exactly what is required for a living learning – it looks for myths. Forgetfulness of the uninterrupted tradition of reading, in favour solely of a knowledge transmitted by the university, makes difficult, if not impossible, for most Jews of the modern era, to see in the Talmud anything else but an anthology, now without any interest other than that of erudition, of particular ideas of the Jewish sages. Levinas thinks, however, that despite its scientific pedigree, this approach toward the text misses the spirit and the truth of Tamudic discussions, without even suspecting it, so great is its self-confidence. In fact these Talmudic discussions aim not at ensuring a meaning beyond myth – the Biblical letter – but at 'establishing a relation between the human being and the sanctity of God and at maintening the human being in this relation'. Whether they concern prescriptive debates (*halakha*) or purely narrative ones (*aggadah*), rabbinic discussions, seemingly so commonplace, so concerned with insignificant or strange details, make sense only within this perspective. None the less, the 'sanctity of God' in relation to which human life must be thought, is foreign to all mythological conceptions – the numinous, enthusiasm, possession by the sacred – all of which, according to Levinas, have to do with idolatry. Idolatry means to think God in terms of the fears and

expectations of human beings. The philosopher thinks that the particular way of the Jewish sages consists precisely in breaking with
this ancient conception of the sacred and in teaching how to seek God
on the basis of a separation or even atheism. This means that this
God has nothing to do with the need of man. He is not proportional
to his fears and expectations, an attitude which despite its extreme
exigency, has a universal value. This is why Levinas constantly insists upon the non-particularistic features of the Talmud: a pagan
who has studied the Torah is declared the equal of the Great Priest,
'to such a degree does the notion of Israel let itself be separated – in
the Talmud – from all historical, national, local and racial notions'
(DF 14 and 22). Israel means, in these texts, an ideal of humanity
chosen to bear the responsibility for the world – as an individual
and as a people – 'but humanity includes what is inhuman and so
Israel refers to the Jewish people, its language, its books, its land'
(DF 223–4). This means that despite all its shortcomings in the course
of history, carnal Israel – denounced by the apostle Paul and his innu-
merable followers – remains through its language, its books, its law
and its land, the guarantor precisely of this original and universal
responsibility toward the other which, according to Levinas, gives
its full meaning to chosenness. This responsibility is older than freedom and sin. No one can abandon it without failing in his or her
human vocation.

It is within this perspective that we must now approach certain
major themes of Levinas's Talmudic readings. The philosopher says,
in fact, that the only faith he is willing to profess publicly has to do
with 'this confidence in the wisdom of the Sages', preceding knowledge and history, which he received from his masters. These Talmudic readings constitute precisely a public testimony to this faith. But
they do not not presuppose an adherence of the intellect to unprov-
able or irrational propositions. Such an adherence would contradict
in its very principle any search for wisdom, whether it be that of the
philosopher (sophia) which Levinas always wanted to be, or that of
the Talmudic scholar (hokhna) whose art he practised with modesty.
On the other hand, this act of faith leads to one's own participation
in 'the millenial effort whose aim is to go beyond the letter of the
text and even its apparent dogma in order to bring back to a truth of
the spirit, even those passages of Scripture considered historical or
ritual or ceremonial or thaumaturgical' (DF 116).[4] This act of faith is

therefore tied to the 'prophetic dignity of Biblical language', whose harmonics the sages make audible.

THE CURVATURE OF SPACE

The figure of Abraham, contrasted to that of Ulysses, is often found in Levinas's work. While the latter dreams at the end of his heroic adventures, of coming back home, to celebrate his reunion with his people and perhaps to forget the time of his long separation from his native land, the former must rise and go without looking back, without hope of coming back. He also knows that this going away involves all his descendants, since he forbids his servant to bring his son back to this land, even if only to find a wife (Genesis 24:6). 'Lekh lekha', 'go towards yourself' (Genesis 12:1), this commandment uproots Abraham from his native realm. It forbids him to believe that he can find himself by cultivating a nostalgia for his past. Abraham discovers his integrity as a man called to be a blessing to all families of the earth, only on condition that he loses himself, that is, only on condition that he gets rid of all that which, by keeping him prisoner of his past – words, images, possessions – would make impossible for him the going forward to the Promised Land. It is a land to which he none the less proceeds, day after day, for his entire humanity lies in his answer to the call he heard. But it is a land which he has no certainty of entering and settling.

In one of his Talmudic readings, *Judaism and Revolution* (NTR 95–119), Levinas interprets a passage of the tractate Baba Metsia (83a–83b), asking himself in particular about the expression 'the lineage of Abraham', present in the Mishna (second century CE) preceding the discussion about it in the Guemara. The Mishna had recalled that he who hires workers immediately has obligations towards them. He must watch over their physical needs (rest, food), according to the custom of the place. The freedom of the master is thus limited by their needs, which are described as rights and thus as duties for him. The Mishna then evokes the case of workers who are of 'the lineage of Abraham, Isaac and Jacob'. Levinas interprets this passage to mean 'a human nature which has reached the fulness of its responsibilities and self-consciousness'. A human nature present in the lowest of social statuses – here, the workers – and toward whom 'our duties are without limits'. The lineage of Abraham thus has nothing to do with social status, and it transcends the nations as well. 'Any man truly human is no doubt of the line of Abraham' (*NTR* 99), affirms Levinas.

What does this proposition mean? Abraham was the one whose tent remained open day and night, the one who fed his guests without asking who they were beforehand. Even beyond this, Levinas says, through all the openings of his tent, 'he awaited passers-by in order to receive them'; for he knew himself to be responsible for their vulnerable bodies which were subject to the harshness of the desert climate, subject to thirst and hunger, as well as to the violence of thieves, or to inner desolation. To descend from Abraham would thus mean to be inhabited by the knowledge, prior to all conscious, reasoned and free commitment, that 'the man who is truly man' is obliged by his neighbour, by the one who passes by, who sometimes doesn't even dare to ask help for his vulnerability as a mortal being. More precisely, according to the expression of Rabbi Israel Salanter[5] which Levinas likes to cite, the descendant of Abraham would know that 'the physical needs of (his) neighbor are (his) spiritual needs'. None the less, this equivalence between the physical needs of the other – his hunger and his thirst, his pain as an abandoned man in a world so often indifferent or cruel – and the spiritual needs of the descendant of Abraham is not self-evident. In fact, according to Levinas, needs express the search for a satisfaction or a happiness for oneself: 'To be cold, hungry, thirsty, naked, to seek shelter – all these dependencies with regard to the world, having become needs, save the instinctive being from anonymous menaces and constitute a being independent of the world'. Needs establish each as the same 'and not as dependent on the other' (*TI* 116), at least for as long as the possibility of satisfying them is within reach. But this remains precarious and it is then that giving drink, feeding, dressing and sheltering the other become 'spiritual needs' for me. But how does one experience such needs? Levinas himself disassociates spirituality from need. The desire for God, he often says, has nothing to do with need. Besides, many human beings live serenely as atheists, without worrying – this would horrify Pascal – about the possible salvation of their souls and without having the silence of God become a source of torment for them. Not to experience the need for God is not, however, an argument for His non-existence or for the illusory or, in any case, very relative character of spirituality. It could even be a liberation, in order to come back freed of the weight of the imaginary, to the lineage of Abraham. To inscribe oneself within this lineage, as this Talmudic lesson teaches, is, in fact, not to want a God *for oneself* – a God whom one would need – but to think the unseverable connection between the quest for this God and the necessity of helping human beings. 'Spiritual need' therefore turns out to be paradoxical and seemingly in contradiction with the Levinasian definition of need – need establishes one as the same – since it tears away from the rule of the same. It, in fact, opens unto the uprightness of a movement without a return to self, unto an up-rooting which gives meaning to the departure without return of Abraham at the heart of one's own life.

The word 'movement' requires some additional precautions and precisions. For it would be to misunderstand the meaning of the expression 'descendant of Abraham' to identify it with spontaneous altruism or generosity. The 'curvature of space' drawn between the son of Abraham and his neighbour, that is to say the asymmetrical distance separating them – Abraham does not know whether the neighbour will feed or shelter him when he will need him – lets itself be bent 'into elevation' (*TI* 291) only on the condition that one hears the call of human weakness as an obligation for oneself. But how is this possible and what does this 'elevation' mean?

In his Talmudic reading, Levinas insists on the importance that the Guemara grants to the contract which precedes the hiring of the worker and which, linked to the custom of the place, specifies the salary owed to him, the food that will be given to him, etc. In other words, the descendant of Abraham knows that there is no limit to his obligations towards the worker. The contract thus comes to limit my obligations toward the worker and not, as one might assume, to institute a minimum of obligation toward him. This means, very precisely, that obligations towards the other are infinite and do not depend on good will or choice. They precede freedom and consecrate the descendant of Abraham to an infinite service, to a responsibility that is greater than the commitments that have actively been taken on. As this Guemara teaches, contracts and customs attempt in fact to introduce some limit to this initial or, more exactly, immemorial, limitlessness. But this is a limitlessness which comes to inscribe itself in the memory of human beings when they hear the Hebrew letter breathing in the interpretations of the Talmudic sages. This limitlessness, they teach, traverses the Abrahamite psyche, giving power and meaning to the history of the patriarch. In this case it means God's call to get up and go toward a land which, for the time being, remains unknown. The Promise to which this call is linked – 'And I will make of thee a great nation, and I will bless thee, and make thy name great: and thou shall be a blessing' (Genesis 12:2) – does not, however, give any guarantees. Abraham does not know whether he will succeed in establishing himself in the Promised Land. The promise does not do away with risks. In this Talmudic lesson, Levinas insists specifically on this point and sees in persecution the major risk that Abraham and his descendants will incur. 'To be responsible despite oneself is to be persecuted. Only the persecuted is responsible for everyone, even for his persecutor.' This, he says, is what 'my text affirms' (NTR 114–15).

To those who object that he forces the page of the Guemara he is studying in order to emphasize this link between a calling to an infinite responsibility not yet limited by contracts or customs and persecution – a central assertion in his philosophy – Levinas answers that this is in fact the task of the Talmudic scholar. He says that the texts of the Talmud themselves force being forced (sollicitent la sollicitation). Their roughness, their silences, their paradoxes demand a permanent deciphering, that must be started all over again but this is a 'deciphering without code'. To find the coherence of meaning in a page of the Guemara, as Levinas always sets out to do in his readings, is in no way self-evident. The one who would want to do without forcing the text – apparently to remain objective – would only preserve before him, under the cover of objectivity, meaningless and strange pages. Without the questioning of the letter by the intellect of a particular person, by a person the quality of whose attention to the possibilities of this letter conditions the bringing to light of these meanings which had hitherto remained unnoticed, these texts 'remain silent or incongruous' (NTR 143).

In several of his lessons, Levinas thus insists on the thought of an infinite responsibility proper to the human psyche – responsible despite itself for the fate of the world – by shedding light upon it by means of the story of Abraham and, correlatively, by shedding light on this story by means of this thought. It seems pointless, however, to seek to clarify whether the thought of responsibility precedes Levinas's reading of the story of Abraham or whether the story inspires this thought in him. Such a search would, in fact, set as its goal the re-establishment of a rigorous border between philosophy – supposed to develop in an autonomous way without being inspired by any particular tradition of thought, in that case Jewish – and traditions of thought which, because they prefer the word to the concept, are supposed to have nothing to do with philosophical rationality. 'I have never understood', says Levinas, 'the radical difference posited between philosophy and simply thinking, as if every philosophy did not derive from non-philosophical sources.' And he continues, not without irony: 'Often, all one needs to do is to define an unusual terminology with words derived from Greek to convince the most difficult to please that one has just entered philosophy' (NTR 122).

Abraham, he who rises in the morning, orients thought to this infinite responsibility and, correlatively, philosophical reflection on responsibility helps better to decipher the Hebrew letter which relates this story as well as the Hebrew commentary about it. Levinas does not stop at elaborating philosophically the *theme* of an infinite human responsibility. He continues to interpret the pages of the Guemara in which, according to him, this responsibility emerges in the thick of the discussion of the sages who, in relation to a concrete problem, ask questions of the Biblical letter and bring out its signifying power. But Levinas's Talmudic readings do not aim, with the help of a given passage, to reveal the premises of a thought which would only take on its full strength and subtlety in his philosophical works. The Talmud makes evident through its discussions a life of the Torah which reminds critical minds that, in its non-conceptual language, the Bible is not merely proposing a 'matter' to elaborate theoretically, which, once accomplished, would in any case make further reading superfluous. The Talmud reminds one that the Torah has 'a mode of being' different from a philosophical exercise, for its interpretation is infinite. The Talmud gives breath to the Bible, Levinas often says, and no philosopher can – without asphyxiating – make himself master of this breathing, notwithstanding the intelligence of his speculations. 'The metaphysics that can be extracted from their apologues, parables and legal lucubrations consists entirely of discussion and dialogue' (OS 130), says Levinas about the dialectic of the Talmudic sages. But in order that this metaphysics not turn into a knowledge *about* what the sages are saying – a knowledge which, as such, would leave life unchanged – it is necessary to 'dive into the sea' of the Talmud, that is to say to inscribe one's own questioning into the heart of these old discussions. The alternative between the living Word and the concept – the saying and the said, in Levinas's words – must remain open, in permanent tension. If no one, of course, has direct access to the fullness of this Word, without coming near madness or death,[6] as far as the philosopher is concerned, he who is concerned with the 'patience of the concept' cannot abandon the hearing of the Word without risking barrenness through speculative excess, but also madness through his claim to master the origin of human beings' speech. It is because knowledge, for Levinas, is not the mode *par excellence* of human accomplishment, and because reason is not the sole source of the meaningful, according to him, that it is fitting untiringly to go back yet again to the non-philosophical sources of philosophy and to propose Talmudic readings. 'I have mainly tried to place due emphasis on an "intelligibility" or a signifying, differing from that of knowledge, and that tends to be construed as a simple lack'. Far from constituting a secondary moment in his thought, therefore, Levinas's Talmudic readings testify to the right of the concern to remember that 'the rationality of discourse is already borne up by the previous signifying of dialogue or proximity' (*TN* 175). And if his philosophy refuses, insistently, the idea of an 'origin' or 'foundation' at the basis of his analyses, if it orients toward a fault line or an anarchy, as he likes to put it, at the beginning of the desire to think, it is precisely in consonance with the infinite quest for original meaningfulness, a meaningfulness forever irreducible to a knowledge about it, a meaningfulness which orients the human being toward the other human being.

The 'curvature of space' drawn by the movement toward the other, a curvature which, by placing the other above oneself, curves the space which separates one from him into elevation, constitutes an error of optics only from the point of view of positive knowledge. But, says Levinas, if this curvature means the impossibility of a 'total reflection', it isn't due to a flaw of knowledge or to the bad qualities of the subject. It is because reflexivity or the return to self lacks the meaningfulness of an absolute orientation toward the other. And it is to answer the call of this orientation that Abraham rises early in the morning. 'Even more should this be the case for the rest of us, who enter into a relation with the other man without having an incontestable mission' (*NTR* 189), specifies Levinas in his Talmudic reading.

TEMPORALITY AS MIRACLE

In another of his Talmudic readings, still in reference to Abraham, Levinas evokes God's choice of the patriarch as 'the miracle of temporality – or of temporality as miracle' (TN 87). Irreducible to the classical idea of a suspension of natural laws on behalf of human beings, a miracle means in this context the 'marvel' of a going out of oneself for the other. It is also the answer to a call which, by removing the 'self' from all its natural anchors and from all identity established under the regime of the 'same', orients it towards an 'unpredictable future'. This is a future which forever postpones the possibility of a return to self, for it obliges one to take the path, with no end in sight, of answering to the otherness of God and human beings. Such would be, according to Levinas, the 'temporality as miracle' to which Abraham testifies.

In the Talmudic page we have just examined I have been especially sensitive to a Judaism that overflows memory, that attempts to conceive of it beyond the Exodus, and senses an unforeseeable future ('no eye has seen it'), but also a future opening up through a new mode of trial, new dimensions of suffering. [TN 87]

What, then, does this Talmudic page say? Bar Kapra teaches : 'Whoever calls Abraham Abram breaks a positive commandment, for it is written in *Genesis* 17:2 : "But thy name shall be Abraham".' Rav Eliezer said : 'He breaks a negative commandment (an interdict), for it is said: "Thy name shall no longer be Abram".' Abram, the father of a people, becomes, in fact, by order of the Eternal, Abraham, the father of all the nations. But the obligation to call him Abraham – or the prohibitions on going back to his original name – has to do with a reflection about time, says Levinas. It has to do, in fact, with hearing

through the relative present, bold anticipations of an absolute future! Hear, in the present's uncertainty, in Israel's misery, Abraham, the father of human universality, hailed as such, invoked as such! Time to accept universality!... But here is the interdict: Do not conceive of Abraham in terms of Abram! Do not constitute the future from traces of memory, mistrusting new things and even the miracle required for universal peace. [TN 85–6]

The Eternal, in addition, specifies to Abraham: 'Saraï (my princess), thy wife, thou shalt not call her name Saraï; but Sarah (princess) shall be her name' (Genesis 17:15). Far from seeing this as a secondary question, Levinas remarks that we have here an 'ontological correction announced by God precisely to the husband' (TN 86). The opening into universality goes through woman's access to the dignity of a human person as well. It in fact even happens that Abraham must listen to Sarah's voice (Genesis 21:12), whose inspiration prevails over his.

Levinas refers back to the commandment to forget old names in favour of new names, open unto universality to think about the awakening of Israel within Jacob. He sees in it a commitment to think human universality in the destiny of Israel, or yet again an obligation to maintain alive the thought of time as open to hope, despite the night which Israel had to live through, especially in the last century. But this hope in no way means the idea of a temporality stretching toward a future that the disasters and the 'new dimensions of suffering' undergone during the *Shoah* supposedly prepared. If temporality as 'miracle' requires elaborating an eschatology – 'an eschatology through the Passion of Israel among the nations' – the latter is completely disassociated from any reference to a teleology. Eschatology is not the end of history; it means its openness, at the heart of present sufferings, to what allows history to be judged today: it is the hearing of the call of the Infinite. As the philosopher's work shows, with an insistence that the passage of time fails to refute, this call is heard in the encounter with the vulnerable face of the other. In this Talmudic reading, Levinas makes this call refer to the story of Abraham as the very model of what it means to be human, and he adds to its weight by invoking the *Shoah* as a reality that memory cannot bear. But, he says, citing the novel *Life and Fate* of Vassily Grossman, from one end to the other of the inhuman apocalypse described by the author 'from out its depths, there can be heard the muffled stirrings of a persistent, invincible humanity. The "I" of men, forced by suffering back into the shackles of the self, breaks forth, in its misery, into mercy. What I called *ahavat Israel'* thought as 'primordial tenderness for the other' or 'gratuitous goodness' 'rises, before hope, from the abyss of despair' (TN 89). This mercy discovered in the torment of the Second World War, a mercy going 'from one human uniqueness to another, independently of, and as if in spite of, structures – political or ecclesiastic – in which they were exhibited', would be 'the sign of a God still unheard-of but who, without promising anything, would seem to assume meaning beyond the theologies of a past shaken to the point of atheism' (TN 89 and 90).

Levinas's move, in this Talmudic reading, is particularly daring but also very revealing of the quality of interpretation he practises in all his readings of the Guemara. He begins, in fact, by seeking the way a given passage is a model of the thinkable on the scale of the human. He thus associates the prohibition against using Abraham's old name with the thought of a time oriented by the word of God in such a way that no turning back could be envisaged. But this thought about time is not exclusive to the Jewish people since, he says, it is precisely what makes Abraham the father of a multitude of nations. The time that opens because of Abraham's election is experienced in his life through the quality of relation he maintains with the other: an availability to him which obliges Abraham to keep his tent open in order not to miss the moment, always unpredictable, of his coming, the moment in which it is suitable to share drink and food. But, far from alienating him, this obligation which makes him pass over into the time of the other – of the one who is hungry and thirsty *now*, of the one whose vulnerable flesh must be protected and cared for *now*, while there is still time – makes Abraham arrive at his inexchangeable uniqueness. According to Levinas, it is precisely in this that Abraham represents a model of the human as such. Time is analysed by the philosopher as a relation. Time is the relation with the infinite or this diachrony which, at the heart of every finite life, presents itself and is experienced as a relationship to the irreducible mystery of the otherness of the neighbour; a diachrony which keeps pace with what remains other and which, in the face-to-face with the other person, calls me and asks for me; time as vigilance and patience, time as awakening and disturbance. This thought about time helps Levinas to give meaning to the prohibition against using Abraham's old name but, correlatively, the story of Abraham and the return to it of the Talmudic commentaries, inspire this thought about time in him. Here, as in the reflection on space sketched previously, it is no more legitimate to posit a priority which would make Levinas's philosophy on time the key to his Talmudic interpretation than it is to make the latter the key to his philosophy. The double fidelity he claims – to the Hebrew source and to the Greek source – does not permit the reader of his work to make up such a hierarchical separation. In contradistinction to Spinoza's enterprise, Levinas's philosophy does not develop the order of its reasons in a rigorously necessary manner, which would be foreign to the language of the prophets. In contrast to the idea that the Talmud is a world sufficient unto itself, however, he thinks that philosophical questioning allows for the extraction of hitherto unexpressed possibilities of meaning. The life of thought – and, no doubt, life itself – passes through this movement which forbids the fixation on the idea of an essence of its own – in this case the essence of philosophy or of Talmud – which, in prideful self-sufficiency, would banish the other from its territory.

As its title indicates, this reading seeks to think 'beyond memory', beyond a historic past which can be remembered, the *trace* of a call which takes hold of the human psyche and orients it toward the other. The Talmudic text is solicited in this sense, as if it had the power, by talking of what we do not remember – Abraham – to make us see this *trace.* Still, at the end of this lesson, Levinas refers to a tragic time which he and the witness he cites, Vassily Grossman, do remember – the unforgettable memory of the exterminating word, the memory of the yawning abyss weighing upon all survivors of the *Shoah.* But the reference to this memory does not constitute only an appendix to what has just been said about Abraham. Asking questions of the Talmud, here, coincides with the memory of the sharpest pain of men and women who, in the total abandonment of 'this inhuman apocalypse', saw the world disappear. But what Levinas notices is 'the possibility within this meaninglessness of a meaning which nonetheless would not be able to guarantee the establishment of a world', or, put another way, the incomprehensible and extraordinary emergence of goodness. Of a goodness without ideology and without arms, but of a goodness which remains invincible despite the astounding excess of evil upon the soul.

In spite of the measured statements of the sages in the passage of the Guemara we have studied here, this good, says Levinas, has a meaning, although it obliges each person to give up all hope in 'the firmness of justice' and to give up on the words which, so it appeared, promised a happy conclusion to the vicissitudes of history. The cruel history of the twentieth century thus intrudes into the Talmudic reading in order to oblige the interpreter – and the reader – to abandon all hope of consolation and to think that the God who called Abraham to the dignity of what is human does not respond to the incommensurable distress of his creatures. The memory of this history and the perception of the catastrophe that befell so many human beings haunts the modern interpreter of the Guemara. According to Levinas he neither can nor should ignore it when he opens one of its pages. The unique situation of the Talmudic scholar – a situation tied to his history and that of his time – plays a major role in his study. It is also with it, with the questions it gives rise to in him, that he asks questions of the text and reveals as yet unnoticed possibilities of meaning in it. Interpretation *is affected* by the sorrows and joys of the times, and it is not appropriate to want to erase the anxiety or hope of a soul for the sake of a revealed truth which supposedly transcends the relativity of history. The human desire to ask questions of the texts, to live one's life in accordance with their saying, emerges almost always from anxiety and hope. It is thus not Levinas's goal to seek, in vain, for a timeless objectivity of the text or for its 'true' meaning, supposedly corresponding to the intention of the first sages. Meaning, he says, stays within the horizon of questions put to the text, arising from the desire of specific persons, in the course of time itself. But if no one can pretend to be the measure of meaning, without a naïve and tyrannical imposture, it is also because no one can hold in his or her grasp the origin of the Word. Each person locates himself or herself in the trace of that origin, a trace which awakens the desire to live and to talk, oriented by this Word, or which gives it back, in an incomprehensible manner, when the desert seemed to be without end. It is a trace which does not spare one the ordeal of suffering.

Thus, the Talmudic discussion on the meaning of the obligation to call the first patriarch Abraham, and on the prohibition to still think of him by naming him Abram, take on an incommensurable seriousness for they are in accordance with the excess of suffering lived in the last century by the descendants of Abraham and by so many others. Levinas opens up this discussion of the sages unto the necessity of a meditation upon the name of Abraham in an age when the Promise that was made to the patriarch seems to sink into an abyss which annihilates it. Are not the theologies of the past shaken up to the point of atheism? For him whose memory remains haunted by the catastrophe of the century, no tangible sign emerges which would give him confidence in history and in the feeling that the

Promise is fulfilling itself, gradually, in the course of time. None the less, in referring himself to the deeds and words of 'the invincible but disarmed goodness of the just and the saints', which persisted, despite the power of the unprecedented destruction which triumphed almost everywhere, Levinas discovers a new mode of understanding the name of Abraham. A bold truth that might have slumbered 'in a forgotten corner of some letters or syllables of the Scripture – only to awaken as Word of God in the Jewish and non-Jewish suffering of the twentieth century, in a time without promise, time of a God without succor' (TN 90).

The trace of the immemorial call which forever made Abram into Abraham and Saraï into Sarah, consecrating them to become, together, the source of blessing for all peoples, can thus be understood, in the fragility we all experience, in the mode of this invincible and disarmed goodness. As if this goodness, from the very centre of its weakness, gave the power to still believe in the human in man, that is in the miracle of a temporality open to the other person. This miracle is required for universal peace, says Levinas, at the beginning of his Talmudic reading. None the less, peace does not appear at the horizon of the events which make up historical becoming, he then goes on to show. But at the moment when despair, derision and nihilism would seem to have the last word and would push one to close the volumes of the Talmud, as works belonging to the past, which can even be blamed for their naïvety, given merciless human reality, the interpreter remembers the contemporary descendants of Abraham. He remembers those men and women who, without thinking of Abraham, for they did not have time for reflexivity – for the return to the self – and, by this very fact, in the trace of Abraham, knew how to behave in the thick of disaster, as if the world continued to exist. According to Levinas, the memory of these people can still bring to mind the idea of the invisible God who called Abraham. It helps in continuing to give meaning to the future coming of the human into being, this Promise made to the patriarch. And, through this, this memory makes possible that to open the pages of the Talmud and to seek in them the trace of the unheard – of God who chose Abraham – can still transmit a light which orients human beings in their thought and in their life.

NOTES

1 Levinas's Talmudic readings were, for the most part, given in the context of the colloquia of French-speaking Jewish intellectuals, whose goal, in the aftermath of the *Shoah*, was to show Jews who were university educated but who had, in almost all cases, gone without traditional Jewish learning, that their heritage was also worth an education.

2 Leo Strauss, 'Théologie et philosophie. Leur influence réciproque', trans. C. Heim in *Le temps de la réflexion* (Paris: Gallimard, 1981), p. 203.

3 The oral law, *Torah Shébèal pe*, consists of all the commentaries – *midrashim* and Talmud – written about the written law, *Torah shébekhtav*.

4 'Were there no Talmud, there would be no Jews today' (*DF* 68 and 175).

5 Rabbi Israel Salanter (1810–1883) is the founder of the Musar movement which originated in Lithuania. It insists above all on moral instruction and is concerned with the moral development of students.

6 See Babylon Talmud, tractate Haguiga 14b, about the four masters who entered the garden of the highest wisdom. One died, one went insane, another became an apostate. Only Rabbi Akiba went in and out in peace.

6 Levinas and language

This chapter attempts to expound Levinas's philosophy of language by seeking to explain the reference made in the final crowded sentence of *Otherwise than Being* to

the trace – the unpronounceable writing – of what, always already past – always '*il*', Pro-noun, does not enter into any present, to which names designating beings or verbs in which their *essence* resounds are no longer suited – but which marks with its seal everything that can be named. [*OB* 185][1]

I begin by giving brief accounts of two of the philosophies of language that dominated the intellectual scene when Levinas's main works were being composed.

STRUCTURALISM

The cluster of ideas that goes under the name structuralism derives largely from Ferdinand de Saussure's *Course in General Linguistics*,[2] though, as Levinas reminds us, structuralism is anticipated by the philosophical ideal of a *mathesis universalis* proposed by Descartes and Leibniz (*OB* 96). While nineteenth-century theoreticians had focused mainly on the evolution of language, Saussure projects a science that subordinates the diachronic to the synchronic. Distinguishing acts of speech (*parole*) from language regarded as a system (*langue*), he aims to show how the units assembled in a linguistic system signify not 'positively' by standing independently for objects signified, but 'negatively' through the combinatorial differences between them. According to Saussure, a sign comprises two distinguishable but inseparable components: a phonetic, graphic or otherwise embodied signifier (*signifiant*) and a signified concept (*signifié*).

He lays down a programme for a general science of signs, a semiology of all systems of signs that extends to other special fields the lessons of the science of language. In this programme relatively simple signs are identified by the places they can and cannot fill, as in chess what matters is the moves that can be made with the pieces, not their shapes or the material of which they are made.

Levinas takes over from structuralism the word *signifiant*. However, prising it away from the *signifié* understood as the conceptual aspect of signs, he applies it to the speaker, but to the speaker not regarded only third-personally or as one of a first person plural *we*. For Levinas the *signifiant* is primarily the speaker in the first person singular subjectivity of its *me*, in the accusative case – except that the word 'case' is misleading. Before being a case, the speaker is a face, the face that speaks. And what the face primarily says, its *signifié*, is nothing but its saying. When I say something there will normally be some semantic signification of a message, but such sense-giving *Sinngebung* is already *signifiance*, where my saying is my saying of my saying. Hence, while on the structuralist theory the positivity of the signs we use depends upon negativity defined by differences between the constituents of the systematic interdependent totalities of *signifiants* and of *signifiés*, *signifiance* as what I shall call 'deep' saying testifies to the positivity of my being accosted by another human being, an event that holds 'the secret of the birth (*naissance*) of thought itself and of the verbal proposition by which it is conveyed' (CP 125). *Signifiance* is without horizon or world. Although or because it is the expression of the face of my neighbour, it infinitely transcends the confines of culture; so its saying is prior to every historical language (CP 122). Other than the countenance, the face has no features or properties or substance, no *ousia*. The *signifiance* of the face is abstract, but its abstractness is prior to the abstractness defined by the structuralist as the separability of the intersubstitutability of propositional signs from a given empirical embodiment.

Precisely because in structuralist semiotics the components or terms owe their meaning to their internal interrelations, it is arguable that there is only one unit, the system as a whole. This suggests an analogy with mathematical systems, where it is arguable that the mathematician reads off from the system as a whole the theorems he calculates or infers. One might say that it is the system that thinks through the mathematician. And something like this is what is said by some of the human scientists who apply Saussure's model to their own special fields. With some structuralists the idea that 'it' (*es*, *ça*) thinks in me turns into the idea of 'the death of man', so that it becomes questionable whether they can properly be called 'human' scientists. Lacan in psychoanalysis, Althusser in political theory, Lévi-Strauss in anthropology and Foucault in the genealogies of knowledge and power are among those whom Levinas would see as representatives of 'modern antihumanism' (*OB* 127). Although this is a description many structuralists embrace, they do so, Levinas maintains, only because they identify humanism with the idea that the human being is first and foremost the author of his acts, including his acts of speech. Kantianism is typical of humanism understood in this way. Spontaneity and freedom are stressed, too, by the existentialism against which structuralism reacts. One of Sartre's titles declares that existentialism is a humanism.[3] For him, as for Kant and for the tradition culminating in them both, humanism is a humanism of the first person singular subject.

ONTOLOGISM

According to Levinas, much the same holds when one turns from the humanism of the subject to a humanism of a being whose way of being is that of being placed, being somewhere, here or there: *Da-sein*. *Da-sein*, Heidegger maintains in *Being and Time*, is in each case mine (*jemeinig*). *Da-sein* is mine-ish. *Da-sein* is a being that interprets itself and its place (*Da*) in its world. Its way of being is for its being to be in question. It is therefore with a questioning of questioning that the analysis of *Da-sein* begins. Heidegger enumerates the elements of investigative questioning – *Untersuchung*, as in the German title of the *Logical Investigations* of Husserl, the dedicatee of *Being and Time*. These components include the topic, which in the case of Heidegger's book is Being; what we seek to discover about the topic, which in this case is the meaning of Being; and that at which attention must be directed in order to discover this, here the beings in which Being resides. The being pre-eminently to be addressed, Heidegger maintains, is precisely the being that is able to raise the question of the meaning of Being, the so-called 'human being' or *Da-sein*. Heidegger also maintains that the question of the meaning of being is first and foremost the question each *Da-sein* puts to itself about its own being. To state this in the terminology of *Being and Time*, ontological and existential questioning begins in questioning that is ontic and *existentiell*. It will turn out to be of importance for our understanding of Levinas's teaching that in Heidegger's analysis the being to whom is put the *existentiell* leading question is none other than the person by whom that question is put. For Heidegger questioning is first self-questioning: not initially *fragen*, but *sich fragen*, *Da-sein*'s ability to ask itself about its own way of being toward its own death.

LINGUISTIC POSSESSIONS

In the 'Letter on "Humanism"'¹ Heidegger calls language the house of Being.⁴ Taking the liberty of reading *Being and Time* in the light of this later remark, but appealing also to Heidegger's demonstration in the earlier work itself that *Da-sein*'s being in the world is its being in language or discourse (*Rede*), could one say that while the point of entry into Heidegger's account of language in *Being and Time* is the question and questionability, the point of entry into Levinas's account of language is the response and responsibility? This would be to oversimplify. For a notion and sense of responsibility (*Antwortlichkeit*) is all pervasive in *Being and Time*.

But the responsibility that figures in that book and in Heidegger's later works is finally the responsibility towards Being, whereas the responsibility that is first and last in Levinas's treatment of language is responsibility to the other human being. And in so far as the target of his 'humanism of the other man' is the 'anti-humanism' he sees in theories like structuralism, it cannot fail to have in its sights at the same time the accounts of language put forth by Heidegger in the course of which we are told both that *Da-sein* has language and that *Da-sein* is, as we might say, had by language.⁵ Language is not merely a competence possessed by a subclass of animals, the rational ones, the *zôon logon echon* of Aristotle. *Da-sein* is and has in its essence to be the place (the *Da*) where language speaks. There is then a mutual belonging of *Da-sein* and language, as is indicated formally by the conjunction of the name *Da-sein* with the statement that language is the house of Being and with the idea that *Da-sein* has to be (*zu sein hat*), to take on, to assume the responsibility for the that and the how of its Being.⁶ Language on this account is not ultimately to be compared, as Wittgenstein compares it, with a toolbox.[7] We speak English or German or French, but that is because we already belong to the linguisticality of which the speaking of natural languages is a manifestation. *Language* speaks, 'die *Sprache* spricht'.[8] Although it is not incorrect to say that we possess this or that language and the ability to speak it, prior to that is our being possessed by language.

Prior to my being possessed by language, Levinas maintains, is my possession by the human being who speaks to me. But, again, this formulation of the difference between Levinas's and Heidegger's doctrines of language is too simple unless we acknowledge the difference between what each of them means by possession and recognize that the difference between Heidegger's and Levinas's doctrines of language is not merely a difference between monologue and dialogue. Already in *Being and Time Da-sein*'s being possessed by language, understood as a basic structure of *Da-sein*'s occupying a place in the world, is a way of *Da-sein*'s being with others, *mit-Da-sein*. Being in the world is Being in dialogue. *Sprache* is *Gespräch*. Heidegger can say this despite his saying that language is monologue,[9] for what he means when he says that language is monologue is that although it is language al*one* (*all*ein) that speaks authentically and although this speaking is l*one*some (ein*sam*), lonesomeness is possible only if one is not alone, not solitary, not cut off from community. Lonesomeness is a way of not being alone; it is a privative way of being *with* others. Therefore our earlier reference to the self-reference of *Da-sein*'s questioning must not be taken to imply that the mine-ishness of each *Da-sein* is incompatible with an original sociality.

However, there is more than one way of understanding this sociality. For both Heidegger and Levinas it is linguistic, and a way of being possessed by language. But, to repeat, whereas for Heidegger possession by language is a way of *being with others*, for Levinas it is also a *possession by others*. This latter possession disrupts my being possessed by language as this is understood by Heidegger. My possession by language is obsession at the same time – or rather from a time beyond recall of which the diachrony is anterior to the diachrony correlatively opposed to synchrony by the structuralist. The other's call to responsibility to her or to him and to the third party, that is to say, to the whole of humanity, is anterior to the call to responsibility to being. Its anteriority is announced in a pluper-fect tense marking the diachrony of a time incommensurable with what a verb in the present tense might have reported. This ab-solute, separated past is contained neither by the structuralist's idea of lan-guage as a synchronous totality nor by the Heideggerian ontologist's description of a historical (*geschichtlich*) dispensation (*Geschick*) as a unitary whole in which *Da-sein*'s having-been, coming-toward and making-present are co-implicated.

Combining Heidegger's turn of phrase with one of Levinas's, we can say that the human other breaks into the house of Being like a thief (*OB* 13). This possession by the other is a dispossession of my home and my belongings, a discomforting that is, to use Heidegger's word, *un-heimlich*, unhomely. I am disconcerted, discountenanced and decentred. Prior to the subject's self-consciousness, prior to the mine-ishness of the self that says 'I', and prior to all consciousness, the self is the me accused by some other human being whose place in the sun I have always already usurped simply by being here, simply as ego or *Da-sein*. Levinas goes as far as to call this obsessive pos-session by the other psychosis, intending us to hear in this reso-nances both of Husserl's *Beseelung*, animation, and of madness or folly, the topic taken up from Freud in the work of Foucault and Lacan.

Another of Levinas's contemporaries who should be mentioned in this context is Ricœur. No less critical of structuralism than Levinas, holding, like him (and John Austin),[10] that the study of language as an object of science must be supplemented by reflection upon mo-mentary acts of speech, Ricœur makes a special analysis of avowals. But this analysis, like psychoanalysis, is conducted within the frame-work of the symbols and primarily Greek myths where the notions of impurity and culpability arise in the West. So the concern with *parole* that Ricœur shares with Levinas is of a sort that leads him to stress the importance of narrative even in his investigation of con-fessions of guilt. Typically, the confession of guilt isolates the person who confesses. In owning up I come to own myself, even if the guilt is shared.[11] On Ricœur's account the isolation effected in the acknowl-edgement of culpability is not itself isolated from the context of a narrative or myth. It therefore serves well to bring out the boldness of Levinas's account. For, according to the latter, culpability is inde-pendent of such narrative or mythological contexts, notwithstanding that Levinas sometimes cites even in his more philosophical writings stories from the Hebrew Bible by way of illustration.

A narrative is a sequence of statements. Among the simplest statements, at least in Indo-European languages, are predicative ones in which something is said about something or somebody. The subject about which the statement says something is represented in the sentence by a noun or noun-like term. What is said about it is expressed in a phrase involving either the verb 'to be' explicitly or a short-form verb, e.g. 'runs', paraphrasable by a long-form copulative expression, e.g. 'is running'. Taking the hint from languages like German, where 'Das Himmel blaut' says 'The sky is blue', some logicians, for instance Quine, have pointed out that long forms can generally be transposed into short forms, as in 'The President of the United States clintonizes', 'The teacher of Plato socratizes', 'Pegasus pegasizes'.[12] Following what he takes to be Heidegger's teaching on the verb and verbal noun (*OB* 189), Levinas gives as examples of identity statements 'Socrates socratizes' and 'Red reds'. Another example given by him orally, but not to my knowledge in print, is 'Le violoncelle violoncellise'. These express, he says, the *fashion* (*façon*) in which, for example, Socrates is (*OB* 41). He italicizes this word in order to bring to our attention that it derives from the Latin *facere*, to do or to make, and in order to help us to hear in predication the time, tense and verbality of being and the adverbiality of being's modalities, its *Seinsweisen*. But here Levinas's word for 'being' is 'essence'. In a note at the outset of *Otherwise than Being* he explains that he does not use the word 'essence' as it is traditionally used, for the nature or whatness of something. He uses it in the verbal sense in which *Sein* is used in German and in *Being and Time* in opposition to *Seiendes*, this latter standing for *a* being, an *étant*. Nevertheless, the second syllable of *étant* retains a trace of the suffix *ance* from which abstract nouns of action are formed through derivation from *antia* and *entia*, for example *naissance*, a word we earlier found him using in the course of explaining this point, and *signifiance*, a word to which we shall return below. Other examples are *tendance*, a word used in *Otherwise than Being* in conjunction with a family of words based on *tendere*, e.g. ostension, and *essance*. This last is a word Levinas says he will not be so bold as to use there, notwithstanding that it would have represented well the verb-noun ambiguity of *Sein* and *Wesen* and the fact that *être* can be either a verb or a noun.

The hidden difference at issue here is what Heidegger calls the ontological difference, the difference between Being and a being present already in the ambiguity of the Greek word *on*. Levinas calls this difference an amphibology. Because there survives in the second syllable of *étant* a hint of the action and verbal-cum-adverbial *fashion* exemplifed in 'Socrates socratizes' Levinas might have had no objection to translating this into 'Socratizing socratizes', by analogy with Borges's Heraclitean verbalizing conversion of 'The moon rose above the river' into 'Upward behind the onstreaming it mooned'. But note in this last example the pronominal 'it' that insists on itself as stubbornly as it does in 'It is raining', 'It reds', 'Es gibt Sein', and 'Es gibt Zeit'. These last two, meaning 'There is Being' and 'There is time' (literally 'It gives Being' and 'It gives time') pose what may seem to be a problem. In his essay 'Time and Being' Heidegger says that the belonging together of these two statements, signalled by the 'and' of his title, is expressed by the word *Ereignis*.[13] In colloquial German this word means a happening or event. Now just as one cannot say either of Being or time that it is or *gibt*, nor can this be said of *Ereignis*. To say any of these things would be to treat Being as a being, time as in time and happening as a happening. The best we can do, Heidegger concludes, is to say 'Das Ereignis ereignet'. Although Levinas may have this apparent tautology in mind when he writes 'Socrates socratizes', it should be observed that the latter is a statement about *a* being in time. Heidegger's statement, on the other hand, purports to be about Being and time, yet, as the definite article *Das* indicates, it puts Being in the same logico-grammatical slot as is occupied by the proper name 'Socrates'. Heidegger's statement fails to mark the ontological difference. Of this he is quite aware. He goes as far as to argue that the history of philosophy is a history of the forgetting of this difference by philosophers and of their failure to become aware of this forgetting. Hence they fail to ask how one can speak of Being without saying the opposite of what one means or wants to say.[14]

Frege raises the question of how one can consistently say either 'The concept horse is a concept' or 'The concept horse is not a concept'.[15] Appearances to the contrary, the first of these is not an analytical truth, and the second is not a contradiction. Both suffer from what he calls the 'awkwardness' that a concept is what the predicate of a statement connotes, whereas in both of these statements the form of words preceding the copula, the grammatical subject of the sentences, converts the alleged concept into an object. What we are calling Heidegger's problem is analogous, but it is more deep-seated than Frege's, because it is about Being as such.

What we are calling Heidegger's problem is not Levinas's problem. But we have been obliged to outline it in order to go on to show now where the crucial difference lies. The relation between saying (*dire*) and the said (*dit*) treated in *Otherwise than Being* is a relation between a verb and a nominal part of speech. It may therefore seem to correspond at the linguistic level with the ontological difference between Being and beings and to be a derivative of this. But Levinas is concerned less with the *dire* that is a speech-act correlative with what is said than with a *dire* that is somehow presupposed by that correlation. That deep *dire* is therefore different both from the pair of correlative dictions and from the pair opposed in the ontological difference. So, if a problem is a question that can in principle be answered, it is not a problem that is raised by the relation between this *dire* and the ontological difference or amphibology. Answerable questions arise as to Being and beings (where among beings are included processes, events and whatever else there is). The question as to how these questions and their answers and topics are related to the uncorrelative saying is not then strictly a question. Deep saying is the expression of answerability prior to the expression of questions and answers. But it must now be acknowledged that Levinasian deep saying has a parallel in the Heideggerian deep being or *Ereignis* of the differentiation *between* Being and a being. If no answerable question or problem can be posed about that, we shall have reached a deeper analogy between Levinas and Heidegger. Nevertheless, this leaves it open for Levinas to maintain that the verbality of the infinitive *dire*, to say – the verb of or for infinity and the unfinished (*OB* 13) – expresses an excluded third infinitely deeper and older than the verbality of to-be-or-not-to-be.

PRONOUNS AND PRONUNCIATION

Like Heidegger and Frege and Wittgenstein, Levinas is confronted with the difficulty of saying or otherwise showing how the philosopher can avoid saying precisely the opposite of what he wants to say. He cites the sentence in which Hegel poses this difficulty (*OB* 84),[16] and would have his readers remember the context in which Hegel's sentence occurs. It occurs in the context of the discussion of the theory of sensible certainty according to which the richest and truest knowledge is the allegedly immediate apprehension of a sensible datum denoted by the demonstrative pronoun 'this'. Hegel challenges the advocate of this theory to write that pronoun down. He does not have to wait long before he is in a position to point out that the unmediated datum the pronoun was supposed to denote earlier may now denote something else, and that the same can be said of 'then' and 'now' as well as of the first person pronoun 'I', should the advocate defend himself by asserting 'This richest and truest knowledge is the sensible apprehension I am experiencing here and now'. For all these pronouns, along with 'my', 'your' and the other possessive adjectives cognate with them, shift from one referent to another. Therefore they do not register a purely immediate apprehension, but import the mediation of comprehension. They do not designate pure sensible receptivity, but engage the conceptualizing activity of the understanding, albeit not in the same way as do common nouns.

The challenge 'Write this down' is the part of Hegel's reply that is very relevant to the understanding of Levinas's teaching on language and pronominality. The written word is especially exposed to interpretation in ways different from what the author intended. The mortal author cannot always be there to forestall the misinterpretation of his intentions. And this holds for any work, whether set down in ink or produced in paint or in bronze or in tablets of stone.

Plato's *Phaedrus* is the work on which Levinas draws in making this distinction between a work (*œuvre*) and the spoken word. Yet in the part of the dialogue that is most relevant here, sections 275-6, this distinction is blurred. Although Socrates is keen to get Phaedrus to agree that there is a kind of discourse that is preferable to writing, this preferable kind of discourse is said to be written in the human being's soul; and Levinas, too, notes how fitting this metaphor is for discourse that expresses knowledge of principles (OB 148). We saw that in the final sentence of *Otherwise than Being* cited at the beginning of this chapter Levinas goes as far as to describe as 'unpronounceable writing' what he wishes to contrast with a work. This is not writing in any ordinary sense. It is related to the archi-writing to which, discussing the same Platonic dialogue, Derrida appealed in 1968 to indicate what is somehow presupposed by both writing and speaking understood in their usual senses as correlatives.[17] Compare Levinas's special use of 'saying' to mark what is called for by both poles of the correlation of saying and what is said. This archi-saying, as we might call it – provided we remember that it is not a formal principle, but an-archic – is the trace of the absolutely third-personal pronoun 'he', the *il* of *illéité* that perhaps, without letting divinity be said, is pronounced by the word 'God'. This word is extra-ordinary. It does not belong to any order. Neither a proper name nor a common name, it names neither nothing nor anything that can be present or represented. It falls within no grammatical category, not even that of the vocative case, perhaps not even the vocative case of prayer (*BV* 128; *OB* 149, 162).

This 'he' is pronounced or invoked as soon as there is language and as soon as there is justice or injustice. And there is justice or injustice as soon as there is a person facing me whom I address as 'you'; for you – as indicated by the French *vous*, a grammatical plural used in polite address to a single person – are one among others, not the 'thou' of the exclusive, intimate duality Levinas takes Buber's I–Thou relationship to be. The violent exclusiveness of preoccupation by a single other person is forestalled by the 'he' implicit in your looking at me, as in an essay in *Difficult Freedom* on the danger of loving God more than the Torah, the written and oral law or teaching is said to come between me and a devotion that runs the risk of becoming a private indulgence, a religious equivalent of the sensible certainty criticized by Hegel. Love of the Torah is practical love of all others. That is a way of saying that they are in the trace of *illéité* (*BPW* 63, *CP* 107). But *illéité* is the third-personality not simply of the third party who looks at me already in your eyes, but the third-personality both of the third party over against me and of myself as a third party over against and thanks to them and you or, as Levinas also writes, thanks to God, blessed be He, *béni-soit-Il* (*BV* 119, 122). Further, if Levinas's neologism *illéité* is built on this upper-case *Il* or lower-case *il*, it is built also on the Latin pronoun *ille* denoting remoteness and disjunction from the speaker, separatedness or absolutely pluperfect pastness (*OB* 12): 'always already past – always "*il*"', says the final sentence of *Otherwise than Being*. It denotes our *parenté*, where this is our being bound in a relationship of fraternity that is neither our being united under a Father in the way of a particular monotheistic religion, nor a biological common descendence, but our being bound ethically in a sociality. In this sociality not only has my responsibility to *you* been complicated by my responsibility to *him* and to *her*; more than this, the hitherto incomparably responsible *me* is now a member of society with comparable rights, one of a *we* that is not and is not founded upon being-with-others as described in *Being and Time* (*OB* 158).

Fraternity means that the other commands me to command, but that the superiority of the other in this relationship consists in the other's face being the face of the poor, the stranger, the widow and the orphan (*TI* 251). I am not commanded as a slave (*TI* 213). I am commanded to serve, to serve the other and the other other. The other assigns me in my responsibility to the third party who looks at me already in the first other's eyes. Because the other's eyes speak, they speak justice, for 'language is justice' (*ibid.*), where the word 'language' translates *langage*, the intersection of *langue* and *parole*. 'Signification signifies in justice' (*OB* 158). Therefore the other's imperative both belongs to and exceeds a systematic *syntax* of tenses and aspects and cases. In Levinas's philosophy of language speaking is primarily but non-foundationally speaking for the other. The *sich fragen* of self-addressed questioning that guides Heidegger's fundamental ontology is superseded. In Levinas's philosophy of first philosophy as ethics, the German pronoun *sich* (and the French pronoun *se* and the English pronoun 'me') is an absolute accusative, not merely a declension from a nominative. Nomination or denomination as the appending of a noun or a name risks stifling the sound of the voice that calls me by name only in order to call me to respond by speaking for the other who addresses me and for the other other for whom that first other speaks. Levinas is thus able to write both that 'language is justice', and that the face is (probably) 'the very essence of language prior to language' without implying that the face is prior to justice (*CP* 122; *BV* 128). 'I am ... necessary for justice, as responsible beyond every limit fixed by an objective law' (*TI* 245). I am in a double bind: the face as saying and responsibility is the 'essence' of language as what is said, of what is, of being and of conceptual essence because the latter require the former if they are not to be a violence; at the same time the former requires the latter in order to meet the demand for justice for every other (*OB* 45, 159).

This last requirement means that there is an ambiguity not only between the different tertialities marked by the two uses of the third-personal pronoun distinguished by Levinas in *Otherwise than Being* discussed in this section so far (*OB* 150), but also between these and an impersonal use like that discussed in the preceding section. It is as though the *il* of the third party is attracted 'upward' toward the *il* of *illéité* and 'downward' to the *il* of what Levinas calls the *il y a*, the 'there is', so that, independently of the fact that *il* can translate 'it' as well as 'he', there is a risk of the extremes being confused (*GCM* 69, *BPW* 141). The impersonal pronoun *il* of the *il y a* is the anonymous *ça*, the anonymous It, one is tempted to say, that susurrates in the interstices of the essance that is sung in the poetic word and in the essence formulated prosaically in the linguistics of structuralism. Through their inevitable liability to lapse from responsibility into the half-sense either of a prejudiced privacy or of a neutral indifferent publicity, the language of the poet (the *Gedicht*) venerated by Heidegger and on the other hand the structures of language abstracted as a topic for science by Saussure (which Heidegger would have called framework, *Gestell*) expose one to suffocation by the utter and unutterable non-sense of what we cannot strictly call 'Itness' on analogy with the translation of 'illéité' as 'He-ness'. 'It' already implies determinacy. So too does 'ness', for it connotes whatness or essence. Determinacy of being, limitation, is a function of negation, whereas the nothingness of the 'there is' is not a nothingness that limits being, but is indistinguishable from being. The 'there is' is beyond contra-diction (*EE* 64). *Apeirôn*, unbounded, its unfinishedness is that of the 'horrible eternity' into which the conceptual diction of essence always threatens to fall (*OB* 176).

Responsibility is interpreted by Levinas, following the *Phaedrus*, as response, and response is interpreted as saying, whether or not out loud. But this speaking responsibility is not unlimited if it is limited to the diction of essence. If it were so limited it would belong to a symmetrical system in which the other and I would be from the start equals before the law. The other and I would be thought together, com-pensated, and there would be no reason why I should not think that a responsibility carried out by me on behalf of another earned for me the right to expect to be treated likewise. In such a case the expectation and the responsibility are supported by a law. *Before* the law, however, prior to the laws of syntax and semantics that regulate the intersubstitutability of pronouns, the responsibility of my unsubstitutability is groundless. And the responsibility grounded in my particular situation is ethical and unviolent only if it is a response to my groundless responsibility, my responsibility toward this other whom I call 'you', and to that other whom I call 'her' or 'him', who is also a you not simply on account of case-law and syntax, but because they all call me. I am called to support all of them and everything on their behalf *without reason*. My being called by them is my owing it to them not to require a demonstration of their right, not to require even that philosophy produce a logical refutation of the conclusion of some anti-humanist sciences that ethical responsibility is a laughable delusion. What is without reason *par excellence* is the anarchic *il y a*. Only thanks to the meaninglessness of its sublinguistic, subliterary and so subpoetic murmuring can meaning and rationality be regained through ethics. Therefore language is rational only in the face of the menace of the non-rationality of the 'there is' – the non-rationality into which language risks slipping if construed in the manner of the doctrines of structuralism and ontologism, with their corollaries that the human being is possessed by language and that what speaks first and last is language in its totality. These doctrines turn out to be of positive assistance in enabling Levinas to describe the fine risk that language on his own ethical doctrine of it must inevitably run. I can only witness to the other in responsibility if, beyond knowing and doubt, there may be no more to illeity than ilyaity. The ambiguity or enigma of this incognitive 'may be' (Levinas's *peut-être*) is necessary to the good beyond being.

SAYING, SAID AND SILENCE

Signifiance is another of those words referred to earlier regarding which Levinas tells us that they preserve the *verbal* sense of 'being' and give rise to abstract nouns of action. It would indeed be quite natural to say that *signifiance* names an action performed in a speech-act understood as the saying that is correlated with something said. But this oppositional correlation is anarchically conditioned by archi-saying, rather as the ordinary opposition of saying and writing is conditioned by what we can just as well call archi-writing as archi-saying. Levinas describes speaking (*langage*) as 'the first action over and above labour, action without action', a generous offering of one's labour and the world to another, 'the first ethical gesture' (*TI* 174). The generosity extends to the exposition of one's very speech-intentions, so that 'The act of speaking is the passivity of passivity' (OB 92).

The correlation of saying and said is an instance of the correlation of mental intending and object intended that Husserl claims to be fundamental to all consciousness. In this noetic–noematic structure the hyphenation, like the bar between the signifier and the signified in Saussure's schema of the sign,[18] marks a distinction that is not a separation. It is, Husserl maintains, the structure of all meaning or intending. It holds where the speech-act is one for which the standard syntactical form expressing it is an indicative sentence. It holds, too, he says, where the standard syntactical form is not an indicative sentence. Speech-acts standardly performed in syntactically interrogative and imperative sentences are based on the same noetic–noematic foundations as assertions. Levinas devotes several pages of *Otherwise than Being* and several paragraphs of the essay 'Language and Proximity' to explaining why there is more than many commentators allow to the Husserlian doctrine of intentionality that 'all consciousness is consciousness of an object'. As applied, for example, to a predicative statement of one's experience of the sensible world, this formula fails to bring out Husserl's point, accepted and indeed insisted upon by Levinas, that no predication merely represents a sensation passively received. Predication, he says, glossing Husserl and up to a point Hegel, is kerygmatic. It proclaims. The intentionality is not only a directedness at an object, but an understanding of an object as such and such, a classification and identification where the intending is a meaning in the sense of the German *meinen* and of the French *vouloir dire*: it is an engagement of will or desire as wanting to say (CP 112–13).

Note again the use here of words based on *tendere*, with the connotations of reaching, tension and tense that are preserved in the stretching and ec-stasis that Heidegger's analysis of tense develops from the notions of temporal retention and protention employed by Husserl in lectures edited by Heidegger.[19] But note, too, that *entendre* can mean either to understand or to hear. This ambiguity has consequences for the interpretation of Levinas's doctrine of deep saying, for it determines what we make of another doctrine he frequently illustrates by citing from Isaiah 65:24 the words 'before they call I will answer' (OB 150). This deep saying, we have seen, is a saying of myself as an unsituated and naked self face to face with another such self in abstraction from empirical paraphernalia behind which I might hide like Gyges concealing himself by twisting his ring (*OB* 145).[20] My exposure of my self to another, whomsoever he or she may be, is an exposure of myself to another in a saying over and above the saying of something said, in the saying of my saying itself. Here the *signifié* is the *signifiant*, the signifying that exposes the sayer, me, as expressed in the Hebrew *hineni* and the French *me voici, envoie-moi*, 'See me here, send me'.

Connected with the indeterminacy of the Greek word *logos*, there is a philosophical tradition extending from Plato to Husserl and Frege according to which phonetic language (*logos*) is the phenomenal exteriorization of a language of thoughts (*logoi*). Levinas is attempting to direct the attention of philosophers to a doubling different from this traditional one in which the phonetic or graphic doubling of the unexpressed or only secretly expressed thought is an otiose extra. He wants to direct attention to a silent saying that is extra because extra-ordinary, but far from otiose (*GCM* 74, *BPW* 145). The 'good silence' of this saying is contrasted with the 'bad silence' of Gyges' secrecy and with the 'sygetic' resounding or ringing of silence, *das Geläut der Stille*, that Heidegger refers to in his essay 'The Nature of Language'.[21] The latter silent saying (*Sage*) is the silence of essence, essance or essencing (*Wesen*) that resounds in the poetic word. The poetic word points to a verbal noun that assembles a world, bringing the things of its different regions into a so-called face-to-face proximity (*in die Nähe des Gegen-einander-über*). But this is the proximity of being in general, not the face-to-face proximity to another human being (*OB* 135). Interpreting Stefan George's poem 'Words', Heidegger says that when the beautiful (*formosus*) words of poetry break off, the formal conceptuality of propositions is disrupted, allowing the language of being to be heard. Levinas says that both that language and the conceptuality of propositions are disordered by the face-to-face language of one human being addressing another.

This brings us back to the methodological difficulty referred to above in connection with Hegel, Frege, Wittgenstein and Heidegger, the difficulty Heidegger attempts to circumvent by turning away from the phenomenological and therefore descriptive mode of discourse of *Being and Time* to a more 'poetic' mode of expression, the difficulty to which Levinas returns repeatedly in the final pages of *Otherwise than Being*.

THE LANGUAGE OF LEVINAS'S PHILOSOPHY
OF LANGUAGE

Am I not, Levinas asks again and again, undermining what I am try-ing to express in the very act of trying to express it? Perhaps the re-sponse to this difficulty may be traced in this 'again and again'. This would be a response that refuses to remain only a theoretical answer which, as such, apparently says the very opposite of what one wants to say. To contradict oneself in this way would indeed be an abuse of language as flagrant as that of which the epistemological sceptic would be culpable if he claimed to know that we can know nothing. Yet it may be through just such an abuse of language that the force of what Levinas desires to say might get expressed. The more I iterate what present themselves unavoidably as constative affirmations of knowledge, opinion or *doxa* with their idealizing identifications of this-as-the-same-as-that and their subsumption of particulars under universals, the more through these very affirmations is my respon-sibility performatively affirmed and confirmed as by the appending of a signature (Italian *firma*) that is both the sign and the trace of my always already having given my word to my interlocutor.

In the forgetting of what Heidegger calls the ontological difference Being again and again gets represented as *a* being, empirical or meta-physical, human or divine. In what Levinas might have called the dictive difference, a trace is what is absolutely forgotten in the sense that it bears witness to what is neither recollected nor forgotten in the epistemic sense of these terms when it is represented as a sign. Strictly speaking, it is incapable of representing any *what* whatso-ever, so full is it of my 'representing' my interlocutor in the sense of my standing for and substituting myself for my interlocutor in response to her or his 'Hear me'. The remembrance without recol-lection of what Levinas calls trace is nevertheless effected in 'body language', in that (to re-echo Hegel) the directness of the trace calls for mediation by the body of a sign, a conventional verbal sign be-longing to the context and structure of a syntactic system. This sign ultimately mediates the sign that is the speaker's body. The speaker's body regarded as the expression of a trace is what Levinas refers to quasi-metonymically as 'face'. Just as the face in his semio-ethical use of the word is distinguished but inextricable from the body, so the trace is different but inextricable from the sign. Hence, if we are to go on talking of a 'deep' saying, we must take care not to think that this entails a level of deep saying below a level of surface saying to which belongs the saying that is correlative with what is said. Rather as the difference of what Heidegger calls the ontological difference does not belong simply either to Being or beings regarded as opposed levels or sides, so, too, the dictive difference in Levinas's philosophy of language is irreducibly ambiguous and enigmatic. This is why the absolute forgetting and unrecollective remembrancing always already effected in the trace does not hark back (anymore than does what Heidegger calls *Ereignis*) to an event like some proto-ethical Big Bang in, at or before the time of historiography. When, against the structuralist's stressing of synchrony, Levinas emphasizes diachrony, he means that every moment of the recollectable time of my going forward toward my own death is cut through (*dia*) by the interlocution of other mortal human beings (*TI* 171).

Levinas's philosophy of language is a philosophy of philosophy according to which, like language quite generally, the language of philosophy is paradoxically prophetic. Prophecy is speaking for another, but in a way that cannot be comprehended by the concepts of philosophy. What they cannot comprehend is that while my speaking is a response to another's command, my perception of that command is my signifying of it in obeying it. The call is understood in the response (*OB* 149). I am diachronically in command and commanded. My commanding is at the 'same' dia-chronic moment an obedience, an *ob-audire* that is a *dire*, a ventrilocution of the other's command; for my command gives voice to the allocution of the other who is like an irritating foreign body 'under my skin' prior to my being myself 'in my skin', *dans ma peau*, comfortably at home. I am in my place, but, ethically speaking, the other has usurped that place before me (*OB* 115). The meaning of my command is not then a straightforwardly intentional *meinen* or *vouloir dire*. Motivated by desire carrying an ethical emphasis that, like the many other ethical emphases given to apparently ontological terms throughout Levinas's writings, postpones Hegelian conceptual elevation (*Aufhebung*), my command is at the same time obedience. This is why Levinas ascribes to it a passivity that is not the passivity of the passive voice or the passivity that is contrasted with activity in theories of knowledge based on a classical construal of subjectivity. In response to the command of an interlocutor, where the reception of the command is in the response, the identity of the constituting and constituted subject is deconstituted and displaced through the deposition of the egoity of its enjoyment of life. That deponent command expresses an incoming, in-ventive intentionality that alters the direction of the ec-static intentionality which, without that alteration, would be, in the words of Pascal cited among the epigraphs of *Otherwise than Being*, the beginning of 'the usurpation of the whole world'. Not usurpation of the whole world, but responsibility for the whole world is what I am called to by the singular categorical imperative with which the other addresses me in an asymmetry without which the symmetry of communication would be the violence either of exclusive intimacy or of purely formal legal universality. The so-called origin of language is 'originally' the non-ontological, non-cosmological and non-theological creation of the world, of 'everything that can be named'. It is not only in the semiotic ways described by generative grammarians that language is infinitely regenerative and creative.[22] In the beginning was the semio-ethical word.

NOTES

1 'Name' here translates *nom*, which can also mean 'noun', as in 'Pro-noun'.
2 Ferdinand de Saussure, *Course in General Linguistics*, trans. Wade Baskin (London: Fontana-Collins, 1974).
3 Jean-Paul Sartre, *Existentialism and Humanism*, trans. Philip Mairet (London: Methuen, 1948).
4 Martin Heidegger, *Basic Writings*, ed. David Farrell Krell (London: Routledge, 1978), p. 239.
5 Martin Heidegger, *Being and Time*, trans. Joan Stambaugh (Albany: State University of New York Press, 1996), p. 165.
6 *Ibid.*, pp. 276, 285, 300.
7 Ludwig Wittgenstein, *Philosophical Investigations*, trans. G. E. M. Anscombe (Oxford: Blackwell, 1953), 11.
8 Martin Heidegger, 'The Way to Language', in *On the Way to Language*, trans. Peter D. Hertz and Joan Stambaugh (New York: Harper and Row, 1975), p. 124.
9 *Ibid.*, p. 134.
10 John Austin, *How to Do Things with Words* (Oxford: Clarendon Press, 1962).
11 Paul Ricœur, 'Guilt, Ethics, and Religion', in *The Conflict of Interpretations* (Evanston: Northwestern University Press, 1974), pp. 425–39.

12 W. V. Quine, *From a Logical Point of View: Logico-Philosophical Essays* (Cambridge: Harvard University Press, 1953), pp. 8, 167.
13 Martin Heidegger, 'On Time and Being', trans. Joan Stambaugh (New York: Harper and Row, 1972), pp. 1–24.
14 G. W. F. Hegel, *Phenomenology of Spirit*, trans. A. V. Miller (Oxford: Clarendon Press, 1979), p. 65.
15 Gottlob Frege, 'On Concept and Object', in P. T. Geach and Max Black (eds.), *Translations from the Philosophical Writings of Gottlob Frege* (Oxford: Blackwell, 1960), pp. 45–8.
16 Hegel, *Phenomenology*, p. 60.
17 Jacques Derrida, 'Plato's Pharmacy', in *Dissemination*, trans. Barbara Johnson (Chicago: University of Chicago Press, 1981), pp. 61–171.
18 Saussure, *Course*, ch. IV. See also Jacques Lacan, 'L'instance de la lettre dans l'inconscient ou la raison depuis Freud', in *Écrits* (Paris: Seuil, 1966), pp. 493–528.
19 Edmund Husserl, *The Phenomenology of Internal Time Consciousness*, trans. James S. Churchill (The Hague: Nijhoff, 1964).
20 Plato, *Republic*, 359–60.
21 Martin Heidegger, *On the Way to Language*, trans. Peter D. Hertz (New York: Harper and Row, 1971), p. 108.
22 See, for example, Noam Chomsky, *Topics in the Theory of Generative Grammar* (The Hague: Mouton, 1966), pp. 11–12.

7 Levinas, feminism and the feminine

Why is it that Levinas's work has attracted so much – and such varied – feminist attention? One answer turns on a historical co-incidence. Philosophical interest in Levinas's work, especially in the anglophone world, blossomed spectacularly in the late 1980s and early 1990s, the years which also saw the first full flowering of 'feminist philosophy', a strange and sometimes exotic plant that has still to establish itself in the academy. Given the intellectual climate (which has now chilled considerably), it would have been surprising if there had been no feminist interest in Levinas.

However, there is also an explanation particular to Levinas's work itself, and one which explains why it was already drawing feminist fire as early as 1949, in Simone de Beauvoir's magnificent and omnivorous study *The Second Sex*. In a move which he may or may not have lived to regret, Levinas chose to make a discussion of what he called 'the feminine' central, or at least integral, to much of his work from the 1940s up to and including *Totality and Infinity* in 1961. Although there has been feminist interest in other aspects of Levinas's work, I will restrict myself here to a discussion of the role and the nature of 'the feminine' as he understands it and the main features of the feminist controversies that this has provoked. For 'the feminine' is a term that has attracted vastly different – indeed diametrically opposed – responses from feminists, ranging from the wholly affirmative to the absolutely dismissive. Reading the feminist responses to Levinas within the terms of a debate over the meaning of the feminine, I will conclude with a suggestion for an alternative contemporary feminist reading.[1]

INTRODUCING SEXUAL DIFFERENCE

Tracking the idea of the feminine through Levinas's work is complicated by the fact that it is co-emergent, although not co-extensive, with other important themes. In wending its sinuous way through Levinas's texts in relation to these themes its place and role also changes considerably over time. Its first discussion occurs in *Existence and Existents* (published in 1947, but composed, Levinas says, some years earlier) in conjunction with an attempt to think 'sexual difference' or 'the difference between the sexes' (*la différence des sexes*) in the context of 'eros' (*EE* 95). (The Platonic terminology already signals the primarily philosophical – as opposed to anthropological or sociological – interpretation that the erotic relation will receive.) Both *Existence and Existents* and *Time and the Other* (also 1947) are preoccupied with the idea that the being of the subject is fundamentally a burden to it, an imprisonment to which all attempts to escape in the direction of the exterior (in intentional relations towards objects) inevitably return. This problem of the transcendence of the subject (arguably still the driving force of *Totality and Infinity* in 1961) would be resolved if not solved in a relation with an alterity that remained absolutely other and yet allowed the subject to retain its identity (that is, not be annihilated as it would be in the 'relation' with death). This is, of course, the relation with *autrui*, the other, the impossible description of which Levinas would attempt – in the Husserlian spirit of infinite recommencement – for the next forty years.

In *Existence and Existents* the relation with the other – or 'intersubjectivity' as he calls it there – is revealed to us in eros. It is not, however, in the erotic quality of the relation itself that its essential asymmetry is located, but rather in the sexual heterogeneity of those related, in the formal structure of sexual difference itself. In what reads as an ironic repetition of the opening paragraphs of *Being and Time*, Levinas cites Heidegger's philosophical misdescription of sexual difference in order to elaborate, through contrast, his own claim. Heidegger is charged with having failed to recognize the 'peculiar form of the contraries and contradictions of eros' because of his tendency to understand 'the difference between the sexes as a specification of a genus' (*EE* 96); that is, 'male' and 'female' would be 'species' of the genus (the general category) 'sex'. Failing to understand the extraordinary – possibly even unique – nature of the subject matter Heidegger fails to see the ontological priority of the question of sexual difference and hence fails to raise the question of the meaning of eros in its originality and profundity. For Levinas, on the other hand, eros understood properly is important phenomenologically in its revelation of the originality of sexual difference: the Ur-form of difference.

It makes sense to think of Levinas as attempting here to carve out a new space for the Heideggerian insistence on ontological differ-ence, located now not between Being and beings but between beings themselves (the 'existents' of the title of the book in English). This ontological difference between existents resists being characterized as a merely ontic difference (as Heidegger, perhaps, would have seen it) by virtue of its specific content: the asymmetry of a specifically *sexual* difference. Perhaps because of this very asymmetry, Levinas then elaborates on this sexual difference from a one-sided perspective on its content, such that sexed alterity (or the other *par excellence*) appears as 'the feminine' (*EE* 85).

This position is more fully worked out in *Time and the Other*, where the transcendence of the subject is, again, accomplished in the relation with the other, prototypically in eros. The originality of eros is located in the experience of the *sexed alterity* of the other:

Does a situation exist where the alterity of the other appears in its purity? Does a situation exist where the other would not have alterity only as the reverse side of its identity, would not comply only with the Platonic law of participation where every term contains a sameness and through this sameness contains the other? Is there not a situation where alterity would be borne by a being in a positive sense, as essence? What is the alterity that does not purely and simply enter into the opposition of two species of the same genus? I think that the absolutely contrary contrary [*le contraire absolument contraire*], whose contrariety is in no way affected by the relationship that can be established between it and its correlative, the contrariety that permits its terms to remain absolutely other, is the *feminine*.

Sex is not some specific difference. It is situated beside the logical division into genera and species. This division certainly never manages to reunite an empirical content. But it is not in this sense that it does not permit one to account for the difference between the sexes. The difference between the sexes is a formal structure, but one that carves up reality in another sense and conditions the very possibility of reality as multiple, against the unity of being proclaimed by Parmenides. [*TO* 85]

Searching for the possibility of a relation with the other in which the subject is neither returned to itself nor annihilated, the erotic relation is posited as primordial because the erotic relation is assumed to be heterosexual. The Levinasian subject, coded masculine or male (the Anglo-American sex/gender distinction blurs in French) finds himself in the erotic relation face-to-face with alterity itself – the feminine. This is an experience with philosophical significance in so far as it highlights the formal structure of sexual difference as an opening on to the possibility of transcendence. At the same time, the disjunctive relationship between the two terms of sexual difference – the moment, precisely, of difference – is the condition of possibility of ontological difference itself.

The feminist response to Levinas's early discussions of the feminine was swift. In a footnote to the introduction of *The Second Sex*, de Beauvoir's description of the relations between the sexes as one in which man is posited as the Absolute, the subject, and woman as the other is justified and illustrated with reference to Levinas, quoting those passages from *Time and the Other* in which the prototypical alterity of the feminine is affirmed.[2] At first sight this would seem to be a misinterpretation, fudging the distinction between the place of the other in Levinas's philosophy and de Beauvoir's quite different (Sartrean) category. More recent readers of Levinas have not been slow to point this out, and a tendency has developed which aims not just to defend Levinas but to make a positive case for a possible feminist appropriation of his work; specifically, of the category of the feminine.[3] The most recent – and in some ways most extreme – example of this tendency is found in Bracha Lichtenberg-Ettinger's conversations with Levinas. Characteristically reticent on the subject of the feminine in his later years, Levinas warns Lichtenberg-Ettinger:

Best to make only a few allusions to the subject of the difference of the feminine ... Above all do not commit yourself too much and do not exhaust this theme too far; you will be attacked, they will say that you have said too much or not enough. It would be better for you not to become entirely involved, stay on the edge. You see, the feminists have often attacked me ... [WES 22]

Lichtenberg-Ettinger, however, insists that 'your [Levinas's] philosophy will be more and more central for talking about difference and the alterity of the feminine, and that we have not really measured its potential in this matter' (WES 22). If Lichtenberg-Ettinger persists, in spite of Levinas's unwillingness and even embarrassment in speaking of the feminine, it is because she discerns an opportunity for a radical reconsideration of the place of 'the feminine' in the history of Western philosophy and in the theoretical discourses (particularly, psychoanalysis) which the latter has spawned.

To explain why this reconsideration should be considered necessary, it is instructive to turn to the work of Luce Irigaray. Viewed from the standpoint of Irigaray's history of Western philosophy, there is a sense in which the foregrounding of the alterity of the feminine in Levinas's early work is an extraordinary move. Apparently using Levinas's terminology, Irigaray claims that it is precisely the alterity of the feminine that has been the victim of philosophy's most systematic enterprise of the reduction to sameness:

Now this domination of the philosophic logos stems in large part from its power *to reduce all others to the economy of the Same.* The teleologically constructive project it takes on is always also a project of diversion, deflection, reduction of the other in the same. And, in its greatest generality perhaps, *of eradication of the difference between the sexes* in systems that are self-representative of a 'masculine subject'.[4]

For Irigaray, the reduction of *sexual* difference to a 'neutral' economy of the same has been the most persistent crime of Western philosophy, and 'it is precisely philosophical discourse that we have to challenge, and *disrupt*, inasmuch as this discourse sets forth the law for all others, inasmuch as it constitutes the discourse on discourse'.[5] If for Heidegger the most pressing question was the question of the meaning of Being, for Levinas it was the question of the other. For Irigaray the question of the other becomes primarily the question of the sexed other or of sexual difference, since it is this difference that has, historically, suffered maximum erasure.[6] The neutralization of sexual difference has, however, taken a peculiar form. Historically, the reduction of sexual difference has been the reduction of the *feminine* other to what Irigaray calls the 'masculine' economy of the same. This economy of the same is not mediated through a neutral term but through the criterion of the masculine itself (hence the allegedly generic use of the masculine pronoun – 'he' – and of the supposedly inclusive 'man'). Within this economy the feminine other is not thought in her alterity or specificity *qua* feminine but only as the dependent opposite of the masculine, the not-masculine. In effect, 'the feminine' translates as the inferior of the masculine, the copy of the original masculine, the pathologized masculine, the castrated masculine and so on.

For Irigaray, then, 'the masculine' refers to that which represents a specious universality in the eclipsed field of sexual difference, that which dissimulates, or does not name, its own difference; an allegedly universal value against which everything (feminine) is to be judged.[7] The feminine is accordingly, for Irigaray, both (1) the traditional representation of the opposite/derivative of the masculine, subordinated to it and its standard, and (2) something posited as incommensurable with the masculine philosophy of the same, something other than the masculine. Irigaray's contention is that, with very few exceptions, the feminine has only been thought within the history of Western philosophy as (1). A possible point of intersection with Levinas is obvious. Levinas's most fundamental assertion that the other has not been thought *as* other, but only as the not-same, becomes Irigaray's fundamental assertion that the *feminine* other has not been thought *as* feminine other, but only as the not-masculine. It is thus clear why Levinas's insistence, in *Existence and Existents* for example, on the dimension of sexual difference in eros might be so important. In saying that it is in eros that the possibility of a radical thinking of transcendence arises, he says that it is in eros that the other is revealed *as* other. Furthermore, he claims that eros reveals the other *par excellence* to be the feminine, or that eros reveals the structure of sexual difference in its radicality. Levinas would seem, therefore, in accordance with Irigaray's feminist demands, to have introduced the thought of the feminine other *as feminine other*, in her difference, or to have attempted to think the question of sexual difference in its radicality.[8]

THE CHANGING FACE OF THE FEMININE

However, for many feminist readers, including Irigaray herself, the possibility of a feminist appropriation of Levinas's category of the feminine is undermined by the more complete descriptions, in *Time and the Other*, and most especially *Totality and Infinity*, of the feminine and its/her role in the 'economy' of lived life according to the

novel analyses of those books. The second of the four sections of
Totality and Infinity, 'Interiority and Economy', is a phenomenological description of the being-in-the-world of *le moi*, or the ego. In
contrast to the following section, 'Exteriority and the Face', it seems
to describe the fundamental relation of the ego to its environment
before the irruption of the other, that is, before the ethical relation.[9]

For Levinas a condition for, or an essential characteristic of, the
ethical relation is the fact of the so-called 'separation' of the ego. The
first half of section II describes this separated ego – the dimension
of interiority or 'psychism' – and its relation to the world primarily in terms of *jouissance* (translated by Lingis as 'enjoyment') and
vivre de ... a 'living from ...' in which the world and the things in it
are not conceived as objects or themes for the ego, but rather 'nour-
ish' it in a relation of happy dependence. Able to fulfil its needs, the
happy ego lives – loving life – as if there were no tomorrow, for the
sake only of enjoyment, consuming and negating the otherness of its
nourishments. There *is*, however, a tomorrow, concern for the uncertainties of which must be addressed today by engaging in relations
with (rather than incorporation/annihilation of) exteriority, raising
oneself, according to Levinas, from the condition of the beasts. These
uncertainties will be overcome in work and the gathering of possessions, but these in turn have their own requirement:

In order that this future arise in its signification as a postponement and a
delay in which *labour*, by mastering the uncertainty of the future and its in-
security and by establishing *possession*, delineates separation in the form of
economic independence, the separated being must be able to recollect itself
[*se receuillir*] and have representations. *Recollection* and *representation* are
produced concretely as *habitation in a dwelling* or a Home. [*TI* 150]

The intimacy of the home is itself assured through the welcome
of the other, revealed not, however, as a shocking alterity but as
'gentleness'. This gentle other is 'the feminine'. At first blush this
would seem to be an echo of the feminine from Levinas's earlier
work – *Autrui* par excellence. But in *Totality and Infinity* her alterity
is immediately qualified. There is a contradiction in the idea that the
gentle welcome, which makes the separation of the human possible,
comes from 'a first revelation of the Other', for as Levinas himself
explains a few pages later, according to the analysis of section I the

other *disrupts* the solitude of the ego, it does not produce it; it is the other that paradigmatically *prevents* the return to self.

The overcoming of this contradiction lies in the description of an other who does not simply reveal itself in/as face, but who simultaneously withdraws and is absent, a simultaneity called 'discretion'. This other is woman: 'And the other whose presence is discreetly an absence, with which is accomplished the primary hospitable welcome which describes the field of intimacy, is the Woman. The woman is the condition for recollection, the interiority of the Home, and inhabitation.' This face-to-face is not a relation that opens up the dimension of height, or transcendence. Such a relation (ethics), 'co-extensive with the manifestation of the Other in the face, we call language. The height from which language comes we designate with the term teaching' (*TI* 171). The other who affords a welcome in the home, however, is

not the *You* [*le Vous*] of the face that reveals itself in a dimension of height, but precisely the *thou* [*le tu*] of familiarity: a language without teaching, a silent language, an understanding without words, an expression in secret. The I–Thou in which Buber sees the category of interhuman relationship is the relation not with the interlocutor but with feminine alterity. [*TI* 155]

Elsewhere, on more than one occasion, Levinas is keen to distance himself from Buber's *je–tu* relation precisely because that relation, in its intimacy and exclusiveness, does not have the dimension of exteriority that would make it ethical.[10] The *tu* of this relation is not the *vous* of the ethical relation, does not command the same respect. Aligning the feminine other with Buber's *tu* amounts, therefore, to an admission that the feminine other is not a 'true' other.[11]

The status of this qualified feminine other is then problematic. *La Femme*, 'wife' as well as 'woman', does not recollect, she is a condition for another's recollection. She is enough of an other to fulfil her function as welcomer and household settler, but not so other that she unsettles the ego; an other domesticated and rendered docile (*TI* 155).[12] And while she apparently exercises her function of interiorization only on the ground of a 'full human personality', this is a full human personality 'which, however, in the woman, can be reserved so as to open up the dimension of interiority'. In opening up the dimension of interiority the woman makes it possible for the subject to labour and acquire property. Furthermore, in order that I am able to free myself from the very possession that the welcome of the Home establishes, in order that I be able to see things in themselves, that is, represent them to myself, refuse both enjoyment and possession, I must know how to *give* what I possess... But for this I must encounter the indiscreet face of the Other that calls me into question. The Other – the absolutely other – paralyses possession, which he contests by his epiphany in the face... I welcome the Other who presents himself in my home by opening my home to him. [*TI* 170–1]

La femme, therefore, is the condition for the ethical relation, but is not herself part of it.[13]

Now, this frank and unself-conscious account of the nature and the place of the feminine in *Totality and Infinity* is gratingly patriarchal. Read in conjunction with the descriptions of the feminine in the 'Phenomenology of Eros' in section IV of *Totality and Infinity* the feminist case for Levinas does not look good:

The feminine essentially violable and inviolable, the 'Eternal Feminine', is the virgin or an incessant recommencement of virginity... The beloved [*L'aimée*], returned to the stage of infancy without responsibility – this co-quettish head, this youth, this pure life 'a bit silly' [*un peu bête*] – has quit her status as a person... The relations with the [feminine] Other are enacted in play; one plays with the Other as with a young animal. [*TI* 258–9]

Although the framework of the earlier (positive) appropriative tendency was couched in Irigarayan terms, Irigaray has in fact been one of the most eloquent feminist critics of Levinas's characterization of the feminine. In 'The Fecundity of the Caress', for example, Irigaray reads Levinas's phenomenology of eros as suggestive of various possibilities which remain undeveloped or are immediately closed off, textually. In particular, Irigaray admires the descriptions of the erotic caress for their privileging of touch over vision, and, implicitly, for the emphasis on incarnation or bodily subjectivity ('they love each other like the bodies they are').[14] However, Irigaray objects, *inter alia*, to the reduction of the feminine in the economy of interiority to a means to an end, to the condition of *another's* possibilities (not her own), and ultimately to the status of object, or at least a non-subject reduced (in the phenomenology of eros) to infancy and/or animality. In so far as she speaks explicitly of the feminine in Levinas, Irigaray places Levinas firmly within the 'masculine economy of the same' which his defenders read him as rejecting. The same is also true in 'Questions to Emmanuel Levinas': 'The feminine, as it is characterized by Levinas, is not other than himself ... The feminine is apprehended not in relation to itself, but from the point of view of man.'[15] The most Irigaray is prepared to concede is, again, that the texts open up a *possibility* (of the approach to the – truly – other sex), but one which they themselves nevertheless reject.

But all, it seems, is not necessarily lost, and Levinas opens the case for the defence himself. Already in *Totality and Infinity*, as if to anticipate future objections, Levinas adds the following disclaimer to his discussion of the dwelling and its feminine welcome:

> Need one add that there is no question here of defying ridicule by maintaining the empirical truth or countertruth that every home *in fact* presupposes a woman? The feminine has been encountered in this analysis as one of the cardinal points of the horizon in which the inner life takes place – and the empirical absence of the human being of 'feminine sex' in a dwelling nowise affects the dimension of femininity which remains open there, as the very welcome of the dwelling. [*TI* 157–8]

With this Levinas clearly rejects the idea that the notion of 'the feminine' refers to empirical women, but offers only a very weak definition instead ('a cardinal point of the horizon in which the inner life takes place'). As the field of interpretation is therefore left wide open, some commentators have taken Levinas's disclaimer in *Totality and Infinity* to be a simple statement of the intended metaphorical meaning of the feminine, separating it out from any reference to literal (empirical) women and thereby, presumably, hoping to neutralize the feminist critique. Adriaan Peperzak, for example, glosses Levinas's words thus: 'we must understand that the "feminine" presence by which a building becomes a home is a metaphor for the discreet and silent presence of human beings for one another that creates a climate of intimacy indispensable for a dwelling'.[16] The presumption, therefore, of this interpretation is that defending Levinas's discussion of the feminine from feminist critique – if not going quite so far as to maintain the possibility of anything like a specifically feminist appropriation of it; a damage limitation exercise – depends on its being distanced from any reference to empirical women.

CAN THERE BE A FEMINIST 'FEMININE'?

Taking an overview of the feminist responses so far, two distinct tendencies, corresponding roughly to Levinas's earlier (*Existence and*

Existents, Time and the Other) and later (*Totality and Infinity*) texts, have emerged: first, an affirmative feminist will-to-appropriation of the category of the feminine; second, a feminist apology for the category of the feminine, in the sense of a formal defence. The two positions pull interestingly against each other at the level of their construal of the constitutive relations between the feminine as a philosophical category and what we will now, in anticipation of a future argument, sceptically call 'empirical women'. The first must assume some such relation in order to construe itself as a feminist position at all, while the second must *deny* it in order to construe itself in the same way. Can they both be right? If not, can they both be 'feminist' positions?

At first glance, this conflict of interpretation of the relation between the feminine and empirical women can be reproduced as a conflict between the appropriative feminist readers of Levinas and Levinas's own intentions in the early texts. If Levinas's earlier discussions of the feminine are to do the *feminist* work his readers want them to do, the relation between the philosophical category and its associated empirical content (its reference, in some sense, to women) must be affirmed. For Levinas, however, in order for the category to do the *philosophical* work he wants it to do, the relation between the philosophical category and its ostensible empirical content must, on the contrary, be denied so that the structure of sexual difference can play its purely formal role.

The fate of the feminine in Levinas's later work, however, is best understood in terms of Levinas's implicit acknowledgement of the impossibility of the separation of the philosophical category of the feminine and the formal structure of sexual difference from its empirical referent. What apparently allows sexual difference to perform its function in the early texts is also what compromises it: the specific *content* of sexed alterity.[17] That this content is crucial is evident in Levinas's slippage from the formal structure of sexual difference to what he will call the 'alterity content' of the feminine. In itself, the idea of sexual difference carries no phenomenological force. The idea of sexual difference must go down, as it were, to the level of eros, to the heterosexual erotic relation of one with another, and from this perspective the phenomenological subject must be sexed in order to experience the other as differently sexed. Unlike Hegel's 'phenomenologist', who as 'we' is meant to be universal, who sees and describes from a point of view above the fray, Levinas's lover has to *be there*, he has to *do it*. As this is a story told by a (heterosexual) man, alterity will be the feminine; the feminine – concretely – will be the other. But this being the case, sexual difference no longer functions as an abstract *formal* structure; it is identified with the *content* of the feminine – which in this context (the actual erotic relation between beings of different sexes) only makes sense with a reference to empirical women – and is compromised or swallowed up by it in such a way that it can no longer perform its metaphysical function. The feminine *is* the content of sexual difference – or sexual difference *is* feminine content: in this identity sexual difference becomes absorbed, immanent to its content, and the formal structure of difference which articulated/produced the possibility of transcendence is lost. By the time of *Totality and Infinity*, and in all of Levinas's work thereafter, sexual difference is no longer originary, eros is no longer the prototypical relation with the other, and the feminine is either given a different role or sidelined entirely.

Ultimately, then, Levinas's feminist readers are right to assume (even if they do not explain) the relationship between the philosophical category of the feminine and empirical women, although it is still the case that what makes the discussion *work* for some feminist readers is precisely what makes it *fail* for Levinas, and what explains the gradual de-emphasis on the feminine, sexual difference and eros in the progression of Levinas's philosophical career. Throughout these changes, moreover, one very problematic presumption remains intact: the identification of the feminine with sexual difference.

This identification is a commonplace of pre- and anti-feminist thinking, the flip side of the presumption of the unmarked neutrality or humanity of the masculine from which the feminine is then derived as supplementary or as a perversion. One sees it particularly clearly in Levinas's 1972 essay 'And God Created Woman'. Here Levinas reads both versions of the Biblical creation myth (one implying simultaneous creation of man and woman, the other the creation of woman from man) as affirming the priority of the human over the significance of the sexual difference of the human. Not only does this rescind the priority of sexual difference and the place of the feminine in his earlier work, it reaffirms the priority of the masculine that Levinas's feminist advocates would read him as overturning. He says, for example, that the meaning of the feminine will emerge 'against the background of a human essence, the *Isha* [woman] from the *Ish* [man]. The feminine does not derive from the masculine; rather, the division into feminine and masculine – the dichotomy – derives from what is human' (*NTR* 167–8).[18] This would only be right, however, if it were indeed the case that the Hebrew *Ish*, man, and its counterpart in numerous languages, really did refer to the neutrality of the human, and was not compromised by the rather obvious fact that it is also the designation of the masculine man. Recognizing this, Levinas concedes that there is a certain priority of the masculine, representing the human, over the feminine, representing sexual difference, but

[i]t is not woman who is thus slighted. It is the relation based on sexual difference which is subordinated to the interhuman relation ... Maybe man precedes – by a few centuries – the woman in this elevation. From which a certain – provisional? – priority of man. Maybe the masculine is more directly linked to the universal, and maybe masculine civilization has prepared, above the sexual, a human order in which a woman enters, completely human. (*NTR* 174, 177)

There is surely very little that the feminist appropriators of Levinas's category of the feminine can salvage here. But even ignoring passages such as this and concentrating on the remarks in Levinas's earlier work, any attempt to maintain a feminist reading would have to account for the effective identification there of the feminine with sexual difference, and explain how this does not repeat the privileging of the masculine that such an identification has, historically, entailed.

It is only left for the appropriative feminist reading of Levinas to refuse to acquiesce with the various unacceptable elements of his discussion of the feminine and to promote a reconceived and repositioned category of the feminine free of the unwanted baggage. Thus eviscerated, however, the resultant conception of the feminine cannot claim to be *Levinasian* at all. In fact, the category of 'the feminine' functions with a variety of often unexplicated but very different meanings in many contemporary feminist discourses.[19] The failure to distinguish between these meanings is also, I would argue, the cause of the misidentification of the category in Levinas's work. Lichtenberg-Ettinger, for example, seems to assume that Levinas's 'feminine' can slip between the specific context of his philosophical work and her own psychoanalytic framework, when the word has for Levinas *none* of the modern psychoanalytic meaning which – with acknowledged differences between authors – refers primarily to a subject position within the symbolic order. Taking all of this into account, the feminist appropriation of Levinas's category of the feminine begins to look like a very thin position. If it were to remain faithful to Levinas's complete descriptions of the feminine such a position would need to explain in what sense it still deserved to be thought of as a *feminist* position. The appropriative literature does not do this. Or, distancing itself from most of what Levinas says about the feminine and from most of the implications of his discussion, filling up with assumptions about and ideas on the feminine from other, often incompatible, discourses, it cannot claim to be a *Levinasian* position in any significant sense.

APOLOGIZING FOR THE FEMININE

It is interesting that in the relatively short preface added to the 1979 edition of *Time and the Other*, Levinas devotes a disproportionate amount of space to the feminine and its attendant themes compared to the length of the discussion in the original text. Perhaps aware of the feminist responses to the treatment of the feminine here and in his later work Levinas says the following of *Time and the Other*:

The notion of a transcendent alterity – one which would open time – is first of all sought starting with an *alterity-content*, starting with femininity. Femininity – and one would have to see in what sense this can be said of masculinity or of virility; that is, of the differences between the sexes in general – appeared to me as a difference contrasting strongly with other differences, not merely as a quality, different from all others, but as the very quality of difference. [*TO* 36]

With this (belated) suggestion of the possibility of a reversal of terms Levinas would seem to be attempting to reinscribe the formal structure of sexual difference in its metaphysical function. The previous emphasis on the feminine could now be seen as merely contingent upon a masculine subject position. If 'the masculine' could function in the same way for a feminine subject, both positions could be reinterpreted on the basis of 'the differences between the sexes in general', an abstract metaphysical principle to which both would have access and of which both would have phenomenological attestation in the experience of their sexual counterpart.[20] However, it is difficult to see how this arrangement is possible without understanding 'the difference between the sexes' in terms of the specifications of a genus – the exact move for which Heidegger was earlier criticized. This would be, moreover, to ascribe to the relation between the sexes a structure of symmetry and reciprocity that would negate the philosophical work that the formal (apparently asymmetrical) structure is meant to do.

But the suggestion of the possibility of reversal is disingenuous anyway. It overlooks the extent to which the association of the feminine with sexual difference is not so much an accident in Levinas's early texts as a fundamental presupposition, an important component of the definition of the feminine in so far as that term may be employed functionally at all. To the extent that this conflation is a historical (theoretical and cultural) commonplace it is easy for it to pass unnoticed. The attempt to re-present the feminine as a term occupying a space which may, under other circumstances, be filled by the masculine, is an attempt to void it of its particular content and make it function as a general signifier of sex, while at the same time disavowing the historical association of the masculine with the unsexed universal or neuter. The suggestion – parenthetical and phrased in the most tentative, even sceptical, manner – is also disingenuous in another sense. Despite this apparent reinvigoration of the idea in the 1979 preface, the formal structure of sexual difference drops out of Levinas's work after *Time and the Other*, except when used in negative comparison with the structure of the relation of 'ethics'. Read carefully, this passage from the preface says as much, in its use of the past tense.

The presumption of the possibility of reversal is also tacitly at play in the second tendency identified above: the feminist apology for the category of the feminine. This second position, as mentioned, consists in the denial of the relation between the category and its *ostensible* empirical content; its major weapon is the metaphor argument. If the interpretation of the feminine as a metaphor is compelling it is because readers of a philosophy such as Levinas's are accustomed to understand words in other than their common or everyday meanings (for example 'care' in Heidegger, 'nausea' in Sartre, 'flesh' in Merleau-Ponty). Even so, quite what it means to claim a metaphorical status for the feminine is unclear. One cannot, for

example, argue that *as a metaphor* the trope of the feminine has no
connection whatsoever, no linguistic or cultural reference at all, to
empirically existing women, as this would deprive the metaphor not
just of its rhetorical force, but of its very sense. Derrida, surprisingly,
overlooks this in *Adieu to Emmanuel Levinas*, when he claims that
while the description of the feminine in section II of *Totality and
Infinity* means that the text may be read as 'a sort of feminist man-
ifesto', the feminine must nevertheless be distinguished from 'the
fact of empirical women'.[21] In this context, the rather obvious point
that the feminine is meant to function as a philosophical category –
that it is not meant to refer only to an empirical content – fudges the
issue. It neither acknowledges that there *is* still some connection,
nor gives any attempt to explain what it might be, while also failing
to consider what the relation *needs to be* in order for there to be any
positive feminist implication. Such remarks are also forced to over-
look the fact that Levinas speaks just as often in *Totality and Infinity*
of *la Femme*. The alterity which opens the dimension of interiority
only does so, he says, 'on the ground of the full human personality
which, in the woman, can be reserved'. This is a statement that it is
very difficult to read metaphorically, or to distance from 'the *fact* of
empirical women'.

So far, however, both the feminist apology and these objections to it
have presupposed a rather simplified account of the relation between
the literal and the metaphorical. John Llewelyn's more sophisticated
account of metaphoricity – one that does not need to deny the relation between the metaphor and its reference to empirical women –
throws new light on the discussion. Llewelyn's reading of Levinas's
category of the feminine is a much more nuanced apology. Alive – indeed sympathetic – to the possibility of a feminist critique, Llewelyn
argues that 'certain avoidable difficulties, though by no means all
difficulties, will be circumvented' if the reader is continually reminded ('it cannot be too often repeated') that the feminine and other
familial terms are not reducible to their biological signification.[22]
For Llewelyn, however, this does not amount to any simple distinction between the literality of the biological ground of the trope
of the feminine and its metaphorical employment. Llewelyn's discussion of Levinas is informed by Derrida's influential deconstruction of the presumed opposition between literal ground or origin
and metaphorical derivation in 'White Mythology'.[23] Furthermore,

Llewelyn quotes Levinas quoting Karl Löwith quoting Bruno Snell to the effect that, in Llewelyn's words, 'instead of thinking of the extended or metaphorical as opposed to the literal or natural we should think of each use as an extension or "metaphor" of the other'.[24] Applied to the notion of the feminine, this means that one could – perhaps even should – equally understand what Llewelyn calls the 'biological signification' as the metaphorical one.

However, neither the assertion of the metaphorical status of the feminine (Peperzak) nor the problematization of the literal/metaphorical (Llewelyn) actually deals with the central problem of the relation between the notion of the feminine and actual women. In distancing the feminine from any empirical or sociological referent, Levinas is not primarily asserting its metaphoricity but rather its status as a philosophical category. In *Time and the Other* and *Existence and Existents* the feminine is explicitly introduced as an ontological category that introduces a plurality into Being itself. And the feminine in section II of *Totality and Infinity* is still, Levinas would insist, a philosophical category. As the condition of possibility for interiority and so on, one might understand its philosophical function as analogous to the relationship between actual historical experience and the 'experience' of consciousness in Hegel's *Phenomenology*. The text need not be understood literally. In reading philosophically a certain level of abstraction is constitutive. However, the feminine is not a category so abstract that it can function *wholly* in abstraction from the content that distinguishes it from a merely functional 'X'. This is true for both immanent and external reasons; that is, both because the intimately welcoming role of the feminine would be negated by the impersonality of an 'X', and because the feminine, as a word or a concept, is only meaningful (and hence only available for use) in terms of its descriptive and/or ideological content. This is why, of course, it is precisely the feminine and not 'the masculine' or 'the androgynous' that plays the role of welcoming gentleness.

Llewelyn's much more sustained engagement with the question of the feminine through the problematization of metaphoricity does not avoid this conclusion; indeed it supports it. Levinas's reference to Snell, which Llewelyn quotes, concerns Snell's comments on a Homeric comparison between the resistance of an army to attack and the resistance of a rock to water. The meaning of resistance,

Snell apparently writes, cannot be assigned originally or naturally to either the human or the rock (that is, the meaning 'belongs' to neither literally, to be transferred to the other metaphorically). In Levinas's words: 'Resistance is neither a human privilege nor a rock's, just as radiance does not characterize a day of the month of May more authentically than it does the face of a woman. The meaning precedes the data [les données] and illuminates them' (BPW 37). If Levinas perhaps says more with the last line than Snell means, it is this 'more' that is interesting. It would mean, for example, that the meaning of the notion of the feminine does not derive unilaterally from empirical women but precedes our understanding of the latter (presumably ideologically) and illuminates it. The difficulty of arguing for a separation between the feminine in its philosophical employment and its reference to empirical women is thus compounded because how we understand what it is to be an empirical woman is influenced – to some extent, that is, constituted – by this (and other) notions of the feminine. The apologetic readings – just because they are apologetic – do not think through the implications of this imbrication of the notion of the feminine and empirical women even when (as in Llewelyn's reading) they highlight the imbrication itself. While aiming to protect Levinas from feminist critique they therefore fail in what one might see as a primary feminist task in philosophy: investigating the often hidden ideological content of philosophical categories and their role in a philosophical text or œuvre.

WHAT NOW FOR LEVINAS AND FEMINISM?

From one angle, the feminist reception of great thinkers in the philosophical canon – especially in the so-called Continental tradition – has tended to pivot around the question of whether any given figure could provide a theoretical 'resource' for feminism. The reception of Levinas has been particularly invited in this respect because the resources allegedly on offer in his work appear as themes or ideas or even a subject matter already recognizable to feminist theory: the feminine, sexual difference, maternity and so on. As I have tried to show, the appropriative feminist tendency does not, however, succeed in explaining, beyond the mere coincidence of words (which is not even a coincidence of terminology), (1) how Levinas's invocation of the feminine is not irremediably compromised by the details of its conventionally patriarchal characterization, its identification with sexual difference as secondary to the human, and its exclusion from the ethical; and (2) how any thinking of the feminine which excludes all of the above is in any sense Levinasian or otherwise indebted to Levinas. The more general problem with such readings – but also the condition of their possibility – is the failure to distinguish between the various senses of 'the feminine' currently circulating in feminist and other discourses; the failure, for example, to distinguish between the use of the term in Levinas, Irigaray, Lacanian psychoanalysis and so on.

The apologetic readings similarly elide the details and therefore the peculiarity of Levinas's discussions of the feminine. They are forced, in particular, to evacuate the feminine of its specific content in a way that deprives it of the possibility of performing its role in Levinas's philosophy or to make claims about the (mostly, metaphorical) status of the term which deflects attention from the role that the term plays. There have been, in this vein, creative reinterpretations of the meaning and the role of the feminine, but like the appropriative readings they have difficulty claiming to be speaking of the feminine *in Levinas's sense* any more. If, therefore, one were to ask whether the thinking of the feminine in Levinas's philosophy could provide resources for feminism, I think the answer would have to be 'no'.

But there is an awful lot more to feminist reading than this, and many reasons why feminists might want to continue to read Levinas. Levinas's texts and the various feminist responses to them reveal – more or less wittingly – intriguing things about the ways in which we think about certain phenomena and suggest intriguing possibilities for rethinking them. For example, the debate about the status of the idea of the feminine leads Llewelyn to consider the nature of metaphoricity. The impossibility of separating out the purely metaphorical form of the idea from its empirical referent not only problematizes the apologetic defence of Levinas, it problematizes the terms involved on both sides, as it were, of the metaphor. The idea of empirical 'women', we may then conclude, is no more purely empirical than the idea of 'the feminine' is purely metaphorical, and there is no purely empirical ground to which one can then refer the metaphor of 'women' (even the idea of 'sex difference' would have its metaphorical element). The categories of 'man' and 'woman' would then be very far from being the natural kinds that we mostly tend to assume they are; sex difference would be much more complicated than our binary presumptions would suggest.[25] That would be very far from anything that Levinas intended when he began his meditations on the feminine and sexual difference. Nevertheless, it is one of its implications.

NOTES

1 Much of the argument of this paper is drawn from ch. 2 of my *The Metaphysics of Love: Gender and Transcendence in Levinas* (London: Continuum, 2000).

2 Simone de Beauvoir, *The Second Sex*, trans. H. M. Parshley (London: Picador, 1988), p. 16; *Le deuxième sexe* (Paris: Gallimard, 1949), p. 15.

3 For defences of Levinas against de Beauvoir see, for example, Richard A. Cohen's footnote to his translation of the offending passage in *TO* 85 (n. 69); Susan A. Handelman, *Fragments of Redemption* (Indianapolis: Indiana University Press, 1991), p. 206; Tina Chanter, 'Feminism and the Other', in Robert Bernasconi and David Wood (eds), *The Provocation of Levinas* (London: Routledge, 1988), pp. 35–6, 52–3; Robert John Scheffler Manning, 'Thinking the Other Without Violence? An Analysis of the Relation Between the Philosophy of Emmanuel Levinas and Feminism', *Journal of Speculative Philosophy*, 5, 2 (1991), p. 136.

4 Luce Irigaray, *This Sex Which is Not One*, trans. Catherine Porter (Ithaca: Cornell University Press, 1985), p. 74 (translation modified); *Ce sexe qui n'en est pas un* (Paris: Editions de Minuit, 1977), p. 72.

5 *Ibid.*

6 See, for example, Irigaray, *Je, tu, nous: Toward a Culture of Difference*, trans. Alison Martin (London: Routledge, 1990), p. 15; *Je, tu, nous. Pour une culture de la différance* (Paris: Grasset, 1990), p. 13.

7 Despite Irigaray's identification of de Beauvoir as *the* exponent of 'equality feminism' (as opposed to the feminism of difference, which sees the aim of the achievement of equality as an attempt to make women the same as men), Irigaray's definition of the masculine is remarkably similar to some of de Beauvoir's comments in the Introduction to *The Second Sex*:

> The terms *masculine* and *feminine* are used symmetrically only as a matter of form, as in municipal registers and declarations of identity. The relation of the two sexes is not like that of two electrical poles: man represents both the positive and the neutral, as is indicated by the way one says in French '*les hommes*' to designate human beings in general and in the assimilation of the particular meaning

of the word *'vir'* to the general meaning of *'homo'*. Woman appears as the negative, such that all determination is understood in relation to her as limitation, without reciprocity. [p. 15, translation modified; *Le deuxième sexe*, p. 14]

8 Tina Chanter's work on Levinas and the feminine has sometimes argued for this reading. See, for example, 'Feminism and the Other', p. 52: 'Levinas's account of the Other provides feminism with a voice that many feminists have already begun to seek', and 'Antigone's Dilemma', in Robert Bernasconi and Simon Critchley (eds.), *Re-Reading Levinas* (London: Athlone, 1991), p. 134: 'By singling out the feminine Levinas makes clear that he is concerned to wrest it from the oblivion to which it has been subjected, and to invest it with a positive significance.' In her most recent contribution to this debate, Chanter's conclusion is substantially unchanged, although the way to it is more critically nuanced. See *Ethics of Eros: Irigaray's Rewriting of the Philosophers* (London/New York: Routledge, 1995), p. 234: 'the feminine functions at the order of the saying in Levinas' text, which remains, in its external appearance, at the order of the said, thoroughly male'.

9 But only *seems* to. Levinas later teaches, in the same text, that the ethical relation is absolutely primordial and grounds all possible relations in/with the world. As Derrida says, in *Adieu to Emmanuel Levinas*, trans. P.-A. Brault and M. Naas (Stanford: Stanford University Press, 1999), p. 28; *Adieu à Emmanuel Levinas* (Paris: Galilée, 1997), p. 59, relations between conditions and the conditioned are always extremely complex in *Totality and Infinity*, and not ultimately decidable.

10 See, for example, *TI* 68–9.

11 Catherine Chalier's feminist reading of the feminine in Levinas, which is both critical and appropriative, makes this point, among others. See Chalier, *Figures du féminin* (Paris: La nuit surveillée, 1982), pp. 65–7, 100. Levinas also seems to confirm this in his conversation with Raoul Mortley; R. Mortley (ed.), *French Philosophers in Conversation* (London: Routledge, 1991), p. 18: 'Sex itself is otherness of genre, but within a relation: so in a relationship with the feminine, a breaking of genre has already taken place. This is a very important *moment* in the accession to the total otherness of the face' (emphasis added). But a moment *on the way* to total otherness, not total otherness itself.

12 The picture is more or less the same in 'Judaism and the Feminine' (*DF* 33–4): '"without woman man knows neither good, nor succor, nor joy, nor blessing, nor pardon." Nothing of what would be required for a soul! Rabbi Joshua ben Levi added: "neither peace nor life." Nothing which transforms his natural life into ethics.' She makes his very soul possible.

13 See Chalier, *Figures du féminin*, p. 93.

14 Irigaray, 'The Fecundity of the Caress', trans. Carolyn Burke, in Richard A. Cohen (ed.), *Face to Face with Levinas* (Albany: State University of New York Press, 1986), p. 235, 'La fécondité de la caresse', in *Ethique de la différence sexuelle* (Paris: Editions de Minuit, 1984), p. 177.

15 Irigaray, 'Questions to Emmanuel Levinas', trans. Margaret Whitford, in Bernasconi and Critchley, *Re-Reading Levinas*, p. 109.

16 Adriaan Peperzak, *To the Other: an Introduction to the Philosophy of Emmanuel Levinas* (Indiana: Purdue University Press, 1993), p. 158. He later adds (p. 195) that this assertion of metaphoricity 'does not yet answer the question of whether it is a good metaphor, and why or why not'; a question that remains unanswered.

17 The claim that Levinas acknowledges both the inevitable relation between the philosophical category and its empirical content and the philosophical implications of this relation may seem precipitous here. The argument is made in much greater detail, and with reference to the changing role of eros in Levinas's work, in ch. 2 of my *The Metaphysics of Love*.

18 See also *NTR*, pp. 164, 169.

19 On the various meanings of 'the feminine' in contemporary feminist discourses see Stella Sandford, 'Feminism Against "The Feminine"', *Radical Philosophy*, 105 (Jan./Feb. 2001).

20 For attempts to argue along these lines see, for example, Manning, 'Thinking the Other Without Violence?', pp. 135–6; Chanter, 'Feminism and the Other', p. 46.

21 Derrida, *Adieu to Emmanuel Levinas*, p. 44; *Adieu à Emmanuel Levinas*, p. 83.

22 John Llewelyn, *Emmanuel Levinas: the Genealogy of Ethics* (London: Routledge, 1995), p. 87. See also John Llewelyn, *The Middle Voice of Ecological Conscience* (Hampshire: Macmillan, 1991), pp. 22, 203, 213; *Emmanuel Levinas*, pp. 87, 98, 99, 117, 119, 122, 137, 139, 146.

23 Jacques Derrida, 'White Mythology: Metaphor in the Text of Philosophy', in *Margins of Philosophy*, trans. Alan Bass (Hertfordshire: Harvester Wheatsheaf, 1982); *Marges de la philosophie* (Paris: Editions de Minuit, 1972). It would be interesting to know how Derrida would reconcile his remarks in *Adieu* on the feminine with the analyses of 'White Mythology'.

24 Llewelyn, *Emmanuel Levinas*, p. 88.

25 Such an idea is not new. See, for example, Monique Wittig, 'The Category of Sex', in *The Straight Mind and Other Essays* (Boston: Beacon Press, 1998) and Judith Butler, *Gender Trouble: Feminism and the Subversion of Identity* (London: Routledge, 1990).

8 Sincerity and the end of theodicy: three remarks on Levinas and Kant*

SINCERE...[...ad. L. *sincer-us* clean, pure, sound, etc.
Cf. Fr. *sincère* (1549)...The first syllable may be the same
as *sim-* in *simplex*: see SIMPLE a. There is no probability
in the old explanation from *sine cera* 'without wax'.]...
[*Oxford English Dictionary*]

In *Difficult Freedom* and elsewhere, Levinas writes of the radically anachronistic nature of Judaism. He sees it as simultaneously the youthfulness that, attentive to everything, would change everything and the senescence that, having seen everything, would seek only to return to the origin of everything. Its difficult, if not impossible, relation to the present is bound up with its refusal of the 'modernist' imperative that one 'desire to conform to one's time'. Simultaneously youthful and aged, engaged (committed) and disengaged, such would be the figure of the prophet: 'the most deeply committed (*engagé*) man, one who can never be silent, is also the most separate, the one least capable of becoming an institution. Only the false prophet has an official function' (*DF* 212). Levinas's religious (Talmudic) writings are always concerned with illustrating, rehearsing and reflecting upon this anachronistic wisdom, finding both in the Biblical expression of monotheism and in its endless rabbinical revisions and interpretations a wisdom that is absolutely irreplaceable. Irreplaceable, above all, by philosophy; but perhaps, above all, not just by *any* philosophy, or, rather, not by philosophy under just *any* name:

(T)his essential content, which history cannot touch, cannot be learned like a catechism or summarized like a credo. Nor is it restricted to the negative and formal statement of a categorical imperative. It cannot be replaced by Kantianism (*kantisme*). [*DF* 213]

Would Kantianism not be a synonym for modernism? And Kant, the least anachronistic of philosophers, the one most concerned that philosophy, in a newly won official capacity, speak to and for its own time, its present? A book could be written on the uses of this word *kantisme* in Levinas's work. But it is not overly disingenuous to propose that one of the differences between the religious and the philosophical writings lies in the fact that the former address a scriptural content that cannot be replaced by this other *-ism* and so remain, as do the religious writings themselves, untroubled by it, whereas the latter in part describe what must always be distinguished from Kantianism and what sometimes perhaps, along with the philosophical writings themselves, cannot avoid resembling or repeating it. If there is a sense in which the sentence 'Judaism cannot be replaced by Kantianism' can be taken as obviously true and as asserting the sort of thing Levinas and Levinasians might sometimes want to say, there is surely also a sense in which the sentence itself need never be said or written. In the religious writings, it is unnecessary or superfluous; in the philosophical writings, it is irrelevant, at least to the extent that the relation to Kant and Kantianism staged in and by Levinas's phenomenological project, especially as we find it in *Otherwise than Being*, can never arrive at such an unequivocal statement of the 'truth' or 'place' of Kantianism. Indeed, were it to do so then arguably that project would cease to be a philosophical one at all. Whatever else it names or entails, Levinas's thought cannot be construed as a prophetic indictment of Kantianism.[1]

THE WORD *KANTISME*

The topic is irresistible. How can the Levinasian call for 'ethics as first philosophy' fail to bring to mind that earlier insistence on the primacy of practical reason which crucially centred around the description of reason's being affected by the moral law, laid low by its own imperative? If we know how Levinas must react to that description, bemoaning the fact that the object of respect remains the moral law, the universality of which tells against the asymmetry of the ethical relation where it would have to be a matter of my respect for the other, might it none the less not be a matter of retrieving something from this description? Apparently not. Of course, it all depends on how and where you begin, and on the context in which you first encounter the word (*kantisme*). But if Levinas's philosophical writings would give a phenomenological exposition of the anachronistic life affirmed in the religious writings, if this would be their *inspiration*, it is hardly surprising if the negative tone is dominant. In *Otherwise than Being*, Levinas pursues his exposition of responsibility. He likens it to 'a cellular irritability' and describes it, crucially, as 'the impossibility of being silent, the scandal of sincerity [impossibilité de se taire, scandale de la sincérité]' (*OB* 143). Responsibility, always asymmetrically and sincerely *for the other*, belongs to the analysis of an affectivity that contrasts sharply and deliberately with that of respect.

Levinas does not need to dispute the fact that one has to learn how to be sincere just as one has to learn how to lie and how to tell the truth. As Wittgenstein puts it, 'a child has much to learn before it can pretend. (A dog cannot be a hypocrite, but neither can it be sincere [*aufrichtig*].)'[2] But Levinas does, it seems, want to suggest that being sincere is not simply one type of linguistic behaviour among myriad others. The uttered (said) 'Yes' and 'Hello', once learnt, do not bring affirming and greeting into the language, nor do they only denote mastery of the language games of affirming and greeting, thereby adding to the stock of games at the speaker's disposal. Rather, in Levinas's hands, they tell us about all language, any language game whatsoever. They provide (phenomenological) insight into what it is for there to be any *said* at all. 'Sincerity' is, perhaps, Levinas's last word on what he calls the saying of the said, the saying of all the – *de jure* and *de facto* – systematizable, theorizable and describable saids. It permits us to speak of the sincerity of the always unsaid 'yes' or 'hello' presupposed in everything that is said. The subject thought in relation to the saying, and exposed *as* this relation, cannot avoid a sincerity that makes of every said, however violent or thoughtless, a bearer of the trace of its saying, a sign of the giving of signs. When I begin to speak, in addition to everything that is said, my words attest to a relation between language and me that is always already underway and that makes of me as a speaking subject a term in a fundamentally asymmetrical relation. Note that Levinas does not want to move from a theory of communication, intersubjectivity and the speaking subject to a more primordial thought of language *as* language, a language that somehow *is* or *speaks* before man, before the subject. Instead of losing the subject in and to language, Levinas's account of subjectivity in *Otherwise than Being* makes of language itself something always already *for the other*. His account attempts to show that, however else it might be analysed and studied, language is first destined to this drama, this *intrigue*. To this end, *Otherwise than Being* proposes two alterations: first, the language that we understand as a system of signs is derived from the thought of an already spoken language (Wittgenstein might agree with this anti-theoretical or pre-theoretical grounding of systematicity); secondly, the philosophical thematizing of signification is derived from a thought of signification in its *signifiance*, its signifyingness – otherwise said, its sincerity.

My words always indicate both that I am speaking and that there is more to this 'I' than a traditional theory of language and subjectivity can disclose or, better, expose. This exposed subject of saying who can never keep silent is also to be thought as 'separation'. This term is deliberately and necessarily opposed to a Kantian conception of autonomy. What prevents the institutionalization of this Levinasian responsibility both from being raised to a level where it is distributed across all subjects and from being referred to the allocation (the equal or fair allocation) of duties, rights and values, derives from an elemental passivity. And although this passivity grants the subject an origin outside the causal mechanisms of nature and so, in some degree, a freedom from that causality, it can never be formulated in quite this fashion. Its subjecthood is not a function of its freedom. It does not stand apart from the sensible and sensibility in the manner of Kant's subject. The passivity of responsibility also implies that that other origin can never be known as such. Moral self-knowledge and knowledge of my origin as a free subjectivity are not prerequisites for ethical life. Neither my origin as a subject nor anything I think I come to know about that origin can stand in my defence. They provide no grounds for excuse.

One of the key subtexts of *Otherwise than Being* will thus be a polemical engagement with Kant, a polemic that reachest its harshest judgement in the final chapter with the book's last reference to Kant and the claim that 'Kantianism is the basis of philosophy [Le kantisme est la base de la philosophie] if philosophy is ontology' (*OB* 179). What is the context? Levinas asks whether there can be a sense of openness that is not one of the disclosure of beings. He recalls Kant's argument concerning the ideality of space and notes that it would make space a non-concept and a non-entity. Would we not have here an exteriority, an outside, that prompts a very different thinking about essence? No. For Kant 'space remains the condition for the representation of beings'. It is thus one more way in which essence continues to be determined as 'presence, exhibition, and phenomenality' and one more way in which thought is held to such determinations. From this Kantian non-entity (space) which serves solely as a condition for the possibility of objectivity, from this exemplary essentializing, Levinas infers that 'one cannot conceive essence otherwise, one can conceive otherwise only the beyond essence' (OB 179). Levinas's project, announced in the title of the book we are just finishing, is not and can never be Kant's or Kantian. There is no way of getting from the Kantian reflection on the subjectivity of space, and time, to a sense of the subject 'outside' ontology. Thus, Levinas writes, 'Kantianism is the basis of philosophy, if philosophy is ontology.'

Recall that in the transcendental aesthetic of the First Critique, Kant's isolating of sensibility and sensible intuition from pure intuition, and indeed, at this moment, pure intuition from the cognitive activity of the understanding, is achieved by way of a challenge to subtract from the representation of a thing all the qualities or attributes to which the sensibility and the understanding, respectively, would relate it. It is a challenge to think spacelessness, and the failure to meet it requires that thought define itself differently in relation to the irreducible remainder. I cannot think spacelessness; my thought spatializes. Interestingly. the move is not dissimilar to that taken by Levinas in *Existence and Existents* when he attempts to show the impossibility of arriving at nothing or nothingness. One runs up against the impersonal *il y a*, existence without existents. In each instance, a methodological subtraction leads to a condition from out of which a different account of subjectivity is to arise. The difference is that, in Kant's case, ontology is strengthened, is made critically possible; knowledge, drastically and critically limited, is nevertheless extended to knowledge of those drastic and critical limits, the conditions of the possibility of the knowledge and the representation of any being whatsoever. In Levinas's case, ontology, and especially a critical ontology, falters. Although replayed in its most convoluted version in *Otherwise than Being*, it would be possible to show that the narrative of *Existence and Existents* still holds a certain sway: from ontology to its faltering, and from its faltering to a thinking other than ontology, a thinking in which neither the being of the subject nor the being of the other is a primary concern and in which the other is never first encountered cognitively. How, then, can it not be a matter of continuing to argue for its non-Kantian motivation and result?

If *Otherwise than Being* closes with a criticism of the manner in which space is still tied to essence in Kant, and since Kant, the main focus of the book has been on time and on the attempt to liberate time from essence. To conceive the temporalizing of time 'not as essence but as saying'. It is 'the equivocation or enigma' of saying that names the book's central topic and contribution. And, again, its exposition requires Kant and Kantianism to be kept at a distance. 'Subjectivity and Infinity', the fifth chapter, continues to describe a subject whose origin can in no way be bound to cognition. When Kant is invoked here it as the author of a thought which can countenance no other origin. In linking the subject with infinity, Levinas effectively unpacks the claim he will later make, 'Since Kant, philosophy has been finitude without infinity', (GDT 36) so as to include Kant. The infinity we can hear in the crucially pre-Kantian 'good beyond being' and that is named in the crucially pre-Kantian 'infinite' of Descartes's Third Meditation has, it seems, no echo in Kantianism.

'Kantianism' for Levinas also seems to denote a break with naïvety, and so the beginning of a whole philosophical discourse of breaks, ruptures, ends and closures. 'Tout autrement', Levinas's essay on Derrida, begins by asking 'May not Derrida's work cut into the development of Western thinking with a line of demarcation similar to that of Kantianism...? Are we again at the end of a naivety?' (WO 3). The end of a naïvety also necessarily problematizes the business of beginning, and Levinas has a fine ear for the way in which philosophers since Kant have laboured to show that their beginnings are anything other than naïve. In the 'itinerary' of *Otherwise than Being*, Levinas appears to concede defeat. He speaks, with Husserl, of 'every movement of thought involving a part of naivety', (OB 20) and the hint is that there might in fact be something misguided about these dreams of a unnaïve beginning. Is it to be a question of Levinas's retrieving a pre-Kantian naïvety, and a pre-Kantian honesty about such a naïvety, not for the sake of ontology but for the sake of a subject whose naïve 'yes' to submission and subjection must always be pitted against the naïveties and immediacies protected in the methodologies (the 'critical' beginnings) of what remain essentially theoretical and ontological undertakings? It would not be difficult to compile two vocabularies or trajectories, a Kantianism and a Levinasianism:

1. Kant: respect (for the moral law); freedom; spontaneity; autonomy;
2. Levinas: responsibility (for the other); sincerity; passivity; separation; heteronomy.

From Kant to Derrida, we could follow the instituting and the radicalizing of a critical ontology of finitude and the gradual dissolution of subjectivity in an ever-renewed thought of language. The second line would recall another subject and subjectivity. It might be read as a polemical retrieval of something pre-modern, anachronistic and naïve, something that elsewhere will be given the religous, scriptural and historical status of the irreplaceable.

But it all depends on how and where you begin, and on the context in which you first encounter the word 'Kantianism'. For we might have begun with the following passage and with this reference to an outside we have apparently just seen being explicitly denied Kant:

If one had the right to retain one trait from a philosophical system and neglect all the details of its architecture ... we would think here of Kantianism, which finds a meaning to the human without measuring it by ontology and outside of the question 'What is there here ... ?' that one would like to take to be preliminary, outside of the immortality and death which ontologies run up against. The fact that immortality and theology could not determine the categorical imperative signifies the novelty of the Copernican revolution: a sense not measured by being or not being; being, on the contrary, is determined from sense. [Si on avait le droit de retenir d'un système philosophique un trait en négligeant tout le détail de son architecture ... nous penserions ici au Kantisme qui trouve un sens à l'humain sans le mesurer par voudrait préalable, en dehors de l'immortalité et de la mort auxquelles achoppent les ontologies. Le fait que l'immortalité et la théologie ne sauraient déterminer l'impératif catégorique, signifie la nouveauté de la révolution copernicienne: le sens qui ne se mesure pas par l'être ou le ne pas être, l'être se déterminant, au contraire, à partir du sens.] [OB 129]

Levinas cites this passage in full in the proceedings to the 1975–6 lecture course on 'Death and time', where we are also told that although the First Critique presents a philosophy of finitude it acknowledges a necessity to questions which require and promise another philosophy. One of those questions, for example, concerns hope: what am I entitled to hope for? A question in which Levinas hears a reference to a beyond, a time after time, irreducible to an ecstatic temporality despite Heidegger's attempts so to reduce it (GDT 61). And might this not be the crux of the matter, Kant bound to ontology by way of his Heideggerian reading? Is it then that the unity of Kant's critical project when construed in terms of a relation to finitude, i.e. when read from the standpoint of a fundamental ontology, will generate a theoretical unity, the gathering of Kantian critical philosophy and of critique itself under the heading of theoretical philosophy? Is Levinas not inviting us to begin to find in Kant's practical philosophy and in the announcement that the critical philosophy is not limited to the conditions of theoretical knowledge, something of a genuine 'outside'?[3] In 'Revelation in the Jewish Tradition', describing an obedience and so an ethics prior to freedom, Levinas writes:

This obedience cannot be assimilated to the categorical imperative, where a universal suddenly finds itself in a position to direct the will; it derives rather from ... responsibility for one's neighbour ... The relationship with the other is placed right at the beginning! Moreover, it is towards a relationship of this kind that Kant hastens, when he formulates the second version of the categorical imperative by a deduction – which may be valid or not – from the universality of the maxim. [BV 146]

A Kant *on the way to* responsibility? Emboldened, now would be the time to embark on a search through Kant's texts looking for signs of ethical asymmetry. One of the places that might usefully be examined is the discussion, in *The Metaphysics of Morals*, of the specific vices that result from a failure to fulfil the duties which follow from my respect for the moral law. Granted that that respect, in its universality and its object, seems to remain immune to a Levinasian retrieval, the same is not so obviously the case with what follows. Kant's concern is with those vices deriving directly from respect. They have no corresponding virtues; I must simply refrain from them. Kant distinguishes three vices: arrogance (*der Hochmut*), defamation (*das Afterreden*) and ridicule (*die Verhönung*). In the second and third of these, it is not primarily, if at all, a matter of lying or slander, but rather of the intentional spreading of what reduces the esteem in which another human being is held by right of being human. There are moral limits to the truths I am entitled to tell about others. In relation to the second, defamation, Kant speaks of 'a mania for spying on the morals of others (*allotrio-episcopia*)' which is 'already by itself an offensive inquisitiveness on the part of anthropology'.[4] There is a sense of my being prevented from enquiring into others in the way in which I am elsewhere obliged to enquire into myself. Note that if there is something of an asymmetry underway here, it is not produced logically; nor does it follow from an empirical or psychological fact, i.e. from my ability to examine myself (to report on my beliefs, desires or whatever) in a way I cannot examine others. If there is asymmetry here, it is imposed morally. This, then, would be one such reading. With a Levinasian eye one might detect many others; and is it not such an eye and such a means of re-encountering the history of philosophy that Levinas, on at least one reading, might be said to provide?

Yet recall the passage: 'If one had the right to retain one trait from a philosophical system and neglect all the details of its architecture... we would think here of Kantianism', which is surely to beg the question of why one does not have such a right. Would not the retention involved in exercising it simply amount to a Levinasian retrieval of the trace or trait of the ethical relation, a moment when, against the dominance of its theoretical and thematizing manoeuvres, ontology can be shown to be ethically oriented? Would ethics as the *sense* or the *saying* of the ontological *said* not depend upon such a selective re-reading? Surely such a re-reading or something extremely close to it is implicit in Levinas's treatment of Descartes's notion of the infinite and Plato's notion of the good beyond being, to give the two best-known examples of the results of what has been taken to be a Levinasian engagement with the philosophical tradition. Do not *these* other interpretations, with their references to certain exceptional words and phrases, presuppose the very right Levinas seems not to want to allow us in the case of Kant? What sort of special case is Kant? There is a difficulty in understanding why Levinas does not take one of two fairly clear alternatives: either, first, to endorse (retrieve, retain) as another exceptional moment, those parts of the description that work despite the universalizing and prescriptive genus implicit in 'practical reason' and in the categorical status accorded the imperative; or, secondly, to argue that such an endorsement cannot come about here at all. Instead, as we have seen, Levinas concedes that there is something that would be retained, had we the right to do so. Perhaps an answer is actually given in the passage, in the slight awkwardness with which the trait, rather than the philosophical system from which it would be retained, seems to be named *kantisme*, as though with Kant it could not be an exceptional word or phrase which once isolated could be added to the list, if list there is, but in some peculiar way the whole system, the *-ism* itself. '*Kantisme* is the basis of philosophy, if philosophy is ontology.' And if one could retain just one trait? Well, it would be *kantisme*.

THEODICY AND THE END OF THEODICY

Levinas's argument against theodicy follows from the description of suffering. He does not begin with, and never really sees the need for, an attack on the actual theoretical content of a theodicy. The description suffices, inviting us to infer the immorality of theodicy from its inability to address suffering as it is exposed in the description. Given what we have seen of Levinas's response to Heidegger's Kant interpretation, it is interesting to realize just how the priority given to a philosophical description has changed from the days when Levinas was content to write to a consciously Heideggerian agenda. In 1930, we were instructed that

in order to go conclusively beyond naturalism and all its consequences, it is not enough to appeal to descriptions which emphasize the particular character, irreducible to the naturalistic categories, of certain objects. It is necessary to dig deeper, down to the very meaning of the notion of being... [*TIHP* 18]

Later, we can say, it is the description of what in its irreducibility always betrays the irrelevance of the question of being that, for Levinas, reawakens the ethical sense of 'first philosophy'.

More than anything else it is suffering that with its exemplary phenomenology brings us straight to the heart of what we now take to be Levinas's own project. For suffering to be thought or described *qua* suffering it must be thought or described in its senselessness, as what everywhere and always resists being given a meaning or context. There can be no thematizing of suffering; if there is or seems to be then it is no longer suffering that is really being addressed or considered but rather something which enables us to move away from suffering. The phenomenology Levinas insists upon here will only ever permit the sense of suffering, the sense such a phenomenology is to work with, to lie in suffering's excessive senselessness, in its capacity to resist the thematic bestowing of a sense. It is in this resistance, this undermining of the very act of sense bestowal, and so in this check to a whole phenomenology of thought based on the essentially meaningful character of mental *acts*, that we begin to see the force and the necessity of the *passivity* that is to play such a key role in Levinas's work. In my inability to give a meaning to suffering, I suffer: I fall back upon a passivity always this side of an active sense-engendering life, a life from which, in so far as I would attend to suffering *qua* suffering, I can gain or claim no support. It is the scene, too, of a radical asymmetry: my suffering here is always referred to the suffering of the other, a suffering whose senselessness provokes my suffering. As Levinas puts it in *Otherwise than Being*, 'The vortex [Le tourbillon] – suffering of the other, my pity for his suffering, his pain over my pity, my pain over his pain, etc. – stops at me. The I is what involves one more movement in this iteration' (*OB* 196, n. 21). Unlike the Kantian transcendental 'I think' that uniquely effects the move away from the recursivity of the empirical 'I think', the regress of empirical reflection, Levinas's I does not 'think': it suffers; it is obsessed; it is nothing but 'for the other'. And the descriptions served by each of these terms and constructions will endlessly exacerbate and underline the passivity and the asymmetry. The I with which the phenomenology of suffering must begin is an I for whom the other's suffering is unthinkable and unjustifiable. Theodicy will be the proper name of a philosophy that seeks to avoid *this* suffering, the suffering of suffering, 'the just suffering in me for the unjustifiable suffering in the other' (*US* 159). Levinas, reluctant to endorse any discourse of ends or the end, will speak unapologetically of *the end of theodicy*. 'For an ethical sensibility... the justification of the neighbour's pain is the source of all immorality' (*US* 163).

Consider epistemological scepticism about another's pain. Here there is, if you like, asymmetry, but it is theoretical. I have to live, the sceptic concedes, as though untouched by my scepticism. But where must one start from in order to arrive at that question, in order to arrive at that as a philosophical problem (How do I know the other is in pain...?)? For Levinas, it is not a matter of knowledge or even of wondering whether or not it is a matter of knowledge, but of being affected. Levinas does not want to describe the world so that this epistemological asymmetry does not arise, in the manner, say, of Heidegger's description of being-in-the-world where *Mitsein* simply is an *existentiale*, part of the structural unity of being-in-the-world. Such a description loses asymmetry altogether, save unsurprisingly in *Dasein*'s relation to what is most its own, its death. Levinas wants to describe the subject as a relation to the other in which this question *must not* arise! It is to be a matter of refusal not refutation.

And Kant? Kant and theodicy? In so far as Kant belongs to a tradition both epistemological and ontological, that either treats the sceptical question as legitimate or else loses it altogether in a more original ontology, and in so far as Kant's subject can only be held accountable under certain knowable and reasonable conditions, the conclusion is straightforward. But again, there are two passages and two stories. The first, and seemingly most straightforward, from *Otherwise than Being*:

The unconditionality of this 'yes' (the naive 'yes' of submission) is not that of an infantile spontaneity. It is the very exposure to critique, the exposure prior to consent, more ancient than any naive spontaneity. We have been accustomed to reason in the name of the freedom of the ego – as though I had witnessed the creation of the world, and as though I could only have been in charge of a world that would have issued out of my free will. These are the presumptions of philosophers, presumptions of idealists! Or evasions of irresponsible ones. That is what Scripture reproaches Job for. He would have known how to explain his miseries if they could have devolved from his faults! But he never wished evil! His false friends think like he does: in a meaningful world one cannot be held to answer when one has not done anything. Job then must have forgotten his faults! But the subjectivity of a subject come late into a world that has not issued from his projects does not consist in projecting or in treating this world as one's project. The 'lateness' is not insignificant. [*OB* 122]

The two trajectories and vocabularies we outlined earlier can be seen in operation throughout this passage. There would be little difficulty in marking a Levinasian naïvety explicitly introduced in opposition to a Kantian naïvety (submission against spontaneity); an exposure to critique that can never itself be the object or theme of critique, and so an exposure or exposition that finds me (exposes me as) pre-critically answerable for what exceeds the possible. Everything falls into place. Levinas sides with scripture, with God (with His angry and silencing

'Where were you when I laid the foundations of the earth...?'), and against Job, his friends and any philosophy that would insist that in the absence of meaning or justification I can be under no obligation. The critical and diagnostic response to suffering is always misplaced; it is never to the suffering that one is so responding. When Job speaks of his suffering he speaks of it as though it could have been justified and understood had he only done something wrong, something to deserve it. Job's complaint concerns neither suffering as suffering nor the idea of a meaning being given to suffering. Its sole object is the fact that there ought to be a meaning but, in this instance, in Job's case, there is none. The Levinasian alternative and challenge to theodicy can here be equated with and read alongside its alternative and challenge to Kantianism. The subject who would define itself solely by its own time and by the origin that ensures that that time is the subject's own will always detect in a certain lateness, a legiti-mate, logical and moral defence (I wasn't here then: that was before my time: I can only be held to account for what is of my time). To this insignificant lateness, to this lateness that the subject is justified in giving no significance, a lateness that would secure the subject in its origin as a rational moral agent, Levinas opposes a paradoxically significant lateness in which the subject is answerable for all it did not know and did not do even when there was nothing it could know and nothing it could do. As with the first of the Kantianisms above, the picture seems clear. But is it? Look at what we have just written: 'When Job speaks of his suffering...' Is it not somewhat churlish to criticize Job – after all *he* is suffering? His is not the just suffering in the face of the unjustifiable suffering of the other, but the unjus-tifiable suffering itself. On what grounds and by what right can we challenge anything that the one (the other) who suffers says about their suffering? It would, to say the least, be strange if Levinas were taken as having provided such grounds and such a right. Unjustifiable surely means unjustifiable by me. The onus is on me not to construct a theodicy, not to thematize or theorize the other's suffering. There must be something wrong with my taking 'unjustifiable' as a means of criticizing the one who is suffering from attempting to survive that suffering by making sense of it. The asymmetry must surely also extend at least this far. There is perhaps a more general worry here about whether and in what sense the suffering one (the other) can be said to speak. Can the other have a theodicy? And when I do come to speak of the other and others, when it is a question of the third, of justice and politics, must I not necessarily rejoin the theoretical language and logic of theodicy? But let us remain with the case of Job. It is a Biblical and literary case. It is a matter of the Biblical staging of a drama between Job, his friends and God in which none of the speeches can be given the ethical status of coming from the mouth of the other. Nevertheless, Job is necessarily represented as suffering. Nothing in the drama would make sense, indeed there would be no drama, were this fact not established from the first. In treating this drama and this representation, Levinas does not argue with or against Job but simply notes the scriptural reproach to him. It is a peculiar moment because there is literally no philosophy in it. Levinas endorses or stands with the unanswerable voice of God, a voice he identifies with the scriptural criticism of Job. That criticism extends not only to the friends but, beyond the text, to all theodicy, all philosophies of the subject apart from Levinas's, all philosophy as such apart from Levinas's. It is a silencing gesture, and what it silences is philosophy. It underlines the authority and, one is tempted to say, the violence of the anti-Kantian Levinas, the Levinas of the first *kantisme*.

This is not, however, Levinas's only reading of Job's predicament. In the final footnote to the essay 'Useless Suffering', he refers both to Job's sufferings as being without reason and unjustifiable and to his consistent oppposition to the theodicy of the friends. 'Job refuses theodicy right to the end and, in the last chapters of the text, is preferred to those who, hurrying to the safety of heaven, would make God innocent before the suffering of the just' (*US* 167). Here Levinas stands with Job and against the theodicy of the friends. This would be a more familiar interpretation. But note that it is not only the friends who stand indicted in their propounding of a theodicy, it is also God. Moreover, it is not only Levinas and Job here teaming up against theodicy. The footnote continues:

It is a little like the reading Kant makes of this book in his quite extraordinary short treatise of 1791, *Uber das Misslingen aller philosophischen Versuche in der Theodicee* ['On the miscarriage of all philosophical trials in theodicy' or 'On the failure of all philosophical attempts at a theodicy'], where he demonstrates the theoretical weakness of the arguments in favour of theodicy. Here is the conclusion of his way of interpreting what 'this ancient book expresses allegorically': for with this disposition he proved that he did not found his morality on faith, but his faith on morality: in such a case, however weak this faith may be, yet it alone is of a pure and true kind, i.e. the kind of faith that founds not a religion of supplication [eine Religion nicht der Gunstbewerbung] but a well conducted life [des guten Lebenswandels]. [US 167]

We will have cause in a moment in the final remark to realize quite how extraordinary this small text of Kant's is. Kant is not concerned with announcing an end to all theodicy but he does want to distinguish between 'doctrinal' and 'authentic' (authentisch) theodicy. It is interesting that Kant puts so much emphasis on speech, on the conversations or non-conversations. He refers both to Job's courage in speaking as he thinks, 'as one can when one is in Job's position', and to the way in which the friends, 'on the contrary, speak as though being secretly listened to by the mighty one'.[5] They never speak to the one who is suffering and never speak of his meaningless suffering. We will return to this. For the present, we seem to have two versions of the battle against theodicy:

1. Levinas, scripture and God contra Job, the friends, Kant and philosophy;
2. Levinas, Kant and Job contra the friends, God and a scriptural justification of theodicy.

Importantly (2) does not deny the presence of theodicy in the Bible. It finds in the Bible, in this instance in the figure of Job, the scriptural inspiration and means to begin questioning the scriptural and theistic basis of theodicy.[6] As in the two Kantianisms above, (2) is less dependent on an extra-philosophical imposition or statement of irreplaceability. But now, on the specific topic of theodicy and suffering, we seem able to go further. For concerning that topic and its description, (2) invites us to call something of (1) into question. It allows us to see that the force and coherence of (1) depends, in part, upon an endorsement of a scriptural and divine reproach to one who is necessarily represented as suffering. (2) suggests an ethical objection to (1) in this respect; and it does so in a manner which (necessarily?) resembles or brings to mind the Kantian reading of Job and the Kantian grounding of faith on morality, of theodicy on the critique of theodicy. (2) is not only more interesting philosophically, it is the only formulation that remains genuinely philosophical!

It demands that there be philosophy, a philosophical critique of theodicy. For the thought of 'the end of theodicy' to have any efficacy, any real purchase on the (philosophical and scriptural) discourse of theodicy, it cannot be a matter any longer of a Levinasianism replacing a Kantianism.

SINCERITY

We have spoken of Levinas's philosophical project as phenomenological, using terms such as 'description' and Levinas's own, deliberately overdetermined, *exposition*. But how do these descriptions and expositions work? What do they do? Suffering is said to be a sensation, but one resistant to synthesis: it is as this sensation, this sensibility, that suffering refuses meaning and confronts consciousness as something consciousness cannot bear (*US* 156–7). In attending to the subject so affected, Levinas moves from a description of suffering as suffering to one of the suffering of suffering, detecting in the doubling (the suffering of suffering) a passivity and asymmetry at the very heart of subjectivity. This order appears as well in the description of obsession, another of Levinas's words for subjectivity. I am obsessed by or with the other. Obsession is not reciprocal. There cannot be a collective subject, a we, whose members, for example you and I, live contentedly and mutually obsessed with each other. Obsession as obsession means that, obsessed by or with the other, I am obsessed by or with their not being obsessed by or with me. Again we move from obsession to the obsession of obsession, and again the subject is disclosed in its passivity and asymmetry.

One could continue. Levinas, of course, does. But where and when does one stop? Is this not the moment when we should follow Levinas's other narratives and raise the issue of application? Ought not we now to begin to ask about those controversial points (politics, the third, justice) where Levinas's texts seem to break into another philosophical register? Perhaps the most frequently debated points in Levinas's later work, they permit us to speak of the implications of the descriptions for, say, politics, the continuation of ontology and theodicy, and all the necessarily theoretical undertakings of a subject who, although now described and exposed as radically answerable, must still continue to philosophize. For the rest of the chapter, however, we shall take a slightly different approach, attempting to say something about the descriptions themselves. We will raise the question of the role and the place of the descriptive both in Levinas's ethical phenomenology and in Kant's critical philosophy.

It may be that Levinas's descriptions do not provide the means for refuting a particular philosophical thesis, but rather for refusing it. Refusal not refutation – we employed the phrase earlier when considering the position of the epistemological sceptic, and it might be usefully recalled in the attempt to clarify the relations between Levinas and Kant. As we have seen, Levinas is consistent in his belief that before being the property of theory, speech is a matter of morality. Concerning speech, the pretheoretical is co-extensive with the ethical. This primacy is set to work in *Totality and Infinity*: 'the essence of discourse is ethical. In stating [*énonçant*] this thesis idealism is refused' (*TI* 216). A refusal of idealism rather than a refutation obviously leaves room for Levinas's intricate redeployment of a sensibility (the sensibility in and of suffering, for example) otherwise cut adrift. Nevertheless are there not worries, both logical and ethical, to this, presumably, ethical refusal of a, presumably, logical refutation? But it does not have to be an anti-logical business; for the stating and refusing of a thesis are not to be separated from description and so from what it is that requires philosophy to be descriptive. Consider why we might need a refusal of evil rather than a refutation and a refusal of hatred and murder rather than a refutation. I want the one I hate to be an object, no longer subject, no longer human. I want them to know that this evisceration is my work, to know that they are nothing. But if they know it, they are not nothing: the hated other is never yet an object. The description yields the thought that it is logically impossible for hatred to achieve its end. Such a description, however, if it serves here as a premise, and the valid conclusion concerning the inherently contradictory nature of hatred that we are able to draw from it, will never put an end to hatred. The description serves a refutation but it can never deliver a release from what is thereby refuted. A similar account, but to different and more complicated ends, can be given of the sceptical thesis concerning truth, a thesis which refutes itself but returns, and returns to refute itself endlessly. Levinas's response to this return of the refuted is twofold. On the one hand, it attests to the saying of the said, to the fact that the self-contradictory nature of the thesis (the said) does not exhaust everything that is going on in and with it. What remains is the saying. On the other hand, it is not a matter of defending the content of the sceptical thesis. Scepticism itself draws no encouragement from Levinas's references to it. The description, if it is successful, shows how little is sometimes achieved when everything is achieved by refutation. There is an ethical sense to the remainder, to what permits the perpetual return despite the inevitability of perpetual refutation. The subject, in and as responsibility, is not silenced or excused by refutation. Responsibility is first and foremost responsiblity as and for the excess of the saying over the said. But, so conceived, this responsibility can only call for the proliferation of the said and the proliferation of a critique of the said, an endless critique in which one is always attempting to catch sight of the saying everywhere and always betrayed in the said. Note that nothing here permits us to assume that we can begin to treat the saying as though it were a topic for speech-act theory. The extensive use of scepticism throughout *Otherwise than Being* demonstrates how the appeal to the saying is not made in order to compensate for any semantic indeterminacy or under-determination in the said. There is nothing lacking: everything is clear. None the less and paradoxically, the saying says that something always remains *to be said*.

Otherwise than Being would constitute an exposition of a subject called to critique. Think of that exposition as the description of suffering and that critique as the critique of theodicy, the announcing of the end of theodicy. We are now in a position to say that what follows from the description is the refusal of theodicy. But *when* does it follow?

What, finally, are we to make of the descriptions of subjectivity as suffering and obsession, as nothing but for the other, in *Otherwise than Being*? Logically and phenomenologically endless, nothing in the matter at hand can do anything but intensify the exposition, the subject they describe can never be reunited with the sort of philosophical project that can specify the right moment (logically or ethically) for judgement, decision and action. If it is part of Levinas's project to address the question of the application of these descriptions, that question and that application cannot by themselves provide the last word on the descriptions. The exposition in *Otherwise than Being* seems to involve four distinct stages. (1) As we have noted, the descriptions of suffering and obsession turn, phenomenologically, into descriptions of the suffering of suffering and the obsession of obsession. (2) These doublings, in their turn, are described in terms of an asymmetry and a passivity that prohibit any phenomenological evidence from serving a return to reciprocity or activity. Thus Levinas describes a further doubling, a 'passivity of passivity' which ensures that the passivity of the subject can never be simply opposed to activity. (3) This passivity of passivity is 'saying', its time is the time of saying which, in its equivocation, is thematized in no said. The exposition needs one more doubling, a saying of saying. (4) The saying which is always and everywhere the saying of the said is available to description and exposition by a certain reduction of the said (the faltering of refutaton, for example). And how are we to describe this saying, this saying *as* saying? The transition from the second to the third to the fourth stages occurs in these difficult sentences:

For subjectivity to signify unreservedly, it would then be necessary that the passivity of its exposure to the other not be immediately inverted into activity, but expose itself in its turn; a passivity of passivity is necessary ... Saying is this passivity of passivity and this dedication to the other, this sincerity. Not the communication of a said, which would immediately cover over and extinguish or absorb the said, but saying holding open its openness [mais Dire tenant ouvert son ouverture], without excuses, evasions, or alibis, delivering itself without saying anything said [se livrant sans rien dire de Dit]. Saying saying saying itself [Dire disant le dire même], without thematizing it, but exposing it again. [*OB* 142–3]

If we have stayed with Levinas this far, and here we find some of the most tortuous moments of the exposition, 'sincerity' comes as the last word on the saying. Resisting description, it concludes the description. Sincerity is not a property of saying; it is not something we simply predicate of saying. 'Sincerity undoes the alienation which saying undergoes in the said.' And 'no said equals the sincerity of saying'. Finally, 'sincerity would be saying without the said' (*OB* 143). There is to be no further doubling, no sincerity of sincerity. The exposition of 'Dire disant le dire même' as sincerity marks the moment when the *itinerary* leads back to the said and to the question of what we are to do with these descriptions.

Is it simply perverse to move from a consideration of Levinas's utterly idiosyncratic and hyperbolic descriptions to a consideration of the role certain descriptions are asked to play in Kant's work? Not

if the exposition of the argument in *Otherwise than Being*, as well
as giving the ethical sense of that argument, also serves as its conclusion; not if the book is organized in such a way that it comprises
a transcendental argument and its conclusion, namely a description.

Even in the *Critique of Pure Reason*, there is a sense that a transcendental argument does not simply conclude. The transcendental
deduction of the categories is not in itself sufficient for a justification of the *a priori* foundations of knowledge. The descriptions
of the schematism are required in order to unpack and expose the
conditions of possibility that have always been the concern of the
argument. But it is in the moral philosophy, above all the Second
Critique and the *Groundwork*, that the descriptive character of critical thought comes to the fore. In the theoretical philosophy, there is
a sense that reason once shown the limits beyond which knowledge
is unattainable prepares itself to work within those limits. Nothing
more is needed; nothing more can be reasonably demanded. Reason
convinces itself to think and work accordingly. To accept the arguments of the antinomies of pure reason, for example, is to become,
in the self-same moment one accepts them, properly critical regarding theoretical knowledge. This is not and cannot be the case in the
practical philosophy. The deduction of the categorical imperative,
the arguments for the moral law, do not in and of themselves bind
reason to acting in accordance with that law. Here something else is
needed, namely a description of reason's coming to feel the force of
that law, a description of what is like a feeling (an intellectual feeling, a moral feeling), respect. It is odd that Levinas, in the passage
we cited earlier from 'Revelation in the Jewish Tradition', when he
comments on Kant's moral philosophy, is drawn to the attempt at
a deduction from the universalizability of the maxim to the obligation to treat the other as an end and not as a means. Levinas implies
that the attempt is bound to fail, it not being properly a matter of
deduction at all. It is odd that Levinas is willing to see in this attempt
at and desire for a deduction, evidence of a move towards ethics as
first philosophy, whereas he has little or nothing to say about the
actual work done by the *description*, deliberately not a deduction,
of respect. Heidegger is attentive to this aspect of Kant's moral phenomenology, recognizing that there is no argument for respect but
an explication or elucidation (*Enthüllung*).[7] It would be tempting to
insist on a certain proximity, if not correspondence, between this

Enthüllung and Levinas's *exposition*, a proximity or correspondence to which Levinas for whatever reason gives little importance.

Kant's 1791 essay on theodicy continues beyond the 'concluding paragraph' quoted by Levinas. It continues with a five-page 'concluding remark' devoted to a 'brief reflection on a big subject', *Aufrichtigkeit*, which we will translate as 'sincerity'. Of course *Aufrichtigkeit* plays on *Richt, richten, richtig* and *Richtung*, that could take us far afield (although 'direction' and 'directedness' are not wholly alien to Levinas's description) and it might be felt that 'uprightness' or even 'rectitude' was the more apposite translation. But let it be 'sincerity' for at least two reasons. First, in *The Metaphysics of Morals*, while treating truthfulness (*Wahrhaftigkeit*) in one's conversation, Kant distinguishes between the truthfulness of declarations, which he calls *Ehrlichkeit*, and the truthfulness of promises, which he calls *Redlichkeit*.[8] In general, however, he continues, the truthfulness attendant upon and in performativity and that underpins the honesty proper to each performative – this is after all Kant's topic here – is to be known as *Aufrichtigkeit*. Truthfulness in whatever guise, in whatever type of conversation, is a matter of sincerity. Secondly, in *The Critique of Judgement*, *Aufrichtigkeit* is associated with a simplicity (*sin-* , *sim-* ; in German, *die Einfalt*). The relevant passage occurs in section 54 where Kant remarks on the way in which the intellectual feeling of respect and a certain bodily gratification are conjoined in naïvety (*Naivität*):

[Naivety is] the eruption of the sincerity [*Aufrichtigkeit*] that originally was natural to humanity and which is opposed to the art of dissimulation [*Verstellungskunst*] that has become our second nature [*zur andern Natur*]. We laugh at such simplicity as does not yet know how to dissemble, and yet we also rejoice in the natural simplicty here thwarting that art of dissimulation . . . [9]

Again, surely this idea of an original, natural and now lost sincerity is undermined by Wittgenstein's claim that you cannot simply be sincere, as it were, from the first any more than you can simply dissemble? Either sincerity ought not to be confused with simplicity or being simple also must name a (linguistic) skill one acquires over time and by practice. But Kant, like Levinas, as the reference in *The Metaphysics of Morals* already implies, wants to suggest that sincerity, being sincere, is not simply one type of behaviour among others.

It is only in the 1791 essay on theodicy, however, written just after the completion of the Third Critique, that its scope and significance for Kant become clear.

Kant is not drawn to the content of the conversations between Job and his friends. The vital factor is not the reasoning of either side but the character of Job's continued insistence on reasoning. Were we to linger with the actual arguments, it is the friends whose pious speculations would most probably triumph. In terms, then, of their respective theoretical positions, Job would almost certainly have to be judged the loser. But it is not their theoretical positions that are or should be at issue, and any court that did so judge would be misled. The 'preeminence of the honest man' has nothing to do with the quality of his reasoning, but with 'sincerity of heart, honesty in openly admitting one's doubts, and repugnance to pretending conviction where one feels none'.[10] These are the properties that elevate Job. It is not with reference to the truth of his theoretical speculations, his theodicy or lack of it, that Job is to be judged but rather with reference to the truthfulness with which he continues to speculate. Job's beliefs may be true or false but they are sincerely held. This latter fact can be known only by Job, and God ('a reader of hearts'). Kant, in the concluding remark, is concerned with how sincerity functions as the last word here. One cannot be mistaken as to whether or not one believes a particular proposition, although one can be mistaken as to its truth or falsity. The 'most absurd lie', Kant says, is when I say untruthfully, or without reflecting on its truthfulness, that I believe something to be the case; here an untruth is synonymous with a lie. It is also the most sinful lie for it 'undermines the ground of every virtuous intention'.[11]

If sincerity names what is presupposed by every virtuous intention and if without it there would be little sense even in speaking of virtue, why are we so moved 'in the depiction of a sincere character'? Why is such simplicity, which as Kant adds 'is the very least we can possibly require of a good character', so surprising that its literary or dramatic representation is deemed especially edifying? Kant answers:

[I]t must be that sincerity is the property farthest removed from human nature – a sad comment [eine traurige Bemerkung] , since all the remaining properties, to the extent that they rest on principles, can have a true inner value only through that one.[12]

It would be tempting to read this sad comment back into the Second Critique and into the description of respect; for might it not be that what necessitates that description, what prevents reason from immediately and straightforwardly becoming virtuous, is the absence of the simplest prerequisite, sincerity? In the Third Critique, sincerity is linked to an original naïvety, one long replaced by another or second nature. Here what has been replaced is described as irreplaceable.[13] Kant shows both why practical reason (morality) can never again be a simple affair and why a faith that would endeavour to make it so must always remain answerable to a moral critique. There is then a Kantian doubling, if not redoubling, of the simple.

On the face of it nothing in this concluding remark on sincerity seems to implicate or concern Levinas. And we might want to go further. Given that Levinas's subject is resolutely not Kant's and given that sincerity, for Kant, seems still to be a matter of inner knowledge and a feeling of conviction, it looks as if we have yet another version of the two trajectories, the Kantian and the Levinasian. In the first, despite the fact that the description of sincerity follows so late in the day, we must surely begin any account of the development of morality with it, in its simplicity and its simple honest characterizing of the original, undeceptive human nature. With Kant, we would move from sincerity to the thought of its absence, difficulty and impossibility, for all of which rational morality must henceforth also function as a compensation. In the second trajectory, the Levinasian, sincerity's coming at the end of the description in *Otherwise than Being* is anything but irrelevant. It is the scandal of sincerity, saying as an endlessly sensitive exteriority, that turns language (speech) into the very site of the ethical encounter. No interior innocence has been lost; the impossibility of interiority is the very condition of sincerity: subjectivity is substitution (one for the other). Sincerity is scandalous, it shocks Levinas and the reader of Levinas's description, precisely because we might have assumed that that description would have had to have run along the lines of Kant's. We might have assumed that it would have had to have described a naïvety unavailable to the critical philosopher and the cultured subject, yet one that subject can always recognize, sometimes sadly and sometimes with a certain amused admiration. Levinas has retrieved sincerity by making it no longer the prize for an inner truthfulness, a prize only available to the naïve or to those in a situation (Job's perhaps) in which naïvety is dramatically restored to them. But can the differences between the descriptions be sustained in quite such a comfortably oppositional form? If we were to leave to one side the respective contexts, Kant's subjectivity versus Levinas's subjectivity, and concentrate solely on the terms in which sincerity is introduced it becomes harder to discern any fundamental disagreements. For example, it follows from Kant's account that 'I believe', 'I say', indeed any speech-act,[14] must be understood as commanding sincerity, an irreplaceable yet always already replaced sincerity. The sad comment, the concluding remark, and the whole essay direct our attention to language, to speech and performativity. Kant even includes an extensive footnote on the oath (tortura spiritualis), arguing against the unreasonable demand that the speaker who swears to tell the truth be committed to the truth of the content of the oath itself. The oath, understood in its performativity, is rather to be taken as a hypothesis: if there were to be an all seeing judge, he would judge what I will say here to have been said sincerely. Given the description of sincerity, the reflection on morality and virtue must now proceed by way of language, that is, by way of a description both of what we say and of that to which our speech *as* speech commits us.

Is the difference simply that Levinas has no need of the 'sad comment'? If the sincerity of saying indicates the pretheoretical and ethical condition of language, if it is thus that the subject enters language, nothing has been lost. It is never too late for sincerity, even the simplest. But the comment is also the moment when Kant's text, in noticing the need for a turn to language and speech as the place where the ethical drama is to be played out, denies itself the luxury of a renewed sincerity. The risk of public morality is compounded by the fact that the appeal to sincerity, perhaps more than anything else, can only be heard as unphilosophical, uncritical and naïve, the exception being the simple and straightforward honesty of someone like Job. We admire a simplicity we can never simply emulate or retrieve. In concluding the exposition by linking the saying to a single (i.e. undoubled) sincerity, does Levinas not momentarily become naïve, and naïve in a way that the Kant of the Third Critique suggests must elicit a partially amused response? Kant, we might say, suggests that reason demands a doubling and complicating of sincerity. Well, if reason cannot be simple here of all places, so much the worse for reason. But if Levinas is proposing to support and be supported by a simplicity that reason can never recognize, is it possible to take him entirely seriously? Such a simplicity would not function as a necessary presupposition or premise, nor would it be of the order of an admission that one always has to start and stop somewhere; each of these gestures already admits to the absence of the sincere simple as it is figured in the saying. We might want to say though that the complexity of *Otherwise than Being* tells against this reading. How else can we begin to do justice to Levinas's variations on and with the exemplary and always legitimate thesis of scepticism? Levinas, as much as anyone, is aware of the intricacies of his exposition and aware that it cannot ascribe to its theme, its said, the character of the saying. There is no sincere said. No said can demonstrate, in its being said, that it is sincerely said. Sincerity can only be thought in relation to the command that there continue to be something said. Put like this, notice how close to Kant's comment we have come, and perhaps have to come. For both Kant and Levinas, sincerity is an exposition to critique, and for Kant this is only made explicit in the wake of his last critical treatment of theodicy just as for Levinas it follows from a description of suffering which entails a refusal of theodicy.

We are left with a final choice. Either Levinas and Kant close a certain descriptive philosophical critique with a very similar word on sincerity, either here the two trajectories become indistinguishable, or else Levinas's would continue to insist on a difference by claiming a pre-Kantian naïvety, an exposition to critique that remains somehow precritical. The sadness in Kant's comment, however, would always make us aware of the inability on the part of the reader simply or naïvely to accept that naïvety or simplicity. The drama already underway in our speech and writing, and which for Kant and Levinas attests to the impossibility of relying any longer on a prelinguistic straightforwardness, must also oblige us to read 'naïvety' and 'sincerity' at least without naïvety. Either here Levinas and Kant are saying the same or else Levinas is saying something to which Kant has already posed a difficult and critical question. However we go about deciding this, it cannot rest on an uncritical claim to the authority of the irreplaceable. Such a claim can only compromise the necessarily philosophical character of Levinas's ethical critique, and 'ethics, in Levinas, still belongs to the philosophical, as it does in Kant'.[15]

NOTES

* An earlier version of this chapter originally appeared in *Research in Phenomenology*, 28 (1998), 126–51, and permission to reproduce it here is gratefully acknowledged.

1 Deliberately not at issue here is the whole question of Kant's relation to a certain Judaism, the Kantian acceptance of a God who although an object of thought or reverence can never be an object of cognition. We are thus not concerned here with the way in which the Hegelian critique of Kant's moral philosophy and philosophical theology seems to draw attention to an irreducibly Judaic aspect in Kant's work, an aspect of particular concern, for example, to Nietzsche and Derrida. Interestingly, the word 'God' – and God is only a word, albeit the first – will not play any real role in Levinas's explicit responses to Kant even though Kant's check to the operations of a theistic ontology in the First Critique, both in the fourth antinomy and in the treatments of the traditional proofs of God's existence, might have been taken as hinting that the word 'God' was henceforth to be employed differently, in the service of another philosophy and in the recognition of another priority. It would be a topic for another study, a comparison of the various ways in which Kant and Levinas justify a continued philosophical use of the word 'God', a use beyond the delimiting of any discourse in which talk of God legitimates or presupposes talk of the being of God. It is not irrelevant for the purposes of the present study, however, to note that something in the reading and reception of Kant's critical project seems to prevent Levinas from endorsing or even making this sort of comparison himself.

2 *Philosophical Investigations*, trans. G. E. M. Anscombe (Oxford: Blackwell, 1967) p. 229e. For some discussion of Wittgenstein and Levinas see J. Greisch, 'The Face and Reading: Immediacy and Mediation', in Robert Bernasconi and Simon Critchley (eds.), *Re-Reading Levinas* (Bloomington: Indiana University Press, 1991), pp. 70ff.

3 Thus again, in *Dieu, la Mort, et le Temps*, we read: 'The practical philosophy of Kant shows that the Heideggerian reduction is not obligatory. That in the history of philosophy there can be a signification other than finitude' (*GDT* 61). The footnote added to these sentences returns us to the passage from OB, 'If one had the right . . .'.

4 Kant, *The Metaphysics of Morals*, trans. Mary Gregor (Cambridge: Cambridge University Press, 1991), p. 258.

5 Kant, 'Of the miscarriage of all philosophical trials in theodicy', in *Religion and Rational Theology*, trans. Allen W. Wood and George di Giovanni (eds.) (Cambridge: Cambridge University Press, 1996), p. 32. 'Über das Misslingen aller philosophischen Versuche in der Theodizee',

Immanuel Kant Werkausgabe XI: Schriften zur Anthropologie, Geschichtsphilosophie, Politik und Pädagogik I (Frankfurt am Main: Suhrkamp, 1978), p. 117. References to the German edition will be given in brackets.

6 This would be a useful moment to recall Levinas's tense relationship with the writings of Simone Weil, whose critical dismissal and opposition to the Jewish Bible prompts some of his angriest remarks. When Weil describes suffering as the evidence of the 'superiority of man over God' and continues 'The Incarnation was necessary so that this superiority should not be scandalous' we seem to be in a discourse diametrically opposed to Levinas's. For Levinas, the superiority of the other man over God and, indeed, the superiority of the law (the Torah) that would compel me to act for the other man does not need its scandalousness to be mitigated or repressed, but rather intensified. In Weil's work, suffering, thought by way of the incarnation, is always either *my* or *our* suffering, and if there is a suffering of suffering it is bound up with my attempts to suffer my suffering uncomplainingly and 'to remain untainted' by it. Cf. Simone Weil, *Gravity and Grace* (London: Routledge, 1952) pp. 72–3, and Levinas 'Simone Weil against the Bible', in *DF*. There are, however, indications that the relationship is not straightforwardly critical. Levinas, after all, is not simply *for* the Bible. Cf. the footnote to *OB*, p. 138, n. 3 p. 198, in which one of Weil's prayers and her notion of decreation is permitted to stand as a partial paraphrase of Levinas's substitution.

7 Martin Heidegger, *The Basic Problems of Phenomenology*, trans. A. Hofstadter (Bloomington: Indiana University Press, 1982), p. 133. See also John Llewelyn, *The Middle Voice of Ecological Conscience* (London: Macmillan, 1991), pp. 70–2.

8 *The Metaphysics of Morals*, p. 226.

9 Kant, *Critique of Judgement*, trans. Werner S. Pluhar (Indianapolis: Hackett, 1987), p. 206.

10 'Of the miscarriage of all philosophical trials in theodicy', p. 33 (119).

11 *Ibid.*, p. 35 (121–2).

12 *Ibid.*, p. 36 (122).

13 See Peter Fenves, *A Peculiar Fate: Metaphysics and World History in Kant* (New York: Cornell University Press, 1991) p. 278. Another discussion of Kant's interpretation of Job can be found in Werner Hamacher, *Premises: Essays on Philosophy and Literature from Kant to Celan* (Cambridge: Harvard University Press, 1996), pp. 106–8.

14 Including prayer. Kant reflects on prayer and sincerity in *Religion within the Bounds of Mere Reason*. Cf. *Religion and Rational Theology*, p. 210.

15 Maurice Blanchot, 'Do Not Forget', in Michael Holland (ed.), *The Blanchot Reader* (Oxford: Blackwell, 1995), p. 245.

9 Language and alterity in the thought of Levinas

A work of literary translation, says Walter Benjamin, exists as though stationed outside of a forest it cannot enter and as calling into 'the wooded ridge' in order to receive an echo that gives back in its own language that which reverberates in the alien one.[1] The work of Levinas is such an invocation, an effort at translating incommensurables, a troping of that which cannot be troped, an unassimilable excess that resists apprehension in propositional discourse. This 'more' that remains beyond spoken or written language is the otherness of the other person, an otherness that cannot be configured as a content of consciousness but that issues an imperative that obliges me to assume responsibility for the other.

Like the otherness of another human being, the more of the infinite overflows the idea that attempts to contain it, its superabundance both traduced and expressed in acts of translation into the language of philosophy. The other human being in the sanctity of her or his manifestation as a human face and the infinite as an *ideatum* whose excessiveness goes beyond any idea we can have of it can only be the objects of an insatiable desire. Any translation (always already merely putative) demands a contraction of this content so that on the one hand it is communicated and on the other retains its ethical authority, the exteriority from which it derives. In order for there to be translation, there must be a pre-existent store of concepts, a speculative language without which translation could not come about, yet one that is disrupted by the more, the exorbitance, of an alterity that is beyond it.

Levinas's enterprise is indebted to Heidegger's forging of a conceptual language that makes accessible the primordial affective relations through which human existents apprehend the world. In bringing to the fore what Levinas calls the pathic elements hitherto refractory to philosophical speculation, Heidegger offers an account of these affects in light of the meaning of Being. Taking the verb 'to be' as active, Heidegger attributes to Being the activity that had generally been ascribed to the existent. Meaning for the Heidegger of *Being and Time* is, in Levinas's view, disclosed in terms of the ontological difference, the difference between Being and beings. Yet it is precisely Heidegger's interpreting of Being as active, as the power of Being, rather than turning to the Good that Plato had discerned as lying beyond Being, that leads Levinas to dissociate his thought from that of Heidegger. Acknowledging his indebtedness, Levinas nevertheless feels compelled to 'leave the climate of that philosophy' (*EE* 19). Heidegger's account of the relationship of human beings to Being as power, Levinas maintains, can only engender political and economic relations founded on violence.

To challenge this violence still another act of translation is required, one that brings to the fore the commanding *kerygma* of the Hebrew Scriptures and the Talmud, the rabbinic commentary on Scripture in the language of Western thought not, *per impossibile*, to exhume their underlying equivalence but rather to correct the hubris of philosophical rationality. The mandate of absolute alterity condensed for him in the synecdoche 'Hebrew' calls into question the self-satisfaction of philosophy that penetrates even philosophy's moments of incertitude. Despite his critical appraisal of philosophy as the conceptual language of ontology and of Being's potential for violence, Levinas never reneges on his allegiance to the rationality of Western thought without which the ethical could not be brought within human purview. The essential task of language is not to express what cannot be expressed, the excess that lies beyond being. Rather thought that betrays as it exposes this excess can be regarded as envisaging a certain difference, as a thinking of the ligature between philosophy and that which transcends it, that separates as it unites them.

In what follows, I shall discuss the multiplicity of meanings attributed to language in Levinas's thought. I shall turn first to the ways in which sensibility, the infra-cognitive world of sensation and enjoyment, and totality, the historical whole, cultural, political and economic as constituted by thought, may be disrupted. In this context, I focus upon the face of the other who is beyond the totality, the other who is seen as elevated and without history and who insinuates her/himself into my world as my interlocutor. Always already language, the face of the other intrudes into the totality that has been historically constituted and issues a call to responsibility. Understood in Hegelian terms, 'the face breaks the system' (*EN* 34).

Next, I shall consider language as gift, as a bestowal of signification upon another. Thence I turn to the 'dionysian' languages of art and of a certain poetics contested by Levinas. Finally I discuss an ethics that becomes discourse, a discourse that becomes ethics. A language that is prior to speech, one that is always already ethical, will be seen in its relation to propositional discourse, the language of linguistic practices and 'semantic glimmerings'. Language is not defined as the transposition of words into referents or by the formalism of the relation of signifiers to one another but as an ethical relation, a responsibility to the other person, 'a semantics of proximity' (*OS* 93).[2] It could be argued that this order of enquiry suggests a developmental sequence in the work of Levinas who denies that there is, in the manner of Heidegger, a significant *Kehre* in his thinking.[3] Yet despite the thematic unity of its preoccupation with the ethical relation, differences of approach may be discerned. *Totality and Infinity* (1961) and the essays of this period consider the disruptions of alterity within the constraints of ontological language whereas *Otherwise than Being or Beyond Essence* (1974) describes the unlimited accusation of self by the other, the radical passivity of subjectivity, the ethical that is the primordial signification of the one-for-the-other that gives rise to the distinction between the Saying and said.[4]

TOTALITY AND ITS UNDOING

Totality is for Levinas a freighted term that includes epistemological, historical and political meanings. In its broadest signification, totality designates a whole, such that 'a multiplicity of objects... or in a homogeneous continuum, a multiplicity of points or of elements [that] form a unity, or come without remainder under a sole act of thought' (*AT* 39).[5] Levinas points to the danger of a thought so encompassing that the intellectual act that intends the whole loses touch with the world in its concreteness and is left with the pure form of the thinkable thus returning to the Kantian problem of the transcendental unity of apperception (AT 41). Hegel, he argues, understands this dichotomization and tries to breach the real and the rational by organizing the parts heuristically into a system, a system of history. 'The true function of totalizing thought does not consist in looking at being, but in determining it by organizing it' (AT 47).[6] For Levinas, such organization or totalization is an expression of freedom, one that is intrinsically time tied, so that totality's historical dimension is not merely incidental but integral to it: history is totalization itself (AT 47).

The politics that Levinas sees embedded in this history is a politics of war and cannot be overcome by way of the fragile peace that supervenes upon war. As in Hegel's phenomenology, 'the trial by force is the test of the real' (TI 21). The totality can be disrupted only by that which lies outside it, a dimension Levinas does not hesitate to call eschatology. The term is not to be understood teleologically as referring to the aim of some future time but rather as the instituting of a relation that is beyond the totality and as a drawing of beings out of history, beings who always already speak (TI 22).

If there is a content whose excessiveness overflows the capacity of consciousness to contain it, one that cannot become the aim of cognitive intention or of a need that can be satisfied, this more must be the object of a desire that precludes satiety. Such an excess is the human face whose exposure is prior to thematization, to phenomenological description. Although beyond discursive formulation, the face discloses itself as language. What is expressed is united with the one who expresses in a ligation that binds and unbinds what can never be made commensurable.

For Levinas, 'to present oneself as other is to signify or to have meaning. To present oneself as signifying is to speak' (TI 65–6). Speech that emanates from another is always already a pedagogy, a magisterial putting into questions of cognition. The arena of ethics is not a level playing field in which all are alike but rather one in which self and other are absolutely asymmetrical. Levinas contends that 'the presentation of the face is not true, for the true refers to the non-true, its eternal contemporary ... The presentation of being in the face does not leave any logical place for its contradictory' (TI 201).[7] In sum, the depiction of alterity seems to thematize the other, but language is always already an address to and from the other who cannot be contained within a common genus as an essence of human being. Discourse is the experience of absolute exteriority, an otherness that is foreign, 'a traumatism of astonishment' (*TI* 73).

ALTERITY AND THE UNIVERSAL

Could it not be argued that even if the other commands me in a relation to which I alone can respond that the other finds her- or himself in a comparable situation so that each one becomes a self in so far as she/he is solicited by another? In that case, each other is like every other other and ethics is in fact grounded in the universal.[8] Otherness in the absence of individual specificity would then become a vacuous concept, an otherness common to all or as one critic would have it: 'To respect the other in his non-objective subjectivity ... means only to respect first the general community which is bound together by [a] generalized otherness', that Levinas, however, means to surmount.[9]

In a complex argument that in part responds to the criticism that undifferentiable alterity entails an empty universality, Derrida points to the inherent necessity of the betrayal of the beyond of ontology. He contends that Levinas takes calculated risks when tying together spoken language and the beyond in such a way that calculation leaves room for the incalculable.[10] It is the language of the ligature between the before and the beyond that attests that there is a beyond, that which cannot come into plenary presence. 'Contamination is no longer a risk but a fatality that must be assumed.'[11] Within this contaminated framework of a language, the self as the irreplaceable one, says, 'At this very moment, here I am [me voici]', thereby offering her-/himself as hostage for the other, as a singularity that defies description yet at the same time speaks.

But, as Derrida reveals, there is still another issue at stake, that of distinguishing the human other from the infinite other. In explaining Levinas's claim, 'Tout autre est tout autre [Every other one is every bit other]', Derrida shows that the sentence need not be read as a tautology, that two senses of *tout* may be distinguished which, in turn, lead to differentiable uses of *autre*:

If the first *tout* is an indefinite pronominal adjective [some, some other one], then the first *autre* becomes a noun and the second [an adverb of quantity (totally, absolutely radically infinitely other)] in all probability, an adjective or attribute. One no longer has a case of tautology but instead a radical heterology; indeed this introduces the principle of the most irreducible heterology.[12]

At the same time, if the homonyms are read tautologously, the sentence can be glossed as a swallowing up of the other, an interpretation that could be seen as an entering wedge into a Kierkegaardian reading. On this view, Derrida claims, the other does not disappear but introduces into a hetero-tautological dimension, the altogether other who is God. To be sure, Kierkegaard attributes homogeneity to human others – the ethical is the universal – whereas God is the altogether other. But in the hope of rescuing human singularity by seeing every human other as other than every other other, Levinas cannot, as he would wish, distinguish between human others and the infinite other. Derrida concludes that no line could then be drawn between the ethical and the religious.[13] This conclusion is borne out by Levinas's remark: 'If the word religion is . . . to indicate that the relation between men, irreducible to understanding . . . in human faces joins the infinite – I accept that ethical resonance of the word with all its Kantian reverberations' (*EN* 8).

THE GIFT OF DISCOURSE

The meaning of gift made thematic in French thought from Marcel Mauss to Georges Bataille is seen by Derrida as a key motif that wends its way through Levinas's understanding of alterity. For Levinas death is the gift that can be given to the other. In his critique of Heidegger's account of mortality, Levinas faults Heidegger for seeing death as one's ownmost possibility and for the additional claim that the call of responsibility is first heard in the *Jemeinigkeit* of my death. In its being-towards-death, *Dasein* answers first and foremost for itself. By contrast, for Levinas, my ipseity, 'the sameness of myself', is constituted *post hoc* through my relation to the other.[14] I am always already included in the death of the other as being called upon to sacrifice myself for the other. As an irreplaceable substitute for her or him, I bestow upon her or him the gift of death. 'Death, source of all myths, is *present* only in the Other, and only in him does it summon me urgently to my final essence, to my responsibility' (*TI* 179). Yet for Levinas gift-giving is bound up with the notion of economy without which the gift cannot be understood. The world as signification opened up by utterance is given to the other as language, a signification that challenges the life of economy. Far from analysing the globalization of economy or the commodification of discourse, Levinas envisages economic relations as rooted in more basic world relations that may be traced to Heidegger's descriptions of the primordial comportments that characterize being in the world, comportments that for Levinas include need, enjoyment, habitation and, as arising out of habitation, work.[15] Levinas contends that work reduces the otherness of the world to the same but the worker does not control what is produced by the activity of labour. 'Works have a destiny independent of the I, are integrated in an ensemble of works ... maintained in the anonymity of money' (TI 176).[16] Bought, sold and interpreted by others, works no longer express the I of my interiority. What is true for me holds also for the works of others.

Work derives from a self that lives in a home, departs from and returns to it. It is as habitation, as home, that a space is opened that enables one to represent things and from which the face of another may be encountered, another who calls the self that has emerged as a separated being into question and who 'paralyzes possession'. By disengaging the self from objects, language contests relations of possession, the realm of economy understood in terms of money, ownership and exchange. 'The calling in question of the I, coextensive with the manifestation of the Other in the face, we call language' (TI 171), Levinas avers.

Far from reflecting the fall of a primordial speech, language as actual discourse is not the regrettable traducing of alterity, a violation of transcendence, but a gift, an offering of that which is thematized to the other. 'To thematize is to offer the world to the other in speech' (TI 209), to manifest beings through representation and concept, to say what they are. Knowledge is the correlation between intending acts of consciousness, a consciousness that posits itself as self-identity, and the objects intended. In its relation with what is other than itself, it reduces the alterity of its object to the same. But language as gift exceeds the speech that brings objects into plenary presence to include the bearer of discourse, the one who calls violence into question. In the absence of the other, the meaning of individuals emanates from the totality whose significance derives from power that is ultimately expressed in war (TI 24). The cessation of violence that supervenes upon war is an ersatz peace, that merely substitutes the violence of exploitation grounded in economy for actual war (EN 37).

Speech in conferring signification brings the world to the other, thereby creating a common world. Far from endorsing an infrarational dissolution of speech in favour of a primordial relation to the world as sensible quality, Levinas sees signification, the capacity to generalize, as an ethical event. An individual entity receives a universal meaning through the word that designates it to another. The *hic et nunc* of the thing is first experienced as possession, thereby presupposing economy. To be sure, the thing is first mine but language which designates it thereby giving it to the other is a dispossession, 'a first donation' (TI 173). Generalization as an invoking of the world in acts of nomination is an offering of the world to another.[17]

THE FACE: PHENOMENON OR ENIGMA?

How does a relation anterior to comprehension, one that is ungrounded and remains refractory to incorporation into concepts, come to us? In concurrence with Husserl's account of phenomena, Levinas maintains that things emerge from a horizon, give themselves perspectively. By contrast, the human face as starting from itself without recourse to form, an outside that enters the sphere of visibility, gives itself otherwise than as a visible configuration. As distinct from Max Picard's poetizing of the face, or from Sartre's account of it as expressing a social role or from Deleuze's interpretation of the face as an icon of imperialist force, for Levinas the face in its very upsurge breaks into a world that is seen and understood but manifests itself otherwise than as idea or image. Is the face, then, a content that in bypassing form gives itself directly as an encounter with pure sensibility in an experience of sheer enjoyment? In relations of pure sensibility the boundaries between self and other are blurred, thereby blocking out the alterity of the other human being. How, it must be asked, does the face overcome the hegemony of ontology, of the being that is cognized to open a new dimension within the sensible?

The face is not an appearance but rather an epiphany that resists conceptual grasp, rending the sensible through which it appears. It proffers itself as defenceless, 'in the nudity of the absolute openness of the transcendent' (*TI* 199) expressing itself in its alterity as destitution and as a solicitation to desist from violence. Challenging the freedom of action that opens the arena of violence, the face unfolds as a discourse that resists violence, as speech 'whose first word is obligation' to the other (*TI* 201). It is not freedom that grounds an ethics of non-violence, of genuine peace, but anterior to freedom, the face of the other reveals the totality as injustice.

It can be argued that if the face belongs to the arena of visibility, its very appearing must somehow be 'disconnected' or bracketed not in the interest of exhuming pure or absolute consciousness through phenomenological reduction, but rather to release its ethical signification. If Levinas remains phenomenological, it is not because he puts the *existence* of the face out of play, as Husserl brackets the existence of the world, but rather because he refuses to grant transcendent meaning to the face as image.[18]

The resistance to images reflects the strenuous opposition to anthropomorphic imagery in conformity with the long Biblical and rabbinic tradition that Levinas affirms. In accordance with this tradition, the most serious theological error consists in the imputation of corporeality to God, an error that undergirds idolatry which, as Maimonides defines it, is the idea that a particular form represents the agent between God and his creatures.[19] Idolatry is precipitated by the unfettering of a figural imagination required by ordinary mortals in order to render theological truths accessible but which disfigures this truth through figuration itself. Maimonides concedes that prophecy requires both the logical and imaginative faculties even if the rational faculty is to predominate. The danger of the hypertrophied imagination cited by Maimonides releases the image's power to unleash a mixture of true and imaginary things.[20] Even in prophetic visions, Maimonides warns, the *viva vox* of God is absent; when thought to be heard, it is only imagined to be present. Moses alone, he contends, is exempt from the mediation of deceptive screening images: 'All prophets are prophetically addressed through an angel except Moses our teacher, in reference to whom Scripture says, "Mouth to mouth I speak to him".'[21] In conformity with this account, for Levinas the other is always already given as unmediated discourse. 'Speech cuts across vision' (*TI* 195).

Levinas could hardly be unaware of the polysemy of the common Hebrew term for face (*panim*) as adumbrated by Maimonides. Not only does the word have a corporeal referent but, in one of its forms, means 'in ancient times' as in the sentence 'Of old (*lephanim*) hast thou laid the foundations of the earth' (Psalm 102:5), a signification reflected in Levinas's account of a past that can never be made present inscribed in the human countenance as a trace. *Panim* in another metonymic expansion can also mean persons receiving attention and regard. The semantic resonances of *panim* from its meaning as archaic time to its meaning as regard for another can be seen as 'translated' into the atemporality of an irrecoverable archaic past and regard for the other.

In sum, the face belongs to the world it inhabits but must in some fashion retain the alterity of a beyond, a transcendence that is inscribed as a trace that attests an indestructible alterity. As signifying the transcendent, the face does not nullify what it signifies in order to force its entry into an immanent order. 'Here on the contrary transcendence refuses immanence as the ever bygone transcendence of the transcendent' (*TIO* 355). The trace (as we have seen) issues from an immemorial past that Levinas calls eternity, a past that can neither be converted to the present of the acts of a self nor incorporated into the diachronicity of the historical process. The face of the other itself becomes a trace whose demands are in excess of any response I may make and before which I inevitably fall short.

If the face is in the trace of that which is beyond, may we not ask whether the trace is not the trace of 'something', perhaps of a God who remains invisible. Levinas rejects any facile imputation of causality to God, so that the trace becomes the sign of a hidden God who 'imposes the neighbor on me' (*OB* 94). Rather the other is always already in the trace of what he calls illeity, the 'He is He', that attests to an unassimilable otherness (*EN* 57).[22] I cannot follow the trace as though it were a path or a way through which one might approach God. Instead I am adjured to turn to the other who stands in the trace of illeity. 'To be in the image of God is not to be an icon of God but to find oneself in his trace' (*BPW* 64). Is the trace as a beyond that falls into immanence not always already contaminated? Derrida suggests:

The contamination of the beyond language and the he within the economic immanence of language and its dominant interpretation is not merely an evil or negative contamination, rather it describes the very process of the trace insofar as it makes a work in a work-making that must neither be grasped by means of work nor of making, [but by what is said of the work] the saying of the said.[23]

ART AND THE POETIC WORD

Because art consists of images that purport to convey truth, to supersede common-sense perceptions of reality, Levinas is compelled to mount an argument against the view that visual art inaugurates signification. First, he contends, in art, the image substitutes for the object and severs the relation of object to concept. Second, the unleashing of a flood of images may lead to expressions of frenzied affect that for Levinas are manifested as paganism, a term he associates with a range of meanings from the exaltation of nature as impersonal fecundity which he identifies with Heidegger's ontology (*TI* 46) to the participation in mystical reality he attributes to non-literate societies as depicted by Levy-Bruhl.[24] Art is seen as a conjuration of images that may effect a return to 'the mythical format of the elemental', a world of pure qualities 'that lies escheat . . . a terrain that is fundamentally non-possessable, "nobody's," earth, sea, light, city' (*TI* 131). The elemental both gives itself and escapes into that in which it is extended, the *il y a*, an existence without existents. 'The aesthetic orientation man gives to the whole of his world represents a return to enjoyment and to the elemental on a higher plane' (*TI* 140). Restated in Adorno's more accessible terms, 'pure' figuration is self-defeating 'for it augments the chaotic moment lurking in all art as its pre-condition'.[25] The world of the elemental is that of faceless gods who do not speak.

Levinas insists that art is a doubling of the real in that a thing is what it is, while the image exists as its double. In the act of representation, I am aware of the absence of the object but in the case of the image I behold a tableau. Anticipating what Guy Debord now calls a culture of the spectacle, Levinas sees the image in art as supplanting the existent. As Deleuze would have it, the problem is one 'of distinguishing between things and their simulacra . . . a question of making the difference, thus of operating in the depths of the immediate . . .'[26] The artwork does not open out into the world that the artist knows in his everyday life, an actual world, but rather precedes it.

It can be said that poetry is not susceptible to the critique of images in that images are infra-discursive and the poem is already language.

But what does language mean in this context? For Heidegger, the essential being of language is a saying that reveals itself as showing, as a letting be seen and heard. The disclosive character of language is not the result of human activity but of a prior letting itself be shown that is 'the mark of everything that is present'.[27] The 'moving force' of the showing of saying that brings beings into their own is owning or appropriation that yields the opening of a clearing in which beings can endure or withdraw. Inexplicable in causal terms, appropriation is not an event that can be represented but the gift of language, of saying as showing, of Being's revealing itself.[28] In what has become a familiar apothegm, Heidegger maintains that 'Language is the house of Being.'[29] The poet experiences his poetic calling as a call to the word as the source, 'the bourn of being'.[30] Things that already exist do not antedate poetic language but, in Hölderlin's words, '"What endures is founded by poets"'.[31] The founding speech of the poet is a speaking that belongs to visibility: to speak is to see. As Blanchot points out, for Levinas the reverse is the case: 'To speak is not the same as to see.'[32] Rather speech frees thought from the imperative of visibility that has dominated it.

For Levinas, a work of literature is an evasion in a world that demands a response to the command for responsibility for the other. Only interpretation, the language of criticism, can call art to order. The critic treats the art work as the product of labour so that it may enter the realm of history. As an attempt to substitute itself for the infinite semantic potential of language, the literary work demands clarification by the critic (CP 12–13).[33] Although it belongs to another realm of discourse, Levinas can be interpreted as making a comparable demand with respect to the exegesis of the text of the Talmud, the rabbinic commentary upon scriptural verses. Interpretation, he insists, must not allow thought to be impeded by 'the picturesque elements' of the text. Since Talmudic language moves back and forth from concrete problems to general ideas, the latter must 'remain in contact with the examples' but are illuminated by the thought which comes to the world of the text from beyond, or outside (BV 103).

FROM SAYING TO SAID

It might be asked whether Levinas and Heidegger are not closer than is apparent from Blanchot's remark cited earlier. In an essay that could be taken as premonitory of Levinas's account of the difference between the Saying and the said as explicated in *Otherwise than Being*, Heidegger maintains that speaking is at the same time a listening, an attentiveness to language itself. Although speech as vocalization appears to be the opposite of listening, listening is no mere accompaniment of speech. Speaking, Heidegger maintains, is a listening that is prior to speaking. That to which listening listens is language itself as that which had been spoken formerly and as that which still awaits speech: 'We let [language] say its Saying to us. Saying grants us the ability to speak.'[34] For Heidegger, 'we let the soundless voice [of saying] come to us and demand, reach out and call for the sound that is already kept in store for us'.[35] Is there not an attentiveness to others, a reciprocal speaking and hearing already inherent in Heidegger's interpretation of a verse by Hölderlin that maintains we have always been a conversation, able to hear from one another? Could it not be argued that Heidegger has broken free of a monological view of language?[36]

Levinas's implicitly anti-Heideggerian account of the Saying and the said in *Otherwise than Being* can be seen *in nuce* in his encomium for the poetry of Paul Celan, for whom the poem does not express an immersion in sensibility but a solicitation to the other. It is not enough to see language as dialogical, as attesting itself as conversation as if language occurs primordially on a level playing field, as it were. For Levinas, Celan's poetry is a speaking to the other that precedes thematization in which 'qualities gather themselves into things'. In a dense passage in which Celan's poetry is seen to bring to the fore the proximity of the other as though the other were encountered in the tactility of a handshake, Levinas writes:

[The poem is situated] at the moment of pure touching, pure contact, grasping, squeezing – which is perhaps a way of giving, right up to and including the hand that gives. A language of proximity... older than the truth of being... by its for-the-other, the whole marvel of giving. [PN 41]

Celan's poetry is not a belonging within language but an estrangement, an expulsion from nature, from the worldliness of the world as it wends its way not towards language but 'along the impossible path of the Impossible' (PN 46). This path is the infinite way of the approach, a delivering of self that is a saying without anything being said.

Saying as offering oneself to the other is not the result of a will act, an outcome of the freedom of the subject. Self-exposure 'breaks with the ring of Gyges', who in the Platonic myth is protected by invisibility. To say *me voici* in this context is not to designate spatial coordinates but rather to place oneself at the disposal of another (OB 145). To maintain a relation with the near one (the neighbour) is to accept a limitless responsibility, to exist as an extreme passivity before the other who lives as her or his freedom. Saying itself is this passivity rather than the activity of assuming liability for the other. Levinas stresses that it does not suffice to invoke the Heideggerian notion that 'language speaks' to account for this passivity. Rather it is necessary to go beyond receptivity so as to desituate the subject (OB 47–8).

Yet saying must find its way into the language that is uttered and written and that identifies entities, the language of the said, in order to make thought and justice in the social order possible (OB 38–9). Saying itself must be thematized, 'contract into thought', show itself as the subject of a sentence. Together the correlation of saying and said manifest the subject–object structure of language (OB 46). If the said betrays the saying in this act of translation, Levinas hastens to assure us that 'the said in absorbing the Saying does not become its master' (OB 190 n. 34). Saying is not exhausted in the said but imprints its trace in the said. The act of thematization itself is thus caught up in a duality, that of the world of things, a world open to historical description, and that of 'the non-nominalized apophansis of the other' (OB 47).

At the core of Levinas's philosophy of language is his complex analysis of the said, language as it exhibits itself in the structure of predicative propositions that express the meaning of being and that at the same time retain the inscription of the trace. In analysing the said, Levinas brings to the fore the intrinsic binarism of being, what he terms its amphibology. Being, he claims, may refer both to real or ideal entities and also may express an entity's way of being. Levinas does not mean to say naïvely that entities can be seen as substances and events or as static and dynamic. Actions and processes are designated by the verb only secondarily, Levinas warns. Rather, being expresses the temporality of the verb: 'The verbalness of the verb that resounds in the predicative proposition [does so] by virtue of its privileged exposure in time' (OB 39). The term essence designates the fact that there is a theme, one that is not merely conveyed but temporalized in predicative statements. Even seemingly tautologous sentences may reflect this amphibology in that verbs can be nominalized and nouns temporalized. Thus Levinas insists, 'A is A' is not a mere assertion of identity but can mean A A's as in the proposition 'The red reddens.' (Consider Heidegger's *Die Sprache spricht*.) The verb as nominalized confers an identity by conjoining that which is time tied into a unit, while at the same time the entity named may be dissolved in the temporalization of essence (*OB* 38–40). It could be maintained that the Saying is lost in this complex web, absorbed in the said, but it can be said in rejoinder that essence itself is an exposing or being exposed in the resounding of temporalization and thus as awakening the Saying in the said.

Levinas envisages saying as a passivity that is extreme but one that is not puffed up in its self-effacement. This passivity, this excess of exposure without reserve in saying, could be seen as an unsaying of the said, a Saying that would seem to unsay the doubling of being and thought.[37] The radical being for another for which I alone am responsible confers upon me a being chosen to responsibility. A crucial question then arises: is being inescapably obliged to the other, hostage to her or him, to be viewed as the extreme possibility of being or is being hostage to the other a subjection to the 'designs of the Infinite' (*BPW* 153)?[38] The trace of infinity in the subject is precisely this ambivalence, a response to another, an-archic, without beginning, another that is 'witnessed but not thematized' (*OB* 148).

Because the order of the infinite enters into the finite, there is always the possibility that one is oneself the author of what is thought to have been received from elsewhere. Is there a mode of speech through which the infinite escapes objectification by the speaking subject? What Levinas calls prophecy effects a conjoining of the one who is commanded with the signification of the command. 'It is as prophecy that the Infinite escapes objectivity... signifies as illeity' (*OB* 150). Saying undoes the dissimulation of the said, gives sign of itself yet remains clothed in the language of the said. Is not prophecy as this questioning mode of unsaying, Levinas asks, the 'blinking light of revelation' (*OB* 154)?

NOTES

1 Walter Benjamin, *Illuminations: Essays and Reflections*, trans. Harry Zohn (New York: Schocken, 1982), p. 76.
2 The phrase is used as the title of ch. 3 in Krzysztof Ziarek, *Inflected Language: towards a Hermeneutics of Nearness: Heidegger, Levinas,*

Stevens, Celan (Albany: State University of New York Press, 1994), pp. 65–102.

3 In an oral communication to me, Levinas denied such a turning, insisting 'Je ne suis pas Heidegger'.

4 For a concise summary of these shifting emphases in the work of Levinas as interpreted by Stephen Strasser, Etienne Feron, Fabio Ciaramelli and Adriaan Peperzak, see Bettina Bergo, *Levinas: between Ethics and Politics* (Dordrecht: Kluwer Academic Publishers, 1999), pp. 132–47.

5 Although this essay first published in 1968 follows *Totality and Infinity* (1961), it succinctly captures some epistemic issues explicated in that work.

6 The now much cited influence upon Levinas of Rosenzweig's revolt against Hegel is here in evidence. In his 'Franz Rosenzweig: a modern Jewish thinker', in *Outside the Subject*, Levinas speculates that whether Rosenzweig had Meinecke's or some other Hegel before him, Rosenzweig was persuaded that 'a history made up of wars and revolutions had a Hegelian face' as did the absence of the person of the thinker in his thought (see esp. pp. 52–3). For an extended analysis of the relation of Levinas to Rosenzweig, see Robert Gibbs, *Correlations in Rosenzweig and Levinas* (Princeton: Princeton University Press, 1992).

7 Robert Bernasconi in 'Skepticism in the Face of Philosophy', in Robert Bernasconi and Simon Critchley (eds.), *Re-Reading Levinas* (Bloomington: Indiana University Press, 1991) points to the bypassing by scepticism of this alternation, its 'secret diachrony' that escapes the synchronous time of contradictories (p. 150). Disagreeing with Jan de Greef's 'Skepticism and Reason', trans. Dick White in Richard A. Cohen (ed.) *Face to Face with Levinas* (Albany: State University of New York Press, 1986) he sees de Greef as trying to 'save Levinas from refutation by reason' and, in trying to do so, 'deny[ing] that skepticism is ever refuted' (p. 161, n. 19).

8 Fabio Ciaramelli, 'Levinas's Ethical Discourse between Individuation and Universality', in Bernasconi and Critchley, *Re-Reading Levinas*, discusses the difficulty of giving universal meaning to one's own particularity (p. 92).

9 John Milbank, *The Word Made Strange: Theology, Language, Culture* (Cambridge: Blackwell Publishers, 1997), p. 223.

10 Jacques Derrida, 'At this very Moment in this Work Here I Am', in Bernasconi and Critchley *Re-reading Levinas*, p. 29.

11 *Ibid.*, p. 30.

12 Jacques Derrida, *The Gift of Death*, trans. David Wills (Chicago: University of Chicago Press, 1992), pp. 82–3.

13 *Ibid.*

14 *Ibid.*, pp. 46–7.

15 One may single out from the extensive literature commenting on Heidegger's influence on Levinas in this regard, Stephen Strasser, *Jenseits von Sein und Zeit. Eine Einfuhrung in Emmanuel Levinas Philosophie*, Phaenomenologica 78 (The Hague: Martinus Nijhoff, 1978); John Llewelyn, *The Middle Voice of Ecological Consciousness: a Chiasmic Reading of Responsibility in the Neighborhood of Levinas, Heidegger and Others* (New York: St Martin's Press, 1991); Gianni Vattimo, *Les Aventures de la Différance* (Paris: Editions de Minuit, 1985).

16 In *Entre Nous*, Levinas's attitude towards money is not altogether negative. He maintains that in an economy singular beings for whom concepts are lacking are totalized. 'It is an ambiguous milieu in which persons are integrated into the order of merchandise but, at the same time, remain persons' (p. 37). Money provides a quantitative measure in the absence of which human violence could be rectified only by relations of vengeance or forgiveness.

17 For an analysis of Derrida's account of the ambiguities of naming, see Simon Critchley '"*Bois*" – Derrida's Final Word on Levinas', in Bernasconi and Critchley, *Re-Reading Levinas*, pp. 162–89. Interpreting Derrida's reading of this issue, Critchley examines the question of what it would mean to return Levinas's work to his proper name. 'To whom should Levinas's work be returned in order to retain ethical alterity? Might not the answer be Elle and not E.L?' (p. 169).

18 The relation of Levinas to Husserlian phenomenology has been described in sources too numerous to list. The following bear on the present problem: Theo de Boer, 'An Ethical Transcendental Philosophy', in Cohen, *Face to Face with Levinas*, pp. 83–115, interprets Levinas's thought as transcendental philosophy that works back from objectifying cognition to that which precedes it; Adriaan Peperzak in 'From Intentionality to Responsibility', in Arleen B. Dallery and Charles E. Scott (eds.), *The Question of the Other* (Albany: State University of New York Press, 1989), pp. 3–22 tracks Levinas's path from intentionality to his later work on language and responsibility; Silvano Petrosini and Jacques Roland in *La Verité Nomade* (Paris: Editions la Decouverte, 1984) describe Levinas's thought as an archaeology of meaning. As preceding essence, meaning is anterior to constituting consciousness (p. 146).

19 Moses Maimonides, *The Guide for the Perplexed*, trans. M. Friedlander (New York: Dover, 1956; reprint of 2nd rev. edn, 1904), pp. 51–2.

20 *Ibid.*, p. 228.

21 *Ibid.*, p. 245. For an account of the way in which the imaging of self and the discourse of the other in a well-known apothegm of the early

Talmudic sage Hillel enters into configuring the structure of *Totality and Infinity*, see Edith Wyschogrod, 'Emmanuel Levinas and Hillel's Questions', in Merold Westphal (ed.), *Postmodern Philosophy and Christian Thought* (Bloomington: Indiana University Press, 1999), pp. 229–45.

22 See Edith Wyschogrod, *Emmanuel Levinas: the Problem of Ethical Metaphysics*, 2nd edn (New York: Fordham University Press, 2000) pp. 158–64; preface to 2nd edn, pp. xii–xiv.

23 Derrida, 'At this Very Moment in this Work Here I Am', p. 38.

24 'Levy-Bruhl and Contemporary Philosophy', in *Entre Nous: Think-of-the-Other*.

25 Theodor Adorno, *Aesthetic Theory*, trans. C. Lenhardt (London: Routledge and Kegan Paul, 1984), p. 219.

26 Gilles Deleuze, *Difference and Repetition*, trans. Paul Patton (New York: Columbia University Press, 1994), p. 60.

27 Martin Heidegger, 'On the Way to Language', trans. Peter D. Hertz (San Fransisco: Harper, 1982), pp. 122–23.

28 *Ibid.*, p. 127.

29 *Ibid.*, p. 63.

30 *Ibid.*, p. 66.

31 *Ibid.*, p. 168.

32 Maurice Blanchot, *The Infinite Conversation*, trans. Susan Hanson (Minneapolis: University of Minnesota Press), p. 57.

33 Emmanuel Levinas, 'Reality and its Shadow'. See also 'Meaning and Sense', in BPW 41.

34 *On the Way to Language*, p. 123.

35 *Ibid.*, p. 124.

36 For accounts of Heidegger as attentive to ethics, see John Llewelyn, *The Middle Voice of Egological Conscience*; Veronique Foti, *Heidegger and the Poets: Poesis/Sophia/Techne* (Atlantic Highlands: Humanities Press, 1992); Gemma Corradi Fiumara, *The Other Side of Language: a Philosophy of Listening* (London: Routledge, 1990).

37 For an analysis of unsaying in Levinas see Jean Greisch 'The Face and Reading: Immediacy and Mediation', in Bernasconi and Critchley, *Re-Reading Levinas*. Levinas is cited as saying '"There is a need to unsay [*dedire*] all that comes after the nakedness of signs, to set aside all that is said in the pure saying proper to proximity"' (p. 70).

38 Emmanuel Levinas, 'God and Philosophy'.

10   The concepts of art and poetry in Emmanuel Levinas's writings

Being's essence designates nothing that could be a
nameable content, a thing, event, or action; it names this
mobility of the immobile, this multiplication of the
identical, this diastasis of the punctual, this lapse. This
modification without alteration or displacement, being's
essence or time, does not await, in addition, an
illumination that would allow for an 'act of
consciousness.' This modification is precisely the
visibility of the same to the same, which is sometimes
called openness. The work of being, essence, time, the
lapse of time, is exposition, truth, philosophy. Being's
essence is a dissipating of opacity, not only because this
'drawing out' of being would have to have been first
understood so that truth could be told about things,
events and acts that *are;* but because this drawing out is
the *original dissipation* of opaqueness.

Otherwise than Being, or Beyond Essence

Emmanuel Levinas's writings are rich in comments and reflections
on art, poetry and the relations between poetry and ethical theory.[1]
Of particular importance is the question of language, because there
appears to be a kind of symmetry between language as an ethical relation and the language of poetry, both of which expose us to regions
of subjectivity or existence on the hither side of cognition and being.
The ethical and the poetic are evidently species of saying (*le Dire*) in
contrast to the propositional character of the said (*le Dit*), yet neither one is translatable into the other, and in fact they are in some
sense at odds with one another. Unfortunately, Levinas never engaged these matters in any sustained or systematic way, and certainly

never without confusion. His friend Maurice Blanchot observed in an early essay that 'Levinas mistrusts poems and poetic activity'.[2] But it is also clear that Levinas could not get such things out of his mind, for he frequently found in poetry and art conceptual resources for his thinking, which perhaps helps to explain why the ethical in his work is never far removed from the aesthetic. But aesthetic in what sense? My purpose here will be to construct as coherent an account as I can of the place and importance that poetry and art have in Levinas's thinking. This account will have three goals. The first will be to sort out, so far as possible, Levinas's often contradictory statements about art. The second will be to clarify the difference between two conceptions of the aesthetic at work in Levinas's writings, which I will call an aesthetics of materiality and an aesthetics of the visible. The argument here will be that, although Levinas found it difficult to distinguish these two conceptions, or did not want to choose between them, his account of the materiality of the work of art is an important contribution to modernist aesthetics for the way it articulates the ontological significance of modern art and its break with the aesthetics of form and beauty that comes down to us from classical tradition and from Kant. Modern art is no longer an art of the visible (which is why it is difficult for most people to see it as art). Possibly we will be able to say that in Levinas both materiality and the beautiful are reinterpreted in terms of the proximity of things, taking proximity to be something like an alternative to visibility. The third aim of this enquiry will be to come to some understanding of the relationship between poetry and the ethical as analogous forms of transcendence in the special sense that Levinas gives to this term. The argument here will be that, if 'Being's essence is a dissipating of opacity' (OB 30), poetry is a 'darkening of being' (CP 9), a thickening, temporalization or desynchronizing of essence that occurs alongside the ethical, if not in advance of it, as 'an unheard-of modality of the otherwise than being' (PN 46).

POETICS ANCIENT AND MODERN

In order to make my account precise and meaningful, however, it will be helpful to have a rough sense of where Levinas appears within poetry's conceptual history, starting perhaps with the early years of modernity when German and British romantics pressed the question of what sort of thing poetry might be if it is not (as both ancient and medieval traditions of poetics had taught) a form of mediation in the service of other fields of discourse – namely, the versifying of meanings derived from various contexts of learning, or the rehearsal of traditional themes of religious and erotic experience.[3] Arguably the great achievement of modernity was not only the development of scientific reason but also the invention of a concept of art that, whatever its philosophical difficulties, provided a space for speculation in which such a thing as poetry could become (and remain) a question for itself – an event that Arthur Danto, interpreting a famous line from Hegel, has characterized as 'the end of art', or the moment when art and poetry turn self-reflexively into philosophy.[4] For what is distinctive about romantic poetics is that it is no longer concerned simply with the art of composing verses but becomes an enquiry into the nature of poetry and the conditions that make it possible. So Friedrich Schlegel (1772–1829), for example, calls modern poetry a *Transzendentalpoesie* that combines the traditional 'self-mirroring' of the lyrical poet with 'the transcendental raw materials and preliminaries of a theory of poetic creativity [*Dichtungsvermögens*]': 'In all its descriptions, this poetry should describe itself, and always be simultaneously poetry and the poetry of poetry.'[5] As if modern poetry were now become the experience of poetry as such, quite apart from the significance or utility it might still have for the church, the court and the schools.

This is not to say that the classical tradition did not have a profound understanding of the nature (and difficulty) of poetry. For example, the ancients typically regarded poetry as an instance of the dark saying, the *ainigma*, a word that sometimes gets translated as riddle; but unlike a riddle, the enigma's darkness is not something that can be illuminated, or eliminated, by reason or interpretation. It is not a puzzle whose solution justifies its formulation but is opaque in the nature of the case, and to that extent it defines the limits of the discursive regions that we inhabit. Poetry is anarchic in the original sense of the word. In the *Republic* Plato formalized this link between poetry and anarchy (and, in the bargain, instituted the discipline of philosophy) when he charged that poetry is not something that can give itself a reason but is exemplary of all that is incoherent with the just and rational order of things, that is, the order of the λογος, where ideally everything manifests (from within itself) the reason why it is so and not otherwise. Following Plato – or, in the event, Aristotle, who found a place for poetry in his *organon* or rule of discourse by reconceptualizing it both as a species of cognition (mimesis) and as a kind of consecutive reasoning (plot) – the justification of poetry became the traditional task of allegory, which is a philosophical way of reading non-philosophical texts by construing them so as to make them coherent with prevailing true beliefs. Henceforward poetry could only justify itself by celebrating or supplementing conceptual worlds already in place. But taken by itself, the poetic text remains exotic in the etymological sense – dense, refractory to the light, not a part of but *a limit of the world and its reasons* – which is perhaps why the classical tradition in poetics has always been concerned to the point of obsession with rules for keeping poetry under rational control.

In the late nineteenth century the French poet Stéphane Mallarmé (1842–1898) renewed this enigmatic tradition for modernity with his famous remark, 'My dear Degas, one does not make poetry with ideas, but with *words*.' Whereas the romantics had conceptualized poetry as a mode of experience or subjectivity, Mallarmé was the first to conceptualize poetry in terms of language. Indeed, Mallarmé can be said to have inaugurated the radical thesis of literary modernism, namely that a poetic work is made of language but not of any of the things that we use language to produce – meanings, concepts, propositions about the world, expressions of feeling, etc. Not that the poem excludes these things, but it is no longer reducible to any of them because in poetry the *materiality* of language is now regarded as essential, no longer part of a distinction of letter and spirit but now the essence of poetry as such. For Mallarmé, poetry is made of writing (*l'écriture*), so that the basic units of the poem include not only the letters of the alphabet but also the white space of the printed page, the fold in its middle, and the typographical arrangements that the letters inscribe.[6] So poetry is not a form of mediation that brings something other than itself into view (not allegory or symbol). On the contrary, Mallarmé distinguished poetry from informative, descriptive and symbolic uses of language by claiming for the materiality of poetic language the power to obliterate the world of objects and events: 'When I say, "a flower!" then from that forgetfulness to which my voice consigns all floral form, something different from the usual calyces arises . . . the flower which is absent from all bouquets' (OC 356). Writing on Mallarmé in 1942 Maurice Blanchot glossed this famous line by explaining that in its propositional form language

> destroys the world to make it reborn in a state of meaning, of signified values; but, under its creative form, it fixes only on the negative aspect of its task and becomes the pure power of questioning and transfiguration. That is possible insofar as, taking on a tangible quality, it becomes a thing, a body, an incarnate power. The real presence and material affirmation of language gives it the ability to suspend and dismiss the world.[7]

What this means is that poetic language is not just an inert mass, not merely a blank or opaque aesthetic 'veil of words'; rather it is a discursive event that interrupts the logical or dialectical movement of signification and thereby opens up a dimension of exteriority or worldlessness – a world without things, or perhaps one should say: things free of the world.

THE ONTOLOGICAL SIGNIFICANCE OF THE MATERIALITY OF ART

Emmanuel Levinas's earliest writings on art and poetry should be read against the background of the resurgence of interest in Mallarmé that began with the publication of Henri Mondor's *Vie de Mallarmé* in 1941 and Blanchot's critical appropriation of Mallarmé's poetics during this same period, which served to sharpen differences among an array of positions in the controversies about the social significance of art that erupted in Paris following the Liberation.[8] For example, in a series of essays published in 1947 in *Les temps modernes*, Jean-Paul Sartre elucidated his theory of writing as a form of social action by opposing it to poetry conceived explicitly in Mallarméan terms as the work of 'men who refuse to utilize language'.[9] The poet, Sartre says, 'is outside language', on 'the reverse side of words', which he treats as mere things to be assembled the way Picasso constructs a collage (S 64–6/WL 30–1). Meanwhile the prose writer is situated 'inside of language', which he manipulates as an instrument for grasping the world. In prose, words become actions, but poetry for Sartre is the 'autodestruction' of language, whose economy is no longer restricted to the exchange of meanings and the production of rhetorical effects but is now an opaque, thinglike thing (S 70–2/WL 35–7).[10]

In 1947 Levinas published *De l'existence à l'existant*, a series of studies of what might be called, after Georges Bataille, 'limit-experiences', that is, experiences (fatigue, insomina, the experience of art) that are irreducible to categories of cognition and whose analyses serve as a way of exploring subjectivity beyond the limits of conventional phenomenology. In the section entitled 'Existence sans existant' Levinas takes recourse to Mallarméan aesthetics as a way of introducing the concept of the *il y a* – if 'concept' is the word, since the term is meant to suggest the possibility of existence without existents, a pure exteriority of being without appearance, and thus a phenomenology without phenomena. As Levinas figures it, the work of art (by which Levinas, in this context, means the *modern* artwork) opens up this possibility of existence without being because it makes everyday things present by 'extracting [them] from the perspective of the world', where the world is that which comes into being as a correlate of intentionality, cognition or conceptual determination (*EE* 52). The idea is that in art our relation to things is no longer one of knowing and making visible. Art does not represent things, it *materializes* them; or, as Levinas would prefer, it presents things in their *materiality* and not as representations. It is clear that Levinas is thinking of the *work* of the work of art as something very different from the work of intentional consciousness, and this is a difference that enables him to formulate in a new way the fundamental question of modernist aesthetics: 'What becomes of things in art?' It is not enough (or even accurate) to say that modern art repudiates mimesis, representation or realism in order to purify itself of everything that is not art – the so-called doctrine of 'aesthetic differentiation' that figures art as a pure work of the spirit.[11] Levinas speaks rather of 'the quest of modern painting and poetry to banish . . . that soul to which the visible forms were subjected, and to remove from represented objects their servile function as expressions' (*EE* 55). This 'banishment of the soul' means, whatever else it means, that the modern work of art cannot be thought of as just another ideal object that consciousness constructs for itself – a non-mimetic or purely formal object, one determined by traditional canons of beauty; on the contrary, the work is now defined precisely as a limit of consciousness: 'Its intention is to present reality as it is in itself, after the world has come to an end' (*EE* 56), as if on the hither side (*en deça*) of the world that consciousness represents to itself. On this analysis modern art can no longer be conceived as an art of the visible. 'Paradoxically as it may seem', Levinas says,

painting is a struggle with sight. Sight seeks to draw out of the light beings integrated into a whole. To look is to be able to describe curves, to sketch out wholes in which the elements can be integrated, horizons in which the particular comes to appear by abdicating its particularity. In contemporary painting things no longer count as elements in a universal order... The particular stands out in the nakedness of its being [EE 56]

This emancipation of singularity from the reduction to an order of things is the essence of Cubism, whose break-up of lines of sight materializes things in a radical way:

From a space without horizons, things break away and are cast toward us like chunks that have weight in themselves, blocks, cubes, planes, triangles, without transitions between them. They are naked elements, simple and absolute, swellings or abscesses of being. In this falling of things down on us objects attest their power as material objects, even reach a paroxysm of materiality. Despite the rationality and luminosity of these forms when taken in themselves, a painting makes them exist in themselves [le tableau accomplit l'en-soi même de leur existence], brings about an absolute existence in the very fact that there is something which is not in its turn an object or a name, which is unnameable and can only appear in poetry. [EE 56–7]

The idea is that in Cubism the spectator can no longer objectify what he or she sees; the work is no longer visible in the way the world is. For Levinas this means that the materiality of the work of art can no longer be contrasted with form or spirit; it is pure exteriority, uncorrelated with any interior, and therefore it constitutes a kind of transcendence (note that it 'can only appear in poetry'). 'For here materiality is thickness, coarseness, massiveness, wretchedness. It is what has consistency, weight, is absurd, is a brute but impassive presence; it is also what is humble, bare, and ugly' (EE 57). For Levinas, the materiality of the work of art is just this implacable 'materiality of being', where 'matter is the very fact of the il y a' (EE 57). What Levinas wants to know is (and this is evidently the source of his interest in the work of art): What is 'the ontological significance of materiality itself'? (CP 8).

Part of this significance emerges when one asks what happens to subjectivity in the encounter with the work of art. What is it to be involved – or, as Levinas prefers, what is it to *participate* – in the moment when the work of art frees things from the conceptual grasp of the subject and returns them to the brute materiality of existence? The point to mark here is that for Levinas the experience of poetry or art is continuous with the experience of the *il y a*, which *De l'existence à l'existant* describes as an experience of a world emptied of its objects. One has to imagine inhabiting a space that is no longer a lifeworld, as if 'after the world has come to an end'. (In *Totalité et infini* Levinas writes: 'When reduced to pure and naked existence, like the existence of the shades Ulysses visits in Hades, life dissolves into a shadow' (*TI* 112).) Levinas figures this experience of exteriority in terms of insomnia and the interminability of the night, as well as in terms of certain kinds of mystical or magical events in which subjectivity loses itself in an impersonal alterity, but he also compares it to certain kinds of realistic or naturalistic fiction in which '*beings* and things that collapse into their "materiality" are terrifyingly present in their density, weight and shape' (*EE* 59–60). Things present in their materiality (like things in the night) are invisible, ungraspable – and horrible, where horror is not just a psychic tremor but a kind of ontological ecstasy, a movement that 'turns the subjectivity of the subject, his particularity qua entity, inside out' (*EE* 61), thus exposing it to 'the impersonal, non-substantive event of the night and the *il y a*' (*EE* 63). This same ontological ecstasy is what characterizes the experience of the work of art, which on Levinas's analysis can never be an *aesthetic object* – never just something over and against which we can maintain the disinterested repose of the connoisseur; rather, disturbance and restlessness are the consequences of art. The experience of modern art is no longer intelligible from the standpoint of an aesthetics of beauty, with its premium upon the integration of discordant elements into a whole. Modern art, with its premium on the fragmentary, is an art of derangement; it does not produce harmony and repose but dissonance and anxiety (think of the noise of the dada drummer).[12] This is part of what it means to say that modern art is no longer an art of the visible. Indeed, Levinas's analysis opens up what one might call the 'non-aesthetic' dimension of the work of art; or, put differently, Levinasian aesthetics is an aesthetics of darkness rather than of light, of materiality as against spirit (or, more accurately, an aesthetics of materiality that is prior to the alternatives of matter and spirit).

Darkness is the thesis of 'Realité et son ombre' (1948), which begins by stipulating that the work of art is, *contra* the Aristotelian tradition, outside all categories of cognition and representation – outside the light and the visible: 'It is the very event of obscuring, a descent of the night, an invasion of shadow. To put it in theological terms... art does not belong to the order of revelation' (*CP* 3). To be sure, a work of art is made of images, but an image is *not* (as in traditional aesthetics, or in Sartre's theory) a form of mediation; on the contrary, it constitutes a limit and, indeed, a *critique* of experience and therefore of subjectivity as such. Levinas writes: 'An image does not engender a *conception*, as do scientific cognition and truth... An image marks a hold over us rather than our initiative: a fundamental passivity' (*CP* 3).[13] An image works like a rhythm, which

represents a unique situation where we cannot speak of consent, assumption, initiative or freedom, because the subject is caught up and carried away by it... It is so not even despite itself, for in rhythm there is no longer a oneself, but rather a sort of passage from oneself to anonymity. This is the captivation or incantation of poetry and music. It is a mode of being to which applies neither the form of consciousness, since the I is there stripped of its prerogative to assume, its power, nor the form of unconsciousness, since the whole situation and all its articulations are in a dark light, *present*. [*CP* 4]

This conversion to anonymity means simply that art turns the sovereign ego out of its house in a deposition that anticipates the trauma or obsession of the ethical relation.[14] In the experience of the image, Levinas says, the subject is no longer a 'being in the world' – especially since 'What is today called "being-in-the-world" is an existence with concepts' (*CP* 5), with all that this entails in the metaphor of grasping things and laying them open to view (*CP* 3). The image implies a reversal of power that turns the subject into a being 'among things', wandering 'among things as a thing, as part of the spectacle. It is exterior to itself, but with an exterior which is not that of a body, since the pain of the I-actor is felt by the I-spectator, although not through compassion. Here we have really an exteriority of the inward' (*CP* 4).[15] Here (as in Blanchot's poetics) the subject is no longer an 'I' but a 'he' – or, as the French more accurately has it, an *il*: he/it, neither one nor the other (neutral, anonymous). The interior of the subject has been evacuated; the subject is no longer correlative with a world but is, so to speak, outside of it. Perhaps one should say: exposed to it.[16]

At any rate the experience of the image is not an intentional experience: the image is not an image *of* something, as if it were an extension of consciousness, a light unto the world. Phenomenology is mistaken, Levinas says, when it insists on the 'transparency' of images, as if images were signs or symbols, that is, logical expressions of subjectivity – products of 'imagination', for example, supposing there to be such a thing (*CP* 5). But images do not come into being according to a logic of mental operations, say by way of comparisons with an original. On the contrary, *every original is already its own image*:

Being is not only itself, it escapes itself. Here is a person who is what he is; but he does not make us forget, does not absorb, cover over entirely the objects he holds and the way he holds them, his gestures, limbs, gaze, thought, skin, which escape from under the identity of his substance, which like a torn sack is unable to contain them. Thus a person bears on his face, along side of its being with which he coincides, its own caricature, its picturesqueness. The picturesque is always to some extent a caricature. Here is a familiar everyday thing, perfectly adapted to the hand which is accustomed to it, but its qualities, colour, form, and position at the same time remain as it were behind its being, like the 'old garments' of a soul which had withdrawn from that thing, like a 'still life'. And yet all this is the person and is the thing. There is then a duality in this person, this thing, a duality in being. It is what it is and is a stranger to itself, and there is a relationship between these two moments. We will say the thing is itself and is its image. And that this relationship between the thing and its image is resemblance. [*CP* 6]

An image is, so to speak, not a piece of consciousness but a piece of the *il y a*: it is a materialization of being, the way a cadaver is the image of the deceased, a remainder or material excess of being: 'the remains'.[17] Levinas writes: 'A being is that which is, that which reveals itself in its truth, and, at the same time, it resembles itself, is its own image. The original gives itself as though it were at a distance from itself, as though it were withdrawing from itself, as though something in a being delayed behind being' (*CP* 6–7). An image is not a reproduction of a thing but (as in Mallarmé) a withdrawal of it from the world; consciousness is stopped in its tracks by an image and cannot get round behind it to an originating intention that would transform it into a meaning (a symbol or stand-in). Thus a painting is not, *pace* phenomenology, a looking-glass on to another world: 'The painting does not lead us beyond the given reality, but somehow to the hither side of it. It is a symbol in reverse' (CP 7). A 'symbol in reverse' means that the gaze of the spectator stops at the surface of the painting and is, so to speak, held there, on the hither side of being, suddenly passive, no longer seeing but gripped by what it sees in an ecstasy of fascination. The image no longer belongs to the order of the visible. 'It belongs to an ontological dimension that does not extend between us and a reality to be captured, a dimension where commerce with reality is a rhythm' (CP 5).

THE WORK OF ART AS A MODALITY OF TRANSCENDENCE

What is the significance of this dimension – this *irrealité* or materiality of being (CP 8)? This question leads in several directions. The work of art is not a mode of revelation but a mode of transcendence – or, as Levinas says (borrowing from Jean Wahl), *transdescendence* (CP 8): in art reality is beside itself, on the hither side of itself, materialized, no longer an object for us but a thing in itself, a pure exteriority. Basically, art is ecstasy. In the third section of 'Realité et son ombre' Levinas figures this ecstasy or exteriority temporally as an interruption of being: the *entre-temps*, the meanwhile in which the present is no longer a traversal or evanescence but an interval that separates the past from the future, as in the interminability of the statue, or in the fate of the tragic hero for whom the catastrophe has always already occurred:

Art brings about just this duration in the interval, in that sphere which a being is able to traverse, but in which its shadow is immobilized. The eternal duration of the interval in which a statue is immobilized differs radically from the eternity of the concept; it is the meanwhile, never finished, still enduring – something inhuman and monstrous. [CP 11]

To experience art is to enter into this 'inhuman or monstrous' *entre-temps*, which is not a 'now' but an event that interrupts what is happening in the way insomnia keeps the night from passing in sleep, or the way the messianic vigil defers the end of history, or (as in Blanchot's poetics) the way dying is the impossibility of death:

Death qua nothingness is the death of the other, death for the survivor. The time of *dying* itself cannot give itself the other shore. What is unique and poignant in this instant is due to the fact that it cannot pass. In *dying*, the horizon of the future is given, but the future as a promise of a new present is refused; one is in the interval, forever an interval. [CP 11]

It is this interval which explains why, as Levinas says in another context, 'incompletion, not completion, [is] paradoxically the fundamental category of modern art' (OS 147).

But if art is a passage on to the 'inhuman and monstrous', what sort of value, if any, can it have, whatever its ontological significance? Levinas begins his conclusion to 'Realité et son ombre' ('Pour une critique philosophique') by saying that the temporality of the work of art 'does not have the quality of the living instant which is open to the salvation of becoming . . . The value of this instant is thus made of its misfortune. This sad value is indeed the beautiful of modern art, opposed to the happy beauty of classical art' (CP 12). Here Levinas is less than clear, but possibly what he means is that it was the good fortune of the classical work to have a place in the human order of things, which it served to illustrate or even complete as a mode of edification. The classical work was part of the economy of redemption. It was at all events a humanist art. Whereas the modern work is anarchic, that is, without reason or the mediation of any principle or ideality, informed by the *il y a* and structured according to 'the inhuman and monstrous' *entre-temps*. So it is no wonder that the work of art is without any place in the world, which is why modernity sets a special realm aside for it: the museum world of the beautiful or, at any rate, the strange.

Is this separation a condition of art, or a misreading of it? We may not find a straightforward answer to this question in Levinas's texts, but here are three considerations.

(1) It is far from obvious what 'the beautiful of modern art' could consist in, or whether any concept of the beautiful could be reconciled with the materiality of art, if one takes seriously the description of the Cubist painting in *De l'existence à l'existant*: 'For here materiality is thickness, coarseness, massivity, wretchedness. It is what has consistency, weight, is absurd, is a brute but impassive presence; it

is also what is humble, bare, and ugly.' Levinas had emphasized that this materiality is outside classical distinctions of letter and spirit or matter and form; it is the materiality of being, outside the visible, whence the experience of art becomes one of dispossession and restlessness, not disinterestedness and repose. Regarding the experience of the modern work of art, recall Kant's account of the experience of the sublime: 'In presenting the sublime in nature the mind feels *agitated*, while in an aesthetic judgment about the beautiful in nature it is in *restful* contemplation. This agitation . . . can be compared with a vibration, i.e., with a rapid alternation of repulsion from, and attraction to, one and the same object.' Moreover, the experience of the sublime (like the experience of the *il y a*) entails a crisis of subjectivity. The sublime object, Kant says, is 'an abyss in which the imagination fears to lose itself'.[18] If one follows categories supplied by Kant's third critique, one has to say that Levinasian aesthetics assigns the work of art to the order of the sublime, not to the beautiful.

(2) Nevertheless, despite the logic of his analysis, Levinas himself seems to prefer the Sartrean ideology of *Les temps modernes* (in which, after all, 'Realité et son ombre' first appeared), namely, as Levinas puts it, that 'art, essentially disengaged, constitutes, in a world of initiative and responsibility, a dimension of evasion' (*CP* 12). Recall the analysis of rhythm in which the subject undergoes a 'reversal of power into participation' (*CP* 4): although earlier the deposition of the sovereign ego had the structure of critique (emphasizing the 'reversal of power'), here it is simply 'la jouissance esthétique', or the private escape of subjectivity from cognition and action in the world (an assertion rather than deposition of sovereignty). 'Art', says Levinas,

brings into the world the obscurity of fate, but it especially brings the irreponsibility that charms as a lightness and grace. It frees. To make or to appreciate a novel and a picture is to no longer have to conceive, is to renounce the effort of science, philosophy, and action. Do not speak, do not reflect, admire in silence and in peace – such are the counsels of wisdom satisfied before the beautiful . . . There is something wicked and egoist and cowardly in artistic enjoyment. There are times when one can be ashamed of it, as of feasting during a plague. [*CP* 12]

Such a view clearly appeals to Levinas's iconoclasm, but does it square with his thought?

(3) The idea that art 'brings into the world the obscurity of fate' summarizes neatly the thesis of the materiality of art (namely that 'the artwork [is] an event of darkening of being... in the general economy of being, art is the falling movement on the hither side of time, into fate' (CP 9–10)). But an argument is missing that would explain how one gets from the 'event of darkening' to 'lightness and grace'. One way to fill the hole would be to isolate the following question: 'Is it presumptuous to denounce the hypertrophy of art in our times when, for almost everyone, it is identified with spiritual life?' (CP 12). The question (with its implication of the monstrosity of modern art – 'hypertrophy' means excessive growth or deformity – a nice anaesthetic concept) suggests that what is really at issue here is not the ontology of the modernist work but the limits of its reception within traditional aesthetics.

Modern art, after all, especially in the various movements of the avant-garde, is a repudiation of the museum, the library and the concert hall; its rhetoric is that of the outrageous performance that calls into question the distinction between art and non-art, not to say the whole idea of the beautiful. The legacy of Duchamp is nothing if not a critique of the aesthetics of pleasure (what Brecht called 'culinary art').[19] Levinas gives little indication of what might constitute a 'philosophical criticism' – 'that would demand a broadening of the intentionally limited perspective of this study' (CP 13) – but it is clear from what he says that it could not be a spiritualizing criticism that isolates the work of art in a private realm of satisfaction and escape. On the contrary, if anything, Levinas's aesthetics of materiality helps to explain why so much of modern art, poetry and music has been and continues to be condemned as unintelligible, degenerate and obscene (and even displayed as such, as in the famous Exhibition of Decadent Art held in Munich in 1937). Thus Levinas says of philosophical criticism that it 'integrates the inhuman work of the artist into the human world... It does not attack the artistic event as such, that obscuring of being in images, that stopping of being in the meanwhile' (CP 12). The 'artistic event as such' would be, following Levinas's analysis, the materialization of things, which is to say 'the darkening of being' or retrieval of things from the panoramic world of representation. In this event the task of criticism would evidently be to acknowledge the inhumanness of art, its material link to the *il y a*. This is, as it happens, the import of Maurice Blanchot's writings on poetry and art, which Levinas understood perhaps better than anyone else. Here (as Levinas suggests in the final paragraph of his essay) the experience of art does not result in 'artistic idolatry' that makes of art 'the supreme value of civilization' (CP 12,13). It means experiencing the limits of the human, which for Levinas means the limits of the ethical.

A POETICS OF PROXIMITY

In the experience of the work of art, Levinas says, we enter into 'a mode of being to which applies neither the form of consciousness, since the I is there stripped of its prerogative to assume, its power, nor the form of unconsciousness, since the whole situation and all its articulations are, in a dark light, present [toute le situation et toutes ses articulations, dans une obscure clarté, sont presenté]' (CP 4). In 'Realité et son ombre' Levinas takes recourse to rhythm and participation to elucidate this mode of being. But how to understand this dark light? What is it for things to be present in a dark light?

This question is part of the larger problem of how I can enter into a relation with a thing without destroying it, that is, without absorbing it into myself as an object of my consciousness or as part of my grip on existing. The figure of light is a way of formulating the problem, and the figure of 'dark light' is a way of resolving it. In Le temps et l'autre (1947) Levinas writes: 'Light [Lumière] is that through which something is other than myself, but already as if it came from me. The illuminated object is something one encounters, but from the very fact that it is illuminated one encounters it as if it came from us. It does not have a fundamental strangeness' (TO 64). Art as 'an event of the darkening of being' (CP 9) would thus be a way of setting things free of the light in which they exist for me. It would be a way of restoring to things their fundamental strangeness.

Heidegger was perhaps the first philosopher to think of art in this way, that is, not in terms of an aesthetics of the beautiful but in terms of an ontology of freedom. In Paris after the Liberation people were catching up with Heidegger's writings, including 'Der Ursprung des Kunstwerkes', with its conception of the work of art as an event that 'holds open the Open of the world'.[20] The *work* of the work of art is the uncovering of ontological difference:

In the midst of beings as a whole an open place occurs. There is a clearing, a lighting [Hofstadter translates one word, *Lichtung*, with two: 'clearing' is his interpolation]. Thought of in reference to what is, to beings, this clearing is in a greater degree than are beings. This open center [*Mitte*] is therefore not surrounded by what is; rather, the lighting center itself encircles all that is, like the Nothing which we scarcely know. [G 39–40/PLT 53]

In this 'lighting' we find ourselves in the midst of things: 'Only this clearing [*Lichtung*] grants and guarantees to us humans a passage to those beings that we ourselves are not, and access to the being that we ourselves are. Thanks to this clearing [*Lichtung*], beings are unconcealed in certain changing degrees' (G 40/PLT 53). So *Lichtung* is an ontological metaphor, a figure of Being. Yet this event of disclosure is not to be understood in terms of representation and cognition; the lighting is also *unheimlich*. For 'each being we encounter and which encounters us keeps to this curious opposition of presence in that it always withholds itself at the same time in a concealedness. The clearing [*Lichtung*] in which beings stand is in itself at the same time concealment' (G 40/PLT 53). The world in which we find ourselves is not transparent; the world is, as Heidegger says, limned by the earth. Things are present, but not for us – not as objects open to view: 'the open place in the midst of beings, the clearing, is never a rigid stage with a permanently raised curtain on which the play of beings runs its course' (G 41/PLT 54). Rather, beings are present *as things*, that is, in their thingly character, which Heidegger had characterized in the opening section of his essay in terms of the resistance of things to the violence of conceptual thinking:

The unpretentious thing evades thought most stubbornly. [Is this a defect in the thing?] Or can it be that this self-refusal of the mere thing, this self-contained independence, belongs precisely to the nature of the thing? Must not this strange and uncommunicative feature of the thing become intimately familiar to thought that tries to think the thing? If so, then we should not force our way to its thingly character. [G 17/PLT 31–2]

In contrast to conceptual thinking, the work of the work of art is non-violent, or rather it disposes us toward things in a non-violent way (G 54/PLT 66), disclosing them in their strangeness or in their earthliness (G 57/PLT 69). Significantly, Heidegger reserves the term poetry (*Dichtung*) for this disclosure: 'It is due to art's poetic nature that, in the midst of what is, art breaks open an open place, in whose openness everything is other than usual' (G 60/PLT 72).

Levinas's objections to Heidegger's phenomenology of disclosure are well known: the world that is opened in Heidegger's analysis has no people in it. *Dasein* listens for the peal of stillness across a post-nuclear landscape. But Levinas becomes implicated in Heidegger's analysis as soon as he asks how any relationship with alterity is possible without reducing alterity to something of mine. He puts this question in an early essay on Blanchot, 'Le regarde du poète' (1956): 'How can the Other (which Jankélévitch calls the *absolutely other* and Blanchot "eternal streaming of the outside") appear, that is, be for someone, without already losing its alterity and exteriority by way of offering itself to view' (PN 130). This question is at the heart of Blanchot's poetics, which is concerned precisely with the alterity of *things*. Already in 'Littérature et la droit à la mort' (1947–8) Blanchot had asked about the price things pay for their intelligibility, given that signification is, as in Hegel, a dialectic of negation that annihilates things in their singularity and replaces them with concepts (PF 313/WF 323–24). The work of the spirit that builds up the world is, paradoxically, 'the speech of death' (EI 49/IC 35). Poetry for Blanchot is a refusal of this speech. By withdrawing into its materiality, poetic language is no longer a form of mediation. Instead it interrupts the dialectical movement in which things are conceptually determined. 'The language of literature', Blanchot says, 'is a search for [the] moment which precedes literature. Literature usually calls it existence; it wants the cat as it exists, the pebble *taking the side of things*, not man but the pebble, and in this pebble what man rejects by saying it' (PF 316/WF 327). 'Literature', Blanchot says, 'is a concern for the reality of things, for their unknown, free, and silent existence' (PF 310/WF 330). Poets are what they are, he says, because 'they are interested in the reality of language, because they are not interested in the world but in what things and beings would be if there were no world' (PF 321/WF 333): existence without a world: the *il y a*. But whereas Levinas considers the *il y a* from the standpoint of the subject's experience of it (ecstasy, horror), Blanchot considers it from the standpoint of things in their freedom from subjectivity.

Levinas searches Blanchot's poetics for 'an invitation to leave the Heideggerian world' (PN 135). In 'Le regard du poète', invoking the figure of the dark light, he writes: 'In Blanchot, *the work uncovers, in an uncovering that is not truth, a darkness*' (*PN* 136):

The literary space to which Blanchot...leads us has nothing in common with the Heideggerian world that art renders inhabitable. Art, according to Blanchot, far from elucidating the world, exposes the desolate, lightless substratum underlying it, and restores to our sojourn its exotic essence – and, to the wonders of our architecture, their function of makeshift desert shelters. Blanchot and Heidegger agree that art does not lead (contrary to classical aesthetics) to a world behind the world, an ideal world behind the real one. Art is light. Light from on high in Heidegger, making the world, founding place. In Blanchot it is a black light, a night coming from below – a light that undoes the world, leading it back to its origin, to the over and over again, the murmur, ceaseless lapping of waves, a 'deep past, never long enough ago'. [*PN* 137]

The contrast that Levinas draws between Heidegger and Blanchot is too broad and misses the strangeness in Heidegger's aesthetics.[21] However, it is true that the Heideggerian world is an opening in which space is a circle or volume to be inhabited, if not altogether familiarly (Heidegger's world is always uncanny), whereas for Blanchot the space of literature is a surface across which one moves endlessly in what Levinas aptly calls 'the exteriority of absolute exile' (*PN* 133). Space here is not open to the light. It is the 'Outside' – which Levinas approaches guardedly in his conclusion to *L'autrement qu'être*: 'the openness of space signifies the outside where nothing covers anything, non-protection, the reverse of a retreat, homelessness [*sans-domicile*], non-world, non-habitation, layout without security' (*OB* 178). But Blanchot does not regard exile as a negative condition, a mere deprivation of place; it is rather a region (let us call it a traversal of ontology and ethics) in which subjectivity no longer presides over things from a standpoint or perspective of the whole, certainly not from the perspective of ownership or conceptual possession.[22] Exile is a relation of intimacy (which Blanchot does not hesitate to call responsibility) with what is nevertheless outside my grasp.[23]

In his second essay on Blanchot, 'La servant et son maitre' (1966), Levinas writes: 'Blanchot's properly literary work brings us primarily a new feeling [*sensation*]: a new "experience," or, more precisely, a new prickling sensation of the skin, brushed against by things [*un "frisson nouveau", ou, plus exactement, une nouvelle démangeaison de l'épiderme, effleuré par les choses]' (PN* 143). This captures something of what Blanchot, in 'Le grand refus' (1959), calls a relation with an 'immediate singularity' that cannot be touched – that which refuses 'all direct relation, all mystical fusion, and all sensible contact' – but to which the subjectivity of the poet or writer is nevertheless exposed as to

the presence of the non-accessible, presence excluding or exceeding [*débordant*] any present. This amounts to saying: the immediate, infinitely exceeding any present possibility by its very presence, is the infinite presence of what remains radically absent, a presence in its presence always infinitely other [*autre*], presence of the other in its alterity. [*EI* 53–4/*IC* 37–8]

The 'other' here is neither the Levinasian *Autrui* nor Heidegger's Being but the outside or foreign, which (philosophy be damned) Blanchot would prefer to think of as neither ethical nor ontological. Nor does Blanchot think of it as the *il y a*; it is simply the singular and irreducible as such. In 'Comment découvrir l'obscur' (1959) he calls it simply 'the impossible' (*EI* 68/*IC* 48).[24] Poetry, he says, is a 'response' to this impossibility – 'a relation with the obscure and the unknown that would be a relation neither of force [*puissance*], nor of comprehension, nor even of revelation' (*EI* 68/*IC* 48).

Poetry in this sense is a relation of proximity, and Levinas appears to pick up on this in 'Langage et proximité' (1967), where he distinguishes between two dimensions of language. The first is kerygmatic, which has to do with the power of language to synchronize things in a structure of identity – the 'as-structure' of hermeneutics, the logical structure of the proposition, the temporal structure of narrative that proclaims the individual as the same over the course of multiple and heterogeneous transformations. The second, however, concerns the movement of subjectivity outside of itself that Levinas has always regarded as an 'original language' on the hither side of discourse (where Blanchot locates poetry). In 'L'ontologie estelle fondamentale?' (1951) Levinas had called it 'prayer'. In 'Langage et proximité' it is called 'contact': 'there is in speech a relationship with a singularity located outside the theme of speech, a singularity that is not thematized by the speech but is approached' (*CP* 115). Heretofore Levinas had always jealously guarded this 'singularity' as a *personal* other, *Autrui*, the face whose 'defenseless eyes' constitute 'the original language' (*BPW* 12); whereas, in explicit argument with

Levinas, Blanchot had always insisted 'that *autrui* is a name that is essentially neutral' (*EI* 102/*IC* 72): neither human nor non-human but inhuman (absolutely without horizon). In *Totalité et infini* things are never singular. They can be enjoyed in sensibility, but sensibility is still an aesthetic (and even economic) concept:[25]

Things have a form, are seen *in* the light – silhouettes or profiles; the face signifies *itself*. As silhouette and profile a thing owes its nature to a perspective, remains relative to a point of view; a thing's situation thus constitutes its being. Strictly speaking it has no identity; convertible into another thing, it can become money. Things have no face; convertible, 'realizable,' they have a price . . . The aesthetic orientation man gives to the whole of his world represents a return to enjoyment and to the elemental on a higher plane. The world of things calls for art, in which intellectual accession to being moves into enjoyment, in which the Infinity of the Idea is idolized in the finite, but sufficient, image. [*TI* 140]

However, in 'Langage et proximité' the sensibility of things takes on an ethical significance within the relation of proximity: 'The immediacy of the sensible is an event of proximity and not of knowledge' (*CP* 116). This means that the sensible no longer belongs to the order of the visible. As Levinas says, 'sensibility must be interpreted first of all as touch' (*CP* 118).

Indeed, perception itself is reconceived as 'immediacy, contact, and language':

Perception is a proximity with being which intentional analysis does not account for. The sensible is superficial only in its role being cognition. In the ethical relationship with the real, that is, in the relationship of proximity which the sensible establishes, the essential is committed. Life is there. Sight is, to be sure, an openness and a consciousness, and all sensibility, opening as a consciousness, is called vision; but even in its subordination to cognition, sight maintains contact and proximity. The visible caresses the eye. One sees and one hears like one touches. [*CP* 118]

And whereas since *Le temps et l'autre* the caress had been exclusively human, now 'the caress of the sensible' spreads out from the human to the world of things, where it is named 'poetry':

The proximity of things is poetry; in themselves the things are revealed before being approached. In stroking an animal already the hide hardens in the skin. But over the hands that have touched things, places trampled

by beings, the things they have held, the images of those things, the fragments of those things, the contexts in which those fragments enter, the
inflexions of the voice and the words that are articulated in them, the ever
sensible signs of language, the letters traced, the vestiges, the relics – over all
things, beginning with the human face and skin, tenderness spreads. Cognition turns into proximity, into the purely sensible. Matter, which is invested
as a tool, and a tool in the world, is also, via the human, the matter that obsesses me with its proximity. The poetry of the world is inseparable from
proximity par excellence, or the proximity of the neighbor par excellence.
[CP 118–19]

Does it make sense to speak of poetry in this way? It depends on
whether one can see the coherence of poetry and the caress as modes
of transcendence. In *Le temps et l'autre* the caress is said to be

a mode of the subject's being, where the subject who is in contact with
another goes beyond this contact. Contact as sensation is part of the world
of light. But what is caressed is not touched, properly speaking. It is not the
softness or warmth of the hand given in contact that the caress seeks. The
seeking of the caress constitutes its essence by the fact that the caress does
not know what it seeks. This 'not knowing,' this fundamental disorder, is
essential. [TO 89]

Compare 'L'ego et totalité', where a 'poetic world' is one in which
'one thinks without knowing what one thinks' (CP 35), and a 'poetic
thought' is a 'thought which thinks without knowing what it thinks,
or thinks as one dreams' (CP 40). The peculiarity is that 'not knowing'
in the case of the caress carries a positive valence, whereas, in the
context of 'L'ego et totalité', the poetic thought that 'thinks without
knowing what it thinks' is something negative, as if Levinas were
simply reciting a line from Plato's *Ion*. But in fact poetry and the
ethical occupy the same priority *vis-à-vis* cognition (both are an-
archic). Thus by the time of 'Langage et proximité' poetry and the
caress are taken up together in a relation of one-for-the-other, no
longer part of 'the world of light' but characters in 'the intrigue of
proximity and communication' (OB 48).

The question is whether assimilating poetry to the ethical in this
way doesn't just allegorize poetry and therefore reduce it in the
usual philosophical style. At the outset of *Totalité et infini* Levinas
says that the purpose of his book is to perceive 'in discourse a non-
allergic relation with alterity' (TI 47). This means reconceptualizing

discourse away from intentionality and the proposition toward what is finally termed saying (*le Dire*), in which 'the subject approaches a neighbor in expressing itself, in being expelled, in the literal sense of the term, out of any locus, no longer *dwelling*, not stomping any ground. Saying uncovers, beyond nudity, what dissimulation may be under the exposedness of a skin laid bare. It is the very *respiration* of this skin prior to any intention' (*OB* 48–9). Meanwhile in his writings since the 1940s Blanchot had been elucidating what looks like much the same thing, namely a theory of poetry as 'a non-dialectical experience of speech' (*EI* 90/*IC* 63) in which the subject (the poet or writer, but also evidently the reader) enters into a relation with what is outside the grasp of subjectivity, and therefore also outside the grasp of language as conceptual determination (hence the need for writing that occurs 'outside discourse, outside language') (*EI* vii/*IC* xii). But alterity for Levinas is always another human being, whereas Blanchot's argument against Levinas is this: to say that only what is human can be other is already to feature the other within a totality or upon a common ground; it is to assemble with the other a possible (workable) community. Blanchot prefers indeterminate or at least highly abstract terms for alterity, namely the 'outside', the 'neutral', the 'unknown' (*l'inconnu*) – not the beggar, the orphan, or the widow, who are, after all, stock characters out of ancient biblical parables. Thus for Blanchot poetry is in excess of ethical alterity; it is a relation of foreignness or strangeness with what is absolutely singular and irreducible (but, for all of that, a relation of proximity or intimacy in which one is in a condition of exposure rather than cognition). As he says in an essay on 'René Char et la pensée du neutre' (1963), poetry means:

To speak the unknown, to receive it through speech while leaving it unknown, is precisely not to take hold of it, not to comprehend it; it is rather to refuse to identify it even by sight, that 'objective' hold that seizes, albeit at a distance. To live with the unknown before one (which also means: to live before the unknown, and before oneself as unknown) is to enter into the responsibility of a speech that speaks without exercising any form of power. [*EI* 445/*IC* 302]

Poetry is thus a species of *le Dire sans le Dit*, but the subject in poetry is exposed to something other than *Autrui* – perhaps it is the *il y a*. Whatever it is, Blanchot leaves it, pointedly, unnamed ('Such is the secret lot, the secret decision of every essential speech in us: naming the *possible*, responding to the *impossible*' (*EI* 68/*IC* 48).

Perhaps in the end the relation of poetry and the ethical comes to this: both are forms of saying (*le Dire*) on the hither side of thematization and are, therefore, *materializations* of language and so, by the same logic, analogous modes of transcendence. But for Blanchot, poetry is the materiality – the literal 'outside' – of language as such, which he epitomizes with the Mallarméan word *l'écriture*, whereas, by contrast, Levinas figures materiality as the corporeality of the subject: *le Dire* is exposure, 'the very respiration of the skin'. Levinas thinks of this saying as 'the original language', which is to say a language that is not yet linguistical, 'a language without words [*mots*] or propositions' (*CP*). Language here is corporeal expression in which 'the face speaks' in 'the language of the eyes, impossible to dissemble' (*TI* 66).

Owing perhaps to his deep-seated iconoclasm, Levinas restricts the materiality of language as such to the sounds of words, as in 'La transcendance des mots. A propos des Biffures' (1949), which begins as if it were to be a review of a volume of Michel Leiris's autobiography, *Biffures* (1948), but which becomes instead an inquiry into the etymology of *biffures*, meaning 'crossings-out' or 'erasures', where what is erased are things in their temporality or irreducibility to spatial and visual contexts. Levinas construes the word *biffures* as a figure of pure spatiality, or of the simultaneity of things held in place – in other words, a figure of totality. As such it can be traced back to 'the visual experience to which Western civilization ultimately reduces all mental life. That experience involves ideas; it is light, it seeks the clarity of the self-evident. It ends up with the unveiled, the phenomenon. All is immanent to it' (*OS* 147). In contrast to sight, which is a modality of worldmaking, sound is a modality of transcendence:

There is ... in sound – and in consciousness understood as hearing – a shattering of the always complete world of vision and art. Sound is all repercussion, outburst, scandal. While in vision a form espouses a content and soothes it, sound is like the sensible quality overflowing its limits, the incapacity of form to hold its content – a true rent in the fabric of the world – that by which the world that is *here* prolongs a dimension inconvertible into vision. [*OS* 147–8]

For Levinas, moreover, sound is not simply an empirical sensation; it is phenomenological. That is, not just any noise can achieve the transcendence of sound. 'To really hear a sound', he says, 'is to hear a word. Pure sound is a word [*Le son pur est verbe*]' (*os* 149).

It is important to notice that Levinas's word for 'word' here is not *mot* but *verbe*, that is, not the word in its spatial and visual fixity as a sign or noun or word-as-image but the word in its temporality, not only in the grammatical sense of the propositional verb but more important as the event of speaking itself, the spoken word as such, where *verbe* entails the power of the word to affect things – to intervene in the world as well as to function in a sentence – as in Rimbaud's *alchimie du verbe* (the writer Michel Leiris, Levinas says, 'est chimiste plutôt qu'alchimiste du verbe' (*os* 145), that is, more analytical than magical; unlike the surrealists he finds causes for his dreams). The *mot* in its transcendence is always more expression than idea, more *parole* than *langue*, more enigma than phenomenon, more *sens* than *signification*, more *Dire* than *Dit*: an open-ended series of Levinasian distinctions is traceable to his iconoclastic theory of the *verbe*. For Levinas, of course, the priority of sound over semantics is meant to indicate the event of sociality: sound means the *presence* of others making themselves felt in advance of what is said. Sound is not the medium of propositional language but of other people. More than this, however, the sound of words is an ethical event, which Levinas does not hesitate to characterize as *critique*, not only because others interrupt me in making themselves felt, setting limits to my autonomy, but because *even when I myself speak* – even in self-expression – I am no longer an 'I', am no longer self-identical, but am now beside myself: 'To speak is to interrupt my existence as a subject, a master' (*os* 149). Of course this is exactly what Blanchot says happens to the subject in the experience of *l'écriture*. Which is why it is most interesting that in Levinas the materiality of language as Blanchot understands it comes into the foreground not as a theme but as an increasingly dominant and controversial dimension of his (Levinas's) own writing.[26] Here, if anywhere, is where poetry and the ethical draw near one another.

NOTES

1 Readers should consult Jill Robbins, *Altered Reading: Levinas and Literature* (Chicago: University of Chicago Press, 1999), and especially Steve McCaffery, 'The Scandal of Sincerity: Towards a Levinasian Poetics', in *Prior to Meaning: Protosemantics and Poetics* (Evanston: Northwestern University Press, 2001).

2 'Connaissance de l'inconnu', in *L'entretien infini* (Paris: Gallimard, 1969), p. 76 (hereafter cited as *EI*); 'Knowledge of the Unknown', *The Infinite Conversation*, trans. Susan Hanson (Minneapolis: University of Minnesota Press, 1993), p. 53 (hereafter cited as *IC*).

3 The most detailed and authoritative study of antique poetics remains that of Ernst Robert Curtius, *European Literature and the Latin Middle Ages* (1948), trans. Willard Trask (New York: Harper and Row, 1953), esp. pp. 145–227, 468–86. Curtius remarks that a 'history of the theory of poetry' remains to be written (p. 468). The statement is as true today as it was fifty years ago.

4 See *The Philosophical Disenfranchisement of Art* (New York: Columbia University Press, 1986), pp. 81–116.

5 Athenäum Fragment 238, *Kritische Ausgabe* (Munich: Verlag Ferdinand Schöningh, 1967), I, p. 204. See *Philosophical Fragments*, trans. Peter Firchow (Minneapolis: University of Minnesota Press, 1991), pp. 50–1.

6 See 'Le mystère dans les lettres', *Œuvres complètes*, ed. Henri Mondor (Paris: Gallimard, 1945), pp. 385–7 (hereafter *OC*). See Maurice Blanchot, 'La poésie de Mallarmé est-elle obscure?' in *Faux pas* (Paris: Gallimard, 1943), pp. 126–31, esp. p. 129.

7 'Le mythe de Mallarmé', *La part du feu* (Paris: Gallimard, 1949), p. 44 (hereafter *PF*); 'The myth of Mallarmé', *The Work of Fire*, trans. Charlotte Mandell (Stanford: Stanford University Press, 1995), p. 37 (hereafter *WF*).

8 See Michael Holland on Blanchot's reception of Mallarmé, 'From Crisis to Critique: Mallarmé for Blanchot', in Michael Temple (ed.), *Meetings with Mallarmé in Contemporary French Culture* (Exeter: University of Exeter Press, 1998), pp. 81–106.

9 *Situations, II* (Paris: Gallimard, 1948), p. 63 (hereafter *s*); *'What is Literature?' and Other Essays* (Cambridge: Harvard University Press, 1988), p. 29 (hereafter *WL*).

10 Sartre's writings on Mallarmé, which stress the idea of poetry as self-annihilating discourse, have been collected in *Mallarmé: or, The Poet of Nothingness*, trans. Ernest Sturm (University Park: Pennsylvania State University Press, 1988). See Dominic LaCapra's discussion of Sartre's changing conceptions of language and writing, *A Preface to Sartre: a Critical Introduction to Sartre's Literary and Philosophical Writings* (Ithaca: Cornell University Press, 1978), pp. 63–91.

11 The term 'aesthetic differentiation' derives from Hans-Georg Gadamer's discussion (and critique) of idealist aesthetics in *Truth and Method*, 2nd rev. edn, trans. Joel Weinsheimer and Donald G. Marshall (New York: Crossroad, 1989), pp. 81–100. Gadamer writes: 'What we call a work of art ... aesthetically depends on a process of abstraction. By disregarding everything in which a work of art is rooted (its original context of life,

and the religious or secular function that gave it significance), it becomes visible as the "pure work of art." In performing this abstraction, aesthetic consciousness performs a task that is positive in itself. It shows what a pure work of art is, and allows it to exist in its own right. I call this "aesthetic differentiation" ' (p. 85).

12 See Arthur Danto, 'Art and Disturbation', in *The Philosophical Disenfranchisement of Art*, pp. 117–33. See also Levinas on 'disturbance' (*le dérangement*) – in contrast to rational discourse – in 'Enigme et phénomène' (*CP* 61–3).

13 Compare Blanchot on fascination and the image in *L'espace littéraire* (Paris: Gallimard, 1955), pp. 28–31; *The Space of Literature*, trans. Ann Smock (Lincoln: University of Nebraska Press, 1982), pp. 32–3.

14 In his interviews with Philippe Nemo Levinas refers to the deposition of the sovereign ego as the mode of escape from the *il y a*, but it is hard to make sense of this statement, since this deposition already occurs in the experience of the work of art, which is to say the experience of materiality, irreality, or the *il y a* itself (*EI* 52). The symmetry between the aesthetic and the ethical in this regard has yet to be studied, but has been noted by Edith Wyschogrod in 'The Art in Ethics: Aesthetics, Objectivity, and Alterity in the Philosophy of Emmanuel Levinas', in Adriaan Peperzak (ed.), *Ethics as First Philosophy: the Significance of Emmanuel Levinas for Philosophy, Literature, and Religion* (London: Routledge, 1995), pp. 138–9.

15 The 'exteriority which is not that of a body' perhaps means that in this event one's body is materialized in such a way that one experiences it from the outside – hence the somewhat incoherent metaphor of the 'I-actor' becoming the 'I-spectator'; but it is no longer obvious that it makes sense to speak of 'experience', since the 'I' is no longer an experiencing subject in the sense of witnessing a spectacle. Indeed, in the next sentence he complains that phenomenology has yet to produce a concept of experience that would do justice to 'this fundamental paradox of rhythm and dreams, which describes a sphere situated outside of the conscious and the unconscious' (*CP* 4). Blanchot's poetics might be called a phenomenology of this sphere of exteriority.

16 The question is whether there is any important difference between exposure to the world and the exposure to others that constitutes the ethical relation. See Jean-Luc Marion on this question, 'A Note Concerning the Ontological Difference', *Graduate Faculty Philosophy Journal*, 20–21 (1998), pp. 25–50, esp. 32–7.

17 Already in *De l'existence à l'existant* Levinas had invoked the figure of the cadaver: 'A corpse is horrible; it already bears in itself its own phantom, it presages its return. The haunting spectre, the phantom,

constitutes the very element of horror' (*EE* 61). See Blanchot's 'Les deux versions de l'imaginaire', in *L'espace littéraire*, pp. 346–9; 'Two Versions of the Imaginary', in *The Space of Literature*, pp. 256–60.

18 *Critique of Judgment*, trans. Werner S. Pluhar (Indianapolis: Hackett Publishing, 1987), p. 115.

19 See Bertold Brecht, 'Modern Theatre is Epic Theatre', *Brecht on Theatre: the Development of an Aesthetic*, trans. John Willett (New York: Hill and Wang, 1964), p. 35. Levinas's conception of *jouissance* in *Totalité et infini* is distinctly culinary – 'Nourishment, as a means of invigoration, is the transmutation of the other into the same, which is in the essence of enjoyment [*jouissance*]' (*TI* 111). It might be possible, nevertheless, to link Levinas's conception of 'jouissance l'esthétique' to conceptions of *jouissance* that derive from the experience of aesthetic modernity. See Paul-Laurent Assoun, 'The Subject and the Other in Levinas and Lacan', trans. Dianah Jackson and Denise Merkle, in Sarah Harasym (ed.), *Levinas and Lacan: the Missed Encounter* (Albany: State University of New York Press, 1998), pp. 79–101, esp. pp. 93–7.

20 *Gesamtausgabe* (Frankfurt am Main: Vittorio Klostermann, 1977), p. 31 (hereafter G); *Poetry, Language, Thought*, trans. Albert Hofstadter (New York: Harper, 1971), p. 45 (hereafter *PLT*).

21 This point is well made by Jean Greisch in 'Ethics and Ontology: Some "Hypocritical" Considerations', trans. Leonard Lawler, *Graduate Faculty Philosophy Journal*, 20–21 (1998), pp. 41–69. See esp. pp. 62–4, where Greisch speculates that art can mediate the breach between ethics and ontology.

22 In 'Etre juif' (1962) Blanchot writes: 'The words exodus and exile indicate a positive relation with exteriority, whose exigency invites us not to be content with what is proper to us (that is, with our power to assimilate everything, to identify everything, to bring everything back to our "I"' (*EI* 186/*IC* 127).

23 Blanchot develops this idea most fully in 'Comment découvrir l'obscur?' (1959), where speech (now called 'poetry') is no longer the expression of sovereignty, power, or conceptual control but is a mode of responsiveness to what is singular and refractory to consciousness. This essay is reprinted in *L'entretien infini* as the second part of 'La grand refus' (*EI* 57–69/*IC* 40–48).

24 In defiance of contradiction, Blanchot says, it is possible to characterize impossibility in terms of three traits:

First this one: in impossibility time changes direction, no longer offering itself out of the future as what gathers by going beyond; time, here, is rather the dispersion of a present that, even while being only passage does not pass, never fixes itself in a present, refers to no past and goes toward no future: *the incessant* [or "meanwhile"]. A second trait: in impossibility, the immediate is a present to which one cannot be present, but from which one cannot separate; or, again, it is what escapes by the very fact that there is no escaping it: the *ungraspable that one cannot let go of*. Third trait: what reigns in the experience of impossibility is not the unique's immobile collecting unto itself, but the infinite shifting of dispersal, a non-dialectical movement where contrariety has nothing to do with opposition or with reconciliation, and where the *other* never comes back to the same. [*EI* 64–5/*IC* 45–6]

25 Interestingly, in 'Realité et son ombre' the sensible was figured as the shadow of being: 'The notion of shadow ... enables us to situate the economy of resemblance within the general economy of being. Resemblance is not a participation of a being in an idea ... it is the very structure of the sensible as such. The sensible is being insofar as it resembles itself, insofar as, outside of its triumphal work of being, it casts a shadow, emits that obscure and elusive essence, that phantom essence which cannot be identified with the essence revealed in truth' (*CP* 7–8).

26 Paul Ricœur calls this dimension Levinas's 'hyperbole' – the 'systematic practice of *excess* in philosophical argumentation' – which in *Autrement qu'être*, Ricœur says, is carried to 'the point of paroxysm'. *Oneself as Another*, trans. Kathleen Blamey (Chicago: University of Chicago Press, 1992), p. 337. See D. H. Brody, 'Emmanuel Levinas: the Logic of Ethical Ambiguity in *Otherwise than Being or beyond Essence*', *Research in Phenomenology*, 25 (1994), pp. 177–203.

11 What is the question to which 'substitution' is the answer?

I

The main text for addressing the concept of 'substitution' is Levinas's essay of the same name. The essay exists in two versions. The first version was delivered as a lecture in Brussels in November 1967 and was revised for publication in the *Revue Philosophique de Louvain* in the following year (*BPW* 79–95). Although the essay was published on its own, as a lecture it had been preceded the day before by a reading of 'Proximity', the contents of which are familiar from the text of 'Language and Proximity' (*CP* 109–26). The second and better known version of 'Substitution' was published in 1974 as the central chapter of *Otherwise than Being or Beyond Essence* (*OB* 99–129). I shall focus on the first version of 'Substitution' in the conviction that Levinas's train of thought is more readily identified in his initial formulation of it, referencing the second version only when it departs from the first in some significant way.

Just as the chapter, 'Substitution', is, as Levinas himself insists, the centrepiece of *Otherwise than Being* (*OB* xli), so the notion of 'substitution' is the core concept of that book, and yet it remains enigmatic. There is not even a consensus about what the question is to which substitution is supposed to be the answer. Only when this is established will it be possible to address with any confidence the questions scholars tend to debate, such as the extent to which the concept of substitution represents a departure from the philosophy of *Totality and Infinity* and the degree to which it should be understood as a response to Derrida's 'Violence and Metaphysics'.

The initial hypothesis to be examined is that Levinas introduces the concept of substitution to address the question of what the

234

subject must be like for ethics to be possible.[1] On this understanding the core argument of the essay is stated near its end when Levinas explains that 'the passage of the identical to the other in substitution... makes possible sacrifice' (BPW 90). The same claim is reformulated a little later as follows: 'It is through the condition of being a hostage that there can be pity, compassion, pardon, and proximity in the world – even the little there is, even the simple "after you sir" ' (BPW 91). This suggests that Levinas is asking what underlies that behaviour which is sometimes called superogatory, gratuitous or, as he prefers to say, ethical. His answer is that at the heart of subjectivity is not a 'for itself', but what he calls 'the one-for-the-other'. This is his working definition of substitution, and when Levinas explains substitution as 'the one-for-the-other' he not only posits an alterity at the heart of subjectivity, but gives it an ethical sense. Levinas is not preaching. He is not saying that one *should* sacrifice oneself. He merely wants to account for its possibility.

Although there is some doubt as to whether this exhausts the positive doctrine of 'Substitution', Levinas clearly identifies the rival accounts that he targets in the essay. There are at least three of them. The first is a form of egoism:

All the transfers of sentiment which theorists of original war and egoism use to explain the birth of generosity (it isn't clear, however, that there was war at the beginning; before wars there were altars) could not take root in the ego were it not, in its entire being, or rather its entire nonbeing, subjected not to a category, as in the case of matter, but to an unlimited accusative, that is to say, persecution, self, hostage, already substituted for others. [BPW 91]

Levinas obviously has Thomas Hobbes in mind, and this is in fact only one moment in an ongoing polemic against Hobbes (e.g. EN 100–1), although Levinas never engages with Hobbes textually. Levinas is strongly committed to the claim that egoism cannot give birth to generosity, but that, by contrast, egoism arises from 'an intrigue other than egoism' (BPW 88). If egoism is true, then sacrifice would be impossible, except perhaps under extreme conditions of self-deception. Levinas moves beyond egoism but without having recourse to altruism (OB 117).

As almost always in Levinas, Heidegger is also a target of his polemics. For Levinas, sacrifice is not possible if the human subject is understood as concerned for its own existence, as Heideggerian

Dasein is on Levinas's interpretation.[2] Levinas's third target is the hypothesis that the condition of the possibility of sacrifice lies in freedom. He rejects the claim that it is because the ego is a free consciousness, capable of sympathy and compassion, that it can take responsibility for the sufferings of the world. The experience of responsibility is not the experience of a free choice, but rather 'the impossibility of evading the neighbor's call' (BPW 95). Some of the claims Levinas opposes echo theses of Sartre's *Being and Nothingness*, and Sartre is named in 'Substitution', as is Hegel, who here again attracts Levinas's critical attention (BPW 84).

'Substitution', as Levinas understands it, cannot be accounted for by the Western philosophical tradition. To the extent that that tradition has largely restricted its purview to whatever is accessible to consciousness, a radical challenge to the subject is excluded by it from the outset. Communication with the other is transcendence only in so far as the sovereignty of consciousness is displaced (BPW 92). In so far as whatever appears to consciousness is a function of the structures of subjectivity, as in Kant's schematism, there are no radical surprises in store for the subject. The self-sufficiency of the subject, its self-satisfaction, is secure because this is a subject who cannot be challenged from the outside. The self-possession of self-consciousness rules as an *arche* and is not submitted to the other's challenge as described in *Totality and Infinity*. It was already clear from *Totality and Infinity* that the relation with the stranger was not conducted through a representation of the other, but in 'Substitution' Levinas radicalizes this account by insisting that one does not know from whom the summons comes. This enables Levinas to accommodate better his hyperbolic notion of responsibility that includes those we do not even know and with whom we cannot therefore have contracted. But, more importantly in the immediate context, it takes responsibility out of the realm of consciousness.

This helps to explain why Levinas believes that it is necessary to depart from the postulates of ontological thinking in order to think 'the in itself of persecuted subjectivity' (BPW 89). This approach is not motivated by a dogmatic rejection of the Western philosophical tradition, still less a fascination for new modes of thinking. Levinas's strategy is philosophically motivated. To break from traditional ontology Levinas speaks of the creature and creation rather than of being. These terms were already introduced in *Totality and Infinity*, but he now emphasizes their role in the analysis. Levinas's previous hesitation about their significance seems to have arisen from his concern to protect his philosophy from being understood simply as Jewish philosophy, largely because he seems to have feared that that would have been a way of dismissing it. His greater confidence on this score is indicated by his comment in 1974: 'It is not here a question of justifying the theological context of ontological thought, for the word creation designates a signification older than the context woven about this name' (OB 113). And it should not go unnoticed that the notion of substitution was already introduced by Levinas into his confessional writings in a lecture he delivered in 1964, three years before it found its way into his philosophical writings (NTR 49).[3]

II

Unlike much contemporary writing on ethics, Levinas does not assume or even expect rationality and morality to be in agreement. Nor does he conceive his project as an attempt to elucidate the way we actually think about morality. Indeed, the good conscience that arises from satisfying the often very restricted demands imposed by conventional morality is one of his central targets. Levinas's radical departure from traditional ethics is signalled by the claim added to the 1974 version, 'The ethical situation of responsibility is not comprehensible on the basis of ethics' (OB 120). Although he never says so in exactly these terms, Levinas suspects that rationality, as ordinarily conceived, serves to tame or domesticate morality. To release a more demanding sense of ethics, Levinas questions the inherited sense of rationality.

Levinas is well aware of how radical his claims are and the burden they place on him as he tries to articulate them. They not only lead him to the difficult thought of substitution, but in preparation for introducing this thought he believes himself compelled to abandon certain theses central to the Western philosophical tradition as he understands it. He identifies one of them when he says that the reduction of subjectivity to consciousness 'dominates philosophical thought' (BPW 83). Levinas announces that, according to the Western tradition, 'all spirituality is consciousness, the thematic exposition of Being, that is to say, knowledge' (BPW 80). The initial task that Levinas sets himself in 'Substitution' is to provide an account of subjectivity that runs counter to that offered by those representatives of the Western philosophical tradition according to which the primary relation to beings takes place in knowledge. This leads Levinas to entertain the possibility of a relation 'with what cannot be identified in the kerygmatic logos' (BPW 80), thereby setting himself on a difficult path.

As I stated earlier, Levinas had prepared the audience of his lecture on 'Substitution' in Brussels by giving an account of proximity in 'Language and Proximity'. When at the outset of 'Substitution' Levinas interprets language not in terms of the communication of information, but as contact or proximity (BPW 80), he is rehearsing one of the claims of the earlier piece (CP 115). It leads directly to Levinas's now familiar distinction between the saying and the said, which is intended not only as a theory of language, but also as a guide to how he himself should be read, albeit on certain interpretations of the distinction this threatens to diminish the content of his thought in a way that makes it virtually irrelevant what is said by the saying. In any event, the account of language presupposed by 'Substitution' makes of it an essay that self-consciously resists any attempt to reduce it to a thematic analysis. This raises questions as to what it means to attempt to elucidate his text as I am attempting to do here.[4] Levinas seems to have foreseen this problem and bypassed it at the outset. The complexity of his strategies, in so far as they can even be identified, are such that one is in no danger of reducing the essay to a theme. It is not only subjectivity as such that cannot be pinned down or identified, but also Levinas himself. And when he says that proximity is a relationship that frustrates any schematism, the reader shares in the frustration (BPW 80). There are times when one wonders if the question to which 'Substitution' is the answer is not 'what is the most obscure philosophical concept of the twentieth century?' The difficulty is that Levinas nowhere clearly sets out the rules under which his exposition is to be judged. The status of his discourse is unclear. However, some indications emerge during the course of the investigation as Levinas expresses his own concerns about the direction it is taking.

Levinas's text is marked by an anxiety that arises from the difficulty of being faithful to the an-archy of passivity (BPW 89). The term 'an-archy' in this context signals that Levinas is not attempting to introduce a new principle or foundation. But his deeper concern is that passivity is constantly threatened by the possibility of an activity, a freedom, being posited behind this passivity (*BPW* 89). This anxiety motivates some of the heavy rewriting that Levinas undertakes between the two versions of the essay, but the anxiety remains (*OB* 113). Indeed, it is extended to embrace the question of whether he had not, in his presentation of persecuted subjectivity, succumbed to the postulates of ontological thought more generally and in particular the sway of eternal self-presence and of self-coincidence (*OB* 113–14). At the basis of responsibility Levinas locates the passivity of the hostage, and not the freedom of an ego that can find in its actions a source of pride.

The 'for' of 'one-for-the-other' of substitution signals a surplus of responsibility that extends even to those one does not know, including people of the past and the future. Substitution is not the psychological event of pity or compassion, but a putting oneself in the place of the other by taking responsibility for their responsibilities. Because substitution is my responsibility for everyone else, including their responsibility, the relation is asymmetrical: 'No one can substitute himself for me, who substitutes myself for all' (*OB* 136). Hence the trope of the-one-for-the-other is contradictory (*OB* 100). My responsibility for the responsibility of the other constitutes that 'one degree of responsibility more' (*BPW* 91), a 'surplus of responsibility' (*OB* 100). Against the traditional notion of responsibility Levinas can claim that I am for the other without having chosen or acted: 'Without ever having done anything, I have always been under accusation: I am persecuted' (*BPW* 89). Levinas likes to quote Dostoevsky's account of the asymmetry of guilt and responsibility: 'every one of us is guilty before all, for everyone and everything, and I more than others' (see *BPW* 102 and 144). Just as Sartre argues that either one is totally free or one is not free at all, so Levinas argues that either one is responsible for everything or one has refused responsibility. This is how Levinas answers those who say that to be responsible for everything is to be responsible for nothing.

In 'Substitution' Levinas focuses on sacrifice, but the limit-case is being accused of and responsible for what others do at the concrete level, even to the point of being responsible for the very persecution that one undergoes (*BPW* 88). What is this but neurosis, mania, obsession? Far from challenging this potential criticism, Levinas accepts its terms even before it has been posed. A subject obsessed with the other is incapable of indifference. One should not suppose that this analysis shifts the blame for violence and murder to the victim, because that would be to confuse Levinas's discussion of ethical responsibility for the legal form of responsibility that Western ethics tends to focus on. The question is not who should be blamed, but 'what am I to do?' (BPW 168). To accept responsibility for the suffering undergone is to be challenged to act, but this action does not have its seat in the spontaneity of a willing subject conceived in artificial isolation. The gift is a good example: the other can be said to dispossess me on occasion so that giving is not an act, but an ethical event whereby I lose my sense of *mine* in the face of the other.[5] Levinas thus introduces an account of how ethical action arises in the extreme passivity of obsession. The relation to the other is now a bond rather than a form of separation, as it was in *Totality and Infinity*. Whereas the structure of desire, which dominates *Totality and Infinity* but not *Otherwise than Being* (cf. OB 88), is that of exteriority, obsession is inscribed in consciousness 'as something foreign, a disequilibrium, a delirium, undoing thematization, eluding *principle*, origin, and will' (OB 81). Obsession is a persecution that reveals the passivity of a subject already in question (BPW 82).

'Obsession' is not the only word that undergoes a transformation as it enters into Levinas's lexicon. Equally striking is his use of the term 'persecution'. Levinas introduces it by equating it with obsession. He then explains: 'Here persecution does not amount to consciousness gone mad; it designates the manner in which the Ego is affected and a defection from consciousness' (BPW 81). The denial seems to suggest that Levinas is trying to distance himself from the idea of a persecution complex, just as he does not want his use of the term 'obsession' to be understood psychoanalytically. Nevertheless, the fact that he invokes these connotations, albeit to warn against them, is evidence that he is fully aware of the danger of these terms and is willing to take the risk. In the context of the opening pages of the essay the terms 'obsession' and 'persecution' seem arbitrary. Only retrospectively, when the argument is complete, is it apparent that the political sense of 'persecution' in all its concreteness is crucial to Levinas. At the outset, all that is clear is that Levinas introduces these terms to assist him in establishing the terms 'passivity' and 'passion' at the heart of the analysis (BPW 82). This enables him to establish a certain distance from the conventional analysis of consciousness as the site of intentionality and of freedom. Levinas also uses these terms to bring into question the traditional assumption that the ego coincides with itself or is equal with itself (BPW 80, 82, 90).

The one who bears the suffering of others and responds to it, no longer has the appearance of a free being but of one who is overwhelmed. So when Levinas counters the hypothesis of a free ego deciding in favour of solidarity for others, he responds: 'At least it will be recognized that this freedom has not time to assume this urgent weight and that, consequently, it appears collapsed and defeated under its suffering' (BPW 95). However, such a claim, like many others in the essay, makes it seem that Levinas is constructing his argument, not as a transcendental or quasi-transcendental investigation, but as a description of experience. But if this is what he is doing, philosophical opponents might appropriately respond by offering alternative descriptions. It is Levinas's attempt to negotiate this dilemma that accounts for much of the complexity of 'Substitution'. Before showing how he addresses it, it is necessary to explore another theme of the essay.

III

Although toward the end of the essay Levinas addresses the question of the possibility of sacrifice, at the beginning of 'Substitution' the dominant philosophical problem is that of identity. The theory that the identity of the I is reducible to a 'turning back' (BPW 84) of essence upon itself is put in question. This conception, identified with both Hegel and Sartre, presents the sovereignty or imperialism of the oneself as an abstraction. Consciousness must lose itself so as to find itself (BPW 85) and it finds itself in the concrete process of truth. That is to say, it finds itself in the return to self that is accomplished across time, through the ideality of the logos (BPW 84) or in the project (BPW 82).

By contrast with the tradition as he understands it, Levinas locates an identity beyond or behind distinguishing characteristics. Unlike consciousness which loses itself to find itself, the Levinasian self is unable to take a distance from itself (BPW 86). It is unable to depart from itself so as to return, once having recognized itself in its past (BPW 89). Traditional theories of identity allow for the individual to become a subject of thematization in language. Levinas does not challenge the conventional accounts of identity directly, so much as undercut them. He proposes an account of what he calls the identity of ipseity or singularity that differs from the identity of identification. The identity of identification, as described by Hegel, involves a return to self, but in the identity of ipseity there is no separation from out of which a unity can be established, except as a unity without rest or peace (BPW 84–5). Levinas gives the name recurrence to this structure. Recurrence 'breaks open the limits of identity' (BPW 89) by being free of duality and Heideggerian *ecstasis*. Recurrence is the simple identity of the reflexive pronoun, itself, free of a system of references (BPW 88). Although the oneself or rather the me (the distinction, although important, cannot be rehearsed here)[6] is 'in itself', it is not 'in itself' like matter, of which it can be said that it is what it is (BPW 86). The me is in itself 'like one is in one's skin' – cramped, ill at ease (BPW 86). The self is the body but not conceived biologically (BPW 87). It is exposure (BPW 89).

The identity of singularity is not conferred by a proper name. It is nameless, identifiable only by a personal pronoun (BPW 85). Unutterable, it is nevertheless said by Levinas to be 'shameful and hence unjustifiable' (BPW 85). These are crucial terms for Levinas because they mark a change of register as he passes from formal description to concretion, which is here, as in *Totality and Infinity*, ethical. In other words, the formal ontological analysis becomes ethical by virtue of the passage to concreteness (cf. BPW 90). Levinas not only wants to insist that the identity of singularity, the recurrence of ipseity, is the condition of the identity of identification as it takes place in the return to self (BPW 85 and 87). He also insists that it is the condition of sacrifice, and this by virtue of its passivity, its susceptibility, its exposure to wounding and outrage (BPW 86). Unable to take a distance from itself (BPW 86) or slip away, the self is responsible prior to any commitment (BPW 87). I am radically responsible for the other prior to any contract, prior to having chosen or acted, indeed prior to my taking up a subject position in relation to an other. In *Otherwise than Being* the responsibility inherent in subjectivity is prior to my encounter with an other, whereas *Totality and Infinity* had located the possibility of ethics in the concrete encounter that realized the formal structure of transcendence. Levinas clarifies this new conception of a responsibility older than interior identification in an essay first published in 1970 under the title 'Sans identité'. Here Levinas explains that if there is a responsibility from which no one can release me, the human being must be 'without identity': 'a uniqueness without interiority, me without rest in itself, hostage of all, turned away from itself in each movement of its return to itself'. Responsible for all, I must substitute for all, substituting for everyone by virtue of a certain 'non-interchange-ability' (*CP* 150).

Levinas's subversion of traditional theories of identity is apparent in his adoption of Rimbaud's phrase, 'Je est un autre'.[7] This formulation, for all its obscurity, avoids the difficulties that arise if the same and the other are understood as ontological categories. Here the subject is not itself but other, to the point of standing in place of the other, of being substituted for the other. Like the idea of proximity that also comes to prominence at this time, substitution as the one for the other runs counter at very least to the rhetoric of alterity that pervades *Totality and Infinity*, although the language of exteriority is retained (*BPW* 80–1). In 'Violence and Metaphysics' Derrida had problematized Levinas's notion of alterity by confronting it with an argument that he drew from Plato's *Sophist*. He appeals to the full force of the Western tradition to say that the other is other only as other than myself. The other cannot be absolved of a relation to an ego from which it is other; it cannot be absolutely other.[8] Rimbaud's phrase serves Levinas as a response. With it Levinas radically transforms the classic opposition of the same and the other and thus the language within which his own thought is framed. To be sure, Levinas does not underwrite Rimbaud's phrase as the latter meant it. Indeed it could have been of that phrase that Levinas writes in *Totality and Infinity*:

The alterity of the I that takes itself for another may strike the imagination of the poet precisely because it is but the play of the same: the negation of the I by the self is precisely one of the modes of identification of the I. [*TI* 37]

That is to say, Levinas in *Totality and Infinity* can be understood as rejecting the phrase that becomes central to *Otherwise than Being*, but in fact he only rejects it in the sense Rimbaud meant it and not in the sense that it comes to be given in the latter text. Levinas emphasizes that by 'I is an other' Rimbaud may have meant alienation (*BPW* 92) or, as he says in 'Sans identité', 'alteration, alienation, betrayal of oneself, foreignness with regard to oneself and subjection to this foreigner' (*CP* 145), but Levinas understands it to mean 'a subjectivity incapable of shutting itself up' (*CP* 151).

Substitution does not do away with the self. Levinas often offers as the paradigm of such responsibility for the other the giving of bread to the other from out of one's mouth. But to give the very bread I eat, one has to enjoy one's bread, 'not in order to have the merit of giving it, but in order to give it with one's heart, to give oneself in giving it' (OB 72). The ethical analysis reveals at the heart of persecution a self prior to the ego, to consciousness, self-possession and knowledge, which is unsuspected by ontology. The significance of this language is clear if one recalls the language of *Totality and Infinity*:

The alterity, the radical heterogeneity of the other, is possible only if the other is other with respect to a term whose essence is to remain at the point of departure, to serve as *entry* into the relation, to be the same not relatively but absolutely. *A term can remain absolutely at the point of departure of relationship only as I (Moi).* [TI 36]

The emphasis of *Otherwise than Being* is somewhat different and can best be summarized by the formula, 'I am "in itself" through the others' (OB 112, translation modified). Or, again, I am 'through the other and for the other' (OB 114).

Obsessed with its responsibilities and accused by everyone, the subject is a hostage (OB 112). 'Responsibility in obsession is a responsibility of the ego for what the ego had not wished for, that is, for the other' (OB 114). This structure of responsibility, which precedes any particular ethics or system of moral imperatives as their condition, transforms the meaning of the 'I' into what Levinas articulates as the '*here I am* [me voici], answering for everything and everyone' (OB 114). That is to say, the *I* now finds itself in the accusative as *me*. To be infinitely responsible is to bear the burden even of the other's own responsibility for me. To be hostage is to bear the burden of 'the responsibility for the responsibility of the other' (OB 117). For Levinas, I am not ultimately someone who chooses, but someone chosen. Furthermore, he would think it a mistake to characterize my being elected as what defines me. The identity of ipseity as recurrence 'breaks open the limits of identity' (BPW 89). It is the breaking open of identity that makes possible sacrifice and responsibility for all, even for my persecutor. 'Uniqueness is without identity' (OB 57). But my lack of identity is not what makes possible substitution: 'it is already a substitution for the other' (OB 57).

The essay 'Substitution' is from its first sentence an essay about identity and our ways of identifying both things and ourselves. This was not a new topic for Levinas. It was a particularly longstanding theme of his philosophical works, as *Existence and Existents* shows, and may indeed have arisen for him in the context of his being persecuted as a Jew. In other words, his approach to philosophical questions of personal identity may have arisen in part because of anti-semitism, the persecution he suffered as a Jew. However, this is not the place to explore this hypothesis that I postpone to another occasion, because of the difficulty, not to say, sensitivity, of these questions that relate absolute identity 'without fatherland' (*OB* 103) to identity *as* this or that. My concern is merely to suggest the possible impact of Levinas's challenge to traditional accounts of identity. But it should be noted that whereas in *Existence and Existents* Levinas had described the arising into consciousness of a solitary being, in 'Substitution' the issue is the arising into consciousness of a being that has always already felt the impact of the relation to the other. Levinas's conception is that once it has been ascertained that the self does not serve as an *arche* in the sense of a foundation and a sovereign principle, then the possibility opens up that it can be construed as a hostage, answerable for everything and everyone (*BPW* 90). The fact of sacrifice and of giving at the concrete level confirms this hypothesis. This is the meaning of the sentence, 'It is through the condition of being a hostage that there can be pity, compassion, pardon, and proximity in the world – even the little there is, even the simple "after you, sir" ' (*BPW* 91).

IV

Does this mean that Levinas has adopted in *Otherwise than Being* a transcendental or quasi-transcendental philosophy? This is suggested not only by the transcendental form of the question about the possibility of sacrifice, but also by Levinas's posing of the question of how communication and transcendence are possible (*BPW* 92). However, to understand how 'Substitution' works it is necessary to return briefly once more to *Totality and Infinity*. In that book Levinas locates the ethical in the way that the other calls the subject in question: 'The strangeness of the Other, his irreducibility to the I, to my thoughts and my possessions, is precisely accomplished as a calling into question of my spontaneity, as ethics' (*TI* 43). The subject is presented as already given prior to the other's calling the self into question, just as the individual within classical forms of the social contract tradition is first presented as outside society. In order to establish the radical alterity of the other, Levinas builds up a conception of the identity of the I in atheist separation. This is necessary, Levinas seems to think, in order to establish an account of the encounter with the other in which the other's alterity does not simply disappear in the encounter, as would be the case if the relation were conceived, for example, in terms of opposition (*TI* 38). Even though Levinas complicates the basic framework of this account by introducing a certain alterity into habitation within the home in a way that I cannot address here, the fundamental impression that emerges from a reading of *Totality and Infinity* is that it is only for an already established 'I' that the other arises. The separated I, the subject, is put in question by the other but it is only with the somewhat problematic analysis of fecundity in the final part of *Totality and Infinity* that there is any real questioning of this 'I' by Levinas himself.[9]

In *Otherwise than Being*, by contrast, Levinas reframes the question of the possibility of ethics by turning from the other to the ethical subject so as to ask about the possibility of such a subject: how could an independent, autochthonous, solitary being be put into question by the other? In other words, he goes behind the back of the consciousness of the I, so that there is no longer any danger that Levinas will be read as if the ethical first arose as a concrete event in the life of an already constituted ego. When Levinas writes in 'Substitution' that the obsessional accusation 'strips the Ego of its self-conceit and its dominating imperialism' (*BPW* 88), he is reformulating the critique of spontaneity and of freedom produced by the arrival of the other on the scene in *Totality and Infinity*. One major difference is that the critique is no longer formulated in such a way that one could suppose, as many interpreters have, that the ethical awaits an empirical encounter, which would seem to leave those who had not had such an encounter free of ethics. And yet this does not mean that experience plays no role in the account.

In 'Substitution' Levinas does more than take up a question that arises from the account in *Totality and Infinity* of the questioning of the self-sufficiency of the subject, which in 'Substitution' is transformed into the question of how the passivity of obsession finds a place in consciousness (BPW 82), how the passivity of self becomes a 'hold on oneself' (BPW 89). He also repeats one of its dominant strategies of the earlier work: in both texts a formal structure is proposed prior to the introduction of a discussion of its concrete realization. However, although the concrete situation is, in each case, identified as that of the advent of the ethical, the formal structure is approached differently. Rehearsing the account of 'a recurrence that breaks open the limit of responsibility' (BPW 89), he asks, 'what can it be if not substitution for others?' (BPW 90). In *Totality and Infinity*, Levinas does not claim that, given that there is transcendence, the ethical is the only or even the preeminent way in which it occurs. Rather his claim is: given that the ethical happens, we should understand its occurrence as the realization of what the Western philosophical tradition called transcendence but misguidedly sought elsewhere, especially in mystical experience. Levinas took from Descartes the idea of infinity as a thought that thinks more than it can produce from its own resources and so a thought that is thought in me.[10] But even Descartes was, at least on Levinas's understanding, offering an account of something like a mystical experience with God. This formal structure is concretized only in the relation to the other human being.

In *Totality and Infinity*, there is, as it were, a tension between the transcendental and the empirical approaches, which are both present. There are passages in which Levinas appears to be offering a concrete description, but much of the language of *Totality and Infinity* seems explicitly to evoke a transcendental reading.[11] In a crucial formulation Levinas describes the procedure of *Totality and Infinity* as follows:

The method practiced here does indeed consist in seeking the condition of empirical situations, but it leaves to the developments called empirical, in which the conditioning possibility is accomplished – it leaves to the *concretization* – an ontological role that specifies the meaning of the fundamental possibility, a meaning invisible in that condition. [TI 173]

The corresponding statement in 'Substitution' is not so direct, but nevertheless shows that the role of the concrete has not diminished:

It is in a *responsibility that is justified by no prior commitment* – in the responsibility for the other (*autrui*) – an ethical situation, that the me-ontological and meta-logical structure of this Anarchy is outlined, undoing the logos framing the apology through which consciousness still recovers the itself and commands. [BPW 82]

What is striking about this passage, over and beyond Levinas's exposure of the apology as an assertion of consciousness rather than its abasement, is Levinas's insistence on how it is in the ethical situation, which is concrete, that the formal structure is outlined. Not only could there not be any transcendental deduction, but experience of the situation, which is already an experience of responsibility that gives ethical meaning to the situation, dictates the structure.

Levinas often questions the term 'experience' (e.g. GCM 162), but here Levinas appeals to 'nonphilosophical experiences' (BPW 92).[12] They are what saves the account from being assimilated to the model of transcendental investigation. It is not simply that certain forms of philosophy seem to have excluded the possibility of such experiences. These experiences are located in an 'ethics beyond politics' (BPW 92), which means beyond being. Sacrifice and giving remain gratuitous on this account, but that does not mean that the relation to being in which the ethical is situated is not crucial. This is why it is not irrelevant what is said in the saying, just as it is not unimportant whether or not one approaches the other with empty hands and closed home (TI 172; cf. OB 74). Levinas's claim here is that if one asks how sacrifice or giving is possible, one will ultimately be led behind consciousness and knowing to the one-for-the-other of substitution, but his thought remains directed toward the concrete, which is where the encounter takes place. The point is not just to show that such acts are impossible for an existence that is concerned only for its own existence, as they would also be on an egoistic account or one oriented on the ego as a free consciousness. Nor is the point to build the ethical into the very structure of subjectivity on the evidence of such actions. The point is that a transcendental account that is not oriented on the ethical situation as the locus of meaning would be open to a series of serious challenges where alternative meanings and alternative experiences would be proposed. Just as critics have argued against *Totality and Infinity* that alternative accounts of alterity might replace the account of ethical alterity, so critics of 'Substitution' could complain that the conditions of ethical action were so divorced from the ethical situation that they also made possible the most extreme subversions of ethics, evil deeds done in the name of the good. To be sure, because such subversions happen, Levinas must be able to account for them as readily as he can account for sacrifice and giving. There can be no 'deduction' in the conventional sense of ethics and politics from 'substitution'. But Levinas must find a way to interweave the formal and the concrete, the transcendental and the experiential.

That 'substitution' is, at least in part, a response to the questions raised by Derrida in 'Violence and Metaphysics' finds confirmation in the transformation that Levinas's thought undergoes. In 'Violence and Metaphysics' Derrida writes that 'According to Levinas, there would be no interior difference, no fundamental and autochthonous alterity within the ego (*dans le Moi*)' (*WO* 109). Derrida's development of the problematic relies on that claim, which is incontestable as a reading of *Totality and Infinity*. But in *Otherwise than Being* Levinas undercuts those earlier formulations. The notion of substitution amounts to saying that 'the other is in me and in the midst of my very identification' (*OB* 125). The only reason why this does not amount to a recantation of Levinas's earlier thought is because 'substitution' operates not at the level of the ego (*le moi*), but of the self (*le soi*), such that the whole notion of identity has to be rethought, to the point where Levinas refers to 'the unjustifiable identity...expressed in terms such as ego, I, oneself' (*OB* 106).

However, 'substitution' can also be understood as an answer to a question that Derrida raised only in 1996 after Levinas's death, indeed on the occasion of a symposium held to commemorate his death. On that occasion Derrida problematized the possibility of a 'deduction' of both an ethical discourse of hospitality and a politics from Levinas's 'ethics of ethics'.[13] However, although Derrida suggests the possibility of thinking politics and right in another way, he does not pursue it in that essay (*A* 20–1). Nor does he recognize it in the interweaving of the formal and concrete. Nevertheless, 'the break-up of the formal structure of thought...into events which...sustain it and restore its concrete significance' is what Levinas calls 'deduction' in *Totality and Infinity* (*TI* 28). Derrida seems not to have recognized this form of deduction which Levinas calls 'necessary and yet non-analytical'. It is the thesis of this paper that Levinas not only remains committed to this effort in 'Substitution', but that he attempts to interweave the strands more rigorously than previously and that this in part accounts for the complexity of the essay, 'Substitution'.

There is more than one question to which 'substitution' is the answer. One of them is, indeed, the question of the transcendental or quasi-transcendental conditions of possibility of sacrifice. It is not wrong to say that the question to which 'substitution' is the answer is that of the condition of the ethical. But by itself the claim is misleading. A second question concerns the ethical situation or the meaning of concrete experience. Levinas is not asking about the conditions of substitution to find what lies behind it. Substitution happens. In some sense it has already happened. But in so far as this is so, then this radically alters the meaning of the transcendental question. To the extent that Levinas seems to have misunderstood Derrida to be saying that transcendence as he presented it is impossible because it is unthinkable (cf. wo 114), Levinas can be understood as responding that because the excessive 'gratuity of sacrifice' (BPW 92) happens, then it is possible and thinking must recast itself to take account of that fact. It is this reorientation of thinking that is Levinas's goal in 'Substitution' but it matters not at all unless it impacts on our approach to concrete situations so that we come to see them as ethical.[14]

NOTES

1 This interpretation is most clearly articulated by Simon Critchley in 'The Original Traumatism: Levinas and Psychoanalysis', in *Ethics–Politics–Subjectivity* (London: Verso, 1999), pp. 183–97. Unfortunately, I am able to address only a few of the important claims made in this rich essay. Some important cautionary warnings about any transcendental reading of the later Levinas are offered by Adriaan Peperzak, *To the Other: an Introduction to the Philosophy of Emmanuel Levinas* (West Lafayette: Purdue University Press, 1993), pp. 231–2. In a brief note in *Adieu* Derrida offers a transcendental reading based on the phrase 'a priori exposed to substitution', but at the same time asks if this can be Levinas's meaning. See Jacques Derrida, *Adieu to Emmanuel Levinas*, trans. P.-A. Brault and M. Naas (Stanford: Stanford University Press, 1999), pp. 150–1. (henceforth A).

2 See R. Bernasconi, 'Levinas and the Struggle for Existence', in Antje Kapust, Eric Nelson, and Kent Still (eds.), *Addressing Levinas* (Evanston: Northwestern University Press, forthcoming).

3 It is also worth noting the role accorded to substitution in the theological context of the 1968 lecture 'A Man–God?' (EN 54).

4 For an excellent review of the difficulty of the essay, see Theodore de Boer, 'Levinas on substitution', *The Rationality of Transcendence* (Amsterdam: J. C. Gieben, 1997), pp. 83–100.

5 On the gift, see R. Bernasconi, 'What Goes Around Comes Around: Derrida and Levinas on the Economy of the Gift and the Gift of Genealogy', in Alan Schrift (ed.), *The Logic of the Gift* (New York: Routledge, 1997), pp. 256–73.

6 Briefly, Levinas explains the distinction between the ego and the self, by saying that persecution strips the ego of its dominating imperialism and so reduces the ego (*le Moi*) to the self (*le soi*). Furthermore, notice that subjectivity is not the ego (*le Moi*) but me (*moi*) (*CP* 150).

7 For example, BPW 92. See Arthur Rimbaud, letter to George Izambard, 13 May 1871, in *Œuvres complètes*, ed. Rolland de Renéville and Jules Mouquet (Paris: Gallimard, 1963), p. 268.

8 J. Derrida, *Writing and Difference*, trans. Alan Bass (Chicago: University of Chicago Press, 1978), p. 126 (henceforth WD). For further discussion, see R. Bernasconi, 'The Alterity of the Stranger and the Experience of the Alien', in Jeffrey Bloechi (ed.), *The Face of the Other and the Trace of* God (New York: Fordham University Press, 2000), pp. 62–89.

9 The analysis of fecundity is problematic primarily because of Levinas's reliance on paternity. See Luce Irigaray, 'The Fecundity of the Caress', *An Ethics of Sexual Difference*, trans. Carolyn Burke and Gillian C. Gill (Ithaca: Cornell University Press, 1993), pp. 185–217.

10 See R. Bernasconi, 'The Silent Anarchic World of the Evil Genius', in G. Moneta, J. Sallis and J. Taminiaux (eds.), *The Collegium Phaenomenologicum: The First Ten Years* (Dordrecht: Martinus Nijhoff, 1988), pp. 257–72.

11 R. Bernasconi, 'Rereading Totality and Infinity', in A. Dallery and C. Scott (eds.), *The Question of the Other*: *Essays in Contemporary Continental Philosophy* (New York: State University of New York Press, 1989), pp. 23–40.

12 For a discussion of this notion that I presuppose here, see R. Bernasconi, ' "Only the Persecuted . . . ": Language of the Oppressor, Language of the Oppressed', in Adriaan Peperzak (ed.), *Ethics as First Philosophy* (London: Routledge, 1993), pp. 77–86.

13 The phrase 'ethics of ethics' can be found at WO 111. On the deduction of politics, see A 20, 32 and 115.

14 I am indebted to many fine scholars who have helped me develop this reading, but special thanks are due to John Drabinski, Stacy Keltner and Max Maloney with whom I have discussed 'Substitution' over a number of years.

12 Evil and the temptation of theodicy

The metaphor that best captures the movement of Levinas's thinking is the one Derrida uses when he compares it to the crashing of a wave on a beach: always the 'same' wave returning and repeating its movement with deeper insistence.[1] Regardless of what theme or motif we follow – the meaning of ethics, responsibility, the alterity of the other (autrui), subjectivity, substitution – there is a profound sense that the 'same' wave is crashing. This is just as true when we focus on those moments in philosophy that indicate that there is 'something' more (and 'something more important') than being and ontology. Levinas keeps returning to Plato's suggestion that the Good is beyond being, and to the moment in Descartes's Meditations when Descartes discovers that the ideatum of infinity positively exceeds its idea, that infinity transcends any idea of finite substances. Or to switch metaphors, no matter which of the many pathways we take – pathways that seem to lead off in radically different directions – we always end up in the 'same' place, the 'same' clearing. This is not the clearing of Being, but rather the 'place' where ethics ruptures Being. But even when the outlines of Levinas's thinking come into sharper focus, our perplexity and puzzlement increase. We want to know how he arrives at his radical and startling claims. What are the considerations and motivations that lead him to insist on our asymmetrical and non-reciprocal relation to the other, our infinite responsibility to and for the other? Some have suggested that the place to begin is with the influence of Heidegger on his thinking, with the way in which much of Levinas's thought can be viewed as a critical dialogue with Heidegger. Others have suggested that we must go back to Franz Rosenzweig's The Star of Redemption, especially to Rosenzweig's critique of philosophy ('from Iona to Jena') and the very idea of totality that never escapes from the horizon of the dialectic of the same and the other. Still others have argued that the primary source for Levinas's understanding of ethics is to be found in his interpretation of the Jewish Bible, and the Jewish rabbinic tradition of commentary on the Bible. There is something right about all these suggestions (which are not incompatible), but frankly I do not think that they go deep enough. They do not answer the question why does Levinas interpret and use these sources in the way he does? The thesis that I want to explore and defend is that the primary thrust of Levinas's thought is to be understood as his response to the horror of the evil that has erupted in the twentieth century. I believe that Levinas's entire philosophic project can best be understood as an *ethical* response to evil – and to the problem of evil which we must confront after the 'end of theodicy'.

At first glance, such a thesis may seem paradoxical, because Levinas does not thematize evil in any of his major works. In the extensive secondary literature dealing with Levinas, 'evil' (*mal*) is barely even mentioned. Yet, like an ever-present ominous spectre, evil casts its shadow over everything he has ever written. It is no exaggeration to assert that Levinas's confrontation with the 'unspeakable' evil of the twentieth century – where Auschwitz is the very paradigm of this evil – has not only elicited his fundamental *ethical response*, but has led him directly to his distinctive understanding of ethics.

I can illustrate what I mean by turning to the provocative opening sentence of *Totality and Infinity*: 'Everyone will readily agree that it is of the highest importance to know whether we are not duped by morality' (*TI* 21). What does it mean to be 'duped' by morality? (Levinas frequently uses the expressions 'morality' and 'ethics' interchangeably, although he prefers 'ethics' which is derived from the Greek *ethos*. Sometimes he does distinguish 'ethics' from 'morality' when he wants to distinguish ethics as first philosophy from the specific rules of morality.) In the paragraphs that follow this dramatic opening, Levinas speak of politics, war and violence, introducing the theme of totality. 'War does not manifest exteriority and the other as other; it destroys the identity of the same ... The visage of being shows itself in war is fixed in the concept of totality, which dominates Western philosophy' (*TI* 21). But the possibility of being duped by morality means more than this. Consider his response to a question he was asked in an interview when he was questioned about the

Greek and Jewish moments in his thought. Levinas insists that his thought is Greek (i.e. philosophical):

Everything that I say about justice comes from Greek thought, and Greek politics as well. But what I say, quite simply, is that it is, ultimately, based on the relationship to the other, on the ethics without which I would not have sought justice. Justice is the way in which I respond to the fact that I am not alone in the world with the other. [PM 174]

But what about the Jewish moment in his thought? He tells us:

If there is an explicitly Jewish moment in my thought, it is the reference to Auschwitz, where God let the Nazis do what they wanted. Consequently, what remains? Either this means that there is no reason for morality and hence it can be concluded that everyone should act like the Nazis, or the moral law maintains its authority . . .
   It still cannot be concluded that after Auschwitz there is no longer a moral law, as if the moral or ethical law were impossible, without promise. Before the twentieth century, all religion begins with the promise. It begins with the 'Happy End'. [PM 176]

But for Levinas, it is not simply a 'rhetorical' question to ask whether we can still believe in morality after Auschwitz. It is a deadly serious question, the most serious question that we must confront. 'The essential problem is: can we speak of an absolute commandment after Auschwitz? Can we speak of morality after the failure of morality' (PM 176)? Perhaps we really have been duped by morality. Both Hannah Arendt and Hans Jonas (two other Jewish thinkers who lived through the Nazi period) raised similar questions. Arendt (like Levinas) believed that the evil that burst forth during the Nazi period indicated a rupture with tradition, and revealed the total inadequacy of traditional accounts of morals and ethics to deal with evil. She declares 'We . . . have witnessed the total collapse of all established moral standards in public and private life during the 1930s and 40s'[2]; 'without much notice all this collapsed almost overnight and then it was as though morality suddenly stood revealed . . . as a set of *mores*, customs and *manners* which could be exchanged for another set with hardly more trouble than it would take to change the table manners of an individual or a people.'[3] And Hans Jonas, in a passage that mocks Hegel, says:

The disgrace of Auschwitz is not to be charged to some all-powerful providence or to some dialectically wise necessity, as if it were an antithesis demanding a synthesis or a step on the road to salvation. We human beings have inflicted this on the deity, we who have failed in the administering of his things. It remains on our account, and it is we who must again wash away the disgrace from our own disfigured faces, indeed from the very countenance of God. Don't talk to me here about the cunning of reason.[4]

As the above quotations from Levinas (and from Jonas) make clear, the question being raised is a question not only of morality, but also of religion – specifically the question of theodicy. The problem of evil, as traditionally conceived by philosophers and theologians, is the problem of theodicy – the problem of how we can *reconcile* the existence of evil (or the *apparent* existence of evil) with a faith in a God who is omniscient, omnipotent and beneficient – a God who is the creator of the universe and all living beings. In his essay 'Useless Suffering', Levinas explicitly takes up the question of theodicy, declaring that we are living in a time after 'the end of theodicy'. 'Perhaps the most revolutionary fact of the twentieth-century consciousness . . . is that of the destruction of all balance between explicit and implicit theodicy of Western thought and the forms which suffering and its evil take in the unfolding of this century' (*US* 161). When Levinas speaks of theodicy, he is not simply referring to the narrow sense of theodicy introduced by Leibniz in the early eighteenth century. Theodicy, in its broad sense, is 'as old as a certain reading of the Bible'. Levinas speaks of theodicy as a *temptation* – the seductive temptation 'in making God innocent, or in saving morality in the name of faith, or in making suffering – and this is the true intention of the thought that has recourse to theodicy – bearable' (*US* 161).

Theodicy, in this broad sense, is not only evidenced in the Christian doctrine of original sin, but is already implicit in the Jewish Bible 'where the drama of the Diaspora reflects the sins of Israel' (*US* 161). Lest we think that theodicy is restricted to religious faith, Levinas emphasizes that, in a secular age, theodicy has persisted 'in a watered-down form at the core of atheist progressivism which was confident, nonetheless, in the efficacy of the Good which is immanent to being, called to visible triumph by the simple play of the natural and historical laws of injustice, war, misery, and illness' (*US* 161). In short, theodicy, in its theological or secular forms, is nothing but the temptation to find some sort of 'justification,' some way to 'reconcile' ourselves to useless unbearable suffering. But intellectual honesty demands that we recognize that theodicy is over.

'The philosophical problem, then, which is posed by the useless pain which appears in its fundamental malignancy across the events of the twentieth century, concerns the meaning that religiosity and the human morality of goodness can still retain after the end of theodicy' (us 163). This is the problem that we must *now* confront.

We can appreciate the radicalness of Levinas's statement of the problem by comparing Levinas with Kant. Kant already criticized theodicy as a *theoretical* problem because theodicy presupposes that we can have some knowledge (no matter how partial) of God's attributes (i.e. that God is (or is not) omnipotent, omniscient and beneficient). But such a *theoretical* knowledge is impossible. Furthermore, Kant begins his *Religion Within the Limits of Reason Alone* by categorically declaring that morality 'stands in need neither of the idea of another Being over him, for him to apprehend his duty, nor an incentive other than the law itself, for him to do his duty.... Hence for its own sake morality does not need religion at all'.⁵ Yet from Levinas's perspective, Kant does *not* resist the temptation of theodicy. He affirms it as the *practical* need to postulate a beneficient God. Lurking in the background here is still the idea of 'reconciliation', the 'promise' – being worthy of 'the Happy End'. This is precisely what we must now give up. The phenomenon of Auschwitz demands (if we are not duped by morality) that we conceive of 'the moral law independently of the Happy End'.

I want to clarify several preliminary issues that will help set the context for probing Levinas's ethical response to twentieth-century evil. There is no doubt that Auschwitz (where most of Levinas's family were exterminated) is the 'paradigm of gratuitous suffering, where evil appears in its diabolical horror' (us 162). But it is crucial to realize that it is not exclusively the Jewish catastrophe that Levinas singles out. Auschwitz itself is a *paradigm* or exemplar of a much more general and pervasive phenomenon of evil. Levinas is explicit about this:

This is the century that in thirty years has known two world wars, the totalitarianisms of right and left, Hilterism and Stalinism, Hiroshima, the Gulag, and the genocides of Auschwitz and Cambodia. This is a century which is drawing to a close in the haunting memory of the return of everything signified by these barbaric names: suffering and evil are deliberately imposed, yet no reason sets limits to the exasperation of reason become political and detached from all ethics. [us 162]

Emphasizing that Auschwitz is a *paradigm* of the more *general* phenomenon of evil enables us to better understand the subtle inter-weaving of Greek and Jewish elements in Levinas's thinking. Some-times the contrast between Greek and Jew is overdrawn (even by Levinas himself). I have already cited the passage in which Levinas insists that his philosophic thought is essentially Greek. (To assert that *philosophic* thought is Greek is redundant.) But it is just as im-portant to realize that when Levinas weaves 'Jewish' elements into his thinking, he is primarily concerned to highlight their *universal* significance:

I do not preach the Jewish religion. I always speak of the Bible, not the Jewish religion. The Bible, including the Old Testament, is for me a human fact, of the human order, and entirely *universal*. What I have said about ethics, about the *universality* of the commandment in the face of the commandment which is valid even if it doesn't bring salvation, even if there is no reward, is valid independently of any religion. [Emphasis added, PM 177]

But for all the distinctiveness of the evils of the twentieth century, we can also hear the voices of Nietzsche and Dostoevsky speaking through Levinas. Nietzsche was one of the most brilliant diagnosti-cians of the human need to 'justify' suffering. And it was Nietzsche who radically criticized theodicy – the 'invention' of God (gods) to give meaning to and 'justify' this suffering:

What really arouses indignation against suffering is not suffering as such but the senselessness of suffering: but neither for the Christian, who has interpreted a whole mysterious machinery of salvation into suffering, nor for the naïve man of more ancient times, who understood all suffering in relation to the spectator of it or the causer of it, was there any such thing as *senseless* suffering. So as to abolish hidden, undetected, unwitnessed suffering from the world and honestly deny it, one was in the past virtually compelled to invent gods and genii of all the heights and depths ... For it was with the aid of such inventions that life knew how to work the trick which it has always known how to work, that of justifying itself, of justifying its 'evil'.[6]

This is an idea that is also expressed by Dostoevsky. When Levinas speaks about our essential asymmetrical relation to the other, he frequently quotes the famous statement of Aloysa Karamazov: 'Everyone is guilty in front of everyone else, and me more than others.' But we can also hear the voice of Ivan Karamazov's diatribe against the suffering of innocents. When Levinas speaks about the scandal of 'useless suffering', he sounds as if he is uttering Ivan's own words:

Western humanity has none the less sought for the meaning of this scandal by invoking the proper sense of a metaphysical order, an ethics, which is invisible in the immediate lessons of moral consciousness. This is the kingdom of transcendent ends, willed by a benevolent wisdom, by the absolute goodness of a God who is in some way defined by this super-natural goodness; or a widespread, invisible goodness in Nature and History, where it would command the paths which are, to be sure painful, but which lead to the Good. Pain is henceforth meaningful, subordinated in one way or another to the metaphysical finality envisaged by faith or by a belief in progress. These beliefs are presupposed by theodicy! ... The evil which fills the earth would be explained in a 'plan of the whole'; it would be called upon to atone for a sin, or it would announce, to the ontologically limited consciousness, compensation or recompense at the end of time. [US 160–61]

Levinas's response to useless suffering is neither that of Nietzsche who calls for a 'transvaluation of values', nor is it the self-laceration of Ivan Karamazov who refuses to accept a world in which there is useless suffering. Levinas's response to the evil of useless suffering that is maliciously inflicted is an *ethical* response – an ethical response that leads to his distinctive understanding of our asymmetrical and non-reciprocal responsibility to and for the other, a response to the suffering of the other, my neighbour:

But does not this end of theodicy, which obtrudes itself in the face of this century's inordinate distress, at the same time in a more general way reveal the unjustifiable character of suffering in the other person, the scandal which would occur by my justifying my neighbour's suffering? So that the very phenomenon of suffering in its uselessness is, in principle, the pain of the other. For an ethical sensibility – confirming itself, in the inhumanity of our time, against this inhumanity – the justification of the neighbour's pain is certainly the source of all immorality. [US 163]

We can see why Levinas's understanding of our ethical relation to the other is at once so demanding and yet so appealing. When confronted with the horrendous evils of the twentieth century, we tend to focus on the actions of the perpetrators and the suffering of the victims. We are much more ambivalent about the responsibility of so-called bystanders – those who allow such actions to take place and who justify their complicity – those who excuse themselves from any direct responsibility. But think how different the course of events might have been in our century, not only during the Nazi period, but in other instances such as the genocide that took place in Rwanda, if so-called bystanders had anticipated and responded to the suffering of their fellow human beings. Levinas's claim is poignantly illustrated by an incident that Hannah Arendt relates in her report of the Eichmann trial in Jerusalem. She tells the story of Anton Schmidt, whose name came up in the course of the trial. Anton Schmidt was a German soldier who helped Jewish partisans by supplying them with forged papers and trucks until he was apprehended and executed by the Germans. Arendt tells us that when Anton Schmidt's story was told in the Jerusalem court, it was as if those present observed a two-minute silence in honour of this German soldier who saved Jewish lives. Arendt's comment is certainly in the spirit of Levinas's insistence on one's ethical responsibility for the gratuitous suffering of one's fellow human beings:

And in those two minutes, which were like a sudden burst of light in the midst of impenetrable, unfathomable darkness, a single thought stood out clearly, irrefutably, beyond question – how utterly different everything would be today in this courtroom, in Israel, in Germany, in all of Europe, and perhaps in all countries of the world, if only more such stories could have been told.[7]

When we think of those instances where an individual ethically responds to the useless suffering of others, we can better understand why Levinas claims that

the suffering for the useless suffering of the other person, the just suffering in me for the unjustifiable suffering of the Other, opens upon the suffering the ethical perspective of the inter-human ... It is this attention to the Other which, across the cruelties of our century – despite these cruelties, because of these cruelties – can be affirmed as the very bond of human subjectivity, even to the point of being raised to a supreme ethical principle – the only one which it is not possible to contest – a principle which can go so far as to command the hopes and practical discipline of vast human groups. [US 159]

In order to probe the relation of evil and ethics, we must explore how Levinas characterizes evil. One of the few places in which there is a sustained explicit discussion of evil is his article 'Transcendence and Evil'. The occasion for this article was the

appearance of Phillippe Nemo's philosophic meditation on evil in the
book of Job. Levinas is primarily concerned with the 'philosophical
perspective opened by this work' (TE 157). He focuses on three moments of the phenomenology of evil: evil as excess; evil as intention;
and the hatred or horror of evil.

Evil as excess initially suggests the excess of its quantitative in-
tensity, 'of a degree surpassing measure'. But Levinas stresses how
'evil is an excess in its very quiddity' (TE 158). Evil is not an excess
because suffering can be terrible and unendurable. 'The break with
the normal and the normative, with order, with synthesis, with the
world, already constitutes its qualitative essence' (TE 158). This is
an extremely strong claim. Levinas is not simply calling attention
to the unbearable torture and suffering that evil deeds may inflict,
he emphasizes that we cannot adequately *comprehend* evil. It cannot be synthesized; it cannot be integrated into our categories of
understanding or reason:

It is as though to synthesis, even the purely formal synthesis of the Kantian
'I think', capable of uniting the data however heterogeneous they may be,
there would be opposed, in the form of evil, the nonsynthesizable, still more
heterogeneous than all heterogeneity subject to being grasped by the formal,
which exposes heterogeneity in its very malignancy.... In the appearing of
evil, in its original phenomenonality, in its *quality*, is announced a *modality*,
a manner: not finding a place, the refusal of all accommodation with – a
counternature, a monstrosity, which is disturbing and foreign of itself. *And
in this sense transcendence!* [TE 158]

Ironically – or perhaps not so ironically – Levinas's claims about
the transcendence of evil parallel some of the claims that Kant makes
about the sublime in his *Critique of Judgement*. The major difference
is that Levinas would argue that Kant treats the sublime as if it can
be integrated into the ideas of reason (*Vernunft*) – although not into
the categories of the understanding (*Verstand*). But for Levinas, 'evil
is not only the nonintegratable, it is also the nonintegratability of
the nonintegratable' (TE 158). Evil is a malignant sublime.

When evil is understood as 'excess in its very quiddity', then we
can discern more clearly why evil doesn't simply resist theodicy, but
opposes all forms of theodicy. Theodicy is based on the presupposition that there is some way of integrating evil into a coherent economy of good and evil. What is so striking about Levinas's discussion

of evil as a non-integratable excess is the way in which his reasoning parallels his critiques of totality and the dialectic of the same and other where Being and ontology are taken to be our ultimate horizon. Just as infinity *ruptures* totality, so too evil *ruptures* totality. I do not think that this 'formal' parallel is accidental. On the contrary, it is *because* of the 'transcendence' of evil, *because* it cannot in any way be integrated or (strictly speaking) comprehended that the *only* adequate response to the malignancy of evil is a response that is 'commensurate' with this transcendence of evil. This is precisely the ethical response that recognizes that the otherness of the other can never be comprehended, that I am infinitely responsible for the other person whose suffering is ethically more important to me than my own suffering.

The content of evil is not exhausted by its excess. The second moment in the phenomenology of evil is the *intentionality* of evil. 'Evil reaches me as though it sought me out; evil strikes me as though there were an aim behind the ill lot that pursues me, as though someone were set against me, as though there were malice, as though there were someone' (TE 159–60). I do not react to evil as if it were something that merely 'happens' to me. I am a *victim* of the evil that is directed to me. Furthermore, there must be some reason why I experience this evil. This is the very phenomenon that tempts us to theodicy, the search to 'justify' or to 'explain away' the evil that I am suffering. But I must resist this temptation. Indeed, the transcendence of evil leads me to realize that the *first* metaphysical question (*pace* Leibniz and Heidegger) is not 'why is there something rather than nothing?' but rather 'why is there evil rather than good?' This second moment provides a glimpse of what is beyond Being, beyond ontology. 'The ontological difference is preceded by the difference of good and evil' (TE 160). There is a priority of the ethical over the ontological; and the ontological presupposes the ethical. Once again, it is evil that leads us to ethics and to the realization of the primacy and priority of ethics.

Throughout Levinas's discussion of evil and its phenomenology there is a subtext. The subtext is his ongoing quarrel with Heidegger. Levinas's thinking – as he himself frequently acknowledges – would not be possible without Heidegger. But when Levinas objects to Heidegger's conception of Being as the ultimate horizon, when in the language of *Totality and Infinity*, Levinas claims that ontology itself presupposes ethics as first philosophy, he is critiquing Heidegger's thinking for its failure to come to grips with evil and ethics. Levinas is not solely critical of Heidegger because of his complicity with the Nazis. Levinas's objection to Heidegger is primarily *philosophical*. Heidegger's thinking lacks the philosophical resources for confronting the non-integratable malignancy of evil. No philosophy that fails to appreciate that there is 'something' beyond Being can adequately confront evil – or elicit the ethical response to evil.

It is the third moment of the phenomenology of evil – evil as the hatred or horror of evil – that is at once the source of the greatest temptation to ontologize evil, to seek an (impossible) reconciliation with evil, and at the same time is the occasion for opening us to an interhuman ethical relation with another person: 'Evil strikes me in my horror of evil, and thus reveals – or is already – my association with the Good. The excess of evil by which it is a surplus in the world is also our impossibility of accepting it' (TE 161). Everything depends on precisely how one interprets this horror of evil. If I interpret it as meaning that there is an economy here whereby evil *must* be counterbalanced by a good, then once again I am being seduced by the temptation of theodicy. I am still operating in a framework where there is an economy of relationships that must be symmetrical and reciprocal. I am still thinking that good is the dialectical *negation* of evil, and/or that evil is the dialectical *negation* of good –.that there is some way of balancing or reconciling good and evil. But Levinas categorically asserts: 'There can be no question of a passage from Evil to the Good through the attraction of contraries. That would make but one more theodicy' (TE 161).

But there is another way (the Levinasian way) of interpreting how the 'horror of evil' leads to the intimation of the good – a good that is beyond Being, a good which is not to be understood as the dialectical negation of evil. The horror of evil opens up and invites an ethical response to evil. The excess of evil, its malignancy that resists all integration, solicits and elicits in me 'a transcendence that shines forth in the face of the other man: an alterity of the non-integratable, of what cannot be assembled into a totality' (TE 163). The following passage eloquently summarizes the movement of Levinas's thinking (the 'same' wave that keeps breaking with renewed insistence):

This is no longer a transcendence absorbed by my knowing. The face puts into question the sufficiency of my identity as an ego; it binds me to an infinite responsibility with regard to the other. The original transcendence signifies in the concreteness, from the first ethical, of the face. That in the evil that pursues me the evil suffered by the other man afflicts me, that it touches me, as though calling on me, putting into question my resting on myself and my *conatus essendi*, as though before lamenting over my evil here below, I had to answer for the other – is not that a breakthrough of the Good in the 'intention' of which I am in my woe so exclusively aimed at? . . . The horror of evil that aims at me becomes horror over the evil in the other man. Here is a breakthrough of the Good which is not a simple inversion of Evil but an elevation. This Good does not please, but commands and prescribes. [TE 163–4]

Levinas's reflections on evil, especially the evil that has erupted in the twentieth century, and the demand for an ethical response to this evil, provide a fresh perspective for appreciating what is at issue in his major books, *Totality and Infinity* and *Otherwise than Being or Beyond Essence*. If we restrict ourselves to the horizon of Being, or if we limit ourselves to the *said* rather than the *saying*, then we cannot adequately respond to the non-integratable evil that we *concretely* encounter, but which nevertheless transcends all categories of comprehension. It is the very concreteness of the 'horror of evil' that calls forth the ethical response that ruptures Being. It is only by ethically responding to the evil inflicted on my fellow human beings that I *become* fully human.

We can further enrich our understanding of Levinas's reflections on evil and ethics by considering what he means by the *conatus essendi*. The expression *conatus essendi* is taken from Spinoza but has a much more general meaning for Levinas. The *conatus essendi* is the 'law of being':

A being is something that is attached to being, to its own being, which is always a persistence of being. That is Darwin's idea. The being of animals is a struggle for life. A struggle without ethics. It is a question of might. Heidegger says at the beginning of *Being and Time* that *Dasein* is a being who in his being is concerned for this being itself. That's Darwin's idea: the living being struggles for life. The aim of being is being itself. [PM 172]

Whatever we may think of this association of Darwin and Heidegger, Levinas's point is clear. The law of being, the *conatus essendi*, is the drive of being to preserve itself – the effort to exist. We, as human *beings*, are, of course, beings. Consequently, qua *beings*, this law of being is our law. But – and this is the crucial point – we are not *exclusively* beings. We are not exclusively what Heidegger calls *Da-sein* (*being* there). We are *human* beings. Levinas emphatically declares 'the human breaks with pure being, which is always a persistence of being. This is my principal thesis' (PM 172). And Levinas – as if he were summing up his entire philosophy in a single sentence – tells us: 'However, with the appearance of the human – and this is my entire philosophy – there is something more important than my life, and that is the life of the other' (PM 172). Levinas is fully aware that there is something 'unreasonable' about this, for it is 'reasonable' to look after oneself – to follow the law of one's being.

But we cannot not admire saintliness . . . that is, the person who in his being is more attached to the being of the other than to his own. I believe that it is in saintliness that the human begins; not in the accomplishment of saintliness, but in the value. It is the first value, an undeniable value. [PM 173]

We can bring out Levinas's meaning by pursuing a 'formal' analogy with Kant. Just as Kant argues that (counterfactually) if we were exclusively natural beings, there would be no categorical imperative and consequently no morality, so Levinas claims that if we were exclusively *beings* there would be no ethical imperative. And just as Kant claims that nature has its own laws, so Levinas claims that being has its own law. Furthermore, for Kant recognizing that there is a moral law, a supreme moral imperative, doesn't mean that we always follow it. Nevertheless, we *can* follow the moral law; we can recognize its authority and obey it. So too for Levinas; although we do not always obey the supreme ethical imperative, we *can* obey it. Ethics presupposes saintliness not as an 'accomplishment', but as a 'value'. In other words, I can always act in such a way so that I respond to other by giving ethical priority to his life and to the suffering that he endures. I stress that this analogy with Kant is a *formal* analogy because the *content* of Levinas's supreme ethical imperative is not to be identified with Kant's categorical imperative. Ethics for Levinas is not 'grounded' in practical reason. It is beyond reason. For Levinas, to be ethical (moral) is not to be autonomous in Kant's sense, it is to be heteronomous – responsive and responsible to and for the other.

But how do these reflections about being, the law of being and the *conatus essendi* enhance our understanding of evil? We are told: 'It is in the human being that a rupture is produced with being's own law, with the law of being. The law of evil is the law of being. Evil is, in this sense, very powerful' (PM 175). But although evil is a powerful *force*, this doesn't diminish the *authority* of the supreme ethical imperative. We must be careful not to misinterpret what Levinas is saying here. There is nothing evil about the law of being in itself. The categories of good and evil do not apply to all beings but only to human beings, although our ethical respsonsibility as human beings extends to all living beings. It is because we, as *human*, know what suffering is that we can have obligations not to cause needless suffering to other living creatures. Furthermore, as human beings, we do and must act to preserve our own being. But if we act as if we were beings exclusively concerned with our own *conatus essendi*, if we fail to respond to the demands, needs and suffering of the other, then we are succumbing to 'the law of evil'. Levinas succinctly sums up his main point about our humanity:

In the *conatus essendi*, which is the effort to exist, existence is the supreme law. However, with the appearance of the face on the inter-personal level, the commandment 'Thou shalt not kill' emerges as a limitation of the *conatus essendi*. It is not a rational limit. Consequently, interpreting it necessitates thinking it in moral terms, in ethical terms. It must be thought outside the idea of force. [PM 175]

If I deliberately violate the (ethical) limitation on the *conatus essendi*, if I act as if I were a being whose sole concern is with the preservation of my own being (or even with Being), then I commit an evil act. It is because I am *human* that I can be good or evil. There is no evil in a world of 'pure being', just as there is no good in a world of 'pure being'. This is why there is not and cannot be any ethics in Heidegger's world. And this is also Levinas's 'answer' to Heidegger's misgivings about humanism. Heidegger treats humanism as if it is limited to the horizon of what he calls metaphysics, and the horizon of Being; Heidegger fails to realize that a *true* humanism – an *ethical* humanism – requires a rupture with Being, a rupture with the *conatus essendi*. To *become* a *human* being is to transcend my own 'law of being', and ethically respond to the non-integratable evil that afflicts my neighbour.

In his essay, 'Signature' which begins with a brief (one paragraph) account of his personal biography, Levinas concludes by telling us that it is dominated by the presentiment and memory of the Nazi horror. The Nazi horror – symbolized by Auschwitz – is the paradigm of that transcendent evil that ruptures all categories of knowledge and understanding, evil as non-integrable excess. We may be reminded of what Levinas's good friend and admirer, Maurice Blanchot, said in *The Writing of the Disaster*, when he tells the story of the young prisoner of Auschwitz who had suffered the worst, led his family to the crematorium, attempted to hang himself but was 'saved' at the last minute, and then was compelled to hold the heads of victims so that when the SS shot them the bullet could more easily be lodged in their necks. 'When asked how he could bear this, he is supposed to have answered that "he observed the comportment of men before death".' But Blanchot declares 'I will not believe it . . . His response . . . was not a response, he could not respond'[8]:

What remains for us to recognize in this account is that when he was faced with an impossible question, he could find no other alibi than the search for knowledge, the so-called dignity of knowledge: that ultimate propriety which we believe will be accorded us by knowledge. And how, in fact, can one accept not to know? We read books on Auschwitz. The wish of all in the camps, the last wish: know what has happened, do not forget, and at the same time never will you know. [*TWD* 82]

Levinas would certainly endorse this moving and perceptive statement. We can never adequately know or comprehend this evil, even though we cannot give up the desire and the attempt to understand it. It transcends and ruptures our categories of knowledge. But this is a transcendence that is not in some 'other realm'. Oxomoronically, it is an *immanent* transcendence – one which we confront in its overwhelming horrible concreteness. When Blanchot says that the survivor's answer was 'not a response', Levinas would certainly agree. It was not a response because nothing that is *said* or *known* can be an adequate response. To think that there is, is to delude ourselves – to be seduced by the temptation of theodicy. But we *can* respond – not by some more refined or sophisticated knowledge, not by reading more graphic accounts of evil, but in the only way that is commensurate with the excess of evil that we concretely encounter. This is the *ethical response*, where I recognize my supreme obligation, my responsibility for the useless and unjustifiable suffering of others, my responsibility to respond to the evil inflicted upon my fellow human beings. This is the ethical response of Anton Schmidt – the obscure German soldier who was executed for helping Jews. The 'same' wave keeps breaking – and all the pathways of Levinas's thinking lead us to the same realization.The only response to the unprecedented evil of the twentieth century is assume 'my responsibility for the other person, without concern for reciprocity, in my call to help him gratuitiously, in the asymmetry of the relation of *one* to the *other*' (*US* 165).

NOTES

1 See Jacques Derrida's 'Violence and Metaphysics', in *Writing and Difference*, trans. Alan Bass (Chicago: University of Chicago Press, 1978), p. 312.
2 See Hannah Arendt's 'Some Questions of Moral Philosophy', *Social Research* 61, 4 (1994), p. 742.
3 *Ibid.*, p. 740.
4 See Hans Jonas's 'Matter, Mind, and Creation: Cosmological Evidence and Cosmogonic Speculation', in Lawrence Vogel (ed.), *Hans Jonas: a Search for the Good after Auschwitz* (Evanston: Northwestern University Press, 1996), p. 188.
5 See Immanuel Kant's *Religion Within the Limits of Reason Alone*, trans. T. M. Greene and H. H. Hudson (New York: Harper Torchbooks, 1960), p. 3.
6 See Frederich Nietzsche's *On the Genealogy of Morals*, trans. Walter Kaufmann (New York: Vintage Books, 1969), p. 68.
7 See Hannah Arendt's *Eichmann in Jerusalem: a Report on the Banality of Evil*, 2nd edn (New York: Viking Press, 1965), p. 231.
8 See Maurice Blanchot's *The Writing of the Disaster*, trans. Ann Smock (Lincoln: University of Nebraska Press, 1986), p. 82 (henceforth abbreviated *TWD*).

BIBLIOGRAPHY

PREPARED BY STACY KELTNER

The bibliography is divided into primary and secondary sources. Levinas's works are divided into, first, books and collections of essays in English translation and, second, articles in English translation. Following the titles of books and collections grouped by Levinas or in a French edition, the dates of original publications appear in square brackets. The secondary work on Levinas is divided topically. After a general section of some important works on Levinas, there follow citations for more specialized topics concerning Levinas, such as Levinas and Derrida, Levinas and feminism, etc. Like the primary source sections, those secondary articles included in edited volumes have not been listed separately, with the exception of important essays by Derrida and Irigaray. For a more extensive bibliography, the reader should consult Roger Burggraeve's *Emmanuel Levinas. Une bibliographie primaire et secondaire (1929–1985) avec complément 1985–1989* (Leuven: Peeters, 1990). A special issue of *Philosophy and Social Criticism*, (23, 6 1997), entitled *Emmanuel Levinas: Ethics of the Other* and edited by Peter Kemp, includes a bibliography by Henrik Peterson (pp. 109–38). There are also Internet resources available: both Peter Atterton and Anthony Beavers have compiled English-language bibliographies of Levinas's work and secondary sources.

PRIMARY WORKS

Books by Levinas and collections

Alterity and Transcendence, trans. Michael B. Smith, London: Athlone Press and New York: Columbia University Press, 1999 [1995].

Beyond the Verse: Talmudic Readings and Lectures, trans. Gary D. Mole, Bloomington: Indiana University Press and London: Athlone Press, 1994 [1982].

Collected Philosophical Papers, trans. Alphonso Lingis, The Hague: Martinus Nijhoff, 1987.

Difficult Freedom: Essays on Judaism, trans. Seán Hand, Baltimore: Johns Hopkins University Press, 1990 [1963].

Discovering Existence with Husserl, trans. Richard A. Cohen, Bloomington: Indiana University Press, 1988 [1949].

Entre Nous: On Thinking-of-the-Other, trans. Michael B. Smith and Barbara Harshav, New York: Columbia University Press, 1998 [1991].

Ethics and Infinity: Conversations with Philippe Nemo, trans. Richard Cohen, Pittsburgh: Duquesne University Press, 1985 [1982].

Emmanuel Levinas: Basic Philosophical Writings, A. Peperzak, S. Critchley and R. Bernasconi (eds.), Bloomington: Indiana University Press, 1996.

Existence and Existents, trans. Alphonso Lingis, The Hague: Martinus Nijhoff, 1978 [1947].

God, Death and Time, trans. Bettina Bergo, Stanford: Stanford University Press, 2000 [1993].

In the Time of the Nations, trans. Michael B. Smith, Bloomington: Indiana University Press and London: Athlone Press, 1994 [1988].

Is it Righteous To Be?: Interviews with Emmanuel Levinas, Jill Robbins (ed.), Stanford: Stanford University Press, 2002.

New Talmudic Readings, trans. R. Cohen, Pittsburgh: Duquesne University Press, 1999 [1996].

Nine Talmudic Readings, trans. Annette Aronowicz, Bloomington: Indiana University Press, 1990 [1968].

Of God Who Comes to Mind, trans. Bettina Bergo, Stanford: Stanford University Press, 1998 [1986].

Otherwise than Being or Beyond Essence, trans. Alphonso Lingis, The Hague: Martinus Nijhoff, 1981 [1974].

Outside the Subject, trans. Michael B. Smith, Stanford: Stanford University Press, 1993 [1987].

Proper Names, trans. Michael B. Smith, Stanford: Stanford University Press, 1996 [1975].

The Levinas Reader, Seán Hand (ed.), Oxford: Basil Blackwell, 1989.

The Theory of Intuition in Husserl's Phenomenology, trans. A. Orianne, Evanston: Northwestern University Press, 1995 [1930].

Time and the Other, trans. Richard A. Cohen, Pittsburgh: Duquesne University Press, 1985 [1947].

Totality and Infinity: an Essay on Exteriority, trans. Alphonso Lingis, Pittsburgh: Duquesne University Press, 1969 [1961].

Important articles not included in any of the above collections

'A Language Familiar to Us', trans. Douglas Collins, *Telos*, 44 (1980), pp. 199–201.

'As If Consenting to Horror', trans. Paula Wissing, Critical Inquiry, 15 (1989), pp. 485–8.

'Beyond Intentionality', trans. Kathleen McLaughin, in Alan Montefiore (ed.), Philosophy in France Today, Cambridge: Cambridge University Press, 1983, pp. 100–115.

'Dialogue with Emmanuel Levinas', trans. Richard Kearney, in Richard A. Cohen (ed.), Face to Face with Levinas, Albany: State University of New York Press, 1986, pp. 13–33.

'Emmanuel Levinas', in Raoul Mortley (ed.), French Philosophers in Conversation, London: Routledge, 1991, pp. 11–23.

'Existentialism and Antisemitism', trans. D. Hollier and R. Krauss, October 87 (1999), pp. 27–31.

'Interview with Emmanuel Levinas: December 31, 1982', conducted and trans. Edith Wyschogrod, Philosophy and Theology, 4, 2 (1989), pp. 105–18.

'Martin Heidegger and Ontology', trans. Committee of Public Safety, Diacritics, 26, 1 (1996), pp. 11–32.

'Phenomenology and the Non-Theoretical', trans. J. N. Kraay and A. J. Scholten, in Marinus C. Doeser and J. N. Kraay (eds.), Facts and Values, Dordrecht: Martinus Nijhoff, 1986, pp. 109–19.

'The Contemporary Criticism of the Idea of Value and the Prospects for Humanism', in Edward A. Maziarz (ed.), Value and Values in Evolution, New York: Gordon and Breach, 1979, pp. 179–87.

'The Primacy of Pure Practical Reason', trans. Blake Billings, Man and World: an International Philosophical Review, 27, 4 (1994), pp. 445–53.

'The Trace of the Other', trans. Alphonso Lingis, in Mark Taylor (ed.), Deconstruction in Context, Chicago: University of Chicago Press, 1986, pp. 345–59.

'The Understanding of Spirituality in French and German Culture', trans. Andrius Valevicius, Continental Philosophy Review, 31, 1 (1998), pp. 1–10.

'What Would Eurydice Say?/Que dirait Euridice?' (bilingual text), interview with Bracha Lichtenberg-Ettinger, Paris: BLE Atelier, 1997.

'Who is my Neighbor? Who is the Other?' in Ethics and Responsibility in the Phenomenological Tradition, Pittsburgh: The Simon Silverman Phenomenology Center, 1991, pp. 1–31.

SECONDARY WORKS

General

Bauman, Zygmunt, Modernity and the Holocaust, Oxford: Blackwell, 1993.

Bayard, Catherine and Joyce Bellous (eds.), Emmanuel Levinas, special issue, Philosophy Today, 43, 2 (1999).

Bergo, Bettina, 'Describing the "Sites" of Desire in Levinas', in H. J. Silverman (ed.), *Philosophy and Desire*, Continental Philosophy 7, New York: Routledge, 2000, pp. 63–82.

Bergo, Bettina and Diane Perpich (eds.), 'Levinas's contribution to Contemporary Philosophy', special issue, *Graduate Faculty Philosophy Journal*, 20, 2/21, 1 (1998).

Bernasconi, Robert, 'Re-reading *Totality and Infinity*', in Arleen Dallery and Charles E. Scott (eds.), *The Question of the Other: Essays in Contemporary Continental Philosophy*, Albany: State University of New York Press, 1989, pp. 23–4.

'The Ethics of Suspicion', *Research in Phenomenology*, 20 (1990), pp. 3–18.

'One-Way Traffic: the Ontology of Decolonization and its Ethics', in Galen A. Johnson and Michael B. Smith (eds.), *Ontology and Alterity in Merleau Ponty*, Evanston: Northwestern University Press, 1991, pp. 67–80.

Bernasconi, Robert and Simon Critchley (eds.), *Re-Reading Levinas*, Bloomington: Indiana University Press, 1991.

Bernasconi, Robert and David Wood (eds.), *The Provocation of Levinas: Re-thinking the Other*, New York and London: Routledge and Kegan Paul, 1988.

Blanchot, Maurice, *The Writing of the Disaster*, trans. Ann Smock, Lincoln: University of Nebraska Press, 1986.

The Infinite Conversation, trans. Susan Hanson, Minneapolis: University of Minnesota Press, 1993.

Bloechl, Jeffrey, 'How Best to Keep a Secret? on Love and Respect in Levinas' "Phenomenology of Eros" ', *Man and World*, 29, 1 (1996), pp. 1–17.

Liturgy of the Neighbor, Pittsburgh: Duquesne University Press, 2000.

Bloechl, Jeffrey (ed.), *The Face of the Other and the Trace of God: Essays on the Philosophy of Emmanuel Levinas*, New York: Fordham University Press, 2000.

Brody, D. H., 'Emmanuel Levinas: the Logic of Ethical Ambiguity in *Otherwise Than Being or Beyond Essence*', *Research in Phenomenology*, 25 (1995), pp. 177–203.

Burggraeve, Roger, *From Self-Development to Solidarity: an Ethical Reading of Human Desire in its Socio-Political Relevance According to Emmanuel Levinas*, trans. C. Vanhove-Romanik, Louvain: Centre for Metaphysics and Philosophy of God, 1985.

'Violence and the Vulnerable Face of the Other: the Vision of Emmanuel Levinas on Moral Evil and Our Responsibility', *Journal of Social Philosophy*, 30, 1 (1999), pp. 29–45.

Casey, Edward, 'Levinas on Memory and the Trace', in John Sallis (ed.), *Collegium Phaenomenologicum: the First Ten Years*, Boston: Kluwer Academic Publishers, 1988, pp. 241–55.

Chalier, Catherine, 'Emmanuel Levinas: Responsibility and Election', in Griffiths A. Phillips (ed.), *Ethics*, (Supp.) 35, Cambridge: Cambridge University Press, 1993, pp. 63–76.

Chanter, Tina, 'The Betrayal of Philosophy: Emmanuel Levinas's "Otherwise Than Being"', *Philosophy and Social Criticism*, 23, 6 (1997), pp. 65–79.

Cohen, Richard A., *Elevations: the Height of the Good in Rosenzweig and Levinas*, Chicago: University of Chicago Press, 1994.

'Difficulty and Morality: Two Notes on Reading Levinas', *Philosophy in the Contemporary World*, 7, 1 (2000), pp. 59–66.

Cohen, Richard, A. (ed.), *Face to Face with Levinas*, Albany: State University of New York Press, 1986.

Critchley, Simon, 'The Original Traumatism: Levinas and Psychoanalysis', in Richard Kearney and Mark Dooley (eds.), *Questioning Ethics*, London and New York: Routledge, 1998, pp. 230–42. Reprinted in Simon Critchley, *Ethics–Politics–Subjectivity*.

'"Das Ding": Levinas and Lacan', *Research in Phenomenology*, 28 (1998), pp. 72–90. Repinted in Simon Critchley, *Ethics–Politics–Subjectivity*, London: Verso, 1999.

Davies, Paul, 'The Face and the Caress: Levinas' Ethical Alterations of Sensibility', in D. M. Levin (ed.), *Modernity and the Hegemony of Vision*, San Francisco: University of California Press, 1993, pp. 252–72.

Davis, Colin, *Levinas: an Introduction*, Notre Dame: University of Notre Dame Press, 1996.

De Boer, Theodore, *Rationality as Transcendence*, Amsterdam: J. C. Gieben, 1997.

De Vries, Hent, *Philosophy and the Turn to Religion*, Battemia: Johns Hopkins University Press, 1999.

Drabinski, John E., 'The Hither-Side of the Living Present in Levinas and Husserl', *Philosophy Today*, 41, 1 (1996), pp. 142–50.

'Sense and Icon: the Problem of *Sinngebung* in Levinas and Marion', *Philosophy Today*, 42 (Supp.) (1998), pp. 47–58.

Sensibility and Singularity: the Problem of Phenomenology in Levinas, Albany: State University of New York Press, 2001.

Durie, Robin, 'Speaking of Time: Husserl and Levinas on the Saying of Time', *Journal of the British Society for Phenomenology*, 30, 1 (1999), pp. 35–58.

Furrow, D., 'Levinas: Ethics Without a Limit', in D. Furrow (ed.), *Against Theory: Continental and Analytical Challenges in Moral Philosophy*, New York: Routledge, 1995, pp. 139–60.

Gibbs, Robert, *Why Ethics?*, Princeton: Princeton University Press, 2000.

Haar, Michel, 'The Obsession of the Other: Ethics as Traumatization', *Philosophy and Social Criticism*, 23, 6 (1997), pp. 95–107.

Hand, Seán (ed.), *Facing the Other: the Ethics of Emmanuel Levinas*, Richmond: Curzon, 1996.

Harasym, Sarah (ed.), *Levinas and Lacan: the Missed Encounter*, Albany: State University of New York Press, 1998.

Hendley, Steve, 'Autonomy and Alterity', *Journal of the British Society for Phenomenology*, 27, 3 (1996).

Horowitz, Asher, ' "How Can anyone Be Called Guilty?" Speech, Responsibility, and the Social Relation in Habermas and Levinas', *Philosophy Today*, 44, 3/4 (2000), pp. 295–317.

Jacques, Francis, 'Primum Relations', trans. Andrew Rothwell, *Difference and Subjectivity*, New Haven: Yale University Press, 1991, pp. 115–61.

Jopling, David, 'Levinas, Sartre and Understanding the Other', *Journal of the British Society for Phenomenology*, 24, 3 (1993).

Kapust, Antje, Eric Nelson and Kent Still (eds.), *Addressing Levinas*, Evanston: Northwestern University Press, 2002.

Keenan, Dennis, *Death and Responsibility*, Albany: State University of New York Press, 1999.

Kemp, Peter (ed.), *Emmanuel Levinas: Ethics of the Other*, special issue, *Philosophy and Social Criticism*, 23, 6 (1997).

Large, William, 'On the Meaning of the Word Other in Levinas', *Journal of the British Society for Phenomenology*, 27, 1 (1996), pp. 36–52.

Levin, David Michael, 'Tracework: Myself and Others in the Moral Phenomenology of Merleau-Ponty and Levinas', *International Journal of Philosophical Studies*, 6, 3 (1998), pp. 345–92.

Lingis, Alphonso, 'Face to Face', *Deathbound Subjectivity; Studies in Phenomenology and Existential Theories*, Bloomington: Indiana University Press, 1989, pp. 135–55.

Llewelyn, John, *Emmanuel Levinas: the Genealogy of Ethics*, New York: Routledge, 1995.

'Levinas's Critical and Hypocritical Diction', *Philosophy Today*, 41 (Supp.) (1997), pp. 28–40.

Lyotard, J.-F., 'Jewish Oedipus', trans. S. Lotringer, in J.-F. Lyotard and G. van Den Abbeele (eds.), *Driftworks*, New York: Semiotext(e), 1984, pp. 33–55.

Maloney, Max, 'Levinas, Substitution, and Transcendental Subjectivity', *Man and World*, 30, 1 (1997), pp. 49–64.

O'Connor, Noreen, 'Intentionality, Analysis and the Problem of Self and Other', *Journal for the British Society of Phenomenology*, 13 (1982), pp. 186–92.

Peperzak, Adriaan, 'Levinas on Technology and Nature', *Man and World*, 25, 3–4 (1992), pp. 469–82.

To the Other: an Introduction to the Philosophy of Emmanuel Levinas, Indiana: Purdue University Press, 1993.

'The One for the Other: the Philosophy of Emmanuel Levinas', *Man and World*, 29 (1996), pp. 109–18.

Beyond: the Philosophy of Emmanuel Levinas, Evanston: Northwestern University Press, 1997.

Peperzak, Adriaan (ed.), *Ethics as First Philosophy: the Significance of Emmanuel Levinas for Philosophy, Literature and Religion*, New York and London: Routledge, 1995.

Rapaport, H., 'Face to Face with Ricoeur and Levinas', in David D. Klemm and W. Schweiker (eds.), *Meaning in Texts and Actions: Questioning Paul Ricœur*, Charlottesville: University Press of Virginia, 1993, pp. 226–33.

Ricœur, Paul, 'What Ontology in View?', trans. Kathleen Blamey, *Oneself as Another*, Chicago: University of Chicago Press, 1992, pp. 297–356.

'Emmanuel Levinas: Thinker of Testimony', in *Figuring the Sacred: Religion, Narrative and Imagination*, Minneapolis: Fortress Press, 1995, pp. 108–26.

'In Memoriam: Emmanuel Levinas', *Philosophy Today*, 40 (1996), pp. 331–40.

Sallis, John, 'Levinas and the Elemental', *Research in Phenomenology*, 28 (1998), pp. 152–9.

Visker, Rudi, *Truth and Singularity*, Dordrecht: Kluwer, 1999.

Wyschogrod, Edith, 'Does Continental Ethics Have a Future?' in Arleen B. Dallery and Charles E. Scott (eds.), *Ethics and Danger: Essays on Heidegger and Continental Thought*, Albany: State University of New York Press, 1992, pp. 229–41.

Emmanuel Levinas: the Problem of Ethical Metaphysics, The Hague: Martinus Nijhoff, 1974; 2nd edn, New York: Fordham University Press, 2000.

Levinas and Derrida

Atterton, Peter, 'Levinas and the Language of Peace: a Response to Derrida', *Philosophy Today*, 36, 1 (1992), pp. 59–70.

Bernasconi, Robert, 'Deconstruction and the Possibility of Ethics', in John Sallis (ed.), *Deconstruction and Philosophy*, Chicago: University of Chicago Press, 1987, pp. 122–39.

'Levinas, Philosophy, and Beyond', in H. J. Silverman (ed.), *Philosophy and Non-Philosophy since Merleau-Ponty*, Continental Philosophy 1, New York: Routledge and Kegan Paul, 1987, pp. 232–58.

'The Trace of Levinas in Derrida', in David Wood and Robert Bernasconi (eds.), *Derrida and Difference*, Evanston: Northwestern University Press, 1988, pp. 17–44.

'The Different Styles of Eschatology: Derrida's Take on Levinas' Political Messianism', *Research in Phenomenology*, 28 (1998), pp. 3–19.

'What Goes Around Comes Around: Derrida and Levinas on the Economy of the Gift', in A. Schrift (ed.), *The Logic of the Gift*, New York: Routledge, 1997, pp. 256–73.

Bernstein, Richard J., 'Incommensurability and Otherness Revisited', *The New Constellation*, Cambridge: MIT Press, 1992, pp. 57–78.

Caputo, John, 'Hyperbolic Justice: Deconstruction, Myth, and Politics', *Research in Phenomenology*, 21 (1991), pp. 3–20.

'Who is Derrida's Zarathustra? Of Fraternity, Friendship, and a Democracy to Come', *Research in Phenomenology*, 29 (1999), pp. 184–98.

Cohen, Richard A., 'The Privilege of Reason and Play: Derrida and Levinas', *Tijdschrift voor Filosofie*, 45, 2 (1983), pp. 242–55.

Critchley, Simon, *The Ethics of Deconstruction: Derrida and Levinas*, Oxford: Blackwell, 1992. Second rev. and expanded edn, Edinburgh: Edinburgh University Press, 1999.

Davies, Paul, 'Difficult Friendship', *Research in Phenomenology*, 18 (1988), pp. 149–73.

Derrida, Jacques, 'Violence and metaphysics', trans. Alan Bass, *Writing and Difference: an Essay on the Thought of Emmanuel Levinas*, London: Routledge and Kegan Paul and Chicago: Chicago University Press, 1978, pp. 79–153.

' "Eating Well" or the Calculation of the Subject: An Interview with Jacques Derrida', in E. Cadava, P. Connor and J.-L. Nancy (eds.), *Who Comes After the Subject?*, London: Routledge, 1991, pp. 105–8.

'At this very Moment in this Work Here I Am', trans. Ruben Berezdivin, in Robert Bernasconi and Simon Critchley (eds.), *Re-reading Levinas*, Bloomington: Indiana University Press, 1991, pp. 11–48.

Adieu to Emmanuel Levinas, trans. P.-A. Brault and M. Naas, Stanford: Stanford University Press, 1999.

Llewelyn, John, 'Levinas, Derrida and Others vis-à-vis', in John Llewelyn (ed.), *Beyond Metaphysics*, Atlantic Highlands: Humanities Press, 1985, pp. 185–206.

'Jewgreek or Greekjew', in John Sallis (ed.), *The Collegium Phaenomenologicum: the First Ten Years*, Dordrecht: Kluwer Academic Publishers, 1988, pp. 273–87.

Perpich, Diane, 'A Singular Justice: Ethics and Politics between Levinas and Derrida', *Philosophy Today*, 42 (Supp.) (1998), pp. 59–70.

Protevi, John, 'Repeating the Parricide: Levinas and the Question of the Other', *Journal of the British Society for Phenomenology*, 23, 1 (1992), pp. 21–32.

Raffoul, Francois, 'On Hospitality, between Ethics and Politics: Review of *Adieu à Emmanuel Levinas* by Jacques Derrida', *Research in Phenomenology*, 28 (1998), pp. 274–82.

'The Subject of the Welcome: on Jacques Derrida's *Adieu à Emmanuel Levinas*', *Symposium*, 2, 2 (1998), pp. 211–22.

Srajek, M. C., *The Margins of Deconstruction: Jewish Conceptions of Ethics in Emmanuel Levinas and Jacques Derrida*, Dordrecht: Kluwer, 1998.

Westphal, Merold, 'Levinas and the Immediacy of the Face', *Faith and Philosophy*, 10, 4 (1993), pp. 486–502.

Wyschogrod, Edith, 'Derrida, Levinas and Violence', in Hugh Silverman (ed.), *Derrida and Deconstruction*, Continental Philosophy 2, New York: Routledge, 1989, pp. 182–200.

Ziarek, Ewa, 'The Rhetoric of Failure and Deconstruction', *Philosophy Today*, 40, 1 (1996), pp. 80–90.

Levinas and feminism

Chanter, Tina, 'The Alterity and Immodesty of Time: Death as Future and Eros as Feminine in Levinas', in David Wood (ed.), *Writing the Future*, Warwick Studies in Philosophy and Literature, London: Routledge and Kegan Paul, 1990, pp. 137–54.

Chanter, Tina, *Ethics of Eros: Irigaray's Re-reading of the Philosophers*, London and New York: Routledge, 1995.

Chanter, Tina (ed.), *Feminist Interpretations of Emmanuel Levinas*, University Park: Pennsylvania State University Press, 2001.

Chapman, Helen, 'Levinas and the Concept of the Feminine', *Warwick Journal of Philosophy*, 1, 1 (1998), pp. 65–83.

Farley, W., *Eros for the Other*, University Park: Pennsylvania State University Press, 1996.

Handelman, Susan A., *Fragments of Redemption*, Bloomington: Indiana University Press, 1991.

Irigaray, Luce, 'Questions to Emmanuel Levinas: On the Divinity of Love', trans. M. Whitford, in Robert Bernasconi and Simon Critchley (eds.), *Re-reading Levinas*, Bloomington: Indiana University Press, 1991, pp. 109–18.

'The Fecundity of the Caress: A Reading of Levinas, *Totality and Infinity*, "Phenomenology of Eros"', trans. C. Burke and G. Gill, *An Ethics of Sexual Difference*, Ithaca: Cornell University Press and London: Athlone Press, 1993, pp. 185–217.

Joy, M., 'Levinas: Alterity, the Feminine and Women – A Meditation', *Studies in Religion*, 22, 4 (1994), pp. 463–85.

Manning, Robert John Scheffler, 'Thinking the Other Without Violence? An Analysis of the Relation Between the Philosophy of Emmanuel Levinas and Feminism', *Journal of Speculative Philosophy*, 5, 2 (1991).

Oliver, Kelly, 'Fatherhood and the Promise of Ethics', *Diacritics*, 27 (1997), pp. 45–57.

Sandford, Stella, 'Writing as a Man: Levinas and the Phenomenology of Eros', *Radical Philosophy*, 87 (1998), pp. 6–17.

The Metaphysics of Love: Gender and Transcendence in Levinas, London: Continuum, 2000.

'Feminism Against "The Feminine" ', *Radical Philosophy*, 105 (2001).

Vasey, C. R., 'Faceless Women and Serious Others: Levinas, Misogyny, and Feminism', in Arleen B. Dallery and Charles E. Scott (eds.), *Ethics and Danger: Essays on Heidegger and Continental Thought*, Albany: State University of New York Press, 1992, pp. 317–30.

Vasseleu, Cathryn, *Textures of Light: Vision and Touch in Irigaray, Levinas and Merleau-Ponty*, London: Routledge, 1998.

Ziarek, Ewa, 'Kristeva and Levinas: Mourning, Ethics and the Feminine', in Kelly Oliver (ed.), *Ethics, Politics, and Difference in Julia Kristeva's Writing*, New York: Routledge, 1993.

Levinas and Heidegger

Bernasconi, Robert, 'Fundamental Ontology, Metontology, and the Ethics of Ethics', *Irish Philosophical Journal*, 4, 1/2 (1987), pp. 76–93.

Chanter, Tina, 'Traumatic Response: Levinas's Legacy', *Philosophy Today*, 41 (Supp.) (1997), pp. 19–27.

'Levinas and Impossible Possibility: Thinking Ethics with Rosenzweig and Heidegger in the Wake of the Shoah', *Research in Phenomenology*, 28 (1998), pp. 91–109.

Time, Death, and the Feminine: Levinas with Heidegger, Stanford: Stanford University Press, 2001.

Greisch, Jean, 'Ethics and Ontology: some Hypocritical Reflections', *Irish Philosophical Journal*, 4, 1/2 (1987), pp. 64–75.

Kemp, Peter, 'Ricœur between Heidegger and Levinas: Original Affirmation between Ontological Attestation and Ethical Injunction', *Philosophy and Social Criticism*, 21, 5/6 (1995), pp. 41–61.

Llewelyn, John, *The Middle Voice of Ecological Conscience: a Chiasmic Reading of Responsibility in the Neighbourhood of Levinas, Heidegger and Others*, London: Macmillan, 1991.

Manning, R. J. S., *Interpreting Otherwise than Heidegger*, Pittsburgh: Duquesne University Press, 1992.

O'Connor, Noreen, 'Being and the Good: Heidegger and Levinas', *Philosophical Studies* (Ireland), 27 (1980), pp. 212–20.

Oliver, Kelly, 'The Gestation of the Other in Phenomenology', *Epoché*, 3, 1/2 (1995), pp. 79–116.

Peperzak, Adrian, 'Phenomenology, Ontology, Metaphysics: Levinas' Perspective on Husserl and Heidegger', *Man and World*, 16 (1983), pp. 113–27.

Sikka, Sonia, 'Questioning the Sacred: Heidegger and Levinas on the Locus of Divinity', *Modern Theology*, 14, 3 (1998), pp. 299–323.

Taminiaux, Jacques, 'The Early Levinas's Reply to Heidegger's Fundamental Ontology', *Philosophy and Social Criticism*, 23, 6 (1997), pp. 29–49.

Wyschogrod, Edith, 'Fear of Primitives, Primitive Fears: Anthropology in the Philosophies of Heidegger and Levinas', in Gerhard Hoffman and Alfred Hornung (eds.), *Emotion in Postmodernism*, Heidelberg: Carl Winter Universitätsverlag, 1997, pp. 401–20.

Levinas and Judaism

Bernasconi, Robert, 'Levinas and Buber: Transcendence and Society', *Sophia: a Journal for Philosophical Theology and Cross Cultural Philosophy of Religion*, 38, 2 (1999), pp. 69–92.

Bergo, Bettina, 'The God of Abraham and the God of the Philosophers: a Reading of Emmanuel Levinas's "Dieu et la Philosophie"', *Graduate Faculty Philosophy Journal*, 16 (1993), pp. 113–64.

Chalier, Catherine, 'The Messianic Utopia', trans. Andrew Slade, *Graduate Faculty Philosophy Journal*, 20, 2/21, 1 (1998), pp. 281–96.

Cohen, Richard A., 'The Face of Truth in Rosenzweig, Levinas and Jewish Mysticism', in D. Guerrière (ed.), *Phenomenology of the Truth Proper to Religion*, Albany: State University of New York Press, 1990, pp. 175–201.

Friedman, Maurice, 'Martin Buber and Emmanuel Levinas: an Ethical Query', *Philosophy Today*, 45, 1 (2001), pp. 3–11.

Gibbs, Robert, *Correlations in Rosenzweig and Levinas*, Princeton: Princeton University Press, 1992.

Meskin, Jacob, 'Toward a New Understanding of the Work of Emmanuel Levinas', *Modern Judaism*, 20 (2000), pp. 72–102.

Mole, Gary D., *Levinas, Blanchot, Jabès: Figures of Estrangement*, Gainsville: University Press of Florida, 1997.

Peperzak, Adriaan, 'Emmanuel Levinas: Jewish Experience and Philosophy', *Philosophy Today*, 27 (1983), pp. 297–306.

   'Judaism and Philosophy in Levinas', *International Journal for Philosophy of Religion*, 40, 3 (1996), pp. 125–46.

Robbins, Jill, 'Alterity and the Judaic: Reading Levinas', *Prodigal Son/Elder Brother: Interpretation and Alterity in Augustine, Petrarch, Kafka, Levinas*, Chicago: University of Chicago Press, 1991, pp. 100–32.
  'An Inscribed Responsibility: Levinas's *Difficult Freedom*', *Modern Language Notes*, 106 (1991), pp. 1052–62.
Rose, G., 'Angry Angels: Simone Weil and Emmanuel Levinas', in G. Rose (ed.), *Judaism and Modernity: Philosophical Essays*, Oxford: Blackwell, 1993.
Van Beeck, Frans Jozef, *Loving the Torah More than God?*, Chicago: Loyola University Press, 1989.
Wright, Tamra, *The Twilight of Jewish Philosophy*, Amsterdam: Harwood, 1999.
Wyschogrod, Edith, 'Emmanuel Levinas and the Problem of Religious Language', *The Thomist: a Speculative Quarterly Review*, 36 (1972), pp. 1–38.
  'From the Disaster to the Other: Tracing the Name of God in Levinas', *Phenomenology and the Numinous*, Pittsburgh: The Simon Silverman Phenomenology Center, Duquesne University, 1988, pp. 67–86.
  'Corporeality and the Glory of the Infinite in the Philosophy of Emmauel Levinas', in Marco O. Olivetti (ed.), *Incarnation*, Padua: Cedam, 1999.
  'Emmanuel Levinas and Hillel's Questions', in Merold Westphal (ed.), *Postmodern Philosophy and Christian Thought*, New York: Fordham University Press, 2000.

Levinas, Literature and Art

Anderson, T., 'Drawing upon Levinas to Sketch out a Heterotopic Poetics of Art and Tragedy', *Research in Phenomenology*, 24 (1994), pp. 69–96.
Bruns, G. L., 'Blanchot/Levinas: Interruption (On the Conflict of Alterities)', *Research in Phenomenology*, 26 (1996), pp. 132–54.
Critchley, Simon, 'Il y a: A Dying Stronger Than Death', *Oxford Literary Review*, 15, 1/2 (1993), pp. 81–131. Reprinted in *Very Little ... Almost Nothing*, London and New York: Routledge, 1997.
  'Il y a: Putting Levinas's Hand to Blanchot's Fire', in C. Gill and L. Hill (eds.), *Blanchot*, London and New York: Routledge, 1997, pp. 108–22. Reprinted in *Very Little ... Almost Nothing*, London and New York: Routledge, 1997.
Davies, Paul, 'A Linear Narrative? Blanchot with Heidegger in the Work of Levinas', in David Wood (ed.), *Philosophers' Poets*, London: Routledge, 1990, pp. 37–69.
Eaglestone, Robert, *Ethical Criticism: Reading after Levinas*, Edinburgh: Edinburgh University Press and New York: Columbia University Press, 1997.

Lingis, Alphonso, 'Fateful Images', *Research in Phenomenology*, 28 (1998), pp. 55–71.

McCaffery, Steve, 'The Scandal of Sincerity: towards a Levinasian Poetics', *Prior to Meaning: Protosemantics and Poetics*, Evanston: Northwestern University Press, 2001.

New, M., R. Bernasconi and R. Cohen (eds.), *Proximity: Emmanuel Levinas and the Eighteenth Century*, Lubbock: Texas Tech University Press, 2001.

Robbins, Jill, 'Aesthetic Totality and Ethical Infinity: Levinas on Art', *L'Esprit-Createur*, 35, 3 (1995), pp. 66–79.

Altered Readings: Levinas and Literature, Chicago: University of Chicago Press, 1999.

Ziarek, Krzysztof, *Inflected Language: toward a Hermeneutic of Nearness: Heidegger, Levinas, Stevens, Celan*, Albany: State University of New York Press, 1994.

Levinas and Politics

Barber, Michael, 'Emmanuel Levinas and the Philosophy of Liberation', *Laval Theologique et Philosophique*, 54, 3 (1998), pp. 473–81.

Bergo, Bettina, *Levinas between Ethics and Politics*, Dordrecht: Kluwer Academic Publishers, 1999.

Bernasconi, Robert, 'The Violence of the Face: Peace and Language in the Thought of Levinas', *Philosophy and Social Criticism*, 23, 6 (1997), pp. 81–93.

'The Third Party: Levinas on the Intersection of the Ethical and the Political', *Journal of the British Society for Phenomenology*, 30, 1 (1999), pp. 76–87.

Butler, Judith, 'Ethical Ambivalence', in B. Hanssen, R. L. Walkowitz, and M. B. Garber (eds.), *The Turn to Ethics*, New York: Routledge, 2000.

Caygill, Howard, 'Levinas's Political Judgement: the *Esprit* Articles', *Radical Philosophy*, 104 (2000), pp. 6–15.

Levinas and the Political, London: Routledge, 2002.

Chanter, Tina, 'Neither Materialism nor Idealism: Levinas's Third Way', in Alan Milchman (ed.), *Postmodernism and the Holocaust*, Rodopi: Amsterdam, 1998.

'The Temporality of Saying: Politics beyond the Ontological Difference', *Graduate Faculty Philosophy Journal*, 20, 2/21, 1 (1998), pp. 502–28.

Ciaramelli, F., 'The Inner Articulation of Origin and the Radical Problem of Democracy', in P. van Haute and P. Birmingham (eds.), *Dissensus Communis*, Kamber, The Netherlands: Kok Pharos, 1995, pp. 52–73.

Critchley, Simon, *Ethics–Politics–Subjectivity: Essays on Derrida, Levinas and Contemporary French Thought*, London: Verso, 1999.

Drabinski, John, 'The Possibility of an Ethical Politics: from Peace to Liturgy', *Philosophy and Social Criticism*, 26, 4 (2000), pp. 49–73.

Simmons, William Paul, 'The Third', *Philosophy and Social Criticism*, 25, 6 (1999), pp. 83–104.

Levinas and the history of philosophy

Beavers, Anthony F., *Levinas beyond the Horizons of Cartesianism: an Inquiry into the Metaphysics of Morals*, New York: Peter Lang, 1995.

Benso, S., 'Levinas: Another Ascetic Priest', *Journal of the British Society for Phenomenology*, 27, 2 (1996), pp. 137–56.

Bernasconi, Robert, 'Levinas Face to Face – with Hegel', *Journal of the British Society for Phenomenology*, 13 (1982), pp. 267–76.

'The Silent, Anarchic World of the Evil Genius', in Giuseppina Moneta, John Sallis and Jacques Taminiaux (eds.), *The Collegium Phaenomenologicum: the First Ten Years*, Dordrecht: Martinus Nijhoff, 1988, pp. 257–72.

"The Truth that Accuses: Conscience, Shame, and Guilt in Levinas and Augustine', in Gary B. Madison and Marty Fairbaim (eds.), *The Ethics of Postmodernity*, Evanston: Northwestern University Press, 1999, pp. 24–34.

Boothroyd, D., 'Levinas and Nietzsche: in between Love and Contempt', *Philosophy Today*, 39, 4 (1995), pp. 345–57.

Cohen, Richard A., 'Justice and the State in the Thought of Levinas and Spinoza', *Epoché*, 4, 1 (1996), pp. 55–70.

Izzi, John, 'Proximity in Distance: Levinas and Plotinus', *International Philosophical Quarterly*, 38, 1 (1998), pp. 5–16.

Llewelyn, John, *The Hypocritical Imagination: between Kant and Levinas*, London: Routledge, 2000.

Sandford, Stella, 'Plato and Levinas: the Same and the Other', *Journal of the British Society for Phenomenology*, 30, 2 (1999), pp. 131–50.

Schroeder, Brian, 'The (Non)Logic of Desire and War: Hegel and Levinas', in Hugh J. Silverman (ed.), *Philosophy and Desire*, Continental Philosophy 7, New York: Routledge, 2000, pp. 45–62.

INDEX

Note: in titles of works, definite/indefinite articles are ignored for alphabetization.

OTHER VOLUMES IN THE SERIES OF CAMBRIDGE COMPANIONS:

AQUINAS *Edited by* NORMAN KRETZMANN *and*
ELEONORE STUMP
HANNAH ARENDT *Edited by* DANA VILLA
ARISTOTLE *Edited by* JONATHAN BARNES
AUGUSTINE *Edited by* ELEONORE STUMP *and*
NORMAN KRETZMANN
BACON *Edited by* MARKKU PELTONEN
DESCARTES *Edited by* JOHN COTTINGHAM
EARLY GREEK PHILOSOPHY *Edited by* A. A. LONG
FEMINISM IN PHILOSOPHY *Edited by* MIRANDA
FRICKER *and* JENNIFER HORNSBY
FOUCAULT *Edited by* GARY GUTTING
FREUD *Edited by* JEROME NEU
GALILEO *Edited by* PETER MACHAMER
GERMAN IDEALISM *Edited by* KARL AMERIKS
HABERMAS *Edited by* STEPHEN K. WHITE
HEGEL *Edited by* FREDERICK BEISER
HEIDEGGER *Edited by* CHARLES GUIGNON
HOBBES *Edited by* TOM SORELL
HUME *Edited by* DAVID FATE NORTON
HUSSERL *Edited by* BARRY SMITH *and*
DAVID WOODRUFF SMITH
WILLIAM JAMES *Edited by* RUTH ANNA PUTNAM
KANT *Edited by* PAUL GUYER
KIERKEGAARD *Edited by* ALASTAIR HANNAY *and*
GORDON MARINO
LEIBNIZ *Edited by* NICHOLAS JOLLEY
LEVINAS *Edited by* SIMON CRITCHLEY *and*
ROBERT BERNASCONI
LOCKE *Edited by* VERE CHAPPELL
MALEBRANCHE *Edited by* STEPHEN NADLER
MARX *Edited by* TERRELL CARVER
MILL *Edited by* JOHN SKORUPSKI
NIETZSCHE *Edited by* BERND MAGNUS *and*
KATHLEEN HIGGINS
OCKHAM *Edited by* PAUL VINCENT SPADE
PLATO *Edited by* RICHARD KRAUT
PLOTINUS *Edited by* LLOYD P. GERSON
ROUSSEAU *Edited by* PATRICK RILEY
SARTRE *Edited by* CHRISTINA HOWELLS
SCHOPENHAUER *Edited by* CHRISTOPHER JANAWAY
SPINOZA *Edited by* DON GARRETT
WITTGENSTEIN *Edited by* HANS SLUGA *and*
DAVID STERN